Unlocking Commercial Financing for Clean Energy in East Asia

DIRECTIONS IN DEVELOPMENT
Energy and Mining

Unlocking Commercial Financing for Clean Energy in East Asia

Xiaodong Wang, Richard Stern, Dilip Limaye, Wolfgang Mostert, and Yabei Zhang

THE WORLD BANK
Washington, D.C.

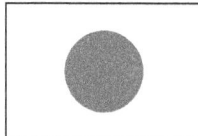

Australian AID

Contents

Boxes

Figures

Tables

Foreword

Overwhelming evidence indicates that climate change, caused in large part by human activities, is already adversely impacting all people, with the very real prospect of worse to come. Nevertheless, a global treaty to curb carbon emissions remains elusive. But many countries—both advanced and developing—have embarked on aggressive action plans designed to reduce their carbon footprints. In East Asia, all middle-income countries have set national targets for energy efficiency and renewable energy, and some even have targets for carbon reduction. The World Bank East Asian flagship report, *Winds of Change: East Asia's Sustainable Energy Future*, concluded that the East Asia region could, with the right policies and sufficient financing, stabilize carbon dioxide emissions by 2025, improve local environments, and enhance energy security without compromising economic growth.

However, a major hurdle to achieving a sustainable energy path is mobilizing the required financing. Given the sheer size of the financing requirements, it is essential that the lion's share of the investment come from the private sector. The challenge facing policy makers is how to unlock these entrepreneurial and financial resources in the most optimal and efficient manner.

First and foremost, accessing commercial financing requires an effective enabling policy and incentive environment. However, it is also clear that once the right policy regime has been put in place, public financing mechanisms designed to provide incentives to investors and mobilize commercial financing can play a major catalytic role in kick-starting substantial investments in energy efficiency and renewable energy. The lessons of experience of public financing for clean energy are beginning to emerge. The learning curve has been steep, and it provides valuable guidance for governments at the national and local levels that are contemplating their own clean energy programs. This report focuses on these recent experiences in applying public financing instruments and tries to draw the lessons to date: *when and how to use the instruments, which instrument to select, and how to design and implement them.*

This report, cofinanced by the Japan Policy and Human Resources Development Fund and AusAID, was originally intended for an East Asian audience, but because it draws from global experience in both developing and advanced countries, it is equally relevant for the rest of the world, particularly for middle- and higher-income countries.

The wide range of financial instruments designed to support and catalyze clean energy investment over the last decade is truly remarkable. Such instruments include credit lines and risk guarantees designed to increase both the capacity and confidence of commercial banks for clean energy lending; dedicated funds and concessional financing mechanisms to kick-start new technologies; mezzanine and equity financing targeted at start-ups, small and medium enterprises, and energy service companies; and various consumer financing instruments designed to lower the up front costs of clean energy equipment. This report systematically reviews the successes and failures of these innovative interventions and distills the lessons of applying them. Although the report does not attempt to be prescriptive, its findings provide a valuable and pragmatic resource for clean energy policy makers, investors, international financial institutions and donors, and practitioners as they design and tailor their own interventions in their respective country environments.

The World Bank Group is committed to supporting governments in East Asia as they make the transformational shift toward a sustainable energy path. The Bank will better integrate its various financial resources and financing instruments to increase its support to energy efficiency and renewable energy, and coordinate with its development partners to meet the region's needs more effectively. We look forward to working with our client countries in the region to bring about the changes that will make a difference locally and globally.

John Roome
Director
Sustainable Development Department
East Asia and Pacific Region
The World Bank

Acknowledgments

This study was undertaken by a team led by Xiaodong Wang and comprising Richard Stern, Dilip Limaye, Wolfgang Mostert, Yabei Zhang, and James Seward, with contributions from Pajnapa Peamsilpakulchorn and Tim Gable. Xiaodong Wang and Richard Stern are the primary authors of the overview, with support from James Seward, Dilip Limaye, and Wolfgang Mostert. The overview (Part 1) is drawn from the key findings in the main report: Part 2, Financing Energy Efficiency (Dilip Limaye is the primary author); Part 3, Financing Renewable Energy (Wolfgang Mostert is the primary author); and Part 4, Clean Energy Financing Case Studies (Yabei Zhang and Dilip Limaye are the primary authors with contributions from James Seward, Pajnapa Peamsilpakulchorn, and Tim Gable). Sherrie Brown edited the report.

The team has interviewed a wide range of clean energy financing experts from the World Bank Group, other multilateral development banks, commercial banks, UN agencies, donors, and others, and wishes to acknowledge their contributions to the report: Andrew Steer, Peter Johansen, Jas Singh, Kyoichi Shimazaki, Bob Taylor, Chandrasekar Govindarajalu, and Richard Hosier from The World Bank; Ajay Narayanan and Jeremy Levin from the International Finance Corporation (of the World Bank Group); Sabine Miltner, Mark Fulton, Silvia Kreibiehl, Susie Shuford, and Jake Baker from Deutsche Bank; Eric Usher from the United Nations Environment Programme; Josue Tanaka and Fani Kallianou from the European Bank for Reconstruction and Development; Arnould Cyrille from the European Investment Bank; WooChong Um and Samuel Tumiwa from the Asian Development Bank; Silvana Capuzzo, David Wilk, Christiaan Gischler, and Juan Perez from the Inter-American Development Bank; Gregory Briffa and Simon Ratcliffe from the United Kingdom Department for International Development; Surender Singh, Mazlina Marmin, and Claudine Lim from InfraCo Asia Development Pte. Ltd.; Richard Parry from InfraCo Africa Pte. Ltd.; Greg Kats from Good Energies Inc.; Mattia Romani from the London School of Economics; and Patrick D'Addario from the Institute for Industrial Productivity.

This work was conducted under the guidance of John Roome and Vijay Jagannathan. Andrew Steer, Charles Feinstein, Peter Johansen, and Aldo Baietti (peer reviewers) provided valuable comments.

Finally, the team wishes to acknowledge the generous support from the government of Japan through a grant from the Japan Policy and Human Resources Development Fund and from Australia through the AusAID grant.

About the Authors

Xiaodong Wang is a Senior Energy Specialist in the East Asia and Pacific (EAP) region of The World Bank. She is the Task Team Leader for the China Energy Efficiency Financing (CHEEF) Project, China Renewable Energy Scale-Up Program (CRESP), Green Energy for Low-Carbon City in Shanghai project, and Energy Saving Measurement and Verification project. She is the lead author for The World Bank East Asia's energy flagship reports: *Winds of Change: East Asia's Sustainable Energy Future* and *Unlocking Commercial Financing for Clean Energy, and the Energy Chapter of the annual World Bank flagship* report: *World Development Report 2010: Development and Climate Change*. She is a coauthor for the Sustainable Low-Carbon City Development Book in China. Prior to joining the EAP region, she worked in the Africa region of the Bank, where she led the Renewable Energy Market Transformation and Low-Carbon Study in South Africa, and rural electrification and off-grid renewable energy projects in a number of African countries. Dr. Wang also worked at the Energy Sector Management Assistance Program (ESMAP) of The World Bank, and led the flagship product of Renewable Energy Toolkit. Prior to joining The World Bank, Dr. Wang managed the Climate Change and Sustainable Energy Program at the UN Foundation, which won a World Climate Technology Award in 2001 and an Energy Globe Award in 2002. She has worked as a climate change specialist at the United Nations Development Program Global Environmental Facility responsible for developing renewable energy and energy efficiency projects in Asia. She holds a PhD in energy and resources from UC Berkeley, and an MS in environmental science and engineering from Tsinghua University.

Richard Stern is a Development Economist by training and a former Vice President of The World Bank. During his 30 years in the institution, he worked as a country economist on East Africa with a particular interest in rural development, and then subsequently managed the Indonesia and China finance and industry divisions. In the early 1990s, as the director of the Bank's Energy, Industry Mining and Telecommunications Department, he oversaw the implementation of a new policy agenda emphasizing the private provision of infrastructure services, developed new rural energy policies, and increasingly integrated environmental concerns into the Bank's energy agenda. He became Vice President of Human Resources in 1997, where he led a major overhaul of the The World Bank's recruitment, staff development, compensation, and pension policies designed to upgrade the skills of the Bank's staff and to align the HR policies and practices to an increasingly decentralized organizational structure. Since 2001, he has undertaken a variety of consulting on development effectiveness, infrastructure, clean energy finance, SME finance, small states, governance, and anti corruption.

Wolfgang Mostert, an independent consultant working out of Copenhagen and has 30 years of experience in developing policy, regulatory, and innovative finance frameworks for energy and environment in more than 70 countries. Mr. Mostert started his international career as researcher in the Science and Technology Policy Instruments Project in 1976, worked as UNDP-JPO in La Paz, Bolivia, from 1978 to 1980, as energy planner in the Danish Ministry of Energy from 1980 to 1981, as Danish Energy and Science attaché to the Danish Permanent Representation to the EU in Brussels from 1981 to 1984, as Head of the Division for Feasibility Studies at the engineering consulting firm Birch & Krogboe from 1985 to 1988, as senior economist at The World Bank's Industry and Energy Department from 1988 to 1990, as management consultant for PA Consulting Group Copenhagen office from 1991 to 1993, and as independent consultant operating out of Copenhagen since 1993.

Mr. Mostert is a member of the Climate Bonds Advisory Panel, the Advisory Panel for the Global Partnership for Output-Based-Aid (GPOBA), and the Technical Advisory Group to ESMAP/ASTEA—The World Bank's applied energy research programs. He has recently concluded a study for ADB on "The Green Climate Fund and Private Sector Engagement."

Mr. Mostert has been the lead consultant for setting up RECREEE, the Middle East and North Africa center for renewable energy and energy efficiency in Cairo, the Climate Technology Innovation Fund for Kenya, the rural electrification funds in Cambodia and in Uganda (REF/REA), and the energy efficiency hub for SE4All. He reviewed UNEP/UNECE/GEF's efforts in establishing a €250 million meazzanine and equity finance fund for clean energy in Eastern Europe and Central Asia.

Mr. Mostert has advised extensively on finance instruments for clean energy. He assisted with the development of national subsidy policies and manuals for renewable energy and rural electrification in Cambodia, Nepal, the Philippines, and Uganda and developed specific finance solutions and instruments in a number of countries (for example, an OBA scheme for reduction of distribution losses in Uganda, the concept for community based ESCOs in Nepal, and the design of the first two public private partnerships (PPPs) in Latvia.

Mr. Limaye is President and CEO of SRC Global Inc. and is internationally recognized as a pioneer and an entrepreneur with over 40 years of experience in energy efficiency, renewable energy, and energy services. He is a senior adviser and consultant to The World Bank, Asian Development Bank, International Finance Corporation, International Energy Agency, United Nations Environment Programme, United Nations Development Programme, U.S. Agency for

International Development, and other donor agencies on financing and implementation of clean energy to mitigate climate change impacts. His recent work has focused on financing clean energy and has included a guidebook on EE financing for China and the development of a UNEP guidebook on financing sources for climate change mitigation. He was the principal author of the International Energy Agency report on PPPs for financing energy efficiency, and is currently the finance team leader for USAID's Partnership for Clean Energy deployment in India.

He has served as a board member of A-Power Energy Generation Systems, the largest alternative energy company in Asia, and is currently Board Chairman of Photonix Solar, a solar PV company in India, and Online Energy Manager, an international energy efficiency technology company. He graduated from IIT-Bombay and was awarded the President of India Gold Medal. He has completed graduate studies in business and in alternative energy at Cornell University and the University of Pennsylvania's Wharton School. He has also completed the Executive Program on Global Climate Change and Economic Development at Harvard University.

He was coauthor of a book published by The World Bank on financing performance contracting projects in the public sector. He has edited or coauthored seven other books and has presented over 40 technical papers at international conferences.

Yabei Zhang is an Energy Economist in the East Asia and Pacific Region of the World Bank. She joined The World Bank as a Young Professional in 2008 and has worked on energy, urban, and climate change issues with a focus on energy efficiency, urban energy, and household energy. She has led or co-led a number of energy efficiency programs including the China Energy Efficiency Financing program and China Provincial Energy Efficiency Program that use financial intermediaries to scale up energy efficiency investments. She is also in charge of household clean cooking programs in China and Indonesia as part of the East Asia and Pacific Clean Stove Initiative. Prior to joining the Bank, Dr. Zhang worked at the Joint Global Change Research Institute (a joint program of Pacific Northwest National Lab and the University of Maryland). She holds a PhD in economics from University of Maryland, College Park, and a master's in city planning from the Massachusetts Institute of Technology.

Unlocking Commercial Financing for Clean Energy in East Asia • http://dx.doi.org/10.1596/978-1-4648-0020-7

Abbreviations

€	euro
$A	Australian dollar
ACT	avoided cost tariff
ADB	Asian Development Bank
ADEME	French Environment and Energy Management Agency
APL	Adaptable Program Loan
ARGeo	African Rift Geothermal Development Program
AU	Administrative Unit
B	baht (Thai)
BA	business angels
BEE	Bureau of Energy Efficiency (India)
BEEF	Bulgarian Energy Efficiency Fund
BEERECL	Bulgaria Energy Efficiency and Renewable Energy Credit Line
BESCOM	Bangalore Electricity Supply Company
BNDES	Brazilian National Economic and Social Development Bank
BOB	Bank of Beijing
BOO	build-own-operate
BOT	build-operate-transfer
Can$	Canadian dollar
CAREC	Central American Renewable Energy and Cleaner Production
CBRC	China Banking Regulatory Commission
CEB	Ceylon Electricity Board
CEEF	Commercializing Energy Efficiency Finance
CfD	Contracts for Difference
CHEEF	China Energy Efficiency Financing Project
China EXIM Bank	Export-Import Bank of China
CFL	compact fluorescent lamp

CHUEE	China Utility-Based Energy Efficiency Finance Program
CO_2	carbon dioxide
CSP	concentrated solar power
CTF	Clean Technology Fund
DEDE	Department of Alternative Energy Development and Efficiency (Thailand)
DKr	Danish kroner
DSM	demand-side management
EAP	East Asia and Pacific (World Bank region)
EBRD	European Bank for Reconstruction and Development
EC II	China Second Energy Conservation Project
ECA	Europe and Central Asia
EE	energy efficiency
EEC	energy efficiency credit
EEG	German Renewable Energy Sources Act
EERF	Energy Efficiency Revolving Fund (Thailand)
EESL	Energy Efficiency Services Limited
EFSE	European Fund for Southeast Europe
EIB	European Investment Bank
EMC	energy management company
EMCA	Energy Management Company Association
EMRA	Electricity Market Regulatory Agency (Turkey)
ENCON fund	Energy Conservation Fund (Thailand)
EPC	energy performance contract
ESC	energy savings certificate
ESCO	energy service company
ESPC	energy saving performance contract
EU	European Union
FI	financial institution
FIDEME	Fonds d'Investissements de l'Environnement et de la Maîtrise de l'Energie (Investment Fund for Environment and Renewable Energy)
FIT	feed-in tariff
FM	fund manager
GCPF	Global Climate Partnership Fund
GDP	gross domestic product
GEEREF	Global Energy Efficiency and Renewable Energy Fund
GEF	Global Environment Facility
GeoE	geothermal energy

GeoFund	Geothermal Energy Development Program
GET-FIT	Global Energy Transfer Feed-in Tariffs for Developing Countries Program
GFA	guarantee facility agreement
GHG	greenhouse gas
GIB	Green Investment Bank
GRI	geological risk insurance
GW	gigawatt
GWh	gigawatt-hour
HEECP	Hungarian Energy Efficiency Co-financing Program
IB	Industrial Bank
IBRD	International Bank for Reconstruction and Development
IDA	International Development Agency
IDB	Inter-American Development Bank
IEA	International Energy Agency
IFC	International Finance Corporation
I&G	China National Investment and Guarantee Co. Ltd.
IGA	International Geothermal Association
IIEC	International Institute for Energy Conservation
IPP	independent power producer
IREDA	India Renewable Development Agency
JVC	joint venture company
KfW	Kreditanstalt für Wiederaufbau (German Development Bank)
KIDSF	Kozloduy International Decommissioning Support Fund
ktoe	thousand tons equivalent
kW	kilowatt
kWh	kilowatt-hour
LIBOR	London Interbank Offer Rate
MDB	multilateral development bank
MEER	Ministry of Energy and Energy Resources
MKE	Ministry of Knowledge Economy
MOL	Hungarian Oil and Gas Company
MSME	micro, small, and medium enterprises
M&V	measurement and verification
MW	megawatt
MWh	megawatt-hour

NDRC	National Development and Reform Commission (China)
NER	National Electricity Regulator
NERSA	National Energy Regulator of South Africa
NGO	nongovernmental organization
NPC	National Power Company
NYSERDA	New York State Energy Research and Development Authority
OECD	Organisation for Economic Co-operation and Development
OM	operational manual
PB	participating bank
PBC	public benefit charge
PBF	Public Benefit Fund
PBG	publicly backed guarantees
PCG	partial credit guarantee
PCI	participating credit institutions
PFI	participating financial institution
PIDG	Private Infrastructure Development Group
PNOC	Philippine National Oil Company
PPA	power purchase agreement
ppm	parts per million
PRG	partial risk guarantee
PV	photovoltaic
PVRP	Photovoltaic Rebate Programme
R&D&D	research and development and demonstration
RE	renewable energy
REAF	Renewable Energy Asia Fund
REC	Renewable Energy Certificate or Renewable Energy Credit
REDP	Renewable Energy Development Project (Vietnam)
REI	Reykjavik Energy Invest
RERED	Renewable Energy for Rural Economic Development
RMF	Risk Mitigation Fund
ROC	Renewables Obligation Certificate
RPS	renewable energy portfolio standards
Rs	Indian rupees
RSFF	Risk-Sharing Finance Facility
SCAF	Seed Capital Assistance Facility

SEFF	Sustainable Energy Finance Facility
SHS	solar home system
SIDBI	Small Industries Development Bank of India
SLSEF	Sri Lanka Sustainable Energy Fund
SME	small and medium enterprise
SOP	Standard Offer Program
SPDF	Special Purpose Debt Facility
SPP	small power producer
SWH	solar water heater
TA	technical assistance
TGC	tradable green certificate
TKB	Turkish Development Bank
TOOR	transfer of operating rights model
TSKB	Turkish Industrial Development Bank
TWh	terawatt-hour
UNEP	United Nations Environment Programme
USAID	United States Agency for International Development
USELF	Ukraine Sustainable Energy Lending Facility
US$	United States dollar
VC	venture capitalists
VCFEE	Venture Capital Fund for Energy Efficiency (India)
VSPP	very small power producer
WBG	World Bank Group
WTO	World Trade Organization
Y	yuan (Chinese)

PART 1

Overview

CHAPTER 1

The Role of the Government: Act Now on Domestic Policy and Financing

Global and Regional Context: Governments Are Taking Action, but Mobilizing Substantial Financing Is the Major Hurdle

Governments should not wait for international climate agreements but should take action now. Impasses in international climate negotiations will increase the costs and difficulties of stabilizing the climate. A low-carbon growth path is in the best interests of each country, yielding the domestic benefits of energy savings, improved local environments, enhanced energy security, and new jobs. The good news is that many countries are already taking action. In 2010, global renewable energy (RE) investment topped US$200 billion. For the first time, the developing world has overtaken the richer countries in new financial investment for clean energy, with China being the largest source of clean energy investment at US$50 billion (UNEP and Bloomberg New Energy Finance 2011). National development finance institutions invested US$42.7 billion in climate financing in 2011, mostly in RE and energy efficiency (EE), more than the climate financing provided by bilateral and multilateral finance institutions combined (Buchner and others 2012).

In East Asia, all middle-income countries have established national targets for EE and RE, and some even have targets for carbon reduction. China has committed to reducing carbon intensity by 40–45 percent from 2005 to 2020; cutting energy intensity by 20 percent from 2000 to 2005 and an additional 17 percent from 2005 to 2010; and increasing the share of nonfossil fuels in primary energy from 8 percent in 2010 to 15 percent in 2020. Indonesia has pledged to reduce its carbon emissions by 26 percent by 2020; improve EE by 30 percent by 2025; and increase the share of RE in primary energy to 17 percent by 2025. Thailand targets supplying 20 percent of final energy demand from RE by 2022, and the Philippines aims to double its RE capacity by 2030 (Wang and others 2010).

The World Bank East Asian flagship report, *Winds of Change: East Asia's Sustainable Energy Future*, concluded that the East Asia region could, with the right policies and sufficient financing, stabilize carbon dioxide (CO_2) emissions

Box 1.1 Key Messages

- **Governments should not wait for international climate deals but should take action now.** Impasses in international climate negotiations will increase the costs and difficulties of stabilizing the climate. A low-carbon growth path is in each country's best interests, bringing the domestic benefits of energy savings, improved local environments, enhanced energy security, and new jobs. Many countries are taking action now. In East Asia, all middle-income countries have national targets for EE and RE, and some even have targets for carbon reduction. In 2011, national development banks invested in more climate financing than did bilateral and multilateral development banks (MDBs) combined.

- **An effective role for government hinges on putting in place a sound enabling environment to attract investment, coupled with public financing mechanisms to provide incentives to investors and unlock commercial financing.** This report focuses on the latter: *when and under what circumstances to use public financing instruments; which instrument to select; and how to design and implement them most effectively.* The report is targeted at (a) the government decision makers who design clean energy policy and financing instruments in middle-income and high-income countries, (b) international donors and MDBs that design global climate financing mechanisms, and (c) energy practitioners who implement these financing instruments.

- **Conducive policies are essential to catalyzing commercial investment in clean energy.** In the absence of such an enabling policy environment, public financing instruments are unlikely to have a sustainable impact. Policy instruments need to be carefully selected and tailored to local conditions, including political realities. EE and RE investments face unique barriers to their adoption, and effective policy measures must be designed to overcome these barriers. Effective EE policies should aim to remove market barriers and overcome market failures, thereby creating market demand. This goal can be achieved through a combination of policy instruments: market-based pricing reforms to discourage energy waste, regulations such as efficiency standards and codes to mandate EE, and financial incentives to defray high up-front costs. RE policies that compensate investors for the cost gap between RE and fossil fuels are a prerequisite to RE financing. When such policies as feed-in tariffs (FITs) are in place, commercial financing for RE becomes the norm.

- **Even with effective clean energy policies in place, public financing mechanisms are still needed to mitigate risks and close financing gaps.** Innovative EE public financing is particularly important to mitigating financiers' risk perception, to aggregating small deals, and to enhancing the interest and capacity of domestic banks. RE financing instruments can provide long-term tenure, mitigate technology risks, and increase access to financing for small and medium enterprises (SMEs). Public financing mechanisms should attract, but not crowd out, private capital.

box continues next page

Box 1.1 Key Messages *(continued)*

- **Financing instruments have to be tailored to the market barriers, the targeted market segments, the existing regulatory environment, and the maturity of the financial market**:
    - *Credit lines* are effective at increasing banks' capacity and confidence in EE and RE investments to large and medium clients and projects, and at providing longer-term tenure for RE projects, but supporting SME EE investments is a challenge.
    - *Risk guarantees* are effective at increasing banks' confidence in clients at the margins of risk ratings, such as first time energy service companies (ESCOs) but with creditworthy clients and viable projects, mitigating technology risks (for example, geothermal); and extending loan tenure, but only reduce banks' *perceived* risks but not their real risks.
    - *Dedicated funds* are effective at increasing access to EE financing for SMEs and public sector projects and when domestic banks are not ready to provide RE financing, but leverage, sustainability, and scale-up of EE and RE financing remain key challenges.
    - *Concessional project financing* is an interim measure for when sound policies are not in place or to kick-start new technologies, but limited public funds cannot lead to large scale.
    - *Mezzanine financing* is a flexible instrument effective at bridging the equity-debt gap for SMEs and clean energy start-ups.
    - *Equity funds* are effective at supporting SMEs, ESCOs, new clean energy technologies, and early-stage technology firms.
    - *Consumer financing* is effective at helping consumers overcome high up-front cost barriers, but regulatory systems need to allow utility on-bill financing.
    - *Carbon financing* plays only a small role in climate finance—it is the "icing on the cake" that can slightly enhance the returns for investment deals.
- **Engaging domestic banks through credit lines and guarantees, mezzanine funds and equity funds, and interest rate buy-downs for consumer financing can catalyze substantial clean energy financing**. Specialized credit lines seem to have had the greatest impact in unlocking private financing, especially for EE. Publicly financed dedicated credit lines have had substantial success in encouraging commercial banks to enter the EE financing market and then to stay in the business once the public credit lines have been exhausted. Publicly supported mezzanine funds and equity funds have also shown similar promise.
- **The impact of public financing instruments can be substantially increased if they are packaged with technical assistance (TA), and in some cases with targeted subsidies**. The experience in China and Eastern Europe certainly provides evidence that the payoff from such packaging can be high. The returns for providing TA to financial institutions and project developers to build their clean energy expertise are significant. And short-term and highly targeted financial subsidies to EE investments, particularly those investments made by SMEs and in the building sector, can accelerate their uptake.
- **Generating sufficient deal flows is not easy**. This is perhaps the most commonly encountered problem. A key reason is the misalignment between the standard financing criteria and terms and risk perception of most financiers and the EE and RE market. Banks need to better align their underwriting criteria with the market segments that are most in need of financing; expand beyond their comfort zones of traditional clients, sectors, and technologies; and motivate their internal organizations to originate projects.

box continues next page

Box 1.1 Key Messages *(continued)*

- **Effective governance and management of publicly funded programs is critical to success.** The use of government funds requires public accountability; however, catalyzing private flows requires that project financing decisions be based on purely commercial considerations. Experience has shown that public representatives in the governance of equity funds often find it difficult to act independently of government. In addition, careful selection of participating financial institutions (PFIs) for credit lines and risk guarantees is a key success factor. Within the PFIs, strong senior management support, dedicated teams, active participation of branches, rewards to investment officers, and training of risk assessment officers are all critical to the success of credit line programs.
- **Promoting SME clean energy investment continues to be a major challenge.** Most publicly sponsored clean energy credit lines and equity funds have had difficulty developing their SME portfolios. Lending to SMEs is often constrained by limited collateral, the relatively high costs of project development and loan processing, and the difficulties of aggregating a portfolio of small loans. However, some financial institutions, for example, the European Bank for Reconstruction and Development and the Small Industries Development Bank of India, have had success in this market segment by bundling loans with small grants and highly targeted TA.

---

by 2025, improve local environments, and enhance energy security without compromising economic growth (Wang and others 2010).

However, a major hurdle to achieving this sustainable energy path is mobilizing the required financing—an estimated additional US$80 billion per year during the next two decades to achieve this goal (Wang and others 2010). Given the fiscal constraints faced by most governments and the inherent profitability of most energy investments, the bulk of the required financing is expected to come from the private sector. To stimulate these private flows, public funds (financed by taxpayers and ratepayers) and international donor funds are needed to cover the incremental costs and risks of EE and RE investment programs. Most of the countries in the region have already reached middle-income status, thus, the bulk of these financing needs will have to be mobilized domestically (see box 1.1). Most East Asian governments have already recognized this reality; for example, the Chinese government spent US$20 billion during 2006–09 on financial incentives for EE and mobilized US$6 billion to subsidize RE in 2012 from the RE levy on electricity consumers. Similarly, Thailand provided a subsidy of about US$140 million per year to RE through its renewable adder program from surcharges on power consumers (see box 2.1 in chapter 2).

Effective roles for government are putting in place an appropriate enabling policy environment along with financing mechanisms designed to catalyze substantial private investment with limited public funds. Most governments in East Asia are facing increasing fiscal constraints as a result of the substantial fiscal stimulus in response to the 2008–09 global financial crisis. The current round of economic turmoil stemming from the debt crisis in the European Union has caused renewed concern among policy makers in the region and has clearly high-lighted the importance of ensuring that the impact of any public financing for clean energy is maximized. Similarly, the design of international climate financing schemes such as the Green Climate Fund must also effectively maximize the leverage of these finite public funds to reduce greenhouse gas (GHG) emissions.

Study Objective and Audience: When to Use Which Financing Instrument

This report focuses on clean energy financing instruments and attempts to help decision makers and practitioners address three key issues: *when and under what circumstances to use public funds, which public financing instrument to select, and how to design and implement the instruments most effectively.* For each financing instrument, the report discusses how it works; what works versus what does not based on lessons learned from actual project implementation; and when to use it to leverage public funds to scale up clean energy most cost-effectively. The purpose of this report is to demonstrate how to apply various public financing instruments to help bridge the financial viability gap and improve the bankability of efficient and clean energy investments, not to identify the sources of such funding.

An enabling policy environment is the most critical element, because a conducive and coherent set of clean energy policies is essential for any successful, targeted, government-supported financing mechanism. However, there is already a considerable body of knowledge, experience, and literature on clean energy policy design, particularly in the *Winds of Change* report. Therefore, this report only briefly presents clean energy policy options, with an emphasis on how to select and most effectively design and implement policy instruments, building on the experience and lessons learned over the past decade.

Because country circumstances and priorities vary considerably, the report is not intended to be prescriptive. Rather, it reviews global experience to date and tries to draw lessons that governments might find useful in designing their own clean energy policy and financing interventions. Although key lessons from existing financing mechanisms are already apparent, judgment will always have to be exercised in interpreting their implications for the design of domestic programs.

Domestic political economy will often dictate which clean energy policies can be applied. For example, pricing reforms, such as removal of fossil fuel subsidies and imposition of fuel or carbon taxes, fundamental to an efficient and sustainable energy sector, are often met with stiff political resistance. Similarly, even though fuel efficiency standards proved to be one of the most cost-effective means of improving the EE of vehicles in Europe, the implementation of such standards may run into strong political lobbying from automobile industries in other countries. For RE, it is critical that policy makers reconcile the need to provide adequate incentives to investors with the political desire to minimize subsidies to renewables and address the affordability issue for consumers, particularly the poor. In some countries, such as China, Germany, and Spain, where RE penetration has increased rapidly, consumers are paying surcharges in their electricity bills to cover the incremental costs between RE over fossil fuels. However, in other countries, RE development is constrained by politicians' and consumers' resistance to paying for such incremental costs.

Although the report has been prepared primarily for an East Asian audience, it draws on worldwide experience and is thus relevant to (a) government decision makers who design clean energy policy and financing instruments in other middle- and higher-income countries; (b) multilateral development banks (MDBs) and international donors that design global climate financing mechanisms; and (c) energy practitioners who implement these financing instruments.

Study Scope: Energy Efficiency and Renewable Energy Face Distinct Barriers and Require Different Policy and Financing Instruments

This study is focused on, and organized around, the twin themes of financing EE and grid-connected RE technologies, and does not cover other emerging new technologies such as carbon capture and storage, second-generation biofuels, and electric vehicles. Policies that put an adequate price on carbon; significant public support to accelerate research, development, and demonstration; public funds to cover the incremental costs of such technologies; and measures designed to help venture capital mitigate some of the related risks are all key elements of govern- ment support programs to these emerging new technologies. However, given the capital-intensive nature of many of these advanced technologies, very large pub- lic transfers are typically required to promote their development. To date, there is limited international experience in financing advanced clean energy technolo- gies in emerging markets and developing countries. Most MDBs and bilateral donor activities are focused on commercially available technologies. Moreover, there remains considerable scope for and a high payoff to government initiatives designed to accelerate the adoption of the latter.

EE and RE require different policy and financing instruments, because of differences in their maturity and in the viability of the technologies (table 1.1). Many EE measures are financially viable, with short payback periods and "negative" lifetime costs (fuel savings are greater than additional investment). EE represents the largest and cheapest source of emission reductions. However, the huge EE potential in East Asia has not yet been fully tapped. The con- straints to investments are usually not the financial viability and maturity of EE technologies, but market failures and barriers, which include (a) low or subsidized energy pricing (for example, fossil fuel subsidies); (b) the small share that energy costs represent in operating costs; (c) a lack of institutional cham- pions due to the fragmented nature of EE measures; (d) limited financing for the high up-front investments; and (e) the inability of some potential investors to capture the returns from EE investments (for example, tenants typically pay energy bills, so landlords have little or no incentive to purchase efficient appliances).

Table 1.1 Policy Instruments and Financing Mechanisms Need to Be Tailored to the Maturity of Technologies

Technology	Description or definition	Issues to be addressed	Policy instruments	Financing mechanisms with public funds
Energy efficiency (mostly financially viable)	Technology is financially viable for project investors—cost-competitive with fossil fuels, or with high financial returns and short payback period for demand-side options	Market failures and barriers hamper adoption	Overcoming market barriers: • Mandatory regulations: targets, standards, and codes; EE portfolio standards and trading • Pricing policies: taxes and financial incentives • Institutional reforms	• Dedicated EE credit line • Partial risk guarantee • Dedicated funds • Utility EE/DSM funds • ESCO financing and equipment leasing • EE equity funds • Consumer financing
Renewable energy (mostly economically viable but not yet financially viable)	Technology is economically viable as justified by a country's development benefits; but it cannot yet compete with fossil fuels without subsidy or internalization of local externalities (or both)	Lack of level playing field between clean energy and fossil fuels, and internalization of environmental external costs required	Providing a level playing field: • Removal of fossil fuel subsidies and imposition of energy or carbon tax to internalize local externalities • Financial incentives for RE: feed-in tariff, RE portfolio standards, tendering mechanism	• Concessional project financing • Dedicated RE credit line • Partial risk guarantee • Dedicated RE funds • Mezzanine financing • RE equity funds and contingent grants

Note: DSM = demand-side management; EE = energy efficiency; ESCO = energy service company; RE = renewable energy.

RE presents a different story. Although most RE technologies are economically viable (when all externalities are included), they may not yet be sufficiently financially viable to attract private investment. The incremental cost of RE over fossil fuels is usually the most important barrier. This cost gap is closing, though, with dramatically lower RE costs (for example, solar photovoltaic [PV] costs have declined more than 50 percent in the past 15 years [Feldman and others 2012]) and rising fossil fuel prices. Therefore, pricing policies—either subsidies to RE such as feed-in tariffs (FITs) or taxes on fossil fuels such as carbon taxes—are essential for making these RE technologies cost competitive with fossil fuels and for continuing to drive down the cost curve of RE technologies.

Effective policy measures and financing mechanisms must be designed to overcome these barriers. It is equally apparent that financing interventions need to be tailored to specific market segments, for example, large or small enterprises, as well as to the local political economy, if their full potential is to be realized. Figure 1.1 summarizes these measures and mechanisms by market barriers, segments, and technologies.

The next section of this overview briefly introduces and compares the main policy instruments for EE and RE, building on lessons learned during the past decade. A more detailed discussion of each of the public financing instruments

Figure 1.1 Financing Instruments Need to Be Tailored to Market Segments and Barriers

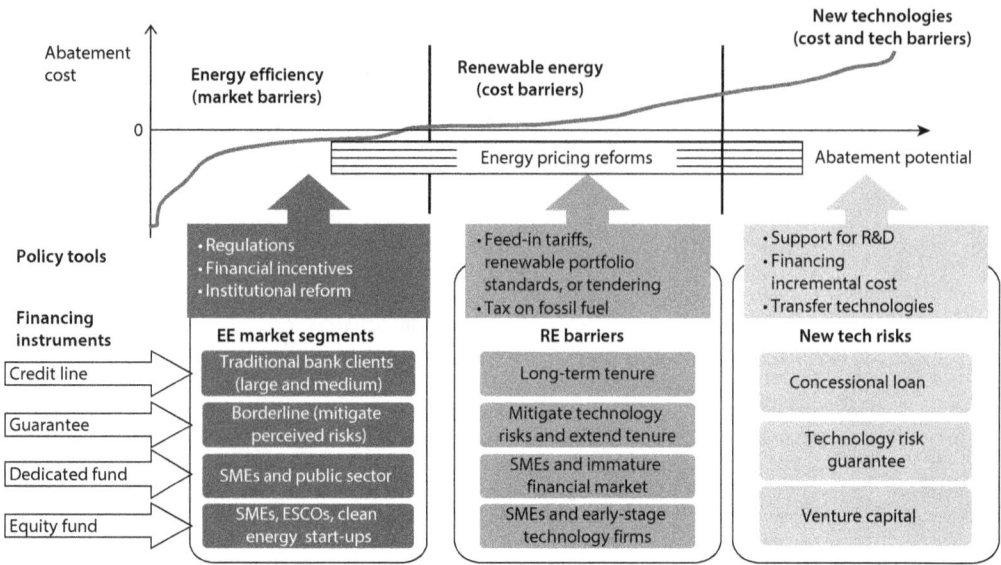

Note: EE = energy efficiency; ESCOs = energy service companies; R&D = research and development; RE = renewable energy; SMEs = small and medium enterprises.

designed to catalyze commercial financing for EE and RE follows. This discussion highlights the specific situational factors that the instruments are designed to address, and assesses their impacts in practice. The final section of the overview summarizes the lessons of experience to date and suggests criteria for government decision makers for selecting appropriate financing mechanisms. A more comprehensive discussion is contained in the main report: Part 2, Financing Energy Efficiency; Part 3, Financing Renewable Energy; and Part 4, Clean Energy Financing Case Studies.

Bibliography

Buchner, B., A. Falconer, M. Herve-Mignucci, and C. Trabacchi. 2012. "The Landscape of Climate Finance 2012." Climate Policy Initiative, San Francisco, CA.

Feldman, D., G. Barbose, R. Margolis, R. Wiser, N. Darghouth, and A. Goodrich. 2012. *Photovoltaic (PV) Pricing Trends: Historical, Recent, and Near-Term Projections.* Technical Report DOE/GO-102012-3839, U.S. Department of Energy, National Renewable Energy Laboratory, Golden, CO.

UNEP (United Nations Environment Programme) and Bloomberg New Energy Finance. 2011. *Global Trends in Renewable Energy Investment 2011: Analysis of Trends and Issues in the Financing of Renewable Energy.* New York: UNEP and Bloomberg New Energy Finance.

Wang, X., N. Berrah, S. Mathur, and F. Vinuya. 2010. *Winds of Change: East Asia's Sustainable Energy Future.* Washington, DC: World Bank.

CHAPTER 2

Conducive Policies: Driver for Catalyzing Commercial Investment in Clean Energy

Energy Efficiency Policy Instruments: Overcoming Market Failures and Barriers

Regulatory Policies

Regulation is one of the most cost-effective measures for improving energy efficiency (EE). Economy-wide energy-intensity targets (energy consumption per unit of gross domestic product [GDP]), appliance standards, building codes, industry performance targets (energy consumption per unit of output), and fuel-efficiency standards are examples of regulatory measures. Some East Asian countries, such as China and Thailand, have adopted such regulatory policies (see box 2.1). Several European countries and states in the United States have gone a step further by implementing EE obligations or EE portfolio standards that oblige utilities to meet specific energy savings targets and allow them to trade energy saving certificates, often called "white certificates."

Weak enforcement of regulations is a concern in many East Asian countries. Regulations are vulnerable to rebound effects—efficient equipment lowers energy bills, so consumers tend to increase energy consumption, eroding some of the energy-use reductions. A white certificates trading scheme is complex to design and administer. Therefore, regulations must go hand in hand with pricing reforms.

Pricing Reforms

Market-based pricing reforms are fundamental to an efficient, sustainable, and secure energy sector. The energy price is a key determinant of the energy future—a driving force to stimulate EE improvements, discourage energy waste, mitigate rebound effects, and encourage the use of clean fuels. Energy prices should remove fossil fuel subsidies and internalize environmental costs through the appropriate use of instruments such as fuel taxes, carbon taxes, or both. Fossil fuel subsidies in East Asia in 2007 (US$70 billion) were close to the estimated additional net financing required for a sustainable energy path (US$80 billion) (IEA 2008; Wang and others 2010). Fuel taxes have proved to be one of the most cost-effective ways to reduce transport energy demand (Sterner 2007). In reality, however, increases in energy prices often face stiff political resistance, and require strong political will, with effective social protection for low-income groups, to make it happen.

Financial Incentives

Financial incentives such as investment subsidies, soft loans, consumer rebates, and tax credits are important mechanisms to overcome the high up-front costs of EE measures. Some Southeast Asian countries provided financial incentives for EE (see box 2.1). In particular, the Standard Offer approach, used in China, some U.S. states, and South Africa, is a transparent and effective approach for providing public subsidies to "acquire" energy savings from end users and energy services companies (ESCOs) using predetermined and prepublished rates (for example, dollars per kilowatt-hour or per tons of coal equivalent savings), once verified energy savings are delivered. But financial incentives require funding from either taxpayers or ratepayers and are increasingly challenging given the lingering financial crisis in many countries.

Finally, experience with EE policy implementation demonstrates that mandatory programs such as energy performance standards are likely to have greater impacts than voluntary programs. In particular, output-based regulations such as energy savings targets are more effective than input-based initiatives such as requirements for energy auditing or requirements for appointing energy managers in energy-intensive enterprises.

Institutional Reforms

Given the fragmented nature of EE measures, a national institutional champion is essential. For example, a dedicated energy-efficiency agency can play an important role in coordinating multiple stakeholders, implementing energy-efficiency programs, and raising public awareness. But they require adequate resources, the ability to engage with multiple stakeholders, independence in decision making, and credible monitoring of results (ESMAP 2008).

Renewable Energy Policy Instruments: Bridging the Cost Gap

Scaling up renewable energy (RE) requires adequate financial incentives for RE or an energy or carbon tax that internalizes local and global environmental externalities (or both) to level the playing field between renewable and fossil fuels. A transparent, sufficient, and secure tariff level with long-term power purchase agreements is a prerequisite for financing grid-connected RE. Effective pricing policies and regulatory frameworks are the key success factors for scaling up RE and a prerequisite for RE financing.

Three Success Ingredients to Scale Up RE

International experience has shown that RE scale-up depends on three critical factors:

- Adequate tariff levels with long-term power purchase agreements
- Mandatory access to the grid for independent power producers
- Incremental costs between RE and fossil fuels (if any) passed through to consumers

Alternative financial incentives include reducing capital and operating costs through investment or production tax credits, improving revenue streams with carbon credits, and providing financial support through concessional loans and guarantees (ESMAP 2006).

Three Mandatory Policies: Feed-In Tariff, RE Portfolio Standards, and Tendering Mechanism

Three major mandatory RE policies are operating worldwide:

- *Feed-in tariffs (FITs)* mandate purchases of RE at a fixed price. The FIT has proved to be the most effective mechanism for generating the highest penetration of RE in a short period, because of its price certainty. At least 50 countries have adopted a FIT approach; half of these countries are in the developing world (REN21 2010), including many East Asian countries (see box 2.1). However, setting tariff levels is a tricky business, and reconciling the need to provide adequate incentives to RE investors with the desire to minimize RE subsidies paid by consumers is a key challenge.

- *Renewable energy portfolio standards (RPS)* mandate that utilities in a given region must acquire a minimum share of power or level of power generation from RE. In theory, market competition drives down costs; in practice, price uncertainty pushes up RE prices. RPS and the trading of green certificates are complex to design and administer, and favor least-cost RE technologies.

- *Tendering mechanisms* allow power producers to bid on providing a fixed quantity of renewable power, with the lowest-price bidder winning the contract. This approach is effective at reducing costs, but signed contracts have not been realized in some countries. Existing experience with auction systems shows that strict selection criteria and approval processes, and penalties for delays and underperformance, are necessary to overcome this challenge (Maurer and Barroso 2011).

Lessons Learned on RE Policies

Affordability and Cost Reduction under FITs

If long-term affordability of RE subsidies is not ensured, the political reality is that the subsidies will not be sustainable. This, in turn, will undermine investor confidence and thus increase the regulatory risk faced by RE financiers. Managing this risk is critical. For example, the sustainable scale-up of RE development in China, Germany, and Spain, where RE has become an increasing share in the power mix, has required that the affordability issue be addressed. In particular, the FIT for solar photovoltaic (PV) must be affordable to consumers or to the government budget to be sustainable. To address this issue, several approaches are being adopted:

- Tendering mechanisms provide a sound basis for establishing cost benchmarks for FIT levels (as in China).
- Consumer price increases can be capped; once the cap is met, the FITs are adjusted downward (as in Thailand).
- FIT rates can periodically be adjusted downward (as in Germany).
- Cost reduction and efficiency improvement measures can be implemented.

The FIT, RPS, and Tendering Policies Are Mutually Exclusive, but Hybrid Approaches Are Emerging under Specific Circumstances

If investor confusion is to be avoided, it is apparent that FIT and RPS cannot be applied to the same RE technology, plant size, or market segment at the same time. However, a recently emerging trend in Italy and the United Kingdom has demonstrated a hybrid approach in which FIT is used to stimulate those technologies not yet financially viable (solar PV, for instance), or those market segments (for example, small RE projects of 1–5 megawatts) that cannot be fully developed under an RPS system.

Box 2.1 Improving the Enabling Environment for Clean Energy in East Asia

China reduced its energy intensity by 70 percent from 1980 to 2010—a remarkable achievement of decoupling energy consumption from economic growth (Wang and others 2010). The Chinese government has mostly relied on regulatory policies to improve EE—setting up a nationwide energy intensity target that is allocated to each province and the nation's top energy-consuming enterprises; implementing stringent EE standards for appliances, buildings, and vehicles (for example, China has higher fuel economy standards than Australia and the United States); and providing generous financial incentives. To capture the remaining EE potential, China needs to (a) promote structural change toward a less energy-intensive economy, (b) increase the use of market-based mechanisms such as reforming energy pricing to complement the administrative measures, and (c) strengthen regulatory and other incentives for EE in urban buildings and transport to complement industrial EE programs.

China is also a global leader in RE, with the largest RE power installed capacity in the world, largely thanks to the RE Law, one of the first in the developing world. China has implemented feed-in tariffs (FITs) for wind, biomass, and solar PV. As a result, wind power capacity has been doubling every year since 2005, reaching 61 gigawatts (GW) in 2012, the largest in the world

box continues next page

Box 2.1 Improving the Enabling Environment for Clean Energy in East Asia *(continued)*

(SERC 2013). However, sustainable and affordable growth of RE in China requires cost reduction, efficiency improvement, and smooth grid integration.

Southeast Asian countries have made less progress toward EE. Indeed, some countries, such as Indonesia, Malaysia, and Thailand, have seen increasing energy intensity since 1996, despite their governments' efforts to improve EE. Most Southeast Asian countries have relied on voluntary measures, financial incentives, and energy managers' programs to improve EE. However, in the absence of mandatory energy performance targets, adequate regulatory regimes, and sufficient pricing reforms, these measures have not achieved the intended results. Virtually all the emerging economies in Southeast Asia have announced EE laws, regulations, or plans. To achieve government targets, Southeast Asian countries need to (a) deepen energy pricing reforms, particularly by removing fossil fuel subsidies; (b) increase the use of mandatory performance-based regulations, such as industrial energy savings targets and fuel economy standards; and (c) reform institutional arrangements by creating national champions for EE and strengthening effective institutional coordination.

Among the Southeast Asian countries, Thailand has implemented FITs (called an RE adder program). As a result, its proposed wind and solar investments have well exceeded the original targets. Malaysia and the Philippines also recently adopted FITs under their new RE Laws. Indonesia, with the largest geothermal resources in the world, has adopted a concession scheme for geothermal, but mandatory requirements for grid access and incremental cost pass-through to consumers will be necessary if RE is to make greater strides.

Bibliography

ESMAP (Energy Sector Management Assistance Program). 2006. *Proceedings of the International Grid-Connected Renewable Energy Policy Forum.* Washington, DC: World Bank.

———. 2008. *An Analytical Compendium of Institutional Frameworks for Energy Efficiency Implementation.* Washington, DC: World Bank.

IEA (International Energy Agency). 2008. *World Energy Outlook.* Paris: IEA.

Maurer, L., and L. Barroso. 2011. *Electricity Auctions: An Overview of Efficient Practices.* Washington, DC: World Bank.

REN21. 2010. *Renewables 2010: Global Status Report.* Paris: REN21 Secretariat.

SERC (State Electricity Regulatory Commission). 2013. *Development Status of Clean Energy in 2012 in China.* Beijing: SERC.

Sterner, T. 2007. "Fuel Taxes: An Important Instrument for Climate Policy." *Energy Policy* 35 (6): 3194–202.

Wang, X., N. Berrah, S. Mathur, and F. Vinuya. 2010. *Winds of Change: East Asia's Sustainable Energy Future.* Washington, DC: World Bank.

CHAPTER 3

Financing Instruments: Tailored to Market Barriers, Segments, and Local Context

Energy efficiency (EE) and renewable energy (RE) financing instruments need to be tailored to (a) the maturity and viability of EE and RE technologies and their specific market and financing barriers, (b) targeted market segments (for example, large and medium or small and medium enterprises, public or private end users, industry or building EE); and (c) the local context, particularly the regulatory environment and the maturity of the financial market.

Tailored to Overcome Market Barriers: Mitigating Risks and Bridging the Cost Gap

Even within an enabling policy environment, innovative EE public financing instruments are needed to mitigate financiers' risk perception, to aggregate small deals, and to enhance the interest and capacity of domestic banks (table 3.1). Many EE developers face substantial financing barriers described as follows:

- *Credit risks*. Most energy inefficient end users and EE project developers such as energy service companies (ESCOs) are small and medium enterprises (SMEs). SMEs face unique barriers in access to financing regardless of the sector, because of their inherent low creditworthiness resulting from limited collateral. Most local banks usually rely on balance sheet financing, which requires that borrowers either have good credit ratings or high levels of collateral, which, in turn, favors large-scale borrowers. The concept of project-based financing that focuses on the cash flows from energy savings has not yet been widely accepted by financial institutions. The end result is that the most creditworthy potential clients do not necessarily need financing for EE, while the customers most in need of financing are typically not creditworthy. Under such circumstances, publicly backed risk guarantee funds can reduce perceived credit risks, and dedicated EE funds can increase access to financing for SMEs.

- **Performance risks**. EE investments also involve perceived performance risk because lenders are not sure whether the expected future savings will be realized or captured by the investors. In such cases, energy saving guarantees can help lessen perceived performance risks.

- *A lack of expertise, interest, and confidence in EE financing on the part of financial institutions*. Most local financial institutions lack the required technical expertise to appraise EE investments, and view EE lending as risky with a strong social cause. Dedicated credit lines have proved to be effective at increasing local banks' confidence and capacity in EE lending, and at changing their perceptions so that they recognize that EE investments are actually a profitable business.

- **Small deals with high transaction costs**. EE investments tend to be small, with high transaction costs. Innovative business models found through the dedicated credit lines and ESCO financing can help aggregate small deals.

For RE, in countries in which sound regulatory frameworks such as feed-in tariffs (FITs) exist, commercial financing for large-scale, grid-connected RE is the norm, and the availability of investment finance is normally not a constraint. However, RE public financing instruments are needed to provide long-term tenure, mitigate RE technology risks, and increase access to financing for SMEs (table 3.2). The reasons for this include the following:

- **Mismatch between short-term tenure and long-term payback**. RE technologies are capital intensive with long-term paybacks, therefore, either direct funding or dedicated credit lines from multilateral development banks (MDBs) can provide the needed long-term financing, and risk guarantees can extend loan tenure.

- **Technology risks**. Emerging RE technologies (for example, offshore wind and concentrated solar power, or CSP) face technology risks, while some RE technologies face unique resource risks such as drilling risks for geothermal energy, and long-term reliability and low-cost biomass fuel supply risks. Risk guarantees are useful for mitigating RE technology risks.

- **Credit risks for SME developers**. RE projects are generally smaller than conventional power projects. Although many large-scale utilities and independent power producers have entered the RE field, small-scale RE projects, such as small hydro and biomass power projects, tend to be developed by local SMEs. Under such circumstances, dedicated credit lines or funds, mezzanine financing, equity financing, and contingent pre-investment grants can help SME developers increase access to financing.

Therefore, although a lack of domestic capital is rarely the problem, the misalignments between the standard financing criteria and term, interest, expertise, and risk perceptions of most financial institutions and the EE and RE market are significant constraints to financing. Many clean energy investments have high up-front capital costs, followed later by savings in fuel costs. However, most investors and end users tend to be biased toward energy choices with lower up-front capital costs, even when such choices eventually result in higher overall costs. As a result, meeting up-front financing requirements is a major hurdle. To this end, carbon financing has been playing a small role in climate financing, as "icing on the cake," because it does not fundamentally address the up-front financing barrier, although it slightly enhances the returns.

Tailored to Meet the Needs of Market Segments: Increasing Access to Financing for SMEs

The target market segment is determined by the program objectives—to maximize reductions in greenhouse gas (GHG) emissions, or to increase access to EE or RE financing. If the former, targeting financing to large and medium enterprises will be most cost effective and will yield the lowest cost per ton of GHG emission reduction. The justifications for public funds are to provide incentives for large-scale enterprises and developers to invest in clean energy, and to increase the capacity and confidence of financial institutions to mainstream clean energy business lines through "learning by doing." This will lead to the highest leveraging of public funds.

If the objective is to increase access to EE or RE financing, the public funds will have real value added if targeted to SMEs, which are often the least efficient energy users and project developers for small-scale EE and RE investments. However, this approach will result in a higher cost per ton of GHG emission reduction. As mentioned, SMEs face unique barriers in access to financing. Experience shows that dedicated credit lines normally favor financiers' traditional creditworthy clients—large and medium enterprises—unless the financiers already have a strong SME client base. Experience also demonstrates that risk guarantees can only reduce banks' *perceived* risks but not their real risks, such as weak borrowers' balance sheets or unviable projects. Dedicated funds targeted to SMEs and mezzanine and equity financing can be more effective at increasing access to financing and bridging the financing gaps for SMEs.

Unlocking Commercial Financing for Clean Energy in East Asia • http://dx.doi.org/10.1596/978-1-4648-0020-7

Table 3.1 Tailoring EE Financing Instruments to Meet the Needs of Market Segments and Overcome Barriers

Financing instrument	Market segments or maturity of financial sector	Market barriers addressed	Leverage and sustainability	Examples
Credit line through local financial institutions	• Targeted at local banks' traditional clients—large and medium enterprises • Lending to SME clients, typically requiring specialized SME banks	• To address a lack of liquidity • To increase the interest and capacity in EE investment of domestic banks through learning by doing	• High leverage (for example, 1:4) • Good prospect for sustainability	• World Bank China Energy Efficiency Financing Program • Thailand Energy Conservation Fund • EBRD Bulgaria Residential Energy Efficiency Credit Line
Partial risk guarantees	Targeted at borrowers with borderline credit ratings, for example, first-time ESCOs but with creditworthy clients and profitable projects	To reduce *perceived* risks and increase confidence of local banks that are interested in new EE business lines and borrowers	• High leverage (for example, 1:7–10) • Good prospect for sustainability	• World Bank China Energy Conservation II • IFC China Utility Energy Efficiency • IFC Commercializing Energy Efficiency Financing
Dedicated EE funds	• SMEs and public sector facilities that local banks normally are not interested in • Immature financial markets	To finance secondary market (SMEs and public sector facilities) in which local banks are not willing to invest with traditional balance sheet financing, with a dedicated team	• Leverage, sustainability, and scale-up are challenges • High cost per ton of emissions reduction	• World Bank Bulgaria Energy Efficiency Fund
Utility EE/ demand-side management funds	Targeted at utility customers and ESCOs	To provide financial incentives to overcome the high up-front cost barrier	Funding from consumer power tariff levy is most sustainable and reliable	• U.S. EE/DSM funds in California, New York, and Vermont • South Africa Standard Offer
ESCO financing and equipment leasing	• ESCOs usually target industries, government and public facilities, buildings • Leasing usually used in relatively mature financial market but underdeveloped EE market	• ESCOs aggregate small deals to reduce transaction costs, and offer performance-based EE services and financing for end users • Leasing helps clients avoid paying for up-front financing	• ESCOs have difficulties accessing financing • Leverage can be high because little public funds are needed • Guaranteed savings model is more sustainable	• China ESCO industry and leasing • Croatia Hrvatska Elektroprivreda, (HEP) Super ESCO • Belgium FEDESCO
Equity funds	• SMEs and ESCOs • EE technology providers • Start-up EE developers	To address limited access to equity funds for SMEs and ESCOs	• Potential large leverage, but in practice often a challenge • Highest risk • Exiting is tricky • Possibility of creating sustainable technologies and business models	• India Venture Capital Fund for Energy Efficiency • European Investment Bank, Global Energy Efficiency Renewable Energy Fund

table continues next page

Table 3.1 Tailoring EE Financing Instruments to Meet the Needs of Market Segments and Overcome Barriers *(continued)*

Financing instrument	Market segments or maturity of financial sector	Market barriers addressed	Leverage and sustainability	Examples
Consumer financing for EE and RE consumer products, such as utility on-bill financing	Targeted at consumer EE and RE products	To overcome the high first cost barrier of EE and RE products	• High leverage • High impacts to increase market penetration of EE and RE products • Good prospect for sustainability	• Tunisia Solar Water Heater Program • Bangalore Efficient Lighting Program • India–UNEP Solar Lantern Program

Note: DSM = demand-side management; EBRD = European Bank for Reconstruction and Development; EE = energy efficiency; ESCO = energy service company; FEDESCO = federal authorities energy service company; IFC = International Finance Corporation; RE = renewable energy; SME = small and medium enterprise; UNEP = United Nations Environment Programme; WB = World Bank.

Table 3.2 Tailoring RE-Financing Instruments to Market Segments and Barriers

Financing instrument	Market segment	Market, policy, and financial sector barriers	Leverage and sustainability	Examples
Concessional project financing by MDBs and development banks	Large-scale RE projects	• When RE policies (for example, FIT) are not in place • When RE market is in an early stage or financial market is not yet mature • To prove or demonstrate new RE technologies • To provide long-term financing in countries where local banks cannot do so	• Medium leverage • Sustainability hinges on policy frameworks	• World Bank CTF for Indonesia Geothermal Development • KfW offshore wind facility • Ukraine Sustainable Energy Lending Facility (EBRD/CTF)
Credit line through local financial institutions	Targeted at SME RE developers, particularly small hydro projects	• To provide long-term financing to RE projects • To increase interest and capacity in RE investment at local banks	• High leverage • Good prospect for sustainability	• World Bank Vietnam Renewable Energy Development Project • World Bank Turkey Renewable Energy Project • World Bank Sri Lanka RE for Rural Economic Development Project
Partial risk guarantees	• RE technologies with resource or technology risks • Emerging technologies, for example, CSP and offshore wind	• To mitigate RE resource or technology risks (for example, as with geothermal) • To extend loan tenure	• High leverage • Good prospect for sustainability	• World Bank Geothermal Guarantee Fund in Africa and Eastern Europe • U.S. Department of Energy Guarantee Fund
Dedicated RE funds for debt financing	Targeted to SMEs, immature financial markets	To finance RE projects that local banks are not yet willing to invest in or for which local interest rates are too high	• Limited leverage • Good prospect for sustainability if local banks gain confidence in the RE sector	• Indian Renewable Energy Development Agency Limited

table continues next page

Table 3.2 Tailoring RE-Financing Instruments to Market Segments and Barriers *(continued)*

Financing instrument	Market segment	Market, policy, and financial sector barriers	Leverage and sustainability	Examples
Mezzanine financing	Targeted to SMEs	• To bridge the debt-equity gap for SMEs • To provide subordinate loans to leverage senior debt	High leverage	• Fonds d'Investissements de l'Environnement et de la Maîtrise de l'Energie (Investment Fund for Environment and RE) • Central American Renewable Energy and Cleaner Production
Equity funds and contingent grants that transform to loans if the project is successful	Targeted to SME developers and early-stage technology firms	• To increase access to equity funds and pre-investment funds for SMEs • To motivate equity funds to move into earlier-stage finance • To partially cover project preparation and development costs • To share risks in uncertain country environments in which private developers are reluctant to take on the development risk fully	• High leverage • Equity funds have the highest risk • Good prospect for sustainability	• European Investment Bank, Global Energy Efficiency Renewable Energy Fund • Berkeley Energy's Renewable Energy Asia Fund • InfraCo Asia • Seed Capital Assistance Facility

Note: CSP = concentrated solar power; CTF = Clean Technology Fund; EBRD = European Bank for Reconstruction and Development; FIT = feed-in tariff; KfW = Kreditanstalt für Wiederaufbau (German development bank); MDB = multilateral development bank; RE = renewable energy; SME = small and medium enterprise.

Tailored to Suit the Local Context: Fitting into the Regulatory Environment and Maturity of the Financial Market

The prevailing regulatory environment

In the absence of effective pricing policies such as FITs for RE, public concessional financing will be needed to cover the incremental costs of RE to demonstrate the potential technologies and set cost benchmarks. When domestic resources from either ratepayers or taxpayers are not sufficient to cover the incremental costs of FITs for RE, global public funds are needed to cover global environmental external costs to support domestic FIT policies. However, given the limited public funds, such instruments are not sustainable and will not lead to the needed scale-up. Without an enabling environment (for example, rational energy pricing and government mandatory policies), EE financing instruments may be difficult to implement because of a lack of demand for EE investments.

The regulatory framework for financial institutions can be another avenue for attracting attention to the clean energy sector. Regulations can run from the most extreme, such as required lending targets for clean energy and restrictions on lending to energy-intensive sectors, to more minor features such as tax breaks and lower risk weights for clean energy loans.

Table 3.3 Financing Mechanisms Need to Be Tailored to the Maturity of the Local Financial Sector

	Level of financial sector development		
	Low	*Medium*	*High*
Country income level in EAP region	Low-income countries (for example, Lao PDR)	Middle-income countries (for example, Thailand)	Upper-middle-income countries (for example, Malaysia)
Banking services	Basic banks	Full range banks	Universal banks
Nonbank financial services	None	• Government bonds • Equity	• Government and corporate bonds • Equity • Alternatives (private equity, venture capital)
Interest rate	Administratively set	Largely market based	Fully market based
Access to finance for SMEs	Limited	Partial	Readily available
Availability of long-term funding	Limited (up to 1 year)	Partial (up to 7 years)	Full (up to 15 years)
Risk management	Weak	Adequate	Robust
Clean energy financing instruments	• Lines of credit (liquidity support) • Concessional financing • Dedicated debt funds	• Lines of credit (demonstration) • Partial risk guarantees	• Lines of credit (demonstration) • Partial risk guarantees • Equity funds • Consumer financing

Note: EAP = East Asia and Pacific; SME = small and medium enterprise.

The overall maturity and sophistication of the national financial sector

The level of financial sector development will be a key determinant of the kinds of instruments that will be most effective. For example, in many low-income countries, the main financial institutions are banks, and the capital markets that might support equity funding are not available. Thus, lines of credit might be most suitable, primarily for liquidity support. When the domestic financial market is not yet familiar or comfortable with clean energy financing or the local interest rate is too high, special purpose public debt funds can be set up as an interim measure to demonstrate the viability of clean energy investments. In slightly more developed financial markets, lines of credit and partial risk guarantees may be more effective at boosting the confidence of the financial institutions in EE and RE investments. Equity funds and consumer financing would have a higher chance for success in fully developed financial markets (table 3.3).

Energy Efficiency and Renewable Energy Financing Instruments: How They Work, What Works, and When to Use Them

This section discusses each public-sponsored EE and RE financing mechanism.

Dedicated EE and RE Credit Lines through Local Financial Institutions
How It Works

- **EE**. Under dedicated credit lines, governments (for example, Thailand Energy Conservation Fund) or MDBs and donors (for example, World Bank China Energy Efficiency Financing Program) provide concessional loans to participating financial institutions (PFIs) in developing countries, which, in turn, on-lend to end beneficiaries at either concessional or market rates. This is by far the largest volume of EE financial support by MDBs.
- **RE**. Dedicated credit lines for RE work the same way as those for EE, except that PFIs usually on-lend to end beneficiaries with longer tenures than those available in the local market to match the long payback period of most RE investments.

What Works

Dedicated credit lines are effective at increasing the capacity, interest, and confidence of participating banks in mainstreaming the EE and RE financing business line through a learning-by-doing process. This approach can achieve a double leverage effect by leveraging substantial debt contributions from the participating banks and equity financing from end beneficiaries, then later revolving the loans that are paid back to the fund. It offers the best prospect for program sustainability. Evidence is accumulating that participating banks continue to provide EE and RE financing after the credit line program is completed. The success formula for the credit line instrument is well established: (a) careful selection of PFIs through a competitive process with well-defined criteria; (b) inclusion of a few PFIs, so developers can shop for the best deal; (c) strong management commitment, dedicated teams at both headquarters and branches, and incentives to staff within the PFIs; (d) technical assistance (TA) to support project pipeline development and capacity building of both PFIs and local project developers; and (e) aggressive marketing and business development as well as new financial products tailored to EE and RE financing, which are critical to generate sufficient deal flows.

When to Use It

- **EE**. A dedicated credit line is usually most effective at increasing EE financing for traditional bank clients, that is, medium and large enterprises. Encouraging commercial banks to support SME EE investments has been a challenge, unless the bank already has a strong SME client base. This is because most banks rely on their traditional underwriting criteria of balance sheet financing. The balance sheets of most SMEs are much weaker than those of larger companies and their risk profiles much higher. Changing banks' underwriting criteria to project-based financing that focuses on energy savings, which could, in turn, increase access to financing for ESCOs and SMEs, has proved to be difficult. In this connection, there is evidence that European Bank for Reconstruction and Development (EBRD)-sponsored EE lines of credit to commercial banks in Eastern Europe have had greater success in reaching SMEs and residential households. The availability of grants to help the banks defray the high costs associated with processing such loans to SMEs to offset a modest portion of their investment costs in some but not all countries seems to be an important factor contributing to this achievement. Finally, for governments and MDBs that intend to use public funds to scale up EE investments, dedicated credit lines are a cost-effective instrument for bundling many small-scale EE projects using a wholesale approach in which PFIs are responsible for managing an EE portfolio.

- *RE.* A dedicated credit line has the following major applications for RE:
  - In financial markets that are still in their early stages of development, dedicated credit lines increase the commercial interest of the participating banks in RE finance through the access to external sources of funds on attractive terms, which enables them to expand the volume of their lending business. Combining the credit line with a TA grant facility removes the obstacle of high costs of finance on the commercial market.
  - For new RE technologies or small-scale RE projects, particularly small hydro projects (for example, the World Bank Vietnam Renewable Energy Development Project and the World Bank Turkey Renewable Energy Project), a dedicated credit line is a cost-effective instrument for public funds from MDBs to invest in a portfolio of small-scale RE projects with a wholesale approach.
  - Providing credit lines with long tenures to participating banks removes constraints on their ability to lend long term caused by mismatches between the short maturity of their own funding and the long payback period of RE investments (for example, the World Bank Sri Lanka RE for Rural Development Project).

Partial Risk Guarantees for EE and RE
How It Works
- *EE.* A risk guarantee scheme can offer individual project guarantees (for example, the World Bank China Energy Conservation II) or portfolio guarantees (for example, the IFC China Utility-Based Energy Efficiency Program), for which the guarantee covers specified losses in the portfolios of participating banks. The partial risk guarantee can be structured in three ways:
  - Pro rata guarantee so that the participating banks and the guarantor share the loss according to a specified formula (typically pari passu or 50/50).
  - A first loss guarantee (typically 10–20 percent) that pays for losses from the first loss incurred until the maximum guarantee amount is exhausted; the lender incurs losses only when the total loan loss exceeds the first loss guarantee amount.
  - A second loss guarantee (typically 40–80 percent) that pays for losses that exceed the nonguaranteed portion of the loan.

- **RE.** A partial risk guarantee can cover specific technology risks, such as partially insuring eligible drilling costs for unsuccessful geothermal exploration wells (for example, the World Bank Geothermal Fund in Eastern Europe and Africa Geothermal Fund in the Rift Valley). Partial risk guarantees can also help extend tenures to match the financing requirements of the RE project developers more appropriately, given that the length of tenure can be a key limitation experienced by RE project developers seeking local financing.

What Works
- **EE.** Partial risk guarantees are effective at reducing lenders' *perceived* risks, thereby increasing their confidence in and familiarity with EE lending. This approach is intended to share and mitigate risks for domestic banks to invest in EE projects, particularly those proposed by ESCOs or SME service providers and developers. It allows borrowers to access commercial funding that may not have otherwise been available to them because of their risk profiles. It also enables them to secure lower interest rates or longer maturity terms as a result of the reduced commercial risks to the lender. This instrument has a high leverage ratio and good prospects for program sustainability. When such guarantee programs are packaged with TA to ESCOs (to help develop and design EE investments) and to financial institutions (to build appraisal and supervision capacity), the impact can be significant (for example, the World Bank China Energy Conservation II and the IFC China Utility-Based Energy Efficiency Finance projects).

- **RE.** Partial risk guarantees can be effective at mitigating geothermal resource risks and unlocking private investment in geothermal, given the high up-front investment requirements and geological risks associated with drilling. As a result of the prolonged global financial crisis, the private sector risk insurance market for geothermal development has not expanded as expected. To date, such public guarantees are provided by the MDBs, bilateral donors (for example, KfW), and some governments; for example, the government of Chile announced in 2009 a program to insure 30–70 percent of the costs of unsuccessful geothermal exploration wells. Therefore, public funds should be willing to take on higher risk to help mitigate risks for private investors. RE policy is a prerequisite for geothermal development and should be part of the policy trigger for the risk guarantee fund. It is also evident that TA should be an integral part of program design.

When to Use It
- **EE.** Partial risk guarantees are most effective at increasing banks' confidence to lend to those potential EE clients that are at the margins of the financial institutions' credit rating lending criteria, for example, ESCOs (whose business model is typically not familiar to banks) that have solid energy performance contracts with host enterprises of good credit standing but no proven track record with commercial banks themselves. Risk guarantees are not a panacea. They only reduce banks' *perceived* risks, but not real risks such as weak balance sheets or unviable projects.

- **RE**. Partial risk guarantees are effective for RE when (a) covering the later maturity of commercial loans to allow extension of longer tenure to RE projects; (b) covering specific RE technology risks such as early-stage geological exploration drilling for geothermal resources; and (c) covering emerging RE technology risks such as the U.S. Department of Energy Loan Guarantee Program for CSP.

Concessional Project Financing for RE by MDBs or Development Banks
How It Works
Under this instrument, MDBs and development banks provide concessional loans directly to RE projects.

What Works
Concessional financing can kick-start RE markets, demonstrate the viability of RE technologies, and establish RE cost benchmarks in countries at the early stages of RE development. If done in connection with loan syndication, it can also enable participating banks to piggyback on the RE project finance experience of development banks. However, conducive RE policy and regulatory environments are essential for sustainability.

When to Use It
This instrument is used when

- Appropriate RE policies (such as FIT) are not in place (for example, the World Bank Indonesia CTF Geothermal Project);
- RE markets are still in their early stages;
- Domestic financial markets are not yet mature; or
- New RE technologies are being piloted (for example, KfW offshore wind facility).

However, because of limited public funds, this approach is not sustainable, and will not lead to the scale that is needed. It is a temporary measure to build the confidence of the market. Governments can also use this instrument to accelerate bank syndication and serve as a safety net to ensure a minimum level of RE finance when overall lending is restricted during financial crises.

Dedicated EE and RE Funds
How It Works
- **EE**. A dedicated EE fund is established with public funding (for example, the World Bank Bulgaria Energy Efficiency Fund) and provides finance through various instruments, such as debt, mezzanine financing, and equity, to secondary EE markets (for example, SMEs and government or municipal facilities) to which local banks have been unwilling to provide traditional balance sheet financing. A professional team is competitively recruited to manage the fund and rewarded on the basis of agreed-on performance criteria.

- **RE**. Specialized RE development banks, such as the India Renewable Development Agency (IREDA) and the New and Renewable Energy Authority in the Arab Republic of Egypt, are created and used as on-lending conduits for foreign concessional loans when domestic banks are not ready to finance RE investments or have very high interest rates. These funds will, in turn, provide loans to RE developers at concessional rates. The intention is to kick-start an RE market that will attract private capital later.

What Works
- **EE**. Dedicated funds are effective at increasing access to financing for SMEs, ESCOs, and government or municipal facilities, and in immature financial markets. The principle of public dedicated funds is that they should only attract and leverage, but not crowd out, private capital, and therefore, should be willing to assume a higher risk to lessen risks for commercial investors and unlock clean energy financing. A key success factor is to have a dedicated team that is committed to bridging the funding gaps for this secondary EE market by providing TA to EE service providers and end users to develop projects and to package financing deals.

- **RE**. Dedicated funds can demonstrate the viability of RE investments and stimulate the RE market at the early stage of RE development. IREDA was almost the only lending institution in the RE field originally in India, but local commercial banks very quickly became involved in financing wind farms. RE developers were able to secure loans from commercial banks once they had a chance to build a track record of developing RE projects by initially receiving loans from IREDA. IREDA should now focus more on promoting less established, higher risk technologies such as CSP plants.

When to Use It
Dedicated funds target markets in which (a) liquidity is an issue; (b) interest rates are very high; (c) the domestic financial market is not yet mature; or (d) local banks have limited interest in lending for EE projects to SMEs, ESCOs, and government or municipal facilities and RE projects. However, if the focus is on small-scale projects, the costs of attaining energy savings and GHG reductions tend to be high. Securing adequate leverage of public funds and ensuring scale up and sustainability, particularly for SME financing, are proving to be major challenges.

Utility Energy Efficiency and Demand-Side Management Funds
How It Works
Utility demand-side management (DSM), widely adopted in many U.S. states, is usually funded through a system benefit charge, also known as a public benefit charge (financed by a tariff surcharge per kilowatt-hour for all electricity customers). These funds are used to finance EE investments by end users and ESCOs, load shifting, research and development, and consumer education. There

are generally three institutional models for managing such funds: (a) the power utility model (as in California); (b) dedicated government agencies (as in the New York Energy Research and Development Authority); and (c) EE utilities (as in Efficiency Vermont), in which state governments competitively select an EE utility as the fund manager with time-bound, performance-based energy savings contracts.

What Works

Utility EE/DSM funds are effective at improving electricity efficiency at the end-user level, but they need strong regulatory initiatives to motivate utilities to implement them. Decoupling electricity sales from profits can provide a very effective incentive to utilities, because utilities normally make profits by selling more electricity rather than saving it. A tariff surcharge is the most financially sustainable and reliable funding source; such a scheme is not dependent on uncertain government budgets. A Standard Offer approach (successfully used in New York and Texas) provides transparency and revenue certainty from energy savings to project developers, which can help them generate EE projects quickly and increase their access to commercial financing.

When to Use It

Utility EE/DSM funds should be seen as an integral component of national clean energy financing programs. However, to be effective, they need a strong regulatory body and utilities that are (or can be) motivated and have the capacity to deliver EE programs. The alternatives to the utility management model are to have an independent government agency manage such funds, as in New York, or to competitively select a fund manager with performance-based contracts, as in Vermont. Finally, such programs need an effective EE service delivery infrastructure.

ESCO Financing and Equipment Leasing for EE and RE

How It Works

Performance contracting is an approach in which ESCOs provide a wide range of EE services, such as energy auditing, recommendations on energy saving measures, project design and implementation, and financing to end users, using performance-based contracts under which the end users pay for these services from the energy savings upon demonstration of successful results. There are typically three ESCO business models:

- Shared savings, in which ESCOs finance projects and share the energy savings with clients according to a specified formula;
- Guaranteed savings, in which ESCOs guarantee performance and clients finance the projects themselves; and
- Outsourcing (also known as chauffage), in which ESCOs assume responsibility for operation and maintenance of energy-using equipment and sell the energy services to the clients at an agreed-on price.

The concept of a Super ESCO has also recently emerged (for example, in Croatia and Ukraine). A Super ESCO is an entity that is established by the government and functions as an ESCO for the public sector market (for example, for hospitals, schools, municipalities, government buildings) and that also supports the capacity development and project development activities of existing private sector ESCOs, including helping create new ESCOs.

Leasing, or hire-purchase, is an approach in which leasing companies install EE or RE equipment at clients' facilities. The clients make monthly payments, and the leasing companies retain ownership of the equipment until the clients have made all payments over the lease period. An emerging trend has seen some ESCOs offering EE and RE equipment leasing.

For RE, this model is most often used for solar PV. Under an ESCO solar PV–financing model for residential and commercial customers, a solar power company installs small PV systems at no up-front cost to the customer. The customer signs a power purchase agreement (PPA) with the ESCO for the purchase of the output of the plant at rates guaranteed to be equal to or lower than the tariffs charged by the local utility. The solar power company retains ownership of the system and responsibility for maintenance; the PPA revenues serve as lease payments. At the end of the PPA, ownership of the PV system transfers to the customer. Staples in the United States is one of the first major corporations to use such a model for solar power.

What Works

Although the experience of ESCOs in developing countries is still limited, a policy and regulatory environment conducive to EE and the provision of financial and technical support for ESCO development seem to be key to success. For example, in China, where these support mechanisms were put in place, the ESCO industry grew from three companies in 1997 to about 560 with more than US$4 billion in energy performance contracts in 2010 (Sun, Zhu, and Taylor 2011). Equipment leasing allows clients to avoid having to obtain up-front equity and debt financing and collateral requirements, because the equipment is owned by the leasing company. Leasing companies also can play a role in project-bundling arrangements.

When to Use It

The ESCO financing model is effective at aggregating small-scale EE and RE projects to reduce transaction costs, and at offering services and financing to convince end users to undertake EE and RE measures. However, the ESCO financing model is not foolproof. In many countries, ESCOs have had difficulty establishing credibility with customers and obtaining adequate financing from commercial banks because of their weak balance sheets, limited physical assets that can be collateralized, and the perceived risks of realizing revenues from energy savings. Guaranteed savings and Super ESCO models are more sustainable in the long run. Equipment leasing is usually used in relatively mature financial markets in which financial leasing companies exist to address the difficulties of securing up-front financing for end users.

Mezzanine Financing for RE
How It Works
A mezzanine loan is unsecured debt, requiring no collateral; instead, lenders have the right to convert their stakes to an equity position or ownership in the event of default on the loan. This is particularly appealing to private companies because mezzanine financiers do not retain an interest in the company except in the event of default (UNEP 2008). Subordinated debt is a type of mezzanine financing structure and may be the most versatile of all public finance instruments. It provides liquidity directly, but at a higher cost. By reducing the risk to senior lenders, it makes commercial bank finance accessible that otherwise would not have been available. Subordinated debt can be used to extend the effective term of loans, thus helping project cash flows and project viability.

What Works
A prime virtue of mezzanine finance is its flexibility. Unlike conventional loans, its repayments are not tied to a fixed amortization schedule. And it can be structured with equity-like features. For example, mezzanine finance for start-up SMEs developing RE technology or providing RE-related services can be structured as royalty payments: a fee per product sold until the mezzanine loan, including interest, is repaid. Such flexibility is a particular advantage for RE power plants with variable resource flows from year to year, such as wind farms or mini-hydropower plants. For example, the Central American Renewable Energy and Cleaner Production (CAREC) mezzanine finance fund managed by E+Co and supported by the Inter-American Development Bank, helps to finance projects that cannot meet the high collateral and project equity requirements for commercial loans. CAREC finances up to 25 percent of project capital costs for RE projects by offering unsecured loans or additional project equity. The terms of CAREC finance are matched to a project's revenue stream.

When to Use It
Mezzanine financing is effective in those countries in which the RE sector is in the early stages of development as well as for SME developers and start-up RE developers.

Equity Funds and Contingent Grants for EE and RE
How It Works
Equity funds have traditionally been the domain of private sector investors. However, many MDBs and donors, such as the European Investment Bank (EIB), the IFC, the Asian Development Bank (ADB), the EBRD, and the European Union (EU), have made significant investments in private equity funds targeted at EE and RE. Recently, a few Asian countries (Thailand and India) have set up public sector equity funds to help finance EE and RE project developers.

An example of a public equity fund for start-up clean energy technology firms is InfraCo Asia Development Pte. Ltd., which is supported by several multilateral and bilateral donors. InfraCo Asia focuses on smaller-scale projects and reduces the entry costs of private sector infrastructure developers by acting as principal, taking an equity stake in the project to shoulder the risks of early-stage development costs, and providing development expertise through its team of experienced developers.

Three methods for public equity involvement can be seen:

- First, a public-private fund-of-funds model, through which the government can invest a relatively small amount of long-term capital and potentially substantially leverage private investment, seems to be a particularly attractive model. Under a fund-of-funds structure, the government invests in a range of private, professionally managed funds that specialize in particular clean energy subsectors, such as RE, and specified regions. Typically, the government investment is a fraction of the total, but it is a strong signal of support and can encourage significant investment from other institutions.

- The second is direct investment in a private equity fund.

- The third is to set up a public-private equity fund managed by a contracted manager selected through competitive bidding, such as the EIB's Global Energy Efficiency and Renewable Energy Fund (GEEREF); alternatively, if a private equity company wants to coinvest from the beginning as lead investor, it will typically also want to be fund manager. Equity funds have high management costs. Fund managers typically charge a fixed annual management fee of 2–2.5 percent of committed capital and a performance fee of 20 percent of profits beyond a minimum rate.

Contingent project preparation grants help SME developers bring financial closure, funding such activities as permitting, power purchase negotiations, and grid interconnection and transmission contracting. These grants can be on a cost-shared basis, or in the form of contingent grants; that is, the grant becomes a loan and must be repaid if the project succeeds (as determined by close of financing or other milestones), but becomes a grant and does not have to be repaid if the project fails (UNEP 2008).

What Works

Given the limited history of publicly sponsored clean energy funds, it is hard to draw firm conclusions. However, raising matching funds from private investors in the public-private equity fund itself has proved to be a major challenge. This is partly a result of the global financial crisis but also reflects the risk aversion of private equity for clean energy. In addition, given that such funds are allocating, at least in part, public money, maintaining fully independent fund investment committees and letting private equity managers make returns-based decisions proved to be a challenge. The funds are also finding it difficult to find EE investment opportunities that match their criteria.

When to Use It

The rationale for a publicly sponsored clean energy equity fund is based on the fact that government funding is generally available for research and development (R&D) and private financing is available for commercialization of mature technologies; but private finance is unavailable for entrepreneurial activities such as new EE and RE technologies and for providing equity support for ESCOs, SME developers, and start-ups. In such situations, public equity funds can provide a stimulating effect to get the results of R&D commercialized to cover the "death valley." However, it should be recognized that such funds face major challenges in governance, transparency, and incentives, particularly in countries with immature financial markets.

Public equity funds and contingent grants are usually targeted at SME EE and RE developers and early-stage EE and RE firms and businesses that often find it difficult to secure sufficient equity. Public equity finance can therefore be used to cover two financing gaps: capital for project preparation and development, and equity capital for start-up clean energy technology firms. Finally, domestic funds make sense only in countries that have moved to a stage in their energy policy at which investors can see the emergence of a viable clean energy market.

Consumer Financing for EE and RE Products

How It Works

Public funds can help overcome the first cost barrier (higher up-front capital investments) for consumers to purchase EE and RE products by offering multi-year consumer financing through financial institutions, microfinance institutions, or utilities. Utility on-bill financing is a commonly used approach—the utility provides or arranges for the financing needed for the investment. The customer signs a loan agreement with the utility and the utility collects the loan repayments on the customer's utility bill. Loan repayments are typically structured to allow the customer to be "cash flow positive" throughout the life of the EE product. Public funds are usually used to buy down the interest rate to further increase affordability (for example, India's Solar Lantern Program) or to build the confidence of PFIs in EE and RE products (for example, Tunisia's Solar Water Heater Program).

What Works

Such schemes give individual users access to funds that may otherwise not be available for investing in EE and RE products or equipment. They allow consumers to pay for EE and RE products and equipment from the resulting energy savings. This approach increases consumers' ability to pay for EE and RE products, because they do not need to make the one-time, lump-sum, up-front investments. The collection of the payments through the utility bill reduces both the transaction cost of recovering the loan repayments from customers and the risk of default.

When to Use It

Given that consumer financing is effective at increasing the market penetration of consumer EE and RE products, which have higher up-front costs, it has almost universal application. However, for this approach to work effectively, utility billing systems may need to be modified to handle the collection of loan repayments, and the regulatory and legal systems need to allow the utility to collect payments for product or equipment loans. Therefore, governments should ensure that any regulatory barriers to the adoption of such schemes are alleviated. Also, for this approach to work effectively through financial institutions, the financial system has to have a certain level of sophistication in retail applications.

Bibliography

Sun, X., L. Zhu, and R. Taylor. 2011. "China's ESCO Industry: Saving More Energy Everyday through the Market." Unpublished. http://ryanschuchard.files.wordpress .com/2011/06/chinas-esco-industry-2010.pdf.

UNEP (United Nations Environment Programme). 2008. *Public Finance Mechanism to Mobilize Investment in Climate Change Mitigation*. Paris: UNEP.

Unlocking Commercial Financing for Clean Energy: Lessons Learned and Ways Forward

This chapter highlights some of the lessons learned and then draws the implications for governments and multilateral development banks (MDBs) as they select and design their clean energy financing interventions.

Effective Clean Energy Policies Are the Driver for Catalyzing Investment in Clean Energy

This point cannot be over emphasized: public financing can only leverage sustainable private investment if the overall incentive environment is favorable. In the absence of conducive clean energy policies, the impact of publicly sponsored financing mechanisms will be minimal. The creation of incentives such as the progressive elimination of fossil fuel subsidies, taxes on fossil fuels or financial incentives for renewable energy (RE) to provide a level playing field, and other measures designed to help overcome market failures and barriers that inhibit energy efficiency (EE) and RE investment is a prerequisite for success. For example, the Chinese government's mandatory performance-based EE targets have created huge demand for EE investments and energy service company (ESCO) service, whereas the absence of such policies in other countries in the region has limited the impact of EE financing initiatives. Similarly, countries that have adopted RE incentives such as feed-in tariffs (FITs) have seen rapid expansion in RE investment mostly from commercial financing without public financing mechanisms.

Another policy area that can help facilitate financing for clean energy investment is financial sector regulation. The banking regulators in many countries use regulation to encourage or discourage lending activities by banks, including what sectors to prioritize or reduce exposure to. The same approach can be taken to encourage banks to lend to underserved market segments, such as low-income urban areas or small and medium enterprises (SMEs) or start-up companies.

Many countries around the world have such regulations, which range from the simplest, such as reporting requirements on target sectors, to the more extreme, such as legal requirements to allocate a certain portion of a bank's loans to a particular target sector.

Several East Asian countries have adopted such banking regulations. The China Banking Regulatory Commission (CBRC) introduced a new "green credit" guideline for commercial banks in February 2012 that requires banks to reduce their lending to energy-intensive industries with high levels of pollution. This new guideline also encourages banks to evaluate and classify the environmental and social risks of their client businesses and to integrate these analyses and ratings into their overall credit risk management processes. It is too early for the impact of the new guidelines to be known, but it is a clear policy direction for banks with regard to the approach to clean energy.

Public Financing Instruments Must Be Tailored to Overcome Market Barriers, Meet the Needs of Targeted Segments, and Suit the Local Context

Financing instruments for each clean energy technology have to be selected and tailored based on careful diagnoses of the regulatory environment, the maturity of the local financial market, the target market segments, and market and implementation barriers. For example, the balance sheet risks and transaction costs associated with SME lending tend to be much higher than those for larger enterprises; financing mechanisms must reflect these realities. Some examples follow:

- *Dedicated credit lines* through local banks have already demonstrated their effectiveness in increasing participating banks' capacity, interest, and confidence in mainstreaming EE and RE investments. They can also provide long-term tenure to RE projects to match their long payback period. To date, this financing vehicle seems to have had the greatest success in unlocking commercial financing, particularly for EE. Publicly financed dedicated credit lines have had substantial success in encouraging commercial banks to enter the EE financing market in both East Asia and Eastern Europe. Banks were able to enter the market on a pilot basis to test the viability of the market with the publicly backed financing. These interventions have proved to have high leverage and good prospects for sustainability. The lessons from countries such as China, Bulgaria, Hungary, Romania, and Thailand are invariably positive. When public credit lines have been fully used, the participating banks have typically stayed in the business. Experience has shown, however, that commercial banks tend to favor their large and medium customers, and special efforts are needed to reach SMEs.

- *Partial risk guarantees* such as those provided by the World Bank and International Finance Corporation in China and Eastern Europe are proving to be effective at increasing banks' appetite for lending to ESCOs, mitigating RE technology risks, such as the risks of geothermal, and enabling investors to secure longer maturities. The availability of public partial risk guarantees has unlocked private investments in EE in China and Eastern Europe. Such initiatives have high leverage and good prospects for sustainability. But they can only reduce banks' *perceived* risks, not the real risks such as weak borrowers' balance sheets or unviable projects.

- *Concessional project financing* made available through mechanisms such as the World Bank Clean Technology Fund (CTF) for Indonesia's Geothermal Project and the KfW (Kreditanstalt für Wiederaufbau, or German development bank) offshore wind facility can be used to kick-start new technologies still in the development or pre-commercial phase, such as concentrated solar power (CSP) and offshore wind, or as an interim measure to support RE projects when a sound RE policy environment is not in place. It is important to emphasize that support for the latter category of investments is temporary because public subsidies cannot be sustained over the long term and will not lead to the needed scale.

- *Dedicated EE or RE funds* such as the World Bank Bulgaria EE Fund and Indian Renewable Energy Development Agency are effective at increasing access to EE financing for SMEs and public sector projects, or when RE is in the early stages and domestic banks are not ready to provide financing. But securing adequate leverage and ensuring sustainability and scale-up are proving to be key challenges.

- *Utility energy efficiency/demand-side management funds* such as the U.S. demand-side management funds in California, New York, and Vermont and the Standard Offer in South Africa are proving to be effective at improving electricity efficiency at the end-user level, but strong regulatory initiatives, such as decoupling sales from profits, are a prerequisite for success. An alternative is to have an independent government agency manage such funds or to competitively select a fund manager with performance-based contracts. A tariff surcharge is the most financially sustainable funding source because it is not dependent on uncertain government budgets. The Standard Offer Approach is an effective and transparent subsidy scheme.

- *ESCO financing* such as is used in China, India, and the United States, and the more recent Super ESCO model in Belgium and Croatia, can be effective at aggregating small EE and RE projects and offering services and financing to convince end users to undertake EE and RE measures. But it is not a panacea—ESCOs in many countries have had difficulty establishing credibility with customers and obtaining adequate financing from commercial banks. Public sector Super ESCOs have emerged as a viable model for retrofitting government facilities. Equipment leasing allows clients to avoid the up-front financing and collateral requirements and is usually used in mature financial markets.

- *Mezzanine financing*, such as Fonds d'Investissements de l'Environnement et de la Maîtrise de l'Energie (FIDEME, or Investment Fund for Environment and Renewable Energy) and Central American Renewable Energy and Cleaner Production (CAREC), is a very flexible instrument and as such attractive to investors. This instrument is effective in those countries where the RE sector is in the early stages of development as well as for SME developers and clean energy start-ups.

- *Equity funds* backed by public funding can be useful vehicles for supporting clean energy investments, including SME RE project developers, ESCOs, new clean energy technologies, and early-stage technology firms. However, the success to date in leveraging public funding has been mixed, managing deal flows has not always been easy, and ensuring the independence of fund managers supported by public finance is a challenge.

- *Consumer financing* such as utility on-bill financing (for example, the Tunisia Solar Heating Program); interest rate buy-downs for consumer financing (for example, the United Nations Environment Programme India Solar Lantern Program); and energy-efficient mortgages used in the United States (which allow borrowers to qualify for a larger mortgage by including home energy-efficiency measures) are effective at helping consumers overcome the high up-front costs of EE and RE products and equipment and increase market penetration of these products. However, governments should ensure that any regulatory barriers to the adoption of such schemes are removed.

Public Financing Mechanisms Should Be Designed to Maximize Private Financial Flows

The principle of public green or clean energy funds is to attract but not crowd out private capital by lowering risks for investors and unlocking clean energy project financing. Therefore, public funds should be willing to take higher risks and to invest in the secondary market in which commercial financing is not interested or willing to invest, such as new clean energy technologies, SMEs, ESCOs, and early-stage technology firms; to provide incentives to investors; to kick-start the market; and to demonstrate the viability of new financial products.

As noted above, experience to date has demonstrated that engaging domestic banks through publicly sponsored credit lines, guarantee instruments, or interest rate buy-downs can leverage substantial clean energy financing. To date, domestic banks, particularly in East Asia, have been the largest source of clean energy financing; therefore, engaging them offers the biggest "bang for the buck" for public funds. This is not surprising, given that domestic banks have the largest network of customers. The evidence also shows that these programs offer the best prospects for program sustainability. Once clean energy becomes an established business line, scale-up is relatively easy. The dedicated credit lines can also have a double leverage effect by attracting substantial debt contributions from the participating banks and equity financing from end beneficiaries, and later revolving the loans that are paid back to the fund. The lessons learned from the World Bank, the European Bank for Reconstruction and Development (EBRD), the Asian Development Bank (ADB), and other clean energy interventions all support this conclusion.

Publicly supported mezzanine funds and equity funds also promise to leverage private clean energy investments. For example, the French FIDEME, a public-private mezzanine fund open to French SMEs that face debt-equity gaps, leveraged private RE investments of more than 20 times its public funding contribution. In particular, public-private funds-of-funds that invest in a number of commercially managed funds, each of which then invests in projects or companies, can achieve a double leverage effect to leverage private capital both into the fund itself and later into the investments that the fund makes.

Despite its potential, the experience of getting private investors to contribute to the publicly sponsored funds has been mixed. Moreover, the leverage potential of particular financing mechanisms is likely to vary across countries and over time. For example, publicly supported Chinese clean energy equity funds appear to have been quite successful in mobilizing equity to match public contributions into the fund itself. However, in other countries in East Asia, South Asia, South America, and Eastern Europe, the results to date have been less encouraging. The financial crises in Asia in the late 1990s and globally in 2008–09 proved to be a major challenge. For example, equity funds sponsored by the ADB, Inter-American Development Bank, and European Investment Bank during those periods found it difficult to mobilize matching funds. There is some evidence that, once these funds become established and fund managers gain experience, the confidence of private investors in these financing mechanisms does increase; however, success is not assured and developments need to be monitored closely.

Public green funds with multiple financing instruments are an emerging trend for scaling up clean energy investments. One such example is the United Kingdom's Green Investment Bank (GIB), which consolidates within a single institution the existing disparate sources of public investment in a low-carbon economy. The primary focus of the GIB should be on lowering risk for investors, rather than simply providing capital. This suggests that the GIB could help catalyze low-carbon investment by unlocking project finance through equity coinvestment, first loss debt, and insurance products for low-carbon technologies and infrastructure.

The lessons of experience to date also indicate that the leverage of publicly sponsored clean energy financing mechanisms can be substantially increased if they are packaged with other products, for example, technical assistance (TA), and in some cases targeted subsidies (see below). The experience in China, Eastern Europe, and the former Soviet Union certainly provides evidence that the payoff from such packaging can be high; financial institutions in countries in these regions have typically responded enthusiastically to such packaged products and demonstrated a willingness to remain in the clean energy financing space once the assistance is withdrawn.

Technical Assistance Is Critical and Has a High Payoff

As noted, many publicly funded clean energy financing mechanisms have been packaged with TA grants to help participating banks defray up-front "learning curve" costs and to build capacity to identify, appraise, and supervise clean energy projects. A major reason for the traditional reluctance of commercial banks to enter the clean energy space is the high up-front costs of building the human capacity to understand the sector, develop the portfolio, and manage associated risks. The overwhelming evidence is that the availability of TA is critical. Indeed, the absence of such TA facilities in some of the European Investment Bank–European Union (EU)–Deutsche Bank–sponsored clean energy funds may explain why their impact, at least to date, has been more limited; this contrasts with the experience of both the EBRD and the World Bank, which routinely include TA in their credit lines. TA efforts can also help participating banks develop new financial products tailored to EE and RE financing, for example, project-based lending for EE projects in which energy savings serve as the primary security for the project loan.

TA has also been provided to build capacity for project developers, particularly SME EE and RE developers, to prepare feasibility studies and bankable investments, as well as for industrial enterprises and building owners to prepare energy audits. Indeed, grant-funded energy audits have the potential to leverage significant EE investment, provided effective policies requiring performance-based energy savings targets and appropriate financing vehicles are available. For example, very modest EBRD grants for energy audits have triggered substantial EE investments financed on fully commercial terms. There is, therefore, a strong argument for continuing grant support to energy audit programs even when clean energy financing has become an established business line for commercial banks and other nonbank financial institutions. From the EBRD's experience, it is also evident that the impact of grant programs is maximized when they are accompanied by strong EE promotional campaigns with the full involvement of local officials and politicians.

The provision of TA to government policy makers also has a high payoff. This TA should be all-encompassing to include not only those agencies directly involved in RE and EE policy making, but also the financial regulatory and supervisory agencies. The purpose of such TA is to help these agencies understand the dynamics of the RE and EE markets, the financing of RE and EE, and what policy and regulatory changes may be needed to facilitate increased RE and EE investment in the future.

The overwhelming evidence is that grant-supported TA has substantial returns. Once their capacity has been built, the commercial banks tend to stay in the business, and industry and property owners continue to seek additional EE improvements. However, TA alone may not be sufficient. It is most effective when packaged with public financing instruments to provide sufficient incentives or credit enhancement for participating banks to scale up EE and RE investments. Given the strong evidence of the high payoff to TA, it is important that MDBs and donors allocate sufficient TA funds and that some governments overcome their reluctance to use fiscal resources for such activities. Together, they should take steps to increase TA grants associated with clean energy financing initiatives.

Generating Sufficient Deal Flows Has Been a Major Challenge

Clean energy funds, managed by either participating financial institutions or dedicated teams, often run into difficulties finding projects that meet their standard financing criteria. This is the most commonly encountered problem with public funds around the world. There are several reasons.

First, a policy environment conducive to clean energy may not exist. Without an enabling policy framework for EE and RE, market demand for and uptake of EE and RE investments will be limited, despite the availability of the funds.

Second, the financing criteria may not match the targeted market segments. For example, financial institutions and EE project developers usually have very different perspectives. Most financial institutions are inherently risk averse, with little appetite for credit risk. As a result, the most creditworthy potential clients do not necessarily need financing, while the customers most in need of financing are typically not creditworthy. Therefore, TA to participating banks and dedicated fund management teams, particularly to risk assessment officers, is essential for improving their capacity in appraisal and risk evaluation of EE and RE projects, and for developing new financial products tailored for EE and RE projects, such as project-based lending.

Third, financial institutions may not have dedicated staff, the required expertise, or the right incentives for project origination. Ingredients that improve the chances of success include strong management commitment, dedicated teams at both headquarters and branches, and incentives and rewards to investment officers for EE and RE financing. TA grants are also critical to help participating banks and dedicated fund teams conduct proactive marketing efforts, training workshops, specific market studies to identify deals, and intensive promotional campaigns using public relations consultants and national and local political and government leaders.

Finally, financial institutions tend to stay in their regular "comfort zones"— among existing clients, in familiar geographic regions, within the client classes they are most used to, or within subsectors that they know best. They need to expand EE and RE business beyond these areas. Partnering with an intermediary agent between the financial institutions and project developers, such as subsector industrial associations and ESCO associations, seems to be an effective means for strengthening project pipelines.

Effective Governance and Management of Publicly Funded Programs Are Critical to Success

Each public financing instrument presents a different governance challenge. The use of government funds requires public accountability; however, these interventions are designed to leverage private financing for clean energy, which, in turn, requires that individual project financing decisions be based on purely commercial considerations. The avoidance of investment decisions based on political criteria is essential, to ensure both the viability of individual investments and the long-term sustainability of the financing programs. In practice, most clean energy lines of credit appear to have avoided such problems. The investment criteria are agreed on up front with the intermediaries, and governments are generally not involved in making financial decisions.

The challenge facing equity funds is more daunting. Shareholders are typically involved in the governance of such funds and government and official representatives often find it difficult to act independently of government. For example, government representatives to EU-sponsored funds have, on occasion, been required to vote against certain categories of investments, for example, biofuels. The MDB-sponsored clean energy funds appear to have less of a problem in this respect. Maintaining independence in a single-country fund when the government is a major sponsor or shareholder is a major challenge.

In light of the above, maximizing fund managers' independent decision-making authority is crucial. Recognizing that full autonomy cannot always be achieved, it is important to design the governance of publicly supported equity funds to ensure that business decisions are commercially driven and independent of government interference, with only light oversight from the government.

Careful selection of fund management is essential. International experience suggests that competitively selected professional and competent fund managers, who have strong relationships and are aligned with domestic banks, are critical to the success of dedicated funds and partial risk guarantees. When selecting participating banks for public support, a strong management commitment to clean energy and interests in ESCOs as well as SMEs are important criteria.

Finally, detailed design of the fund management evaluation and compensation criteria is critical. For example, some publicly financed fund managers have been too passive, waiting for project proposals to arrive, rather than actively marketing their products. Effective incentive instruments include compensating fund managers through fees based on committed investments rather than a fee structure exclusively based on a percentage of paid-in capital. Such modified formulas can demonstrate the fund manager's confidence in the business model of the fund, as well as make it easier to convince potential investors to place money into the fund. The Global Energy Efficiency and Renewable Energy Fund has attempted to meet this governance challenge by creating an incentive scheme designed to align private equity managers' compensation with the public interest.

SMEs Remain the Toughest Market Segment to Finance

Most publicly sponsored clean energy credit lines and equity funds have had difficulty developing their SME portfolios, as in China, Thailand, and Eastern Europe. Even though EE investments typically have short payback periods, SME lending is often constrained by limited collateral, the relatively high costs of project development and loan processing, and difficulties aggregating a portfolio of small loans. For example, Deutsche Bank found aggregating a portfolio of EE projects under the EU-sponsored European Energy Efficiency Fund to be a major challenge. Moreover, SME lending and investment is typically inherently risky; money is fungible, and potential SME lenders and investors may face *real* balance sheet risks that they cannot mitigate, irrespective of the fact that specific clean energy investments may be very attractive. In these cases, any sort of publicly sponsored clean energy financing mechanism is likely to fail.

In this connection, the EBRD's success in promoting SME EE projects is notable. The EBRD has a significant clean energy portfolio targeted at SMEs and small property owners. The bundling of loans with small grants, coupled with highly targeted TA, has played a major role in ensuring client uptake. TA is particularly important in SME financing projects, both to assist SMEs with capacity building and developing business models to bundle small deals, and to help the financial institutions develop special product lines for SMEs to reduce transaction costs. Similar success has also been achieved by KfW and the Agence Française de Développement, in cooperation with the Small Industries Development Bank of India, in financing SME projects in a number of industrial SME clusters in India.

Although aggregating smaller EE and RE projects and loans is feasible, it can be costly. The high transaction costs of dealing with small-scale projects do not go away, but are simply transferred to someone else. Mechanisms designed to minimize transaction costs include the following:

- A market aggregation business model can be used by domestic banks to target large-scale industrial enterprises and aggregate smaller-scale EE projects at their subsidiary plants, for example, the World Bank China Energy Efficiency Financing Project.

- ESCOs and EE equipment vendors play an essential role in aggregating small deals, particularly in the building sector, because building retrofit investments tend to be very small. ESCOs can package building retrofit investments by ownership (in retail shopping chains or hotel chains under the same owner group, for instance); or EE equipment vendors can bundle EE investments in enterprises or buildings with the same type of EE technology or product, for instance, the ADB Building Energy Efficiency Project in Shanghai.

- Under the Super ESCO model, a government-sponsored Super ESCO is established for public sector markets such as hospitals, schools, municipalities, government buildings, and other public facilities. A Super ESCO can also support development activities of existing private sector ESCOs. The government capitalizes the Super ESCO with sufficient funds to undertake public sector energy saving performance contract projects and to leverage commercial financing, including loans, risk guarantees, and leasing instruments. The World Bank Armenia and Croatia Projects provide examples of Super ESCOs.

Targeted Subsidies Can Play a Catalytic Role

Given the high rates of return and short payback periods that typically characterize EE investments, there is a generally accepted view that financing subsidies are not needed for such investments. The same reasoning applies to the more mature RE technologies. However, based on experience to date, and as noted above, there is some evidence that targeted, short-term financial subsidies to these investment categories can accelerate their uptake, particularly by SMEs and in the building EE sector. Many of the EBRD lines of credit have incorporated subsidies (up to 15 percent of total investment costs) for SMEs and residential EE projects. These have typically been financed through EU grants; however, some governments, for example, Bulgaria, have continued these programs once donor funds have been exhausted. The subsidies are justified to cover the high transaction costs and high risks for SME financing as well as to demonstrate the return on investment to other potential investors. Where such subsidy programs have been available, and in contrast to other countries where only investment financing mechanisms are provided, the SME response appears to have been quite encouraging. Experience also shows that building-retrofit projects have much longer payback periods than industrial EE projects; therefore, government subsidies to shorten the payback period to investors are crucial to increasing market demand and uptake for building-retrofit investments. Although EE public subsidies may not be sustainable in the long term, and care must be taken to ensure that they are phased out once the "demonstration effect" has been achieved, they have the potential to have a major SME impact.

MDBs Have Been Pioneers in Innovative Clean Energy Financing Mechanisms, and National Development Banks Have the Potential to Play a Significant Role

In reviewing the lessons of experience, it is apparent that the MDBs have been pioneers in developing and implementing innovative clean energy financing mechanisms designed to leverage private financing. Within a comparatively short period, they have developed a range of products and have begun to systematically evaluate the impact of those products. Their development mandate has given them the necessary space and ability to pilot new approaches and begin to evaluate their effectiveness. Box 4.1 lays out the World Bank Group's role in spurring clean energy investments in developing countries.

MDBs can also play a bank syndication role, particularly during the ongoing global financial crisis when local banks are more cautious and reluctant to finance capital-intensive, large-scale projects or new clean energy technologies such as offshore wind and CSP. Loan syndication is typically required for financial closure in large-scale projects. The participation of an MDB in loan syndication facilitates bank participation because local banks can piggyback on the development bank's experience in RE project finance, and foreign banks find the participation of development banks in project finance politically reassuring.

Box 4.1 The World Bank Group's Role in Catalyzing Clean Energy Investment

The WBG has been a pioneer in financing clean energy projects in developing countries and is well positioned to provide policy advice, TA and concessional long-term financing to spark EE and RE investments. The WBG investment in EE and RE hit an all-time high at nearly US$5 billion in 2012, accounting for 60 percent of the Bank's energy portfolio.

The lessons drawn from this report show that policy advisory services, TA, and financing need to go hand in hand for any clean energy project to have a significant and sustainable impact. Therefore, better integration of various financing sources (for example, from the International Bank for Reconstruction and Development, the International Development Association, the Global Environment Facility, the Clean Technology Fund [CTF], and carbon financing) can increase the magnitude and speed of the shift to a sustainable energy path. In addition, the conclusions of this report support the importance of first setting the program objective, diagnosing the barriers, and identifying targeted market segments before selecting the appropriate financing instrument.

The fact that the WBG's RE lending was nearly three times its EE lending volume in 2012 indicates the difficulties with EE projects, which face substantial market barriers and failures in many developing countries because of their small and fragmented nature, even though they are often labeled as "low-hanging fruit." Dedicated credit lines have proved to be an effective financing instrument for the WBG to bundle these small-scale fragmented EE investments using a "wholesale" approach. Experience shows that dedicated credit lines provide real value added by mainstreaming EE business lines in participating banks through a "learning-by-doing" process, rather than by providing liquidity support as many had thought, particularly in middle-income countries. If the objective of such a program is to reduce GHG emissions, the targeted market segment should not shy away from large and medium end users, which will cost-effectively achieve substantial emission reductions. The most commonly encountered problem with credit lines is the difficulty in finding bankable deals, and this report provides valuable recommendations in this regard. In addition, a risk guarantee instrument is useful for mitigating the *perceived* risks of financial institutions but is not a panacea. The Global Environment Facility or CTF may be more appropriate financing sources for risk guarantees.

Effective RE pricing policies such as FITs are a prerequisite to financing, particularly in middle-income countries. Therefore, policy dialogue and TA to help client countries put in place such policies are the first priorities. Concessional financing is valuable for kick-starting new RE technologies in emerging economies, such as the Bank's CSP portfolio in North Africa. But such public subsidies cannot be sustained over the long term and will not lead to the needed scale. Again, a dedicated credit line is useful for bundling a portfolio of small-scale RE projects, such as small hydro. Finally, if the objective of such programs is to reduce GHG emissions, a substantial scale-up in grid-connected RE investments in the WBG is warranted, particularly in middle-income countries.

The challenge of replicating this MDB role at the national level is well recognized. The performance of state-owned development banks has been decidedly mixed: they are often poorly managed, have weak corporate governance, are frequently saddled with bad assets, and are subject to inadequate supervision. Moreover, development banks are frequently politicized; they typically end up doing a variety of market-distorting operations through subsidized lending in areas in which commercial banks are active, and often move away from their intended mandates. Paradoxically, despite their development mandate, some of these institutions have been unwilling to pilot innovative financing mechanisms.

Notwithstanding these realities, development banks can be an important instrument for governments to promote economic growth. They can provide credit and loan guarantees together with other financial and technical services to targeted groups, such as low-income households and SMEs, or to priority sectors, such as infrastructure. Even in advanced economies, in which private financial institutions and capital markets cover most of the financial needs of households and enterprises, development banks continue to play an active role by fostering investment in public goods such as clean energy, biotechnology, and the environment.

The good news is that national development banks are playing a growing role in enabling the transition to low-carbon development, especially in emerging economies, such as the Brazilian and the Chinese development banks. Indeed, national development banks invested US$42.7 billion in climate financing in 2011, mostly in RE and EE—more than half of the total climate financing by public actors (Buchner and others 2012).

Where strong, independent, and robust national development banks or specialized energy financing institutions do exist, exploiting their potential to pioneer new and innovative clean energy financing products would appear to be an avenue worth exploring. Governments could support and encourage such institutions to enter the clean energy financing market together with developing the necessary professional expertise to design and promote clean energy financing products and to carefully and systematically evaluate their impact. Finally, it is also critically important for governments to strengthen their own capacity to develop and evaluate clean energy financing programs.

Bibliography

Buchner, B., A. Falconer, M. Herve-Mignucci, and C. Trabacchi. 2012. *The Landscape of Climate Finance 2012*. Climate Policy Initiative, San Francisco, CA.

CBRC (China Banking Regulatory Commission). 2009. "Guidelines on Credit Underwriting for Energy Conservation and Emission Reduction." http://www.cbrc .gov.cn/chinese/home/docView/200908050CE9DC53F577564BFF554AF1CD E5E600.html.

PART 2

Financing Energy Efficiency

CHAPTER 5

Barriers to Energy Efficiency

Introduction

Improved energy efficiency (EE) is increasingly being recognized as the most cost-effective short- to- medium-term option for meeting the energy needs associated with increased economic growth, enhancing energy security, and reducing the cost of future energy supply. Enhanced EE will also contribute to mitigation of global climate change impacts without compromising economic development. EE can be particularly important in the East Asia and Pacific region, which is experiencing unprecedented economic growth. EE options can reduce the need for expensive new electricity generation capacity and, because much of the generation capacity is coal based, reduce greenhouse gas (GHG) emissions from energy production and use.

Role of Energy Efficiency in Mitigating Climate Change

The potential role of EE in mitigating climate change was defined by the International Energy Agency, which estimated that an additional US$10.5 trillion investment is needed for the "450 parts per million (ppm) scenario" required to limit the temperature rise to 2°C (IEA 2009). Measures to boost EE account for most of the abatement through 2030, as illustrated in figure 5.1, which shows the 450 ppm scenario.

As shown in figure 5.1, the needed GHG abatement by 2020 is 3.8 gigatons, of which 65 percent is expected to be contributed by EE. By 2030, the needed GHG abatement is 13.8 gigatons, of which 57 percent is expected to be contributed by EE. Although detailed statistics on the actual contribution of EE to global climate change mitigation are not available, most experts agree that market implementation of EE has not kept pace with these GHG abatement requirements because of a number of barriers that limit investment in EE projects.

Barriers to Scaling Up Energy Efficiency

Many studies have identified the various barriers to large-scale implementation of EE in developing countries (see, for example, IEA 2010; Limaye 2009;

Figure 5.1 Role of Energy Efficiency in Mitigating Climate Change

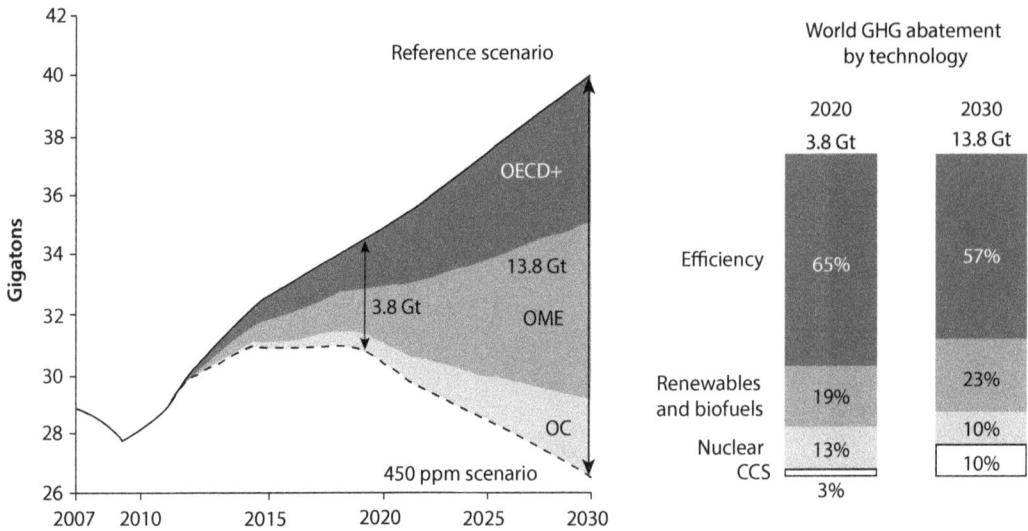

Source: Adapted by the World Bank from IEA 2009, *World Energy Outlook 2009,* © OECD/IEA.
Note: CCS = carbon capture and storage; GHG = greenhouse gas; Gt = gigaton; OC = other countries; OECD+ = Organisation for Economic Co-operation and Development countries plus European countries that are not OECD members; OME = other major economies (China, Russia, Brazil, South Africa, and the countries of the Middle East); ppm = parts per million.

Singh and others 2010; Taylor and others 2008). These barriers have been classified into five broad categories (see table 5.1):

- Policy and regulatory barriers,
- Barriers related to energy end users (both public sector and private sector),
- Barriers related to providers of energy equipment and energy services,
- Institutional barriers, and
- Financing barriers.

In addition to the policy and regulatory barriers in table 5.1—low or subsidized energy prices, distorted fiscal and regulatory policies, rigid procurement and budgeting policies in the public sector, limitations of public financing, ad hoc planning, and limited data availability and quality—a key policy and regulatory issue is the failure to internalize the impacts of energy use in the pricing of energy. In particular, the "price" of carbon emissions is not reflected in energy prices. The *Report of the UN Secretary-General's High-Level Advisory Group on Climate Change Financing* concluded that unless the carbon price is set at US$25 per ton, raising the funds to achieve the target levels of 450 ppm will be difficult (UN 2010).

Barriers related to public sector end users include limited incentives to save energy, lack of discretionary budgets for special projects or upgrades, unclear ownership of cost and energy savings, limited availability of financing, lack of

Table 5.1 Barriers to Large-Scale Implementation of Energy Efficiency

Policy and regulatory barriers	End-user barriers	Barriers related to equipment and service providers	Institutional barriers	Financing barriers
Low or subsidized energy prices	High cost of energy efficient products	Limited development of EE services market	Lack of formal institutional framework for developing and implementing energy efficiency strategies, policies, and programs	Small project size
Distorted fiscal and regulatory policies	Consumer preferences for non-EE attributes	High project development and transaction costs		High transaction costs
Rigid procurement and budgeting procedures	Split incentives	Limited risk management skills	Emphasis on increasing energy supplies, not on reducing consumption	Limited availability of funds
Limitations of public financing	Low management priority on EE	Limited access to equity capital	Lack of confidence in EE improvements to deliver savings	High perceived risks
Ad hoc planning	Limited technical knowledge of EE	Lack of credibility with consumers and financial institutions	Lack of "champions" for promoting EE	Lack of interest on the part of banks and financial institutions
Limited data availability and quality	Lack of internal funds for EE investments	Limited M&V capacity	Limited knowledge and understanding of EE by consumers	Limited development of targeted financial products for EE

Note: EE = energy efficiency; M&V = measurement and verification.

awareness and technical expertise, and behavioral biases. Barriers related to private sector energy users include higher yields on alternative capital investments, low management priority on EE relative to other corporate needs, limitations on internal capital for investing in EE, and lack of knowledge and awareness of new and innovative technologies for EE. Other major barriers in both the public and private sectors include the high cost of energy efficient equipment, consumer preferences for product attributes other than EE, and the "split-incentive" issue (IEA 2007), wherein the beneficiary of the EE savings is not the investor in the EE measures.

With respect to EE equipment and service providers, the barriers include the limited development of the EE services delivery infrastructure; high project development and transaction costs for EE projects; limited technical, business, and risk management skills; limited availability of equity financing; and lack of credibility with both large energy users and financial institutions. Furthermore, the formal measurement and verification procedures and protocols upon which energy savings performance contracts crucially depend are neither sufficiently developed nor widely accepted in most developing countries.

Institutional barriers in developing countries include the lack of a formal institutional framework for developing and implementing EE strategies, policies, and programs; the emphasis on increasing energy supplies rather than reducing energy consumption; the lack of confidence in the ability of EE improvements to offset the need for new capacity; the lack of "champions" who will promote EE; and limited knowledge and understanding of EE by the general public.

Financing barriers (discussed in more detail below) include high perceived risks, the need for new financial products and appraisal tools, small project size leading to high transaction costs, and lack of interest and motivation on the part of bank loan officers and risk managers in EE project financing.

Financing Barriers

Many of the financial barriers to EE arise from the unique characteristics of such projects relative to traditional investment projects. Because EE reduces energy costs, it improves the "bottom line" of enterprises and does not increase the "top line." Thus, corporate or government executives and managers, as well as bankers and other members of the financial community, find it difficult to clearly perceive the benefits of EE and to determine how to capture them by using conventional financing mechanisms. Furthermore, EE projects are typically much smaller than conventional projects related to plant expansion, new product development, research and development, or facility modernization. Other novel characteristics of EE projects include high project development and transaction costs, use of new or innovative technologies, relatively small value of project assets, and use of new business models involving performance contracting and third-party implementation (by energy service companies or other types of energy service providers).

The typical barriers encountered by EE project implementers in obtaining the needed financial resources follow:

- *Limited availability of internal funds.* Internal funds (equity) are generally not readily available for procurement of the equipment or products needed for EE project implementation, in either the public or private sectors. Also, private sector energy users are unwilling to commit their balance sheets as collateral for EE project borrowing because of the potential impacts such commitments may have on their total borrowing capacity for other investments.

- *Lack of perceived incentives for EE projects.* Neither public sector nor private sector energy users recognize the financial benefits of investing in EE or committing to borrowing funds for EE projects.

- *Small project size leading to high transaction costs.* The relatively small size of EE projects (compared with, for example, energy generation projects or plant expansion projects) leads to relatively high transaction costs (compared with other conventional lending by banks and financial institutions[1]), which, in turn, makes them less attractive for conventional bank financing. This factor also limits their appeal to international financial institutions (such as multilateral and bilateral donor organizations) to whom the scale of financing is important.

- *Lack of knowledge and awareness.* Conventional lenders (such as commercial banks and financial institutions) do not have sufficient knowledge and understanding of EE technologies and their technical, economic, and financial characteristics, and have not fully developed approaches and techniques for project appraisal and risk assessment.

- *Risk perceptions*. Lenders may perceive EE projects as being more risky than their other conventional lending.

- *High project development costs*. EE projects have a relatively high proportion of "soft costs" that lenders are reluctant to finance. Such soft costs include project evaluation, project development, and contract negotiation costs as well as costs of equipment replacement, plant shutdown, and training of equipment operating and maintenance personnel.

- *Requirement for collateral or balance sheet financing*. Lenders usually require high levels of collateral or strong borrower balance sheets to provide financing. Energy users and energy service companies may not have collateral or strong balance sheets (or may not be willing to commit their available collateral for EE projects).

- *Limited application of "project financing" for EE projects*. The concept of "project financing" has not yet been widely accepted for EE projects in developing countries.

- *Limited results from financing programs of international donor agencies*. Multilateral development banks and bilateral aid agencies have undertaken many EE project development and financing programs in developing countries and have implemented a range of financing mechanisms. However, the total volume of investment in the projects implemented by these initiatives has been far short of that needed to meet national and global goals.

- *Communication between financiers and project developers*. Lenders have limited knowledge and awareness of EE project characteristics, while EE project developers often are unaware of the project packaging and presentation requirements of the financial community. This creates a difficult communication gap.

- *Measurement and verification of energy savings*. Adequate methods and tools are not readily available to demonstrate the achieved energy savings.

- *Limitations of capacity of various market participants*. The capacity of various market actors in EE project implementation is limited. The limitations include the following:
  - Capacity of loan officers and risk managers to understand EE project characteristics and the need to develop new or innovative financial products and project appraisal and risk management approaches and techniques.

– Capacity of EE service providers in the technical, business, project manage-ment, and risk management skills needed for efficient project development and execution, and in the ability to develop "bankable projects" that can be presented to and understood by loan officers.
– Capacity of project proponents or "hosts" to understand the basic concepts of performance contracting and the need to appropriately structure energy services and financing agreements for EE projects.

Classification of Financing Barriers

This part of the book groups the above barriers into the following major classifications:

- Availability of funds to invest in EE projects,
- Information, awareness, and communication,
- Project development and transaction costs,
- Risk assessment and management, and
- Lack of capacity.

Figure 5.2 illustrates these classifications.

The next chapter examines the types of government policy and regulatory instruments that could address some of these barriers. Chapter 7 of the book identifies the range of financial mechanisms developed to support the policy instruments to address the barriers. A discussion of each of these financing mechanisms is then presented in chapter 8, along with lessons learned.

Figure 5.2 Classification of Financing Barriers

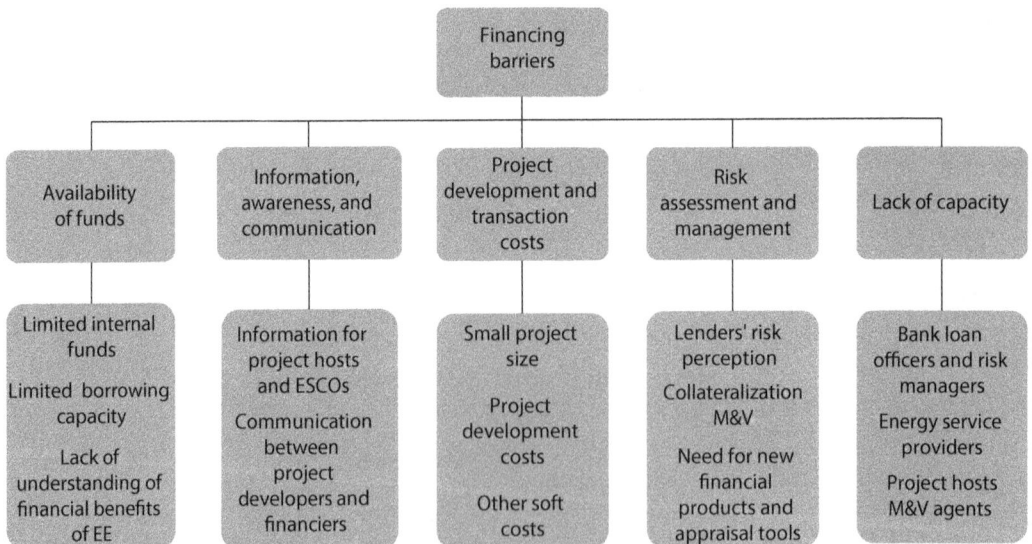

Note: EE = energy efficiency; ESCO = energy service company; M&V = measurement and verification.

Note

1. Throughout part 2, the term "lenders" will often be used to encompass both banks and financial institutions.

Bibliography

IEA (International Energy Agency). 2007. *Mind the Gap—Quantifying Principal Agent Problems in Energy Efficiency.* Paris: OECD/IEA.

———. 2009. *World Energy Outlook 2009.* Paris: OECD/IEA.

———. 2010. *Money Matters: Mitigating Risk to Spark Private Investments in Energy Efficiency.* Paris: OECD/IEA.

Limaye, Dilip. 2009. *DSM Financing Annex: Financing DSM and Energy Efficiency Programs in China.* Washington, DC: USAID ECO-Asia Clean Development and Climate Program.

Singh, Jas, Dilip R. Limaye, Brian Henderson, and Xiaoyu Shi. 2010. *Public Procurement of Energy Efficiency Services: Lessons from International Experience.* Washington, DC: World Bank.

Taylor, Robert, C. Govindarajalu, J. Levin, A. Meyer, and W. Ward. 2008. *Financing Energy Efficiency: Lessons from Brazil, China, India and Beyond.* Washington, DC: World Bank.

UN (United Nations). 2010. *Report of the Secretary-General's High-Level Advisory Group on Climate Change Financing: Work Stream 3: Revenue Options from Carbon-Related Sources.* New York: UN.

CHAPTER 6

Policy Instruments to Enhance Investments in Energy Efficiency

Introduction

Governments have adopted a wide range of policy initiatives to overcome the barriers to large-scale implementation of energy efficiency (EE). A number of reports have provided extensive compilations and discussions of EE policy instruments (APERC 2010; World Energy Council 2008). This chapter provides an overview of some of the policy instruments, classified as shown in figure 6.1.

Legislative Instruments

An overview of the legislative and policy instruments outlined in figure 6.1 is provided below.

Energy Efficiency Laws

Many countries have implemented specific EE laws that address a number of barriers related to EE implementation. Several international reviews of EE legislation have been compiled (IEA 2010; Limaye, Heffner, and Sarkar 2008; SRC Global Inc. 2009). Although EE laws are generally broadly based and are designed to address a number of different barriers, some of them have specific elements relevant to financing. For example, India's Energy Conservation Act, 2001, requires the establishment of EE funds at the state level. Vietnam's Law on Energy Efficiency and Conservation provides for preferential financing rates for EE projects. A key element of most EE legislation is the development of a new institutional structure for implementing EE—most EE laws establish a dedicated EE agency or unit with responsibilities for coordinating multiple stakeholders, implementing EE programs, and raising public awareness (Limaye, Heffner, and Sarkar 2008).

Mandatory Energy Audits

To identify opportunities for EE improvement, many countries have undertaken legislative initiatives to require large energy users (generally referred to as

Figure 6.1 Policy Instruments to Overcome Barriers to Energy Efficiency

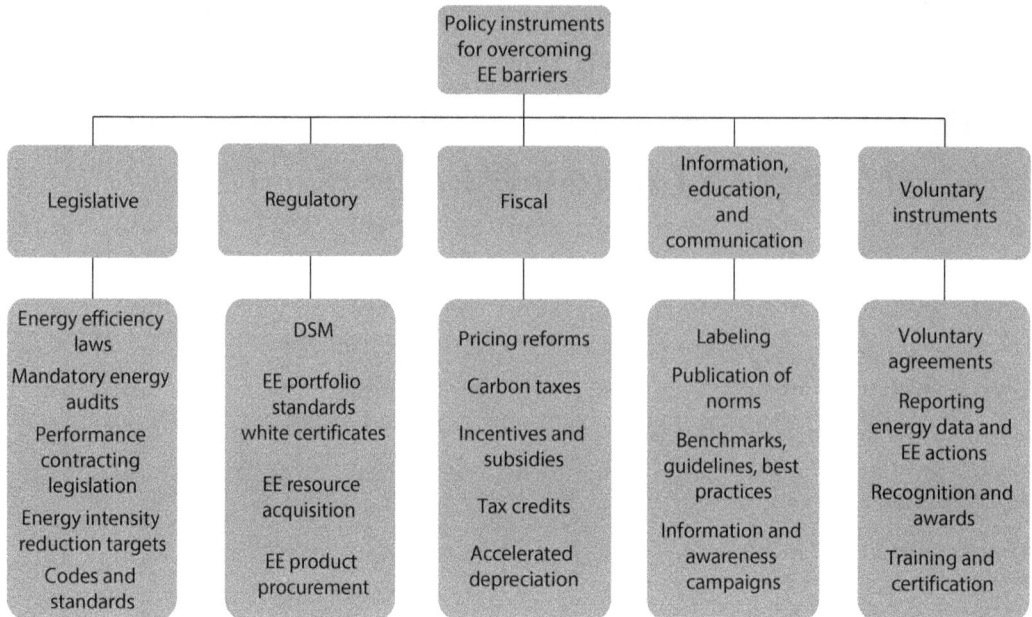

Note: DSM = demand-side management; EE = energy efficiency.

"designated consumers") to undertake energy audits. Such audits are required to be conducted by trained and certified energy auditors. Examples of such mandatory audit requirements can be found in Thailand, India, and Vietnam. Some legislation, such as that in Vietnam and Thailand, goes further and requires the designated consumers to develop and submit EE action plans.

Legislation Facilitating Performance Contracting

Energy saving performance contracting (ESPC) is recognized as a potential mechanism for overcoming EE barriers, including financing barriers. Under the ESPC concept an energy service provider (commonly known as an energy service company or ESCO) provides a complete range of services related to implementation of EE projects and assumes much of the technical and performance risk. Payments for the services are contingent upon the successful demonstration of performance, generally as defined in a performance guaranty provided by the ESCO. The ESPC process can be particularly useful for helping public sector EE projects to overcome a number of financial and institutional barriers (Singh and others 2010). Some governments have taken legislative and regulatory actions to facilitate ESPCs.

Energy Intensity Reduction Targets

A national policy to establish EE improvement targets is another example of a legislative measure to promote large-scale implementation of EE projects. Typically, in developing countries, such targets are for energy intensity reduction (expressed by indicators such as energy consumption per unit of gross domestic product [GDP]). China successfully established and achieved energy intensity reduction targets in its 11th Five-Year Plan, which ended in 2010.

Codes and Standards

Many governments have legislated EE building codes for new construction (Deringer 2005) and minimum energy performance standards for appliances and equipment.[1] Although codes and standards do not directly address specific financing barriers, they stimulate demand for efficient appliances, equipment, or buildings, which require greater investment than corresponding inefficient options, and increase awareness of improving EE.

Regulatory Instruments

Regulatory instruments include measures to encourage or require utilities to undertake EE programs (including demand-side management initiatives, EE portfolio standards, and mechanisms to acquire demand-side EE resources); market-based systems such as white certificates; and regulations to require energy efficient product procurement by government agencies.

Demand-Side Management

Demand-side management (DSM) refers to activities initiated by utilities to change the amount and pattern of energy use by their customers in a way that creates benefits for the customers, the utilities, and society as a whole. EE programs are an important component of DSM, and regulators around the world, including in India, Thailand, and Vietnam, have required utilities in their jurisdictions to implement a wide range of DSM programs.

Energy Efficiency Portfolio Standards

Regulators in a number of western countries and several U.S. states[2] have imposed EE portfolio standards (also known as portfolio obligations) that require utilities to meet specified EE goals (International Confederation of Energy Regulators 2010). These standards or obligations are similar to the older DSM activities but focus on outcomes (such as specific energy savings targets) rather than funding levels and program designs. In Europe, the schemes are combined with trading mechanisms for energy savings certificates (known as "white certificates"; see below).

White Certificates

A white certificate, also referred to as an energy savings certificate (ESC) or energy efficiency credit (EEC), is an instrument issued by a government agency or a regulatory authority certifying that a specified amount of energy savings has been achieved. Each certificate is a unique and tradable commodity carrying a property right over a certain amount of additional energy savings and guaranteeing that the benefit of these savings has not been accounted for elsewhere. These certificates can be traded in the marketplace between sellers (who get the certificates by exceeding their EE savings obligations or commitments) and buyers (who need to buy the certificates to meet their EE savings obligations or commitments). In Europe, the white certificates are associated with utility portfolio obligations. In India, the white certificates will be traded among the "designated consumers" for each of whom the Bureau of Energy Efficiency has established an energy savings target (Lees 2010).

Acquisition of Energy Efficiency Resources

Some regulatory mechanisms impose a requirement that utilities "acquire" EE resources by paying for verified energy savings achieved by customers or energy service providers. The early examples of EE resource acquisition focused on peak load management using acquisition of load reductions through a "standard offer" or the use of "demand-side bidding." These mechanisms have also been used for acquisition of EE resources using a standard offer or bidding procedures that are analogous to feed-in tariffs for renewable energy resources (see part 10 of this volume). Such programs have been used in the states of California, New York, Texas, and Wisconsin (Greany 2009) and the recent Standard Offer Program in South Africa (World Bank 2010). See the case study in chapter 20 for details on South Africa's program, known as Eskom.

Energy Efficient Product Procurement

Government agencies purchase large amounts of energy equipment, and until recently most equipment procurement was based on first cost. Energy efficient equipment is generally more expensive than inefficient equipment; however, because efficient equipment yields lower operating costs over its operating life, some governments are now requiring public agencies to change their procurement procedures to allow for its purchase. The European Council has adopted a regulation that requires European Union (EU) institutions and central government authorities to use EE criteria no less demanding than those defined in the EU Energy Star program[3] when purchasing office equipment. A discussion of the mechanisms for public sector procurement of EE services is provided in the World Bank book and the World Bank Institute e-learning course on this subject (Singh and others 2010; WBI 2011).

Fiscal Instruments

Various types of fiscal instruments have been developed and implemented to promote EE. The two major types of fiscal instrument are taxes and subsidies. A good overview of these instruments is provided in the World Bank review of initiatives for green infrastructure finance (Baietti 2012).

Pricing Reforms

Low energy prices caused by subsidies or inefficient pricing structures discourage investment in EE. Therefore, governments have initiated various regulatory reforms to move toward market-based pricing to promote efficient, sustainable, and secure energy sectors. Energy pricing reform can stimulate EE improvements, discourage energy waste, and encourage the use of clean technologies. The most common pricing strategies consist of removing fossil fuel subsidies, restructuring prices to be market based, and introducing innovative pricing such as two-part tariffs and time-of-use pricing. Some governments have also attempted to internalize the environmental externalities of energy use through taxation or by providing subsidies for EE (discussed below).

Carbon Taxes

Carbon taxes are levied on fossil fuel carbon content, thereby taxing carbon dioxide emissions.[4] Carbon taxes are intended primarily to internalize environmental costs and encourage energy conservation. The resulting revenues may be used in various ways—to reduce other taxes, finance rebates, or provide incentives and subsidies to low-carbon technologies and EE programs.

Incentives and Subsidies

Subsidies may be offered to encourage consumers to move toward more efficient products, technologies, and equipment. According to IEA (2010), fossil fuel subsidies totaled US$557 billion in 2008. Phasing out these subsidies and phasing in subsidies to EE through programs such as rebates and incentives can create a positive impact on EE implementation.

Tax Credits

Tax credits have proven to be an effective instrument for stimulating investment. The U.S. government stimulated energy efficient investment with a 30 percent tax credit program (up to a maximum of US$1,500).[5]

Accelerated Depreciation

Accelerated depreciation is a taxation option under which a business is allowed to depreciate a fixed asset for tax and financial accounting purposes such that the amount of depreciation taken is higher during the earlier years of an asset's life. The benefit of this approach is that the business can lower its taxes in the early years of the asset's deployment. This valuable tax incentive encourages businesses to purchase new assets, particularly when these assets require high levels of capital investment. Accelerated depreciation has been used to promote investment in renewable energy options, but it can also be very useful for investment-intensive EE options such as cogeneration, waste to energy, and industrial process EE improvement.

Information, Education, and Communication

As indicated in chapter 5, the lack of adequate information, lack of knowledge regarding the costs and benefits of EE technologies, and the misperceptions about the risks of EE options are important barriers to scaling up EE. Therefore, governments have initiated a number of energy information, education, and awareness programs to address these barriers.

Appliance and Equipment Labeling

One of the most common and perhaps most useful approaches to informing consumers of the efficiency of appliances and equipment is through labeling. Many countries have introduced labeling programs for domestic appliances and for commercial energy-using equipment. An initial assessment of international labeling programs was conducted by UN-ESCAP (Huh 1999). The Collaborative Labeling and Appliance Standards Program database provides up-to-date information on worldwide labeling programs.

Publication of Norms

In the industrial sector, energy intensity (expressed as energy used per unit of production) varies widely across firms within the same sector. Although some of the variation may be attributable to differences in age of the facility, process type, and product mix, EE can be a major factor. Therefore, the publishing of energy norms by process type may provide useful information to industrial plant engineers and managers about the potential for energy intensity improvement. India has established industrial energy norms for major industries as part of its Perform, Achieve, and Trade program (BEE 2011).

Benchmarks, Guidelines, and Best Practices

International experience with EE improvement efforts can also provide useful information about its potential. Many governments, in collaboration with international donor agencies, have published benchmarks, guidelines, and best practices related to EE in industry and buildings. UNIDO (2010) published a report on industrial energy benchmarking as a tool for EE improvement.

Public Information and Awareness Campaigns

In addition to the above measures, governments have undertaken public information and awareness campaigns to promote EE using a wide range of instruments, from brochures, billboards, and advertising campaigns to targeted workshops and seminars.

Voluntary Instruments

Voluntary instruments include collaborative efforts between governments and private sector organizations to improve EE. Examples include voluntary agreements, reporting of energy data and EE actions, public recognition and rewards for exemplary EE performance, and training and certification programs.

Voluntary Agreements to Improve Energy Intensity

In some countries, governments and energy users have signed voluntary agreements targeted at EE improvement. Generally, such initiatives involve (a) establishment of targets negotiated between industrial firms and governments for reducing energy consumption or greenhouse gas (GHG) emissions, (b) specification of government support to industry, (c) commitment by industry to meet the established targets, and (d) definition of the approach for monitoring and evaluation. Examples of such agreements can be found in Australia, Canada, Finland, Germany, and the Netherlands (Price 2005).

Reporting of Energy Data and Energy Efficiency Actions

To assess progress toward EE targets, data on energy consumption and related information on the factors affecting energy consumption must be collected. Although some countries have included mandatory reporting of data as part of their energy legislation, others have relied on voluntary reporting, particularly from small and medium enterprises, for which a mandatory reporting program would be difficult, cumbersome, and expensive to monitor and enforce.

Public Recognition and Awards

Many national and state government agencies use public recognition and awards to reward exemplary EE performance. This mechanism is particularly useful for public sector personnel who may not be directly remunerated for outstanding performance, but it is also useful for recognizing individuals in the private sector who have substantially contributed to improving EE in their organizations. These awards are generally presented at highly publicized events.

Training and Certification Programs

Scaling up of EE requires enhancing the capacity for the delivery of EE services. National legislation often mandates that large energy consumers conduct energy audits and develop EE action plans. In most cases, the legislation specifies that audits be conducted by certified energy personnel. To facilitate compliance with this requirement, a number of countries have implemented training and certification programs, particularly for energy auditors and energy managers. The United States–based Association of Energy Engineers has developed internationally recognized training programs for certified energy managers, certified energy auditors, and certified measurement and verification Professionals. These programs have been implemented in many countries.[6]

Addressing Barriers to Energy Efficiency

Table 6.1 illustrates the influence of the policy instruments reviewed above on addressing the barriers to EE.

Conclusion

This chapter reviews a wide range of policy instruments to help promote scaling up of investments in EE.

- Experience in the development and implementation of these policy instruments in developing countries points out that mandatory programs are likely to have a greater impact than voluntary programs. For example, mandatory

Table 6.1 Policies and Regulations to Address Barriers to Energy Efficiency

Policy instruments	Barriers				
	Policy and regulatory	End-user related	Equipment and service providers	Institutional	Financing
Legislative					
Energy efficiency laws	•	•	•	•	•
Mandatory audits	n.a.	•	o	o	o
Legislation facilitating performance contracting	n.a.	n.a.	•	•	•
Energy intensity reduction targets	•	•	n.a.	•	n.a.
Codes and standards	•	•	•	•	o
Regulatory					
Pricing reform	•	•	•	•	•
Demand-side management	•	•	•	•	•
Energy efficiency portfolio standards	•	o	o	•	o
White certificates	•	o	o	n.a.	o
Acquisition of energy efficiency resources	•	•	•	•	•
Tradable energy savings certificates	•	o	o	n.a.	o
Energy efficient product procuremnt	•	n.a.	•	•	o
Fiscal					
Carbon taxes	•	•	•	•	•
Incentives and subsidies	o	•	•	•	•
Tax credits	o	•	o	n.a.	•
Accelerated depreciation	o	•	o	n.a.	•
Information, education, and communication					
Appliance and equipment labeling	•	•	•	•	o
Publication of norms	•	•	•	•	o
Benchmarks, guidelines, and best practices	•	•	•	•	o
Public information and awareness campaigns	•	•	•	•	o
Voluntary					
Voluntary agreements to improve energy intensity	o	•	o	o	•
Reporting of energy data and EE actions	o	o	n.a.	o	n.a.
Public recognition and awards	o	•	o	o	o
Training and certification programs	o	•	•	o	•

Note: EE = energy efficiency.
• Strong influence.
o Moderate influence.

minimum energy performance standards are likely to be more effective in encouraging investment in energy efficient products and equipment than voluntary standards or labeling programs. Similarly, mandatory auditing programs will be more effective than voluntary ones.

- Output-based mandates such as mandatory energy savings targets are more effective than activity or input-based initiatives such as requirements for energy auditing.
- Fiscal instruments, such as elimination of fossil fuel subsidies and imposition of carbon taxes, can effectively provide positive market signals to promote

investment in EE, but they may face institutional and political difficulties in implementation.

- Policy instruments use a mix of "carrots" (incentives) and "sticks" (penalties). Many developing countries appear to be moving toward increased use of sticks such as EE laws, mandatory energy performance standards, and energy savings targets.

Notes

1. Collaborative Labelling and Appliance Standards Program (CLASP), http://www.clasponline.org.

2. The European countries with EE portfolio obligations include Belgium, France, Ireland, Italy, and the United Kingdom. The leading U.S. states with EE portfolio obligations include Connecticut, Nevada, and Pennsylvania.

3. http://www.eu-energystar.org.

4. Carbon Tax Center, http://www.carbontax.org.

5. This tax credit expired at the end of 2010 and is now 10 percent up to a maximum of US$500.

6. Association of Energy Engineers, http://www.aeecenter.org.

Bibliography

APERC (Asia Pacific Energy Research Center). 2010. *Compendium of Energy Efficiency Policies of APEC Member Counties*. Tokyo: APERC.

Baietti, Aldo, Andrey Shlyakhtenko, Roberto La Rocca, and Urvaksh D. Patel. 2012. *Green Infrastructure Finance: Leading Initiatives and Research*. Washington, DC: World Bank.

BEE (Bureau of Energy Efficiency of the government of India). 2011. "National Mission on Enhanced Energy Efficiency: Perform, Achieve and Trade, Consultation Document 2010–11." January 10.

Deringer, Joseph. 2005. "Survey of Energy Efficiency Building Codes." Paper prepared for Vietnam Energy Efficiency Building Code Project.

Greany, J. 2009. "Distributed Energy through Distributed Effort: Harnessing the Power of the End-User through Standard Offer Programs and Feed-In Tariff Systems." International Sustainable Energy Policy Project.

Huh, Kwisun. 1999. "Initial Experiences with Energy Labelling Programmes: Evaluating the Effectiveness of Energy Labelling." In *Compendium on Energy Conservation Legislation in Countries of the Asia and Pacific Region*. Bangkok: UNESCAP.

IEA (International Energy Association). 2010. *Energy Efficiency Governance*. Paris: OECD/IEA.

International Confederation of Energy Regulators. 2010. "A Description of Current Regulatory Practices for the Promotion of Energy Efficiency." International Confederation of Energy Regulators.

Lees, Eion. 2010. *European and South American Experience of White Certificates*. Report prepared for ADEME and World Energy Council.

Limaye, Dilip R., Grayson Heffner, and Ashok Sarkar. 2008. *An Analytical Compendium of Institutional Frameworks for Energy Efficiency Implementation.* Formal Report 331/08, ESMAP, World Bank, Washington, DC.

Price, Lynn. 2005. "Voluntary Agreements for Energy Efficiency or GHG Emissions Reduction in Industry: An Assessment of Programs Around the World." Paper prepared for the "2005 ACEEE Summer Study on Energy Efficiency in Industry," West Point, NY, July 19–22.

Singh, Jas, Dilip R. Limaye, Brian Henderson, and Xiaoyu Shi. 2010. *Public Procurement of Energy Efficiency Services: Lessons from International Experience.* Washington, DC: World Bank.

SRC Global Inc. 2009. "Review of Energy Efficiency Legislation and Energy Efficiency Units." Paper prepared for UNDP-Mauritius.

UNIDO. 2010. "Global Industrial Energy Efficiency Benchmarking: An Energy Policy Tool." Working Paper, United Nations Industrial Development Organization, Vienna.

WBI (World Bank Institute). 2011. "New e-Learning Course on Climate Change." World Bank, Washington, DC. http://wbi.worldbank.org/wbi/Data/wbi/wbicms/files/drupal-acquia/wbi/energy_efficiency_brochure2011_final.pdf.

World Bank. 2010. "Implementing Energy Efficiency and Demand-Side Management Programs: South Africa's Standard Offer Model." ESMAP Briefing Note 007/11, World Bank, Washington, DC.

World Energy Council. 2008. *Energy Efficiency Policies Around the World: Review and Evaluation.* London: World Energy Council.

CHAPTER 7

Overview of Financing Mechanisms for Investments in Energy Efficiency

Introduction

The previous chapters identified the major financing barriers to scaling up investments in energy efficiency (EE) projects and the various policy and regulatory instruments adopted by governments and international donor agencies to overcome these barriers. This chapter discusses experiences with different mechanisms designed and implemented in a number of countries to facilitate and enhance financing of EE projects. Many different financing programs are used in developed and developing countries. This report classifies them into the following types:

- Energy efficiency funds,
- Utility demand-side management (DSM) programs,
- Utility consumer financing programs,
- Dedicated credit lines for EE projects,
- Risk-sharing programs,
- Leveraging of commercial financing through performance contracting and energy service companies (ESCOs), and
- Equity funds.

This chapter provides an overview of each of the financing mechanisms and reviews how they support the policy and regulatory instruments that are focused on addressing the various financing barriers.

Need for Financing Mechanisms

Although energy-using organizations have funded EE projects using their own resources, the competing demands for internal funds lead to lower priority and limited resources for EE projects. Equipment suppliers sometimes provide financing for the purchase of equipment, but it is limited to the specific equipment and to a short term (generally up to one year). National and local governments as well as donor agencies have provided financing for many EE projects in developing countries to promote and enhance the knowledge of, understanding of, and experience with these projects, but this funding has usually been program specific and therefore of limited duration. Similarly, nongovernmental organizations, foundations, and others have financed a limited number of pilot and demonstration projects.

Many efforts have been undertaken to encourage ESCOs to implement EE projects using the performance contracting approach, and these ESCOs have been responsible for providing or arranging financing for the projects. Efforts have also been made to encourage commercial financial institutions (FIs) to participate more actively in financing EE projects either directly or in collaboration with ESCOs. Despite substantial efforts devoted by governments and donor agencies to these approaches, the available financing for EE projects has been limited, and there has been increasing recognition that more sustainable financing mechanisms need to be developed and implemented.

Public Sector Role versus Market Role

As discussed above, governments and international donor agencies have developed a number of policy and regulatory instruments to overcome the barriers to EE and facilitate the scaling up of investments in EE projects. In developing countries, the public sector role, represented by government agencies and supported by technical assistance from international donors, has broadly focused on a three-pronged approach to promoting EE:

- Developing policies and programs;
- Providing incentives or subsidies, or both;
- Stimulating market development for delivery of EE services and for EE investments by commercial lenders.

Public sector initiatives can help to create an enabling environment in the short term to promote and facilitate financing of EE projects, (see figure 7.1), but the scaling up of EE investments to meet the needs of developing countries, particularly in the East Asia and Pacific region, requires sustainable project development and commercial financing approaches (Limaye 2011). The long-term growth and development of the market for delivering EE financing and implementation services requires the active participation of commercial banks and FIs. To leverage commercial financing, a number of innovative financing mechanisms have been developed and implemented.

Financing Mechanisms

Figure 7.2 provides an overview of the seven financing mechanisms discussed in this report.

Figure 7.1 Public Sector versus Market Roles in Scaling Up Energy Efficiency Investments

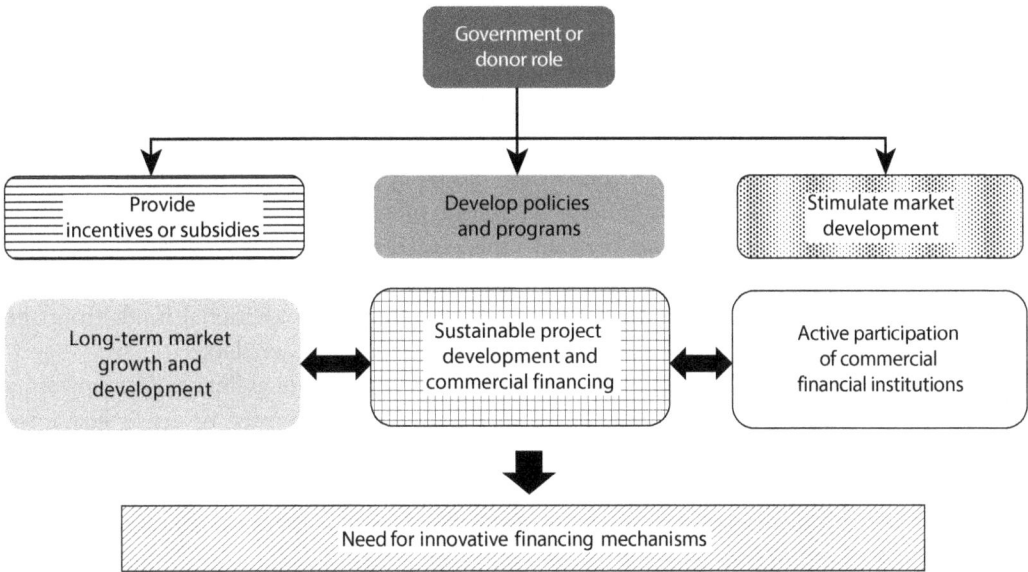

Source: Limaye 2011.

Figure 7.2 Innovative Financing Mechanisms

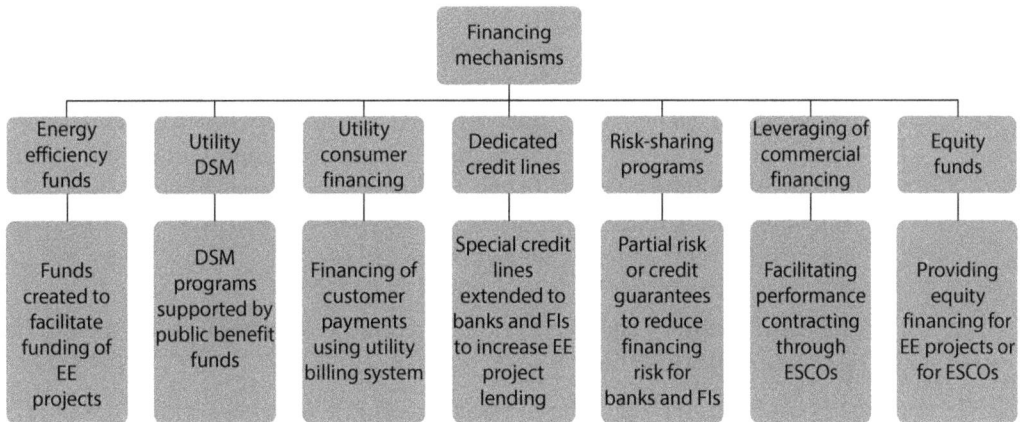

Note: DSM = demand-side management; EE = energy efficiency; ESCO = energy service company; FI = financial institution.

1. *Energy efficiency funds* are special purpose funds established by governments, regulators, and donor agencies (often jointly) for financing EE projects. The experience with such funds indicates that a wide range of financing approaches have been used to deploy the funds for EE projects. Some funds have been established by donor agencies such as the World Bank.[1] Others have been created by national governments as in Thailand.[2] In the United States, electricity regulators have established Public Benefit Funds using the public benefit charge mechanism.[3]

2. *Utility DSM* activities are undertaken by utilities to finance and implement EE projects in customer facilities. Utility DSM programs are supported by funds authorized by regulators, such as Public Benefit Funds, and are used to provide rebates, subsidies, or financing assistance to implementers of EE projects.

3. *Utility consumer financing.* Electric and gas utilities in many countries have been required by their regulators to finance customers' investments in energy efficient products, technologies, and equipment and to use the utility billing mechanism to accept customers' repayment of the funds.

4. *Dedicated credit lines* are funds made available generally by donor agencies to local banks and FIs to increase the funding available for EE project investments. The donor funds are usually leveraged by additional funds from the participating banks and FIs to increase the amounts available.

5. *Risk-sharing programs.* In this approach, an international financing organization or government agency develops a partial risk guarantee or credit guarantee program to share the risk faced by the bank or FI in financing EE projects. Such programs are designed to address lenders' perception that EE projects are riskier than traditional investments and to induce them to increase lending for EE projects.

6. *Leveraging commercial financing through ESCO performance contracting.* This approach promotes EE project implementation services offered by private sector ESCOs. ESCOs address some of the financing barriers because they can provide, or facilitate access to, capital from lenders for implementation.

7. *Equity funds* are generally provided by private sector venture capital firms to finance entrepreneurial ventures related to development or deployment of new EE technologies, but some equity funds have also been established by the public sector for financing ESCO projects or investments in ESCOs. These funds may be used to provide "last mile" equity investment[4] for EE projects or to provide funding to ESCOs to facilitate project implementation. Public equity funds are designed to partner with private sector venture funds to leverage private sector expertise and resources.

Table 7.1 provides an overview of how these financing mechanisms address some of the barriers to EE.

Moving from Public to Commercial Financing

The seven financing mechanisms entail different levels of public sector and private sector financing. Figure 7.3 illustrates the range of public and commercial financing for the seven mechanisms.

EE funds are generally publicly funded (although some of these funds may include some private sector cofinancing). Utility DSM funds provide "public funds" through a regulatory public benefit charge but generally offer only partial financing of projects and therefore might involve a greater degree of private sector financing than do EE funds. Utility consumer financing allows the use of the utility billing mechanism for customer payment to the private sector

Table 7.1 Financing Mechanisms and Barriers Addressed

Financing mechanism	Barriers to financing EE projects				
	Funds availability	Information, awareness, and communication	Project development and transaction costs	Risk assessment and management	Lack of capacity
Energy efficiency funds	Provide funds for investments in EE	Generally include TA to increase awareness by banks, energy users, and ESCOs	n.a.	n.a.	Enhance capacity of banks, energy users, and ESCOs
Utility DSM	Provides utility funds for investments in EE	Utility will generally conduct information and promotion campaign	Some reduction in project development and transaction cost due to utility's scale of operations	Utility may provide technical assistance to customer and lender	Utility may provide capacity building to energy service providers
Utility consumer financing	Provides the consumer the ability to pay for the EE investment through the utility bill	Utility will provide information to consumer	Cost of collection is reduced by using utility billing system	Low risk of nonpayment by use of utility billing mechanism	n.a.
Dedicated credit lines	Leverage bank financing for EE projects	Generally include TA to increase awareness of banks, energy users, and ESCOs	Some reduction in project development and transaction cost due to standard forms and templates	Uses banks' appraisal criteria and innovative financial products	TA enhances capacity of banks, energy users, and ESCOs
Risk-sharing programs	Reduce banks' risk perception and achieve high leverage	Generally include TA to increase awareness of banks, energy users, and ESCOs	Some reduction in project development and transaction cost due to standard forms and templates	Uses banks' appraisal criteria and stimulates innovative financial products	TA enhances capacity of banks, energy users, and ESCOs
Leveraging of commercial financing (ESCOs)	Accesses debt funds from private banks or FIs for EE projects	ESCOs provide information to energy users and to banks or FIs	Some reduction in project development and transaction cost due to ESCO activities	Most of the technical and financial risk is assumed by ESCOs	Government programs generally include ESCO capacity building
Equity funds	Access private equity and venture funds to provide equity funding for projects or ESCOs	n.a.	n.a.	Reduce project risks and ESCO risks by providing equity capital	n.a.

Note: DSM = demand-side management; FI = financial institution; n.a. = not applicable, that is, does not address barrier; TA = technical assistance.

Figure 7.3 Range of Public and Commercial Financing

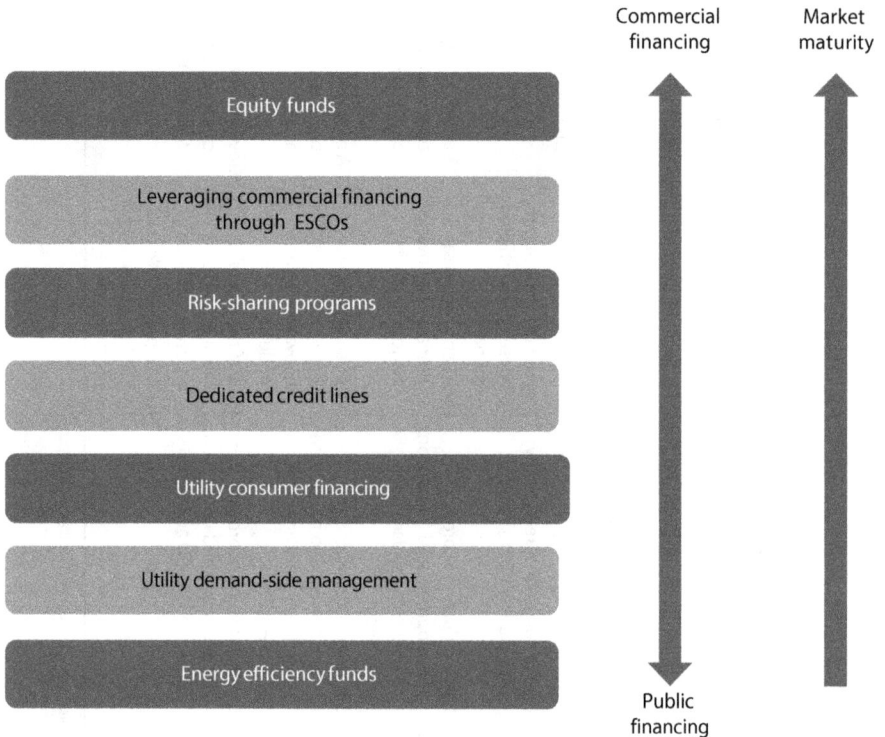

Source: Adapted from Limaye 2011.

suppliers of the EE product or equipment. Dedicated credit lines provide public funding to banks or FIs but generally leverage the public funds with additional bank or FI financing.

Leveraging commercial financing through ESCOs using performance contracting requires the creation of appropriate legislative and regulatory mechanisms to encourage and facilitate private sector financing of EE projects implemented by ESCOs. Public funding may be used to provide technical assistance and capacity building, to develop supporting tools and materials such as standard auditing and contract templates, and to assist in contract negotiation. Finally, equity funds might use a small amount of public funding to leverage large amounts of private capital for financing EE projects.

Designing the Financing Mechanisms

In view of the broad range of financing mechanisms, an important step is to determine the best option to use in an East Asia and Pacific country. International experience with development and implementation of these financing mechanisms illustrates that no standard solution is universally applicable. The applicability and effectiveness of any of the mechanisms in a specific country depend on

Figure 7.4 Designing the Financing Mechanisms

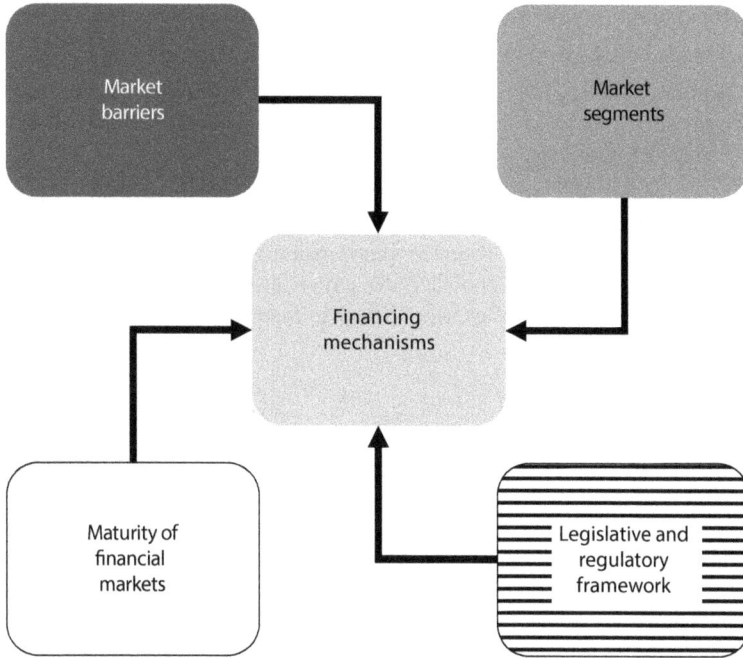

a number of factors, including market barriers, market segments targeted by the financing program, the existing legislative and regulatory framework, and maturity of the commercial financing market (figure 7.4).

International experience further illustrates the following:

- Selection of a financial mechanism depends on local conditions. For example, when the commercial financing market is not yet mature, EE funds or dedicated credit lines may be appropriate and risk-sharing programs may not be effective.
- Different mechanisms may be needed for different end-use sectors. For example, for large and medium end users, a dedicated credit line may be effective, whereas leveraging commercial financing through ESCOs or the establishment of a public ESCO may be more appropriate for public sector EE projects.
- Combinations of mechanisms might, in theory, be more effective than a single mechanism. For example, some EE funds have set aside a portion of available resources to provide risk sharing. An equity fund may be a useful supplement for leveraging commercial financing using ESCOs. However, practical experience with combining instruments, as in the Bulgarian Energy Efficiency Fund program, has been mixed at best (World Bank 2010).

International experience provides useful information but must be adapted and customized to local conditions. The application and effectiveness of a particular financing mechanism depends on many country-specific conditions.

Notes

1. For example, the World Bank established the Bulgarian Energy Efficiency Fund.
2. Thailand established the ENCON Fund to finance EE projects.
3. A public benefit charge (also known as a system benefit charge) is a regulatory mechanism that imposes a levy on electricity sales and uses the funds from the levy to finance EE programs.
4. Most lenders will provide only a part (generally no more than 70 percent) of the investment needed for an EE project as debt financing and will require the project developer or promoter to invest the remaining 30 percent as equity. If the project developer is unable to mobilize the entire 30 percent equity, an equity fund may provide the balance as "last mile" equity to make the project financeable.

Bibliography

Limaye, Dilip. 2011. "Lessons Learned from Innovative Financing of Energy Efficiency Programs." Paper presented at the Asia Clean Energy Forum, Regulatory and Policy Dialog, Manila, June.

World Bank. 2010. *Implementation, Completion and Results Report on a Grant from the Global Environment Facility Trust Fund in the Amount of US$10 million to the Republic of Bulgaria for an Energy Efficiency Project.* Washington, DC: World Bank.

CHAPTER 8

Financing Mechanisms for Energy Efficiency: Characteristics and Lessons Learned

Introduction

This chapter discusses the seven financing mechanisms introduced in chapter 7. It includes reviews of the major characteristics of each mechanism, implementation experience, and lessons learned, and provides illustrative examples.

Dedicated Energy Efficiency Funds

One approach that has received increasing acceptance throughout both developed and developing countries is the establishment of special purpose funds by national or state governments for financing energy efficiency (EE) projects. National funds include the ENCON Fund in Thailand, the Korea Energy Management Fund, and the Energy Conservation Fund in Sri Lanka. In some countries, international donor agencies such as the World Bank or the European Bank for Reconstruction and Development (EBRD) have established these funds. In the United States, electricity regulators have established Public Benefit Funds (PBFs). All of these funds are referred to as EE funds in this chapter.

Public Benefit Funds in the United States and Other Countries

A review of international best practices in EE funds was conducted by the U.S. Agency for International Development (USAID) ECO-Asia program to examine the approaches and methods used in many different countries for establishing such funds (Limaye 2008). Perhaps the best examples of EE funds are in the United States. Most of these funds were created at the state level, using various mechanisms. The most common approach is to assess a surcharge on electricity sales. The funds are collected by the electric utility and either used directly to finance EE projects (as in California) (California Public Utilities Commission 2008), handed over to a specially created agency to administer the financing programs (as in New York State),[1] or entrusted to a third-party energy service

Table 8.1 Examples of Energy Efficiency Funds in Selected U.S. States

State	Energy efficiency spending as percentage of annual utility revenues
Vermont	4.4
California	2.9
Washington	2.5
Utah	2.4
Oregon	2.3
Massachsetts	2.3
Minnesota	2.2
Idaho	2.1
Iowa	1.8
New York	1.7
Wisconsin	1.6
Connecticut	1.4
New Jersey	1.2
Colorado	1.1

Source: Molina and others 2010.

provider (as in Vermont).[2] Some states have used taxes, general revenues, or state revenue bonds to create EE funds. In a few cases, petroleum taxes have been the funding source.

The most common, reliable, and sustainable source of funding is a tariff levy, known as a public benefit charge or a system benefit charge, established by the regulator and collected by the utility via the customer's bill (Limaye and Patankar 2011). The level of funding varies from state to state. The more progressive states have assessed a levy of 1–3 percent of electricity sales revenue to finance their EE funds (see table 8.1).

Examples of similar EE funds in other countries include the following:

- Bulgaria – Bulgarian Energy Efficiency Fund (BEEF)
- Romania – Romanian Energy Efficiency Fund
- New South Wales, Australia – Sustainable Energy Fund
- New Zealand – Sustainable Management Fund
- Czech Republic – Energy Savings Fund
- Brazil – Energy Efficiency Charge
- South Africa – Energy Efficiency and Demand-Side Management Fund

An illustration of the structure of EE funds is provided in figure 8.1. An overview of BEEF is provided in box 8.1, and more details are available in the case study in chapter 19.

Energy Efficiency Funds in Asia

There are a number of examples of EE funds in Asia:

- *The Republic of Korea.* In 1980, the Korean Ministry of Knowledge Economy (MKE) established the Korea Energy Conservation Fund to promote the development of EE initiatives by providing long-term, low-interest loans for investment in EE projects (Korea Energy Management Corporation 2008).

Figure 8.1 Illustrative Structure of an Energy Efficiency Fund

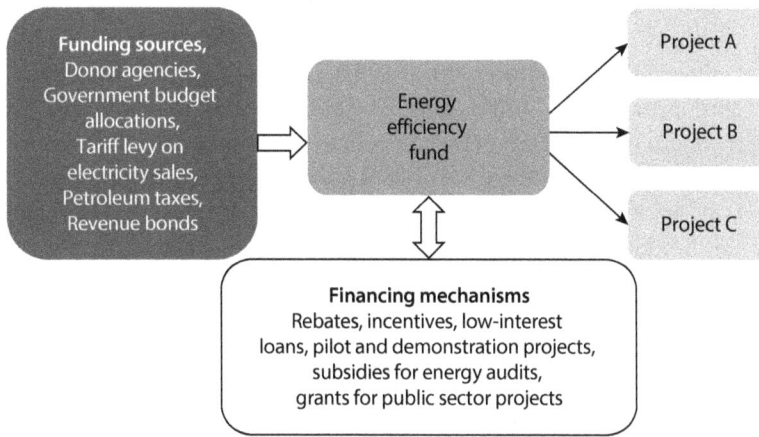

Box 8.1 Bulgarian Energy Efficiency Fund

The Bulgarian Energy Efficiency Fund (BEEF) was established under the Bulgarian Energy Efficiency Law of 2004. The fund was designed as a dedicated, revolving EE facility with in-house technical and financial evaluation capabilities. BEEF was to be operated as a not-for-profit entity, and income from fees charged to the clients of the fund need only cover the operating costs and losses from defaults. BEEF aimed to complement existing lending facilities of local commercial banks to achieve higher leverage on its investments.

BEEF was capitalized with US$10 million of Global Environment Facility (GEF) funding, which was designed to support the establishment and operation of BEEF as a commercially oriented public-private finance facility. GEF funds were used to provide seed capital for BEEF and cover setup and operating costs until BEEF reached financial self-sufficiency; and also to partially cover initial costs of EE capacity building. Additional financing was secured from the Bulgarian government (US$1.5 million), and other donors provided an additional US$5.5 million.

BEEF was designed to provide both loans and partial credit guarantees for EE projects. At the time, Bulgarian banks lacked both liquidity and credit risk assessment tools to extend dedicated EE financing to borrowers. Within the first two years of operation, the fund became the EE financier of choice for the public sector and for hospitals and universities. Energy service companies (ESCOs) and small enterprises were also attracted to BEEF's financing because of relaxed collateral requirements and assistance in the project development process.

The projects financed by BEEF included EE improvement in industrial equipment, building retrofits, district heating substations, thermal insulation, heat distribution systems, street lighting systems, and small cogeneration plants.

The total volume of projects financed using BEEF was US$48 million. The BEEF loan portfolio was US$24 million. Greenhouse gas savings were reported to be 1.1 million tons per year.

Sources: Klev 2007; World Bank 2010b.

MKE assigned Korea Energy Management Corporation to manage the fund, which offers loans for a wide array of projects.

- *Thailand.* Thailand established the ENCON Fund under the Energy Conservation Promotion Act of 1992. The funding came from a levy on petroleum products sold in Thailand. The aim was to fund sustainable energy initiatives and incentive programs as well as research and development.
- *Sri Lanka.* The government of Sri Lanka established the Energy Conservation Fund under the Ministry of Power and Energy to finance EE projects. In 2007, this fund was transferred to the newly created Sustainable Energy Authority of Sri Lanka.[3]
- *India.* India's Energy Conservation Act, 2001, requires all Indian states to establish a State Energy Conservation Fund to satisfy their obligations to promote EE under the act. The first such fund was established in the state of Kerala in 2010 (Limaye and others 2008).
- *China.* China has established aggressive targets for reducing energy intensity and has designated the responsibility to implement these targets to the provincial governments. Some of the provinces, such as Hebei, have established EE funds through a levy on electricity consumption. Hebei is using its fund to provide incentives and subsidies to enterprises that implement EE measures.

Characteristics of EE Funds
Management and Operation
Responsibility for management and operation of EE funds may be assigned to the utilities that are collecting the monies through the tariff or may be assigned to other organizations such as

- Existing government agency;
- Specially created statutory agency;
- Public-private partnership;
- Municipalities;
- Third parties, including
  - Independent entities (with a board of directors comprising stakeholders),
  - Financial institutions, and
  - Nongovernmental organizations (NGOs).

Selection of the organization to manage and operate the fund may be based on some or all of the following criteria:

- Compatibility with public policy goals;
- Credibility with funders and customers;
- Technical, financial, and administrative capacity;
- Management incentive structure;
- Ability to realize economies of scale and scope;
- Minimal start-up requirements;
- Ability to work collaboratively across agencies; and
- Ability to engage with demand-side management (DSM) and EE stakeholders.

Project Financing Mechanisms

The project financing mechanisms used by the EE funds to finance project implementers for specific EE projects include the following:

- Grants,
- Loans,
- Subsidies,
- Equity funds,
- Loan guarantees,
- Credit guarantees, and
- Supplier credits.

Criteria for Selecting Projects

The criteria used for selecting projects for financing generally include

- Technical feasibility,
- Compliance with environmental standards,
- Financial characteristics,
- Acceptability of the level of risk,
- Replicability,
- Contribution to developing sustainable EE markets, and
- Documentation of project characteristics.

Lessons Learned

The lessons learned from international experience with EE funds demonstrate that they can address a number of financing and implementation barriers, as illustrated in table 8.2.

The major lessons follow:

The United States and many other countries have successfully used EE funds, establishing them using the following mechanisms:

- Regulations establishing a tariff surcharge on electricity consumption,
- Special taxes,
- General state tax revenues,
- State bonds,
- Petroleum taxes, and
- Certification fees.

Many EE funds in the United States have been established by regulators using public benefits charges. These funds, sourced via a tariff levy established by the regulator and collected by the utility, have proved to be the most common, reliable, and sustainable sources of funding because they are not dependent on uncertain government budgets and are thus financially sustainable. The level of such funding varies. The more progressive EE funds have assessed a levy of 1–2 percent of electricity sales revenue. EE funds are widely used in conjunction with utility DSM programs.

Table 8.2 Addressing the Financing and Implementation Barriers

Barrier	How an EE fund addresses the barrier
Lack of knowledge and awareness	Fund demonstration projects. Publicize success stories.
New DSM-EE technologies	Finance projects with innovative technologies. Provide training; publicize success stories.
Limited availability of conventional financing	Provide funds for projects. Supplement conventional financing.
Small project size	Facilitate financing of small projects. Standardize and aggregate projects.
Limited applications of project financing	Educate banks on applicability of project financing. Provide risk guarantees.
Lenders' lack of experience	Provide information and training to lenders. Work with lenders to finance demonstration projects.
Perception of high risk	Provide risk guarantees. Document and publicize success stories.
Collateral or strong balance sheet requirement	Provide credit guarantees. Assist ESCOs in project financing.
High transaction costs	Standardize project financing application forms. Create forum for interaction among lenders and ESCOs.
High development costs	Finance or subsidize energy audits. Educate consumers on benefits of DSM-EE and on role of ESCOs.
Monitoring, measurement, and verification methods and tools	Develop guidelines and procedures for monitoring and verification. Demonstrate the applications in early projects.
Limited infrastructure for DSM-EE implementation	Provide a clear signal to the market that the energy fund will be financing projects on an ongoing basis.

Source: Limaye 2010.
Note: DSM = demand-side management; EE = energy efficiency; ESCO = energy service company.

EE funds have also been established by governments using legislative mandates, by donor agencies, or by a combination of these. Such funds are effective in markets in which liquidity is an issue and where local banks have been unwilling to provide financing for EE projects. A government-resourced EE fund can provide finance through various instruments such as debt, mezzanine financing, and in some cases, equity. In many cases, donor agencies have provided funding for establishing EE funds. The EE funds are generally operated by existing financial institutions, or a professional management team is competitively recruited to manage the fund and compensated on the basis of agreed-on performance criteria.

Utility DSM Funds

Under the DSM approach, a regulatory agency requires the utilities under its authority to develop and implement programs to modify customers' energy consumption. These programs typically address EE along with other load-modification objectives, including peak clipping, valley filling, load shifting, energy conservation, load building, and flexible load shape (IIEC 2008). The utility's costs for developing and implementing the DSM programs are included in the calculation of the utility's tariff and are recovered through a tariff increase paid by all utility ratepayers.

The concept of DSM was originally developed in the United States in the 1980s in response to the problems faced by utilities, including staggering capital requirements for new generation capacity, significant fluctuations in demand growth rates, and customer and regulatory concerns about rising electricity prices (Edison Electric Institute and Electric Power Research Institute 1984). In the 1990s, many developing countries and donor agencies recognized the potential benefits of DSM for reducing electricity shortages, mitigating the impacts of climate change, and contributing to sustainable development. DSM involves cooperative activities between the utility and its customers (sometimes with the assistance of third parties such as energy service companies and various trade allies) to implement options for increasing the efficiency of energy use, with resulting benefits to customers, the utility, and society as a whole (see table 8.3).

Rationale for DSM

DSM programs increase the efficiency of energy service delivery and create economic benefits for utilities while simultaneously creating substantial benefits for customers and for society (figure 8.2). Tapping into this energy resource

Table 8.3 Demand-Side Management Benefits

Customer benefits	Societal benefits	Utility benefits
Satisfy electricity demands	Reduce environmental degradation	Lower cost of service
Reduce or stabilize costs	Conserve resources	Improve operating efficiency, flexibility
Improve value of service	Protect global environment	
Maintain or improve lifestyle and productivity	Maximize customer welfare	Reduce capital needs
		Improve customer service

Source: IIEC 2008.

Figure 8.2 Benefits of Demand-Side Management

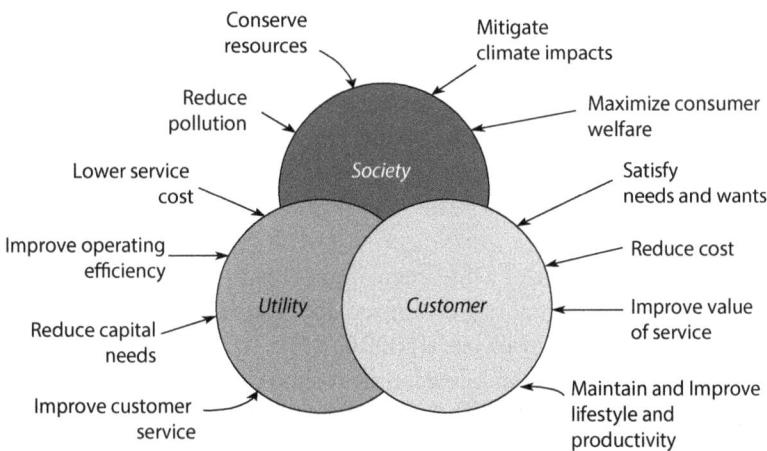

Source: IIEC 2008.

requires special programs to mobilize cost-effective changes in energy demand. Without such programs, these impacts either would not have occurred or would have materialized only with significant delay, forcing society to obtain potentially less optimal sources of supply. The historic justification for the pursuit of DSM was the presumed existence of market barriers that limited the adoption of cost-effective options.

During the 1980s and early 1990s, utilities in the United States and Europe implemented a wide range of DSM programs under regulatory oversight and supervision. The early DSM programs consisted primarily of rebates and incentives for various types of energy efficient products, technologies, and equipment. Regulators also created EE funds (discussed above) that were managed by utilities as a part of their DSM activities.

DSM in Restructured Utility Markets

A major restructuring of the electricity industry began in the 1990s in the United States and Europe, leading to the creation of new entities and the realignment of industry players (generators, transmission businesses, distribution or "wires" businesses, and retail suppliers) relative to customers.

With utility restructuring, two distinct types of DSM programs emerged (IEA 1996):

- *Public-policy-based DSM and EE* programs carried out to achieve public policy objectives, such as to reduce environmental damage, to increase overall energy system efficiency, and to create jobs, among many others.
- *Business-based DSM and EE* programs carried out by energy businesses or their partners to achieve commercial corporate objectives, such as improving the profitability of existing business areas, improving market positioning, retaining customers, improving public relations, and increasing profitability of new business areas.

DSM in Asia

Most Asian countries are facing the challenge of meeting the increasing energy needs that accompany high economic growth rates. The supply of energy (particularly electricity) has not kept pace with demand growth in many countries, and electricity shortages are becoming common, causing electricity load shedding or curtailments. As a result, regulators are starting to consider the implementation of DSM programs, as in these examples:

- China issued a set of DSM regulations "for the purpose of improving power use efficiency, promoting optimized allocation of power resources and guaranteeing order of power use" (NDRC 2010, 1). These regulations specify that "both conservation and development should be taken into consideration, but conservation should come first" (NDRC 2010, 1), and require the power grid companies in China to achieve a savings of 0.3 percent in sales volume and in maximum electrical load compared with the previous year.

- In India, states regulate utilities. The state of Maharashtra issued DSM regulations that require utilities to develop and implement a range of DSM programs (Maharashtra Electricity Regulatory Commission 2010).

U.S. Experience with DSM Implementation

Three basic models of DSM implementation are used in the United States. The first model is best exemplified by California. Regulators assign responsibility to the utilities to design and implement a wide range of DSM programs.

In the second model, the regulators assign responsibility for DSM to a government agency (existing or newly created). For example, in New York state, DSM programs are administered by the New York State Energy Research and Development Authority (NYSERDA). This agency receives the DSM funds collected by the utilities through the public benefit charge mechanism. NYSERDA designs and implements the DSM programs and reports to the regulators annually.

In the third model, the responsibility for managing the EE fund is assigned to a competitively selected independent third party (usually an NGO or nonprofit organization). This agency (sometimes called an EE utility) is held responsible and accountable for program design and implementation under a contract with the regulatory agency (generally a performance-based contract). The first such EE utility was Efficiency Vermont, established by the Vermont Public Service Commission.

The three implementation models are illustrated in figure 8.3.

A summary of DSM in California, New York, and Vermont is presented in table 8.4.

Lessons Learned

- To be effective, DSM programs require strong regulatory initiatives (such as decoupling electricity sales from profits) and utilities that are (or can be) motivated and have the capacity to deliver EE programs. DSM

Figure 8.3 Demand-Side Management Implementation Models

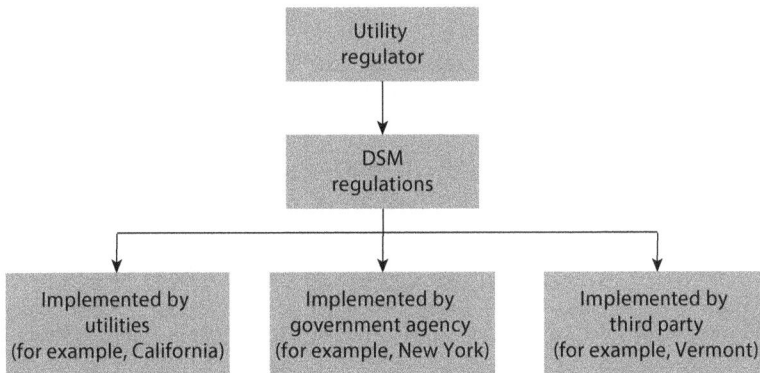

Note: DSM = demand-side management.

Table 8.4 Summary of Demand-Side Management in Three U.S. States

	California	*New York*	*Vermont*
Regulatory oversight	California Public Utility Commission	New York State Public Service Commission	Vermont Public Service Board
Implemented by	Utilities (PG&E, SCE, and SDG&E)	NYSERDA	Efficiency Vermont
Funding provided by	Public benefit charge	System benefit charge	System benefit charge
Annual budget (2010)	$1 billion	$378 million	$31 million
Annual budget per capita	$49.4	$19.0	$19.4
Energy savings (2008)	3,044 GWh	471 GWh	149 GWh
Peak reduction	6,000 MW (through 2008)	1,200 MW (through 2007)	45 MW (in 2007)
Levelized cost of energy efficiency	3.0 cents per kWh	~ 3 cents per kWh	< 2.0 cents per kWh

Note: GWh = gigawatt-hour; kWh = kilowatt-hour; MW = megawatt; NYSERDA = New York State Energy Research and Development Authority; PG&E = Pacific Gas and Electric; SCE = Southern California Edison; SDG&E = San Diego Gas and Electric.

programs also need an EE service delivery infrastructure. Therefore, the DSM approach has not yet been widely used in the East Asia and Pacific region, where utilities have limited motivation to engage in EE and very limited capacity to implement EE programs. In addition, regulatory authorities in many of these countries are relatively new and have not yet focused attention on DSM.

• The emerging EE utility model managed by competent third-party organizations (as in Vermont) can provide a way to overcome the issues related to utility motivation and capacity.

• DSM programs have successfully delivered substantial energy savings in many U.S. states, and the experience can be customized and adapted to East Asia and Pacific countries.

Utility Consumer Financing of Energy Efficiency Programs

Utility consumer financing is a mechanism under which the electric utility provides financing for the implementation of EE projects. The funds are loaned to the customer for equipment purchase, and loan repayments are recovered by the utility through the customer's electricity bill (Limaye 2009). The cost of the EE equipment is borne by the individual customers in whose facilities the EE equipment is installed (and who are the direct beneficiaries of the energy savings and related cost reductions).

Utility consumer financing (also known as "on-bill financing") is designed to overcome the first cost barrier (lack of internal funds) for customer investment in EE. The utility provides or arranges for the financing needed for investment in the project. The customer signs a loan agreement with the utility and repays via a line item on the bill. In most cases, the loan repayments are arranged to be smaller than the customer's cost reduction from the energy savings created by the energy efficient equipment. This allows the customer to be "cash flow positive" throughout the life of the EE project.

Some of the advantages of this mechanism, based on experience in 20 U.S. states, follow (Bell, Nadel, and Hayes 2011):

- On-bill financing provides consumers access to financing using the utility's relationship with its customers.
- It generally provides the customer the advantage of paying for the EE investment from the savings in utility costs resulting from that investment.
- Such programs may be able to extend financing to otherwise underserved markets, such as consumers renting their facilities and residents of multifamily dwelling units.
- Financing can be provided to consumers whose weak credit limits their ability to obtain conventional financing.
- The costs and risks related to the collection of loan repayments from consumers are reduced because very few consumers are delinquent on their utility bill payments.

Key Characteristics

Important characteristics of utility consumer financing programs include the following:

- The financing structure is generally on favorable loan terms. The interest rate is based on the utility's cost of capital, usually below the commercial market rate. Some utility financing programs charge no interest.
- The length of the loan is determined by the type of EE equipment being financed and is designed so that the consumer's monthly loan repayment is less than the savings generated by the equipment. For example, financing for compact fluorescent lamps (CFLs) may be for 9–18 months, which is commonly the payback period for these efficient lamps.
- The equipment is generally owned by the consumer, and the utility has a lien on the equipment under the loan agreement.
- The utility's financing and administrative costs can be rolled into the equipment price and paid by the consumer as a part of the loan repayment.
- The risk of default is low because consumers are usually diligent about paying utility bills. In some cases, the utility may threaten to cut off electricity service for nonpayment of the equipment loan, providing a major incentive to the consumer to avoid default.
- Some utilities have found it difficult and cumbersome to modify their billing systems to add loan repayments for EE equipment to the electricity bills.

Illustrative Examples

Utility financing of EE projects through the billing mechanism was undertaken for the Bangalore Efficient Lighting Program launched by the Bangalore Electricity Supply Company (BESCOM) in India and for the Programme Solaire (PROSOL) program in Tunisia for installation of solar water heaters.

In the Bangalore program, the electric utility competitively selected manufacturers of energy efficient CFLs based on price, quality, and warranty. BESCOM's residential customers were able to obtain the CFLs from the manufacturers' retail outlets. Customers signed agreements with BESCOM to pay for the CFLs over nine months through their electric bills (IIEC 2006).

The Tunisian program PROSOL was a joint effort involving the Tunisian Ministry of Industry, Energy, and Small and Medium Enterprises and the National Agency for Energy Conservation. Solar water heating manufacturers and suppliers worked with commercial banks to arrange financing for customers interested in purchasing solar water heating systems. The customers agreed to repay the loans through their electricity bills. The electric utility collected the customer payments and repaid the banks (Touhami 2006). This program is summarized in box 8.2.

Box 8.2 Tunisia's PROSOL Program

The PROSOL project was initiated in 2005 by the Tunisian Minister for Industry, Energy, and Small and Medium Enterprises and the National Agency for Energy Conservation, with the support of the United Nations Environment Programme Mediterranean Renewable Energy Programme Finance Initiative. The objective of PROSOL was to revitalize the declining Tunisian solar water heater market. The innovative component of PROSOL was its ability to actively involve the finance sector, turning it into a key player for the promotion of clean energy and sustainable development. By identifying new lending opportunities, banks were able to build dedicated loan portfolios, thus helping to shift from a cash-based to a credit-based market.

The main features of the PROSOL financing scheme were the following:

- Loan mechanism for domestic customers to purchase solar water heaters;
- Cost subsidy provided by the Tunisian government, up to 100 dinars (about US$75 at the prevailing exchange rate in 2005) per square meter (m^2) of installed solar panels;
- Discounted interest rates on the loans, progressively phased out; and
- A series of accompanying measures, including an awareness-raising campaign, a capacity-building program, and carbon finance.

Key partners included

- Société Tunisienne de Banque;
- Two commercial banks (UBCI and Amen Bank);
- The state electricity utility Société Tunisienne d'Electricité et du Gaz;
- Manufacturers, importers, and installers of solar water heaters; and
- Local consultants.

Launched in April 2005, the PROSOL project achieved immediate success. By December 2005, sales reached the record figure of 7,400 solar water heating systems, for a total surface installed of 23,000 m^2. By the end of 2006, an additional 11,000 units were sold, corresponding to approximately 34,000 m^2. In less than two years, the solar water heater market surpassed 57,000 m^2, representing as much as 50 percent of the cumulative surface area installed from 1985 to 2004.

Sources: MacLean 2008; Touhami 2006.

Advantages and Limitations

The main advantages of utility financing follow:

- Allows the customer to purchase EE equipment and pay for it from savings generated by the equipment,
- Facilitates the customer's repayment of the equipment purchase by collecting the payments through the electric bill,
- Reduces the transaction cost of recovering the loan repayments from customers,
- Reduces the risk of default, and
- Improves the relationship between the utility and the customer.

There are also some limitations and challenges related to the utility consumer financing approach:

- Many utilities are unwilling to finance equipment purchase through the electricity bill.
- The utility billing system may not be structured to handle the collection of loan repayments, and the cost of modifying the system may be high.
- The regulatory system may not allow the utility to collect payments for equipment loans.
- Although default risks are low, issues may arise with respect to what actions the utility can take if the customer does not pay the finance charge or only pays a part of the utility bill. Some utilities have included provisions to cut off service for nonpayment of the EE finance component, but consumer advocates have questioned the legal basis for doing so.
- Other challenges include accurately estimating the utility financing and administration costs, ensuring that the monthly payment is less than the savings on the bill, addressing the issue of change in ownership of the property, and addressing non electric savings such as gas or oil savings or reductions in operating costs.

Dedicated Credit Lines for Energy Efficiency

Dedicated credit lines for EE address the issues related to insufficient lending by banks and financial institutions (lenders) for EE projects. Most energy users are unwilling to invest their own funds for EE improvement because of competing demands for internal capital, lack of awareness of the characteristics and benefits of EE, and perceptions of the risks of such projects. Lenders are also reluctant to mobilize lending for EE projects because of their limited experience and familiarity with EE projects and their perceptions that such projects are highly risky. A dedicated credit line for EE uses government or donor funds to leverage an increase in lending for EE projects.

Rationale and Structure

Dedicated credit lines may be established by governments, international donor agencies, or governments in cooperation with international donor agencies. These credit lines are provided to one or more participating lenders, with the following basic objectives:

- Increase the interest and confidence of participating lenders in financing EE projects,
- Enhance the technical capacity of lenders to scale up EE lending,
- Leverage cofinancing from participating lenders for EE financing,
- Strengthen participating lenders' capacity for identifying and managing project risks, and
- Assist participating lenders in exploring business opportunities in other low-carbon lending and carbon-financing businesses.

The basic structure is illustrated in figure 8.4. An example of the EBRD's Sustainable Energy Financing Facility (SEFF) is provided in box 8.3.

The donor agency or government provides a credit line to one or more participating banks. The credit line is generally provided at a low interest rate to the banks, which on-lend at either a concessional rate or the market rate. The bank may be required to add its own funds to increase the total resources available. The bank will generally charge a fee for loan processing and may charge market rates for its funds, but the total interest cost for financing projects will be lower than the market interest rate as a result of the low-interest funds from the donor or government. Banks use their standard project appraisal criteria to evaluate and process the loans. The banks generally finance about 70 percent of the total project investment, requiring the project developer to invest 30 percent as equity.

Assuming that the banks match the donor or government funds on a 1:1 basis and require a 30 percent equity investment for each project, the donor or government is able to obtain a leverage ratio of about 285 percent on the funds it provides to the total investment in EE projects.

Figure 8.4 Illustration of Dedicated Credit Line

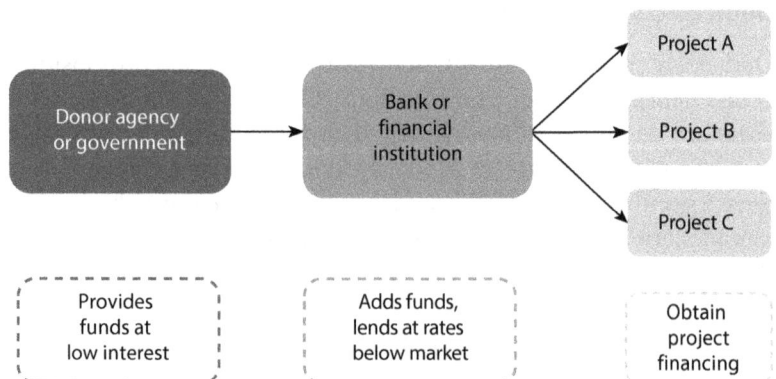

Box 8.3 The European Bank for Reconstruction and Development (EBRD) Sustainable Energy Financing Facility

The EBRD's Sustainable Energy Financing Facility (SEFF) is a credit line made available to partner banks in member countries for financing EE improvements, at their own risk, in commercial and industrial enterprises and, in some countries, in residential buildings. The SEFF is supported by a comprehensive technical assistance (TA) package under which each loan applicant receives free TA from a team of consultants. Each country has its own tailored approach reflecting local requirements and energy savings needs. The dedicated country TA teams, comprising international and local consultants, support interested companies and borrowers in identifying the best technical solutions for their energy savings requirements, preparing suitable loan documentation, and providing assistance through the application process. The teams also help familiarize local partner bank loan officers with sustainable energy investment opportunities.

Since launching the first SEFF in Bulgaria in 2004, the EBRD has committed almost US$1.7 billion of commercial funding to 15 facilities in 12 countries. The Slovak Republic is a typical example. SloSEFF was launched in 2007 when the EBRD provided €60 million (about US$78 million) through four partner banks to encourage Slovak enterprises to make better use of energy resources. To respond to the high demand, the EBRD extended another €90 million (about US$ 117 million) in 2010. By the end of 2011, the EBRD had financed more than 350 sustainable energy projects in the residential and industrial sectors under this facility.

Although experience is still relatively limited in some countries, the SEFF model has proved to be a highly effective approach for helping businesses to optimize energy solutions, reduce energy costs, and enhance competitiveness. It is still too early to assess what happens once the loans are fully disbursed, but it is clear that an increasing number of SEFF partner banks have recognized the business opportunity. Some have launched their own sustainable energy loan products, allocated staff to focus on originating sustainable energy opportunities, or even established dedicated departments, for example, United Bulgarian Bank and Ukreximbank.

The EBRD's independent evaluation department has concluded that the credit lines have also been effective in introducing commercial banks to the financing of renewable energy and EE. They note, however, wide variations between banks, but some have effectively integrated EE and renewable energy into their operations, and are likely to continue financing these projects after the credit lines end. State-owned banks seem to have performed better in this respect, perhaps because of their broader development mandate.

The following factors have been critical to the SEFF's success:

- Free TA for energy audits, investment design, and loan facilitation;
- A comprehensive and sustained promotional effort with strong national and local support from government leaders; and
- The provision of grants to offset a modest portion of small and medium enterprise investment costs in some but not all countries.

The EBRD's independent evaluation department questioned the efficacy of the subsidies. Specifically, it noted that participation by small and medium enterprises appeared to be

---

box continues next page

Box 8.3 The European Bank for Reconstruction and Development (EBRD) Sustainable Energy Financing Facility *(continued)*

similar in Ukraine, where no subsidies are available, and Bulgaria, where subsidies are provided. However, despite this finding, and despite the attractiveness of the high internal rate of return and short pay-back period of most small and medium enterprise EE investments, the availability of these grants still appears to be a major factor in securing interest from small entrepreneurs.

Source: EBRD, Sustainable Energy Financing Facilities (SEFF), http://www.ebrd.com/pages/sector/energyefficiency/sei/financing.shtml.

To be eligible for financing under such a credit line, projects need to satisfy certain criteria. For example, in the China Energy Efficiency Financing (CHEEF) Project, the simple payback was required to be less than 10 years. The line of credit for small and medium enterprises (SMEs) provided by KfW (Kreditanstalt für Wiederaufbau, or German development bank) in India required both a 20 percent minimum energy savings and a minimum level of greenhouse gas (GHG) reduction per unit of investment.[4]

Examples in Asia

Three examples of dedicated credit lines for EE are summarized below (two are included as case studies in part IV this book; see chapters 14 and 15).

China Energy Efficiency Financing (CHEEF) Project

In the CHEEF project, the World Bank provided a line of credit for EE project financing to three banks in China—China EXIM Bank, Minsheng Bank, and Huaxia Bank[5]—that were selected to be the participating lenders. The line of credit was structured as a financial intermediary lending operation with a sovereign guarantee provided by the government of China (Ministry of Finance) (World Bank 2008, 2010c). The World Bank loan product for the project was a London Interbank Offer Rate (LIBOR)-based, US$-denominated, single currency, variable-spread loan at US$100 million (for each of the three banks), to be repaid in 17.5 years, including a grace period of 5 years. The World Bank funds were on-lent by the Ministry of Finance to the three banks at the same financial terms and conditions, and were in turn loaned by the banks to industrial enterprises and energy service companies (ESCOs) for EE investment subprojects at market rates. The participating banks are fully responsible for debt servicing and for bearing all financial risks associated with the World Bank loan.

The World Bank required the banks to co-invest at least US$100 million in EE projects. The World Bank project was supported by a Global Environment Facility (GEF) grant that was used to provide TA (see details in the case study in chapter 14). As a result, the project has disbursed US$115 million in International Bank for Reconstruction and Development (IBRD) funds, which leveraged US$462 million from participating banks and industrial enterprises, with a leverage ratio

Figure 8.5 Illustrative Overview of China Energy Efficiency Financing Project

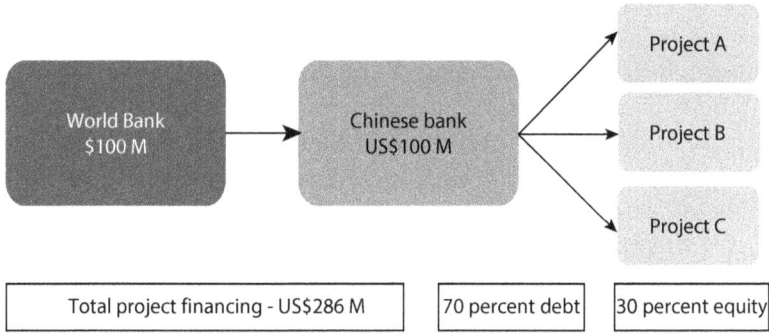

of 1:4. These investments are expected to save 1.7 million tons of coal equivalent and reduce CO_2 emissions by 4.2 million tons per year.

Figure 8.5 provides an illustrative overview of the CHEEF project.

Thailand Energy Efficiency Revolving Fund

Thailand's Energy Efficiency Revolving Fund (EERF) was established by the government of Thailand to stimulate and leverage commercial financing for EE projects and to help commercial banks develop streamlined procedures for project appraisal and loan disbursement. The source of the government funds was the Energy Conservation (ENCON) Fund managed by the Department of Alternative Energy Development and Efficiency (DEDE), the original fund created under Thailand's Energy Conservation Promotion Act of 1992. The EERF provides capital to Thai banks to fund EE projects, and the banks provide low interest loans to EE projects in industries and buildings.

Phase I of the EERF was launched in 2003 as a three-year program and has been renewed for two additional three-year terms. It has been working with 11 participating banks. By April 2010, the EERF had financed 335 EE projects and 112 renewable energy projects. The total investment in these projects was US$453 million, with an average leverage ratio of about 1:1 from the ENCON Fund investments. The estimated annual energy cost savings were US$154 million, providing an average payback of about three years (Sinsukprasert 2010). The leverage ratio increased to about 2:1 as participating banks became more familiar with and confident in EE and renewable energy projects, and thus more willing to take risks.

KfW SME Credit Line

The KfW of Germany has provided a dedicated credit line of €50 million (about US$65 million) to the Small Industries Development Bank of India (SIDBI) to finance EE projects in micro, small, and medium enterprises (MSMEs) in India. The main purpose of this credit line is to provide SIDBI the capacity to encourage MSMEs to undertake energy saving investments in plant and machinery and production processes. KfW also provided a TA component to support SIDBI in identifying key target MSME clusters, setting up the credit lines, providing technical support, and conducting awareness campaigns in MSME clusters throughout India. The overall objective of the program is to reduce the emission of GHGs, especially CO_2, and thus to contribute to climate change mitigation. Specifically, the program seeks to (a) increase MSME investments in EE, (b) increase the contribution of MSME to ecologically sustainable economic development, and (c) broaden SIDBI's financial instruments (KfW and SIDBI 2010).

A key requirement of this dedicated line of credit is that each project should achieve a minimum level of energy savings and GHG emission reduction. The targets established by KfW are a 20 percent energy intensity reduction and 30 tons of GHG emissions reduction for every 1 million rupees (about US$20,000) invested.

A comparison of the three dedicated credit lines is provided in table 8.5.

Lessons Learned

The following major lessons emerge from a review of dedicated credit lines:

- Dedicated credit lines can be successful in enhancing bank pursuit of and confidence in financing EE projects through a learning-by-doing process.
- Donor agencies and governments can leverage additional financing from banks to increase the total size of the loan portfolio. In CHEEF, every US$1 IBRD loan has leveraged US$4 of cofinancing from participating banks and industrial enterprises. Credit lines can double the leverage effect when participating banks revolve the loans that are paid back into EE investments again.
- Most dedicated credit lines have a TA component that helps build capacity in banks and thereby contributes to future increased bank lending.

Table 8.5 Comparison of the Three Dedicated Credit Lines for Energy Efficiency

Feature	China energy efficiency financing project	Thailand energy efficiency revolving fund	KfW/SIDBI
Funding agency	World Bank	Government of Thailand ENCON Fund	KfW Bank
Participating banks	China EXIM, Huaxia, and Minsheng Banks	11 commercial banks in Thailand	SIDBI
Amount of credit line	US$100 million to each bank	US$192 million	€50 million
Cofunding from banks	Minimum $100 million each	Varies by bank	None required
Sectors targeted	Medium and large industries and ESCOs	Industrial and commercial energy users and ESCOs	Micro, small, and medium enterprises
Percent debt financing	70	Maximum 70	70
Maximum loan size	—	$1.4 million	—

Note: — = not available; ESCO = energy service company; KfW = German Development Bank; SIDBI = Small Industries Development Bank of India.

- Credit lines offer a high rate of leverage of public funds and the best prospect for program sustainability by increasing the interest and capacity of commercial banks in EE financing.
- This instrument has been most effective in increasing EE financing for traditional bank clients—medium and large enterprises. It has been less effective in encouraging commercial banks to enter the SME sector because most banks rely on their traditional risk assessment criteria and focus on balance sheet financing. The balance sheets of most SMEs are much weaker than those of larger companies and their risk profiles are generally much higher.
- Commercial banks have been unwilling to consider project financing for EE projects using the cash flow stream from the energy savings as a major criterion in their underwriting process.

Risk-Sharing Programs

Risk-sharing programs are designed to address the perception held by lenders that EE projects are inherently riskier than their traditional investments. This perception creates a major barrier to commercial financing of EE projects. A risk-sharing program provides partial coverage of the risk involved in extending loans for EE projects. The risk-sharing facility generally includes a subordinated recovery guarantee and might also have a "first loss reserve" to be used to absorb up to a specified amount of losses before the risk sharing occurs.

The risk-sharing facility directly enables increased financing of EE projects by

- Addressing credit risk and barriers to structuring the transactions involved in financing EE projects and
- Engaging commercial lenders and building their capacity to finance EE projects on a commercially sustainable basis.

A partial risk guarantee facility, provided by a government, donor agency, or other public agency, can assist the beneficiaries (EE projects) by (a) providing them access to finance, (b) reducing the cost of capital, and (c) expanding the loan tenor or grace periods to match project cash flows (Mostert 2010). By reducing the banks' risk in financing EE projects and informing and educating the lenders through parallel TA programs, the risk-sharing facility leverages commercial financing for EE projects.

Rationale and Structure

The primary rationale for a risk-sharing program is to induce the participating lenders to increase their lending for EE projects by providing partial coverage of the potential losses from loan defaults. The basic structure of the risk-sharing program is summarized in the following:

- A public agency (government or donor agency) signs a guarantee facility agreement (GFA) with participating lenders to cover a portion of their potential losses.

- Under the GFA, the public agency provides a partial guarantee covering loan loss from default. Although the actual amount or percentage of the loss covered by the guarantee may vary, the typical guarantee is for a 50/50 (pari passu) sharing of the losses between the bank and the public agency.
- Some GFAs also include a "first loss" facility that absorbs 100 percent of the losses up to a specified amount.
- Participating lenders sign agreements specifying loan targets and conditions.
- Lenders are responsible for conducting due diligence and processing the loans. The public agency may specify certain terms and conditions for the project appraisal.
- The public agency generally approves each project (or project portfolio) for each lender.
- In case of loan default, the guarantee facility covers the specified portion of the loss.
- Substantial TA is usually provided to lenders, project hosts, and project developers (ESCOs) to help facilitate the financing transactions.

Key features of such programs follow:

- Eligible lenders' credit risk for EE financing is reduced (making transactions possible and gaining credit approval for use of their own funds).
- Targeted TA stimulates deal flow and uptake of financial products offered under the guarantee facility (in support of both partner lender marketing and delivery of EE financing services and of ESCOs in the preparation of projects and programs for investment).
- Transaction costs borne by project participants are reduced.
- Longer-term financing is enabled (to reduce annual finance payments, finance longer-payback "deep retrofit" projects, and make EE projects more attractive to end users by allowing the projects to be self-financing from energy cost savings).
- A long-term sustainable market for financing of EE projects is created.

This process is illustrated in figure 8.6.

Types of Guarantees

The risk-sharing program may offer individual project guarantees or portfolio guarantees. For individual project guarantees, the public agency is involved in each transaction, appraising the eligibility of the applicant borrower for the guarantee in parallel with the lender's due diligence to determine eligibility for a loan. The process is illustrated in figure 8.7.

For a portfolio guarantee, the public agency covers all loans made by the lender to a class of borrowers (the portfolio). Figure 8.8 illustrates the portfolio guarantee. The guarantor and lender agree on loan underwriting criteria in

Figure 8.6 Overview of Risk-Sharing Program

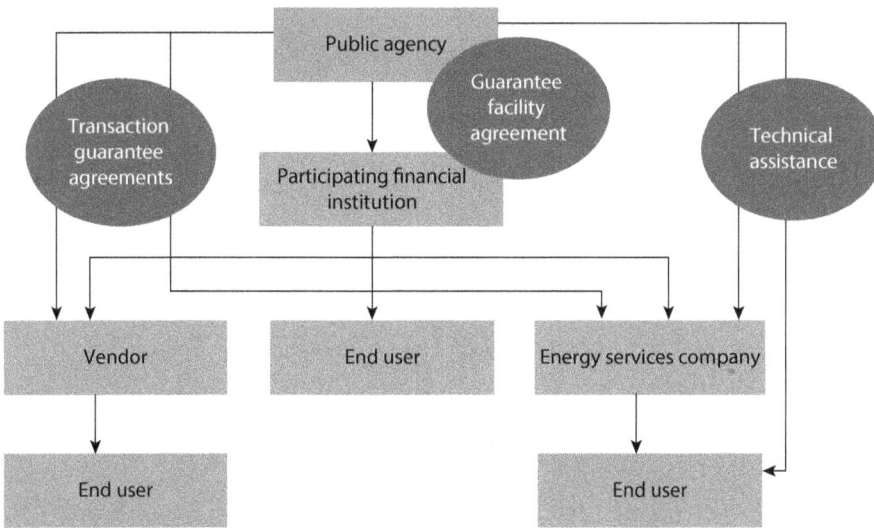

Source: Taylor and others 2008.

Figure 8.7 Individual Project Guarantee

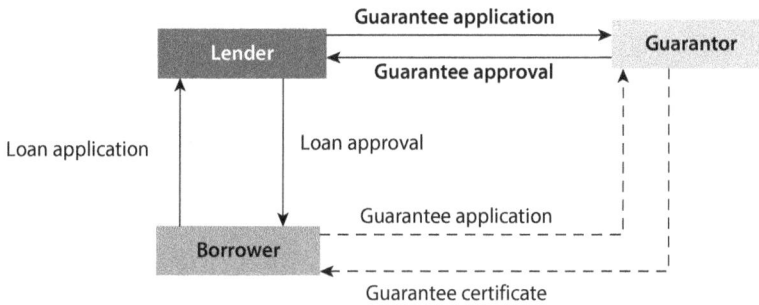

Source: Mostert 2010.

advance, and the lender can automatically include new loans meeting these criteria.

Risk-Sharing Approaches
Because the lender is responsible for project appraisal and due diligence, the public agency should never provide a 100 percent guarantee to cover loan losses. All risk-sharing programs are designed to provide a partial risk guarantee. There are three types of partial guarantees:

- Pro rata guarantee,
- First loss guarantee, and
- Second loss guarantee.

Figure 8.8 Portfolio Guarantee

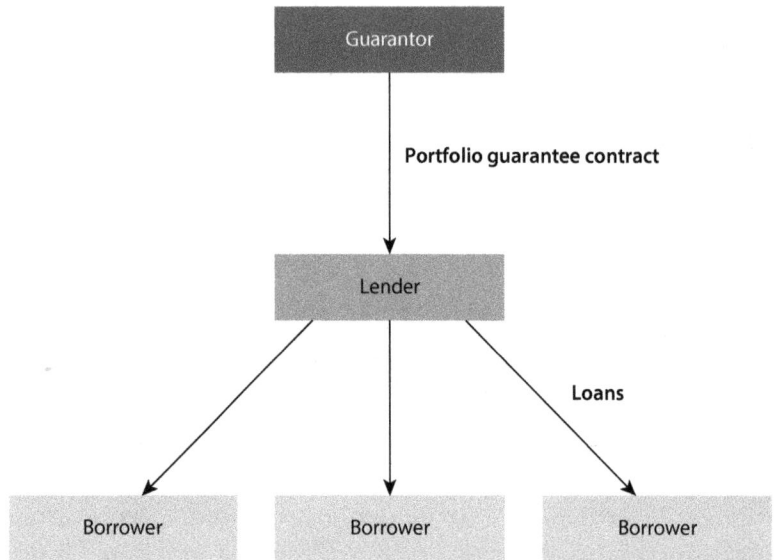

Source: Mostert 2010.

A pro rata guarantee apportions the loss between the lender and the public agency according to a specified formula. Typically, the public agency's share is between 50 and 80 percent. The pro rata formula is the normal procedure for individual project guarantees, however, it can also be used for portfolio guarantees. In some programs, the pro rata share may be variable—higher during the first period of a program, or up to a certain amount of the loss, and lower during a subsequent period. An example of such a program (called the "learning curve formula") is shown in figure 8.9 (from the IFC and GEF China Utility-Based Energy Efficiency Finance [CHUEE] Program) (World Bank IEG 2010).

This scheme allows the lender to incur a lower proportion of the potential loss during its early "learning" phase and a higher proportion after it has gained more experience with financing EE projects.

A first loss guarantee pays for losses from the first loss incurred until the maximum guarantee amount is exhausted; the lender incurs losses only if the total loan loss exceeds the guarantee amount. By covering a large share of first losses and sizing the definition of first losses to be a reasonable proportion of the loan portfolio (usually higher than the estimated default or loss rate), a first loss portfolio guarantee can provide meaningful risk coverage to the lender, but with low levels of total guarantee liability relative to the total size of the portfolio. This approach, therefore, provides a stronger incentive than either the pro rata or second loss guarantees.

Figure 8.9 Pro Rata Sharing with Variable Percentage

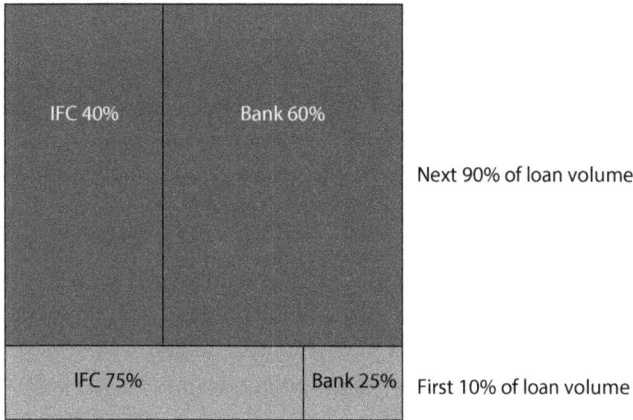

IFC 40%   Bank 60%

Next 90% of loan volume

IFC 75%   Bank 25%   First 10% of loan volume

Source: World Bank IEG 2010.

Table 8.6 Comparison of Guarantee Payments under Different Order of Loss Terms

	Pro rata guarantee	First loss guarantee	Second loss guarantee
Loan amount	US$500,000	US$500,000	US$500,000
Guarantee percentage	60	60	60
Order of loss paid	Pro rata	First	Second
Actual loss	US$200,000	US$200,000	US$200,000
Guarantee paid	US$120,000	US$200,000	0

Source: Seidman 2005.

A second loss guarantee pays for losses that exceed the nonguaranteed portion of the loan. The main purpose is to cover incremental losses beyond the normal loss rate. For example, suppose a lender has an average loss rate of 1 percent of its loan portfolio; when asked to move into a new business segment that it perceives to have higher risk (such as EE loans) the lender would expect the average loss rate to be higher. Because the guarantee is partial, the second loss coverage starts at a loss at or somewhat below 1 percent of the loan portfolio.

Table 8.6 shows how the order of loss affects guarantee payments for a 60 percent loan guarantee on a US$500,000 loan that incurs an actual loss of US$200,000 in a portfolio of US$10 million with a 5 percent first loss guarantee and a 2.5 percent threshold for the second loss guarantee (adapted from Seidman 2005). Under these assumptions, the pro rata guarantee covers 60 percent of the loss or US$120,000; the first loss guarantee covers up to US$500,000 of the total loss and therefore covers the entire loss of $200,000 on this project; and the second loss guarantee covers none of the first US$250,000 and therefore does not cover any loss on this project.

Key Characteristics and Issues

The key characteristics and issues of risk-sharing approaches are summarized below:

- *Guarantee facility agreement.* A GFA needs to be executed between the lender and the guarantee provider. The provisions of this agreement are critical because they will determine how the overall risk guarantee program will succeed in leveraging investment from the lenders.

- *Project selection criteria.* The guarantor will generally specify the project eligibility criteria, which may include types of technologies or projects, minimum savings requirements, maximum payback, and the like. Once these are agreed on and specified in the GFA, the participating lender assesses and selects projects consistent with these criteria.

- *Operational manual.* An operational manual (OM) is generally developed to specify the detailed procedures to be followed by the lender. The OM describes the project eligibility selection criteria, appraisal requirements, responsibilities of the lender and the guarantee provider, and other procedures governing how the risk-sharing program will function.

- *Management of the guarantee fund.* The guarantee fund is managed by the guarantor. Any claims for payments from the guarantee fund have to be made by the lender using the procedures defined in the GFA. Generally, the lender will have to demonstrate that appropriate actions have been taken to attempt to correct the default.

- *Counter guarantees.* The participating banks in the China Energy Conservation II program (see the examples in the next section) required a counter guarantee to cover the banks' risk exposure[6] (the portion that was not covered by the guarantee). Such a requirement may make it difficult to find sufficient qualified projects. The participating banks in the International Finance Corporation (IFC) programs (such as CHUEE, see below) did not require counter guarantees.

- *Collateral requirements.* Once the GFA is signed, the lenders use their normal project appraisal and risk assessment criteria to evaluate projects. Collateral requirements will be consistent with their guidelines and procedures for other types of loans. The concept of project financing using cash flows from the energy savings has generally not been used as collateral in these programs.

- *Project approval process.* The lenders select the projects using their appraisal and risk assessment criteria, and the guarantor generally makes final approval. This process can become cumbersome, time consuming, and expensive unless the procedures are streamlined.

- *Guarantee fee*. The guarantor charges a fee for the guarantee, and the lender will pass on the fee as part of the cost to the borrower. Although the guarantee reduces the lender's risk, and should reduce the borrower's interest rate, the addition of the fee will increase the effective interest rate. Therefore, the guarantee fee must be reasonable. The IFC charges guarantee fees of 1.0–1.5 percent of the guarantee amount.

- *Monitoring and evaluation*. The guarantor generally needs to monitor and evaluate the results of the risk-sharing program. Thus, certain requirements may be added to the lender's normal data collection and documentation procedures. The monitoring and evaluation requirements must be specified, agreed to, and documented in the GFA and the OM for the program.

Examples of Risk-Sharing Programs

Three examples of risk-sharing programs are provided below and are included in chapters 16, 17, and 18 of this book.

IFC/GEF Commercializing Energy Efficiency Finance Program

The Commercializing Energy Efficiency Finance (CEEF) Program was launched in April 2003 as a joint program of the IFC and the GEF, with the IFC acting as the executing agent for the GEF. CEEF was initiated based on the experience with the Hungarian Energy Efficiency Co-Financing Program (HEECP), which had begun in Hungary in 1997. The countries included in CEEF were the Czech Republic, Estonia, Latvia, Lithuania, and the Slovak Republic. In 2005, Hungary was added and HEECP was merged into CEEF. The CEEF program was successfully completed in December 2008.

CEEF was designed to work in partnership with local lenders by providing partial guarantees to share in the credit risk of EE loan transactions that the partner lenders would fund with their own resources. The transactions eligible for the program included capital investments aimed at improving the efficiency of energy use in buildings, industrial processes, and other energy end-use applications.

Risk sharing was achieved through a partial guarantee structure under which the IFC guaranteed 50 percent of the project risk on an equal basis with the participating lenders. The GEF committed US$17.25 million to the program, of which US$15 million was for the guarantee facility. (The remaining US$2.25 million was used for program operating costs and TA.)

Technical assistance was an important component of the program. The TA had two main purposes: (a) to help prepare projects for investment and (b) to build capacity in the EE and lender industries in each country. Assistance was provided

- To participating lenders, to help market their EE finance services, prepare projects for investment, develop new EE finance products, and build their capacity to originate EE project financing;

- To EE and ESCO businesses, for building their corporate capacity and developing EE projects; and
- To support targeted EE market promotion activities, generally undertaken in cooperation with other organizations.

IFC/GEF China Utility-Based Energy Efficiency Finance Program

The IFC, in cooperation with the GEF, initiated the China Utility-Based Energy Efficiency Finance Program (CHUEE) in June 2006 (World Bank IEG 2010). See the case study in Chapter 17 for more details on CHUEE. The program was aimed at stimulating EE investments in China through two main instruments: (a) bank guarantees for EE loans and (b) TA to market players, including utilities, equipment vendors, and ESCOs, to help implement EE projects. Both types of interventions relied on subsidies funded by donors. CHUEE attempted to bring together lenders, utility companies, and suppliers of EE equipment to create a new financing model for the promotion of EE.

CHUEE cooperated with two Chinese commercial banks (Industrial Bank and Bank of Beijing) and offered them a facility whereby the IFC shared part of the potential loss for all loans within the GHG emissions reduction portfolio. The program also provided technical advisory services related to marketing, engineering, project development, and equipment financing services to banks, project developers, and suppliers of EE and renewable energy products and services.

The structure of the risk-sharing facility is illustrated earlier, in figure 8.9. In this scheme,

- The IFC provided the "loss-sharing agreement," with the IFC sharing 75 percent of the first losses, defined as 10 percent of the total original principal amount of the loan portfolio; and
- The IFC and the bank shared 40/60 for second losses, that is, potential losses after the first losses.

The IFC managed the CHUEE TA and advisory service programs through its Beijing office, including the development of marketing strategies, training in credit underwriting for the banks, and support for loan origination and structuring for marketing partners and energy end users. CHUEE also conducted market research for particular regions or industries to help major players in the sector identify potential business opportunities and design tailored financial products. In addition, CHUEE supported research in the EE regulatory environment, to benefit a wide range of stakeholders.

Although the initial IFC model was to work with a utility (Xin'ao Gas), the IFC found that there was a strategic mismatch between the utility and the financing partners. The gas utility's customers were primarily smaller customers and the participating banks preferred to work with large customers.

World Bank China Second Energy Conservation Project

Following the completion of Phase I of the World Bank/GEF China Energy Conservation Project, in which the World Bank provided loans, grants, and TA to

Figure 8.10 Schematic of the China Energy Conservation II Program

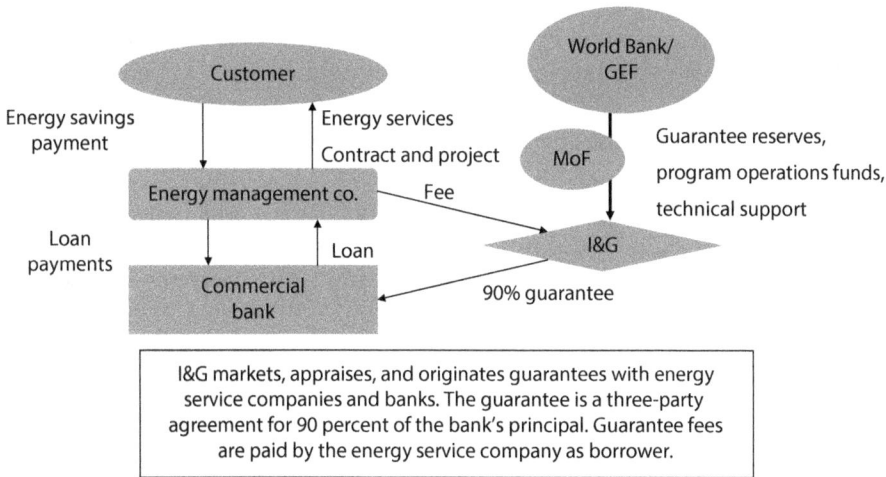

Source: World Bank 2002.
Note: GEF = Global Environment Facility; I&G = China National Investment and Guarantee Company Ltd.; MoF = Ministry of Finance.

three demonstration ESCOs, the Bank set a goal of mobilizing local banks to provide ESCOs with debt financing for EE projects (World Bank 2002). The project used a loan guarantee mechanism, with China National Investment and Guarantee Company Ltd. (I&G), a state-owned national guarantee company, acting as guarantor. World Bank/GEF funds were provided through the Ministry of Finance to serve as guarantee reserves and were made available on a formula basis for I&G to pay guarantee claims (see figure 8.10). Using these resources, I&G provided 90 percent loan guarantees to commercial banks that made loans to ESCOs for qualified EE projects. In addition, the World Bank supported establishment of the Energy Management Company Association of China, to provide support to ESCOs, and as a way to provide TA to newcomers to the market and to represent the emerging industry to the Chinese government and other parties.

The ESCO Loan Guarantee Program has helped create a bridge for many ESCOs into the world of formal financing. With the backing of US$20 million placed in a special guarantee reserve fund held by the Ministry of Finance, I&G issued loan guarantees totaling about US$104 million from 2004 through June 2010, in particular providing support for energy performance contracting project investments. Nearly 40 Chinese ESCOs received loan guarantees for one or more of their projects, and many of them received a bank loan for the first time. So far, 12 banks have participated.

The key features of the program follow:

- GEF funds, through the Ministry of Finance, were used for program operations, TA, and guarantee reserves.

- The World Bank and China's Ministry of Finance entered into a guarantee program operations agreement with I&G.
- I&G marketed, appraised, and originated guarantees with ESCOs and banks. The guarantees were three-party agreements and covered 90 percent of the bank's principal.
- Guarantee fees were paid by the ESCO as borrower.

Table 8.7 illustrates how the CEEF risk-sharing facility addresses some of the financial barriers. Table 8.8 shows a comparison of the three risk-sharing programs. For more details on the EC II, CHUEE, and CEEF programs, see the case studies in chapters 16, 17, and 18, respectively.

Lessons Learned

The review of risk-sharing programs in several regions underscores the following:

- The risk-sharing programs implemented by the IFC in Eastern and Central Europe have been successful and are now being replicated in Asia.
- Risk sharing has successfully addressed the negative risk perceptions of bankers with respect to EE projects.
- To be successful, a risk-sharing program for EE projects needs a strong complementary TA and capacity-building component.

Table 8.7 Addressing the Financing Barriers: Commercializing Energy Efficiency Finance (CEEF) Program

Barrier	How the CEEF program addresses these barriers
Lack of debt financing due to experience and capacity deficit in host country financial sector	Provision of guarantee to induce and support lending; TA to lenders to develop understanding of market opportunity, to develop credit analysis skills and financial products, and to facilitate introduction to ESCOs
High perceived risk for SME borrowers and EE projects by lenders	TA to develop credit analysis skills for appraising EE project risk; provision of partial guarantee to mitigate actual risk to lender
Lack of collateral value associated with EE projects or equipment	Provision of partial guarantee to mitigate lender risk; TA to lenders to develop project finance capabilities and value the positive security features of EE projects such as cost savings that improve free cash flow of end user, and essential-use nature of EE equipment
Excessive collateral requirements imposed by lenders	Provision of partial guarantee to mitigate actual risk to lender
Extraordinarily risk-averse financial markets resulting from historical experience with poor credit procedures	Provision of partial guarantee to mitigate actual risk to lender; selection of priority markets, e.g., SMEs, in which project finance techniques can be applied, viability of borrowers can be demonstrated, and competition between lenders can result in new lending
Lack of well-prepared projects	Selection of markets in which fundamental economics of EE projects are attractive; TA support to ESCOs to assist in project structuring and presentation to lenders

Source: IFC 2004.
Note: EE = energy efficiency; ESCO = energy service company; SME = small and medium enterprise; TA = technical assistance.

Table 8.8 Comparison of CEEF, CHUEE, and China EC II Programs

	CEEF	CHUEE	China EC II
Public agency	IFC/GEF	IFC/GEF	World Bank/GEF
Participating banks	14 participating banks	Industrial Bank and Bank of Beijing	China National Investment and Guarantee Company and 12 participating banks
Risk sharing	50/50	First 10% at 75/25 After 10% at 40/60	90%
First loss reserve	GEF: US$15 million	GEF: US$16.5 million	GEF: US$22 million
Target markets	Commercial and industrial firms and ESCOs	Large industries	ESCOs
Total project investments	US$208 million	US$936 million	US$131 million
Total value of guarantees provided	US$49.5 million	US$197 million	US$74 million
Estimated CO_2 reduction	145,700 tons/year	14 million tons	4.7 million tons of coal equivalent
Cost per ton of CO_2 reduction	US$2.50	Not available	US$4.68

Note: CEEF = Commercializing Energy Efficiency Finance Program; CHUEE = China Utility-Based Energy Efficiency Finance Program; CO_2 = carbon dioxide; EC II = China Second Energy Conservation Program; CGEF = Global Environment Facility; IFC = International Finance Corporation.

- Risk-sharing programs, coupled with TA to lenders, can contribute toward building capacity for future sustainable commercial EE project financing.
- A first loss reserve provides an attractive incentive to lenders by substantially reducing their risk, and can be a strong factor for obtaining their participation in the risk-sharing program.
- Experience in Hungary and other countries indicates the potential for sustainability; participating banks expanded lending for EE projects after expiration of the IFC risk guarantee program.
- A risk-sharing program needs a somewhat mature commercial banking sector to be effective.
- Risk guarantees are not a panacea. This instrument is most effective in increasing banks' confidence to lend to those potential EE clients who are at the margin of the lenders' credit ranking and lending criteria, that is, SMEs with reasonably good credit ratings but no established relationship with commercial banks, or ESCOs (whose business model is typically not familiar to banks) that have energy saving contracts with enterprises with good credit.
- Such programs only reduce lenders' risk perceptions and do not change the actual project risks that might be associated with uneconomic projects, noncreditworthy borrowers, or unproven technologies.

Leveraging Commercial Financing through Performance Contracting

Performance contracting is an increasingly popular approach to financing and implementing EE projects. This approach addresses some of the major barriers to the implementation of EE projects, such as the lack of awareness and knowledge of EE opportunities by some energy users, lack of technical expertise and capacity for implementation, limited internal capital, and inability to access external capital for implementation.

Overview of Performance Contracting and ESCOs

Performance contracting refers to EE implementation services offered by private sector ESCOs under energy saving performance contracts (ESPCs) that are characterized by the following key attributes (SRC Global Inc. 2005):

- ESCOs offer a complete range of implementation services, including design, engineering, construction, commissioning, and maintenance of the EE measures, and measurement and verification of the resulting energy and cost savings.
- ESCOs also provide or arrange financing (often 100 percent) and undertake "shared savings" or "guaranteed savings" contracts, such that the payments to the ESCO are less than the cost savings resulting from implementation of the project.
- Under a performance contract, an ESCO offers specific performance guarantees for the entire project (as opposed to individual equipment guarantees offered by equipment manufacturers or suppliers) and generally guarantees a specific level of energy or cost savings.
- Payments to the ESCO are contingent upon demonstrated satisfaction of the performance guarantees.
- Most of the technical, financial, and maintenance risk is assumed by the ESCO, thereby substantially reducing the risks to the energy user.

The potential benefits of the performance contracting approach offered to energy users (customers) by ESCOs include the following:

- Performance contracts provide guarantees to ensure the successful implementation of the EE measures.
- ESCOs generally provide operation and maintenance services to ensure that the installed equipment continues to perform at a high efficiency level.
- A mutually agreed upon measurement and verification scheme is established to allow for actual measurement, verification, and demonstration of the energy and cost savings.
- The ESCO provides breadth and depth of capabilities as well as training to the staff of the customer.
- The ESCO facilitates access to external capital for project implementation.

Alternative Models of Performance Contracting

Although the specific approaches to performance contracting can vary widely, they can generally be characterized into three basic models—shared savings, guaranteed savings, and energy supply contracting (also known as chauffage) (Singh and others 2010). In all of these models, the ESCO provides a wide range of services related to EE and generates energy and cost savings. The differences between the models arise from the manner in which the customer makes payments to the ESCO and the way the savings are allocated between the ESCO and the customer.

Shared Savings Model

In the shared savings model, the ESCO provides or arranges for most or all of the financing needed for project implementation. The ESPC specifies the sharing of the cost savings (which are measured and verified using a defined protocol) between the ESCO and the host facility during a specific period. The host facility generally makes no investment in the project and gets a share of the savings during the contract period and 100 percent of the savings after the contract period, thus maintaining a positive cash flow throughout the life of the project.

In this model (see figure 8.11) the end user enters into an energy services agreement with the ESCO for project financing and implementation. The ESPC specifies the energy user's payment obligation based on project performance, savings, delivered energy, or the value of capital and services provided. The loan is typically on the ESCO's balance sheet. The ESCO assumes the energy user's credit risk and may need lender assistance to assess the risk.

The ESCO generally needs to fund a portion of the project with equity, typically 10–30 percent, given that the lender is not likely to provide 100 percent financing. The end user may make a capital contribution of 0–10 percent. The balance of project financing comes from debt taken out by the ESCO.

Figure 8.11 Shared Savings Model

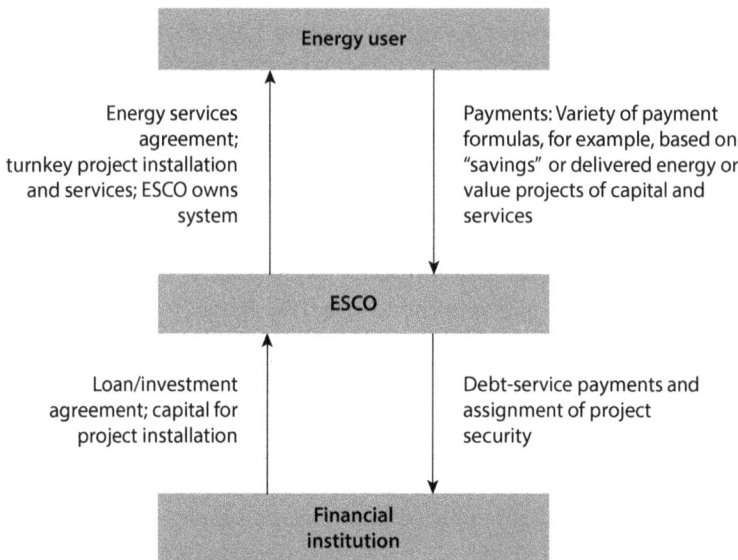

Source: USAID 2009.
Note: ESCO = energy service company.

Figure 8.12 Guaranteed Savings Model

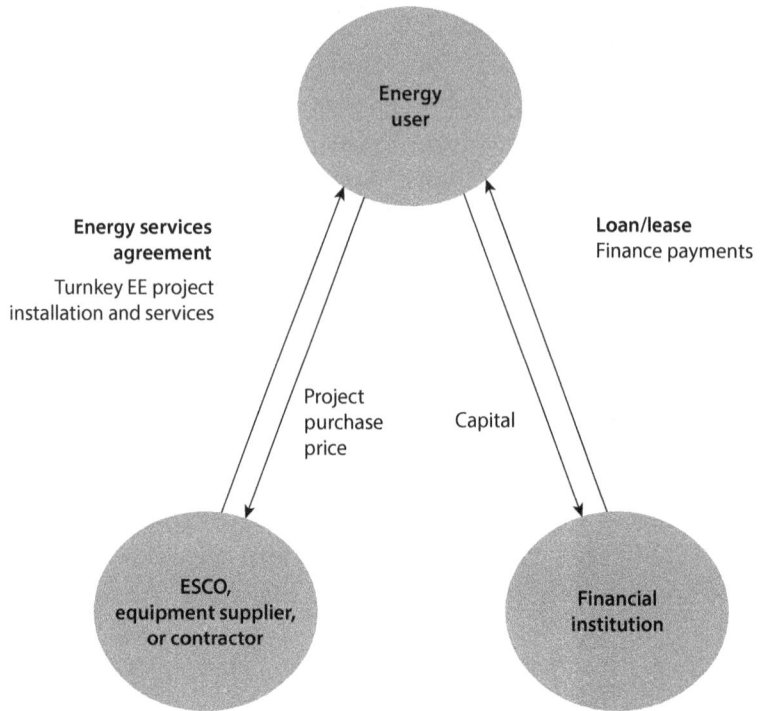

Source: USAID 2009.
Note: EE = energy efficiency; ESCO = energy service company.

Guaranteed Savings Model

In the guaranteed savings model, the host facility generally takes the loan on its own balance sheet. The ESCO guarantees certain performance parameters in the ESPC, and specifies the methods for measurement and verification. Payments are made once the measurement and verification confirms that the project performance parameters have met the guarantees. The typical structure is depicted in figure 8.12.

The project is implemented under two separate agreements, one for turnkey project implementation services between the energy user and the ESCO (energy services agreement), and the other for project financing (financing agreement) between the energy user and the lender. The energy user's credit risks are separated from project performance and project technical risks. The lender assumes the energy user's credit risk, whereas technical and performance risks are addressed in the energy services agreement. The energy user is obligated to make fixed loan payments. The loan payment amount is calculated to amortize the loan regardless of project performance.

The energy user generally assumes responsibility for equipment maintenance and repair. Provision for equipment operations and maintenance services, warranties, and performance guarantees can be included in the energy services agreement.

Energy Supply Contracting or Chauffage

In this model, the ESCO takes over operations and maintenance of the equipment and sells the energy output (e.g., steam, heating or cooling, lighting) to the customer at an agreed-on price. This model is a form of "outsourcing," in which the costs for all equipment upgrades, repairs, and the like are borne by the ESCO, but ownership remains with the customer. The fee paid by the customer under a chauffage arrangement is calculated on the basis of its existing energy bill minus a percentage savings (in the range of 3–10 percent), or a fee may be charged per square meter of conditioned space. Thus, under the chauffage arrangement, the client is guaranteed an improved level of energy service at a reduced price. Contracts for this type of arrangement tend to be substantially longer than others, ranging from 10 to 30 years (Bertoldi and Rezessy 2005). An illustration of the energy supply contracting model is provided in figure 8.13.

The term ESCO has been used to designate a wide range of organizations that may offer the performance contracting mechanism for implementing EE projects. Such organizations may include design and engineering firms, construction management firms, equipment manufacturers and suppliers, or teams comprising two or more of the types of organizations. ESCOs need both equity financing for project development and risk sharing, and debt financing for project costs and working capital. Therefore, ESCOs need to develop relationships with commercial lenders and work with them to arrange the needed financing for EE projects.

Experience with Performance Contracting in Organisation for Economic Co-operation and Development Countries

The concept of performance contracting originated with the chauffage model in France in the 1950s, but much of the development of the model occurred in North America during the 1980s and 1990s. Performance contracting has also

Figure 8.13 Energy Supply Contracting Model

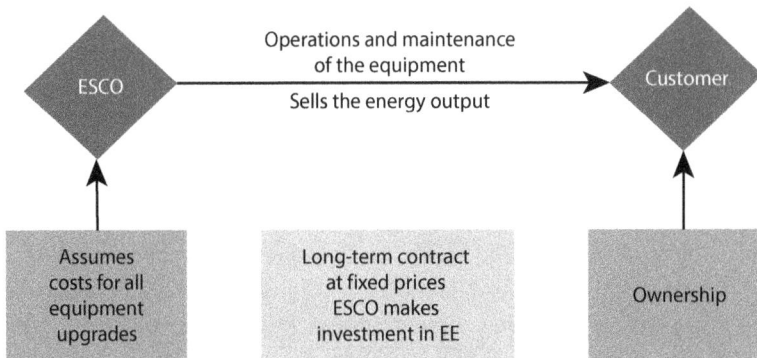

Source: Singh and others 2010.
Note: EE = energy efficiency; ESCO = energy service company.

Table 8.9 Performance Contracting Results in Selected Countries

Country	Market size	Projects	Results
United states	US$3.8 billion	500+	• Energy savings ~ 30 trillion BTU • US$11.7 billion cost savings
Canada	Can $320 million	85	• 20% reduction in energy intensity • an over Can $40 million cost savings
Germany	€200 million	2,000 properties	• 20–30% reduction in energy costs • €30–45 million cost savings
Japan	¥10 billion	50	• 12% reduction in energy intensity
Republic of Korea	223 billion won	1,400	—

Source: Singh and others 2010.
Note: — = not available; BTU = British thermal unit.

been successfully implemented in many European countries (such as Germany), as well as in Japan and the Republic of Korea (Singh and others 2010).

Significant results have been achieved with performance contracting in some countries (see table 8.9). For example, in the United States more than 500 ESPC projects have saved US$11.7 billion in energy costs.

In Canada, 85 projects have been completed in more than 7,500 buildings with energy cost savings exceeding US$40 million. In Germany, ESPC projects have been implemented in more than 2,000 properties with savings of €30–45 million (about US$40–60 million). Japan has completed 50 ESPC projects producing a 12 percent reduction in energy intensity, and about 1,400 projects have been implemented in the Republic of Korea.

Performance Contracting in Asia
China

In China, the World Bank, the IFC, and the Asian Development Bank have devoted considerable efforts and funding to establishing and growing ESCOs. The ESCO industry in China has experienced three phases of growth (Taylor and others 2008). The first phase consisted of assistance from the World Bank and the GEF to establish three ESCOs to demonstrate the performance contracting approach. After the successful demonstration, the second phase involved a credit guarantee program to help establish new ESCOs and enable them to develop collaborative financing schemes with lenders. The third phase, currently under way, is likely to allow ESCOs to work with lenders without the need for a guarantee mechanism.

With energy performance contracting investment in 2010 totaling more than US$4.24 billion, the business volumes of China's ESCO industry are on par with those of the U.S. ESCO industry. China's energy performance contracting business has grown remarkably fast during its history, developing contractual practices, business models, and market approaches that are distinctly adapted to the Chinese market. China's ESCO industry is unique in its concentration of almost three-quarters of energy performance contracting investment in industrial sector projects. China's ESCO industry is poised for continued sharp growth in the coming years (Sun, Zhu, and Taylor 2011).

The Energy Management Company Association maintains industry statistics and reported that in 2010 there were more than 900 ESCOs operating in China. The total investment in EE projects by ESCOs in 2010 was US$4.2 billion. These projects generated annual energy savings of more than 10 million tons of coal equivalent and annual GHG emission reductions of more than 6 million tons of CO_2 equivalent. Industrial projects represented about 50 percent of the number of projects and about 75 percent of the project investment.

India

The first ESCO in India was established in 1995 following a market assessment by USAID (SRC International 1995), and 89 ESCOs were registered in India as of October 2010.[7] However, a number of barriers have prevented the ESCO market in India from growing like the market in China. The Bureau of Energy Efficiency (BEE) is undertaking a number of new initiatives to enhance and promote ESCO activities, including the establishment of a Partial Risk Guarantee Fund and a Venture Capital Fund for Energy Efficiency (VCFEE) (BEE 2010b). BEE has also funded, in cooperation with HSBC Bank, a capacity-building program for Indian banks and lenders on EE project financing focusing on performance contracting (IIEC 2011).

Thailand

Thailand's ESCO industry was formed after passage of the Energy Conservation Promotion Act and received impetus from the establishment of the EERF (Sinsukprasert 2010). However, most of the projects financed with funds from the EERF were in larger enterprises with strong balance sheets, and ESCOs were allotted a very small share of the EERF funds. In 2008, Thailand established an ESCO fund to provide specialized financing (including equity financing) to promote increased ESCO activities (Chintakananda 2010).

Public ESCOs and Super ESCOs

Despite the potential for creating thriving energy services business, the growth and advancement of the ESCO industry in developing countries has been constrained by a number of barriers. Box 8.4 defines some of these barriers.

To overcome some of these barriers, particularly in countries in which the ESCO industry is nascent or nonexistent, or where ESCOs have difficulties working with public agencies, some governments have established public ESCOs. Examples include UkrESCO in Ukraine and HEP ESCO in Croatia (Singh and others 2010; World Bank 2010a). A public ESCO facilitates contracting with other public agencies, helps reduce transaction costs associated with complex public sector procurements, allows for financing of performance contracts from international donor agencies, and helps concentrate ESPC expertise. However, a potential drawback is that these public ESCOs may not provide services as

---

Box 8.4 Barriers to ESCOs in Developing Countries

- Most independent energy service companies (ESCOs) have small capital bases and have difficulties accessing project funding from commercial lenders because they can mobilize only limited equity financing.
- The concept of financing ESCO projects is not commonly accepted by lenders in developing countries. Lenders require collateral and are generally unwilling to accept the savings stream generated by the project as appropriate collateral. Energy efficiency (EE) projects are generally small relative to other investment projects lenders consider, and they also have a relatively large proportion of "soft costs" that cannot be easily collateralized.
- As a result of the immaturity of the EE market in developing countries, the costs of project development are relatively high, and most small ESCOs find it difficult to finance them.
- The ESCO model is new in developing countries and, because of limited experience with successful ESCO projects, ESCOs have not yet developed credibility with energy users.
- Lender staff typically have limited knowledge and understanding of EE projects and the ESPC concept. Lenders also (incorrectly) perceive EE projects to be inherently riskier than other investments, and generally require a large proportion of equity funding from the ESCO for a project.

The combination of high project development costs; limited access to long-term, low-cost project financing; high equity requirements for project financing; and lack of credibility with customers has led to a "market failure" with respect to the ESCO industry's ability to implement EE on a large scale (Hasnie 2009).

Source: Limaye and Limaye 2011.

---

efficiently as fully private ESCOs, and that they may inhibit the growth of the private ESCO industry.

The concept of a Super ESCO (see figure 8.14) has evolved as a mechanism for overcoming some of the limitations and barriers to the large-scale implementation of EE projects. A Super ESCO is an entity established by the government that functions as an ESCO for the public sector market (hospitals, schools, municipalities, government buildings, and other public facilities). A Super ESCO also supports capacity development and project development activities of existing private sector ESCOs, and helps to create new ESCOs. The government capitalizes the Super ESCO with sufficient funds to undertake public sector ESPC projects and to leverage commercial financing. A primary function of the Super ESCO is to facilitate access to project financing by developing relationships with local or international lenders. The Super ESCO may also provide credit or risk guarantees for ESCO projects, or act as a leasing or financing company to provide EE equipment to ESCOs and customers on lease or on benefit-sharing terms.

A Super ESCO can be uniquely positioned to overcome a number of the barriers faced by smaller ESCOs. With their size and credibility as public institutions, Super ESCOs have the capability to support the growth of a nation's private domestic ESCO business and the capacity to provide financing for EE

Figure 8.14 Illustration of a Super ESCO

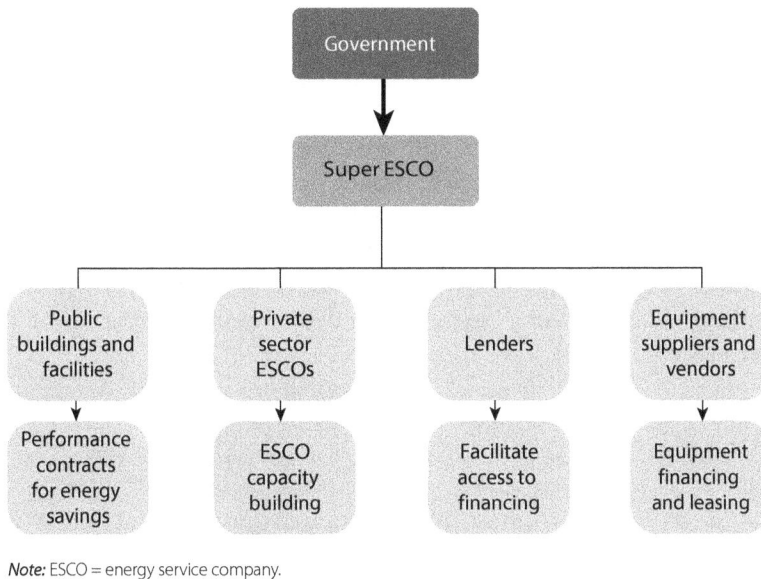

Note: ESCO = energy service company.

projects. An exemplary Super ESCO is Energy Efficiency Services Limited (EESL), established by the government of India as a public corporation owned by four power sector public undertakings[8] with the objective of meeting the market development and implementation functions of India's National Mission for Enhanced Energy Efficiency.

A Super ESCO can target the largely untapped EE market in the public sector. The efficiency potential in the public sector is substantial, but the implementation of energy savings programs is complicated by numerous factors, including public agencies' lack of commercial orientation, limited incentives to lower energy costs, complex and strict budgeting and procurement procedures, and limited access to budgetary or commercial project financing.

A Super ESCO can also play a major role in the private sector. It can be mandated to work as a partner with private ESCOs, build their capacity, and create a competitive private market for ESCO services. An appropriate role for the Super ESCO may be to engage private ESCOs as contractors for portions of implementation (such as installation, commissioning, and performance monitoring), thereby helping to build their capacity. The Super ESCO may also be in a position to arrange financing for small private ESCOs to help them implement projects and build their capacity and credentials (Limaye and Limaye 2011).

Equipment Leasing

A lease is a contractual arrangement in which a leasing company (lessor) gives a customer (lessee) the right to use its equipment for a specified length of time (lease term) and specified payment (usually monthly). Depending on the lease structure, at the end of the lease term the customer can purchase, return, or continue to lease the equipment. All imaginable types of organizations, including proprietorships, partnerships, corporations, government agencies, and religious and nonprofit organizations, use leasing throughout the world. More than 80 percent of American businesses lease at least one of their equipment acquisitions, and nearly 90 percent say they would choose to lease again.

Equipment leases are broadly classified into two types: operating leases and finance or capital leases (Lee 2003). In an operating lease, the lessor (or owner) transfers only the right to use the property to the lessee. At the end of the lease period, the lessee returns the property to the lessor. Because the lessee does not assume the risk of ownership, the lease expense is treated as an operating expense in the income statement and the lease does not affect the balance sheet.

In a capital lease, the lessee assumes some of the risks of ownership and enjoys some of the benefits. Consequently, the lease, when signed, is recognized both as an asset and as a liability (for the lease payments) on the balance sheet. The firm gets to claim depreciation each year on the asset and also deducts the interest expense component of the lease payment each year. In general, capital leases recognize expenses sooner than equivalent operating leases.

Equipment Leasing for EE Projects

Because EE projects generally involve the installation of new equipment, leasing can be a viable option. Depending on local tax and leasing laws, leasing companies can provide an important vehicle for commercial financing of EE projects. Many banks have leasing subsidiaries. Stand-alone leasing companies are often more aggressive than banks in probing new market segments. Leasing company partnerships with EE equipment companies can facilitate implementation of EE technology with a financing solution. Such partnerships can provide important secondary markets and recourse vehicles to support credit structuring. In particular, leasing can be a useful financing option when a large part of the project capital cost is for specific equipment (such as variable speed drives or industrial process equipment).

World Bank Lease Financing Project in Shandong, China

China's rapid economic growth has provided an opportunity for the development of its equipment leasing industry, which has created rapid growth in the underlying equipment market. Equipment manufacturers and vendors are increasingly recognizing the need to provide an equipment finance solution to complete their offering to their customers. Although the information technology and construction equipment segments are in general more mature, lease finance is emerging for energy saving equipment financing using performance contracting concepts (Scholtz 2009).

The World Bank initiated the Shandong Energy Efficiency Project in 2011 to support financial leasing and energy performance contracting for EE investments in selected industrial enterprises. IBRD funds will be on-lent to two leasing companies: the Shandong Rongshihua Leasing Company, Ltd. (US$64 million) and the Guotai Leasing Company, Ltd. (US$50 million).[9] Both companies have acquired pilot leasing licenses and offer an opportunity to leverage the World Bank loan severalfold to accelerate EE investments. These two leasing companies were selected based on their operational performance, financial strength, market position, interest in the EE market, and potential to scale up EE investments.

The project is designed to support the Shandong provincial government's EE service industry development program through the demonstration of successful use of financial leases for EE investments.

Lessons Learned

- The performance contracting model has many attractive features for Asian countries.
- Considerable success has been achieved in Western countries (and in China) with performance contracting, but experience in other Asian countries has been limited.
- Legislative and regulatory initiatives are needed to facilitate performance contracting in the public sector.
- Successful implementation requires a mature banking sector and a viable energy services delivery infrastructure.
- The shared savings model has limitations because ESCOs face difficulties in obtaining financing. A recent trend shows a shift from a shared savings model to a guaranteed savings model.
- Capacity building in both banks and ESCOs is important.
- Alternative models such as public ESCOs or Super ESCOs may be useful in Asia.

Experience with ESCOs in developing countries is still limited, but it is clear that a major success factor is a policy and regulatory environment that is conducive to EE and that provides financial and technical support for ESCO development. For example, in China, where these support mechanisms were put in place, the ESCO industry grew from three companies in 1997 to about 560 with more than US$4 billion in energy performance contracts in 2010 (Sun, Zhu, and Taylor 2011). However, the ESCO model is by no means perfect. In many developing countries, ESCOs have had difficulty establishing credibility with customers and obtaining adequate financing from commercial banks because of their weak balance sheets, limited physical assets that can be collateralized, and the perceived risks associated with providing finance to entities whose income stream is dependent on cash flows from energy savings.

Equity Funds

Equity funds provide equity capital to EE projects or to EE companies. Most equity funds are established by private sector venture capital organizations and are designed to finance investments in early-stage, high-potential, and high-growth companies to generate a return through an eventual "liquidity event" such as an initial public offering or trade sale of the company. Key advantages of venture capital finance include the following:

- It injects long-term equity finance, which provides a solid capital base for future growth.
- The venture capitalist is a business partner, sharing both the risks and the rewards of business success and the capital gain.
- Venture capitalists provide a source of practical advice and assistance to the company and also provide a network of contacts in many areas of business that can add value to the company.
- In some cases, venture capital can leverage additional rounds of funding that may be required to finance growth.

Equity Funds for Energy Efficiency Financing

Although equity funds have traditionally been established by private sector investors, some donors (e.g., the European Investment Bank, the IFC, the Asian Development Bank, and the European Union) have made significant investments in private equity funds targeted at EE (as well as renewable energy). The rationale for an equity fund established by a public agency (government or donor) is that government funding is generally available for research and development, and private financing is available for the commercialization of mature technologies, but funding is generally unavailable for entrepreneurial activities—such as proof-of-concept, piloting, firm building, and marketing—that are needed between these two stages. Given this void, an equity fund for EE could provide a stimulating effect, particularly in developing countries in which the EE market encounters many barriers, such as the following:

- Absence of established venture capital firms specializing in EE projects;
- Unfamiliarity with the risk profiles of energy users and energy service providers such as ESCOs;
- Business environments that discourage entrepreneurship;
- Generally inadequate awareness of and expertise for EE projects among lenders; and
- Limited availability of equity capital on the part of project developers, particularly ESCOs.

Public Versus Private Sector Roles in Equity Funds

Equity financing is typically the domain of private sector investors. However, many of the characteristics of EE may make equity investments in EE projects or companies unattractive to private investors because of characteristics such as limited experience, small project size, returns that are less attractive than investments in other sectors (for example, information technology or biotechnology), and relatively high transaction costs. Under such circumstances, a case can be made for public sector equity funds for EE.

A public sector equity fund may be appropriate in the following situations:

- The fund could provide equity investments in public sector projects to facilitate (in combination with other mechanisms such as risk-sharing agreements) performance contracting projects implemented by ESCOs in the public sector. Funding could also include public-private partnership projects.
- The fund could provide equity financing for promising small ESCOs to help them develop and implement projects (primarily in the public sector but could also include private sector). The selection of ESCOs would be based on their unique technologies or experience.
- Equity investments could be made in companies with promising new technologies (for example, light-emitting diodes) that offer significant potential for EE.

Examples of Equity Funds

Public sector equity funds for EE in developing countries are scarce. One, however, is the ESCO fund established in Thailand to encourage private investment in EE and renewable energy projects that are viable but need equity investment support to obtain project financing (Chintakananda 2010). This fund has focused only on renewable energy projects.

Other examples are the proposed VCFEE being established by the BEE in India and the Global Energy Efficiency and Renewable Energy Fund (GEEREF).

India's Planned Venture Capital Fund for Energy Efficiency

The objective of the VCFEE is to accelerate the adoption of proven energy efficient technologies (business models involve both manufacturing and services) having large-scale impacts on EE in India (BEE 2010a). Although the design of the VCFEE had not been finalized as of June 2012, it is expected that the minimum equity participation will be 20 percent with a maximum equity participation of 50 percent on a co-investment basis with other funds as a lead or support for companies related to EE. The fund will also provide last-mile equity support to specific EE projects, limited to 25 percent of total equity required or 50 percent of total project cost, whichever is lower, through a special purpose vehicle.

The government of India is allocating 738 million Indian rupees (Rs) (about US$16.5 million) and expects that the fund manager (to be selected competitively) will substantially increase the size of the fund. An individual investment is expected to range between Rs 10 million (about US$225,000) and Rs 100 million (about US$2.25 million).

The VCFEE will invest in early-stage-growth-phase companies engaged in manufacturing of energy efficient technologies or products. The fund will take stakes in specific projects through special purpose vehicles and in companies that execute EE projects, develop and sell products, or develop and license technologies for projects. The expected characteristics of this fund are that it will

- Provide risk capital support to EE investments in new technology, goods, and services;
- Leverage private venture investments in the EE sector by identifying possible co-investment opportunities in collaboration with other venture capitalists;
- Seek a comparatively lower expected return on its share of investment in specific projects;
- Allow capitalization of the transaction costs associated with specific EE investments; and
- When co-investing on an equal return on investment basis with other investors, could be "last to be paid" if there were to be a liquidation of investment in projects; when investing with a lower expected return on investment, it could be the "first to be paid" in case of liquidation.

The Global Energy Efficiency and Renewable Energy Fund

Launched in 2008 as a public-private partnership fund worth €200 million to €250 million (about US$260 million to US$325 million), the GEEREF uses a private equity fund-of-funds model to catalyze renewable energy and EE investments. The fund is designed as a 50/50 public-private venture with the initial €108 million coming from the EU budget. A fund-of-funds investment strategy allows GEEREF to invest public monies indirectly across a range of private equity managers to fully leverage returns and manager expertise. GEEREF's broader policy objective is to "accelerate, transfer, develop and use environmentally sound technology to the world's poorer regions" and "supply clean and affordable energy to local people." The fund primarily uses patient capital at market rates with a long-term time horizon aimed at SMEs, small projects, and specific developing regions. Proposal preparation and project development assistance is also available through GEEREF's technical support facility. As part of its public-private partnership structure, GEEREF complies with official development assistance rules that require public returns to revolve back into GEEREF or into another similar fund.[10]

GEEREF matches private capital from its equity partners at a 1:1 ratio. GEEREF carefully selects private equity managers who commit to provide up to €10 million (US $13 million) in equity finance, demonstrate a proven track record of supporting SMEs and clean energy projects that fill significant market gaps, and have developed a robust pipeline. These investments are, in turn, expected to attract additional private investment at a 3:1 ratio. To best leverage private equity manager expertise and to offer high returns for private investors, GEEREF has created an incentive scheme designed to align private equity manager compensation with the public interest.

Lessons Learned

Limited information is available on publicly financed equity funds for EE, particularly in developing countries. The India VCFEE is not yet operational and the

Thailand ESCO fund has been used primarily for renewable energy investments. Coupled with the limited history of equity funds in Organisation for Economic Co-operation and Development countries, it is hard to draw firm conclusions. However, raising matching funds from private investors has proven to be a major challenge, partly because of the 2008 global financial crisis but also as a result of the risk aversion of private equity for clean energy. Given that such funds are allocating, at least in part, public monies, maintaining fully independent fund investment committees and letting private equity managers make returns-based decisions have also proved to be challenges. The funds are also finding it difficult to uncover EE investment opportunities consistent with their risk-return criteria.

In summary,

- It has not been easy to find viable investment opportunities for equity investments in EE projects or companies,
- The cost of the needed due diligence for EE projects can be relatively high compared with the total equity investment,
- It may be necessary to provide some TA to project developers to prepare investment proposals, and
- The development of an appropriate "exit strategy" has been complex.

Notes

1. See New York State Energy Research and Development Authority, http://www.nyserda.org/About/default.asp.
2. The Vermont Public Service commission competitively selected a nongovernmental organization named Efficiency Vermont to manage the Public Benefit Fund (Efficiency Vermont 2009).
3. Sri Lanka Sustainable Energy Authority, http://www.energy.gov.lk/.
4. The requirement was specified as 30 tons of CO_2 equivalent per 1 million rupees (about US$20,000) of total project investment.
5. China EXIM Bank is wholly government owned, Minsheng Bank is privately owned, and Huaxia Bank is a commercial bank.
6. Such counter guarantees may be provided by the project proponent, local government, or a guarantee company engaged by the project proponent.
7. http://www.beeindia.in/schemes/documents/ecbc/listofESCOs.pdf.
8. EESL is a public corporation owned by NTPC Ltd, Powergrid Corporation, Power Finance Corporation, and Rural Electrification Corporation.
9. Rongshihua was created by Shandong Province to successfully introduce energy performance contracting, with Bank support, in 1997. Guotai is part of the Xinwen Mining Group, which is one of China's top 1,000 energy-intensive enterprises and is one of nine enterprises that piloted Shandong's energy management system standard.
10. Global Energy Efficiency and Renewable Energy Fund (GEEREF), http://geeref.com/.

Bibliography

BEE (Bureau of Energy Efficiency, India). 2010a. "Invitation for Expression of Interest for Hiring of Consultant for Operationalisation of Venture Capital Fund for Energy Efficiency (VCFEE)." New Delhi.

———. 2010b. "National Mission on Enhanced Energy Efficiency." New Delhi. http://www.beeindia.in/NMEEE/NMEEE2.ppt.

Bell, Catherine J., Steven Nadel, and Sarah Hayes. 2011. *On-Bill Financing for Energy Efficiency Improvement: A Review of Current Program Opportunities, Challenges, and Best Practices*. American Council for an Energy-Efficient Economy, Washington, DC.

Bertoldi, Paolo, and Sylvia Rezessy. 2005. *Energy Service Companies in Europe: Status Report 2005*. EUR 21646 EN, Luxembourg: European Commission Joint Research Centre.

California Public Utilities Commission. 2008. *California's Long-Term Energy Efficiency Strategic Plan*. San Francisco, CA.

Chintakananda, Asavin. 2010. "The ESCO Fund by the Energy Conservation Foundation of Thailand." Paper presented at the ECO-Asia Conference on Establishment of the Kerala State Energy Conservation Fund, Thiruvananthapuram, India, July.

Edison Electric Institute and Electric Power Research Institute. 1984. *Demand-Side Management: Volume 1—Overview of Key Issues*. Palo Alto, CA.

Efficiency Vermont. 2009. *Efficiency Vermont, Annual Report 2009*. Burlington, VT.

Emergent Ventures India. 2010. *International Survey of Partial Risk Guarantee Funds for Energy Efficiency*. Report prepared for the Bureau of Energy Efficiency, Haryana, India.

Hasnie, Sohail. 2009. "ESCOs in the Philippines." Paper presented at the Workshop on ESCOs and Energy Efficiency Projects, Asian Development Bank, January.

IEA (International Energy Agency). 1996. *DSM Implementation Agreement: Annex IV: Review of Existing Mechanisms for Promoting DSM and Energy Efficiency in New Electricity Business Environments, The IEA DSM Implementing Agreement, A Report of Task IV—Development of Improved Methods for Integrating Demand-Side Options into Resource Planning and Government Policy*. Paris.

IFC (International Finance Corporation). 2004. "Commercializing Energy Efficiency Financing Project Brief." International Finance Corporation, Washington, DC.

IIEC (International Institute for Energy Conservation). 2006. *Report of the Committee Set-Up to Review the BESCOM Efficient Lighting Program*, Report to the BELP Evaluation Committee. http://www.esmap.org/esmap/sites/esmap.org/files/55.%20BELP_Evaluation_Committee_Report_10March2006.pdf.

———. 2008. *Demand-Side Management Best Practice Guidebook*. Prepared for USAID and Bureau of Energy Efficiency, New Delhi.

———. 2011. "Capacity Building of Bank Staff for Energy Efficiency Project Financing: Capacity Building Modules." Unpublished. Paper prepared for the Bureau of Energy Efficiency, Mumbai.

KfW and SIDBI (Kreditanstalt für Wiederaufbau and Small Industries Development Bank of India). 2010. "Operating Guidelines for KfW Energy Efficiency Line of Credit—Assistance for Energy Efficiency Projects."

Klev, Kolio. 2007. "Policy for Energy Efficiency Implementation and Integration of EU Directives in Bulgaria." Bulgaria Energy Efficiency Agency.

Korea Energy Management Corporation. 2008. "Korea Energy Conservation Fund." Paper presented at the Asia Clean Energy Forum, Manila.

Lee, Susan. 2003. *Capital and Operating Leases*. Washington, DC: Federal Accounting Standards Advisory Board.

Limaye, Dilip. 2008. "Energy Conservation Funds: International Best Practices." Paper presented at the "Roundtable on Establishing a State Energy Conservation Fund," US Agency for International Development, ECO-Asia Clean Development and Climate Program, Kerala, July.

———. 2009. *DSM Financing Annex: Financing DSM and Energy Efficiency Programs in China*. Washington, DC: USAID ECO-Asia Clean Development and Climate Program.

———. 2010. "Financing DSM and Energy Efficiency: The Role of State Energy Conservation Funds." *Energy Manager*, April–June 2010.

Limaye, Dilip R., Bhaskar Natarajan, B. Anil Kumar, Swati Lal, and Pradeep Tharakan. 2008. *Establishment of the Kerala State Energy Conservation Fund*. Report prepared for ECO-Asia Clean Development and Climate Program.

Limaye, Dilip., and Emily Limaye. 2011. "Scaling Up Energy Efficiency: The Case for a Super ESCO." *Energy Efficiency* 4 (2): 133–44.

Limaye, Dilip R., and Mahesh Patankar. 2011. "Clean Energy Funds: A Review of International Experience." Paper presented at the Workshop on Design and Road Map for State Clean Energy Funds, Mumbai, August.

MacLean, John. 2008. "Tunisia Solar DHW Finance Program." In *Mobilizing Commercial Financial Institutions for Energy Efficiency and Small-Scale Renewable Energy Finance in Developing Countries: Financial Products, Program Designs, and Scale-Up Strategies*. Paper prepared for KfW Financial Sector Development Symposium Greening the Financial Sector: How to Mainstream Environmental Finance in Developing Countries? Berlin, December 4–5.

Maharashtra Electricity Regulatory Commission. 2010. "Regulations: DSM Implementation Framework." Maharashtra Electricity Regulatory Commission, Mumbai.

Molina, Maggie, Max Neubauer, Michael Sciortino, Seth Nowak, Shruti Vaidyanathan, Nate Kaufman, and Anna Chittum. 2010. *The 2010 State Energy Efficiency Scorecard*. Report No. E107, American Council for an Energy-Efficient Economy, Washington, DC.

Mostert, Wolfgang. 2010. *Publicly Backed Guarantees as Policy Instruments to Promote Clean Energy*. UNEP—Sustainable Energy Finance Alliance, Basel.

NDRC (National Development and Reform Commission, China). 2010. "Demand-Side Management (DSM) Implementation Measures." Beijing, November 4.

Scholtz, Axel. 2009. "The Chinese Equipment Leasing Market." *World Leasing News*, February.

Seidman, Karl F. 2005. *Economic Development Finance*. Thousand Oaks, CA: Sage.

Singh, Jas, Dilip R. Limaye, Brian Henderson, and Xiaoyu Shi. 2010. *Public Procurement of Energy Efficiency Services: Lessons from International Experience*. Washington, DC: World Bank.

Sinsukprasert, Prasert. 2010. "Financing Energy Efficiency and Renewable Energy: Thailand's ENCON Fund." Paper presented at the International Energy Efficiency Forum, Astana, Kazakhstan, September 27–30.

SRC Global Inc. 2005. *A Strategic Framework for Implementation of Energy Efficiency Projects for Indian Water Utilities*. Report prepared for the World Bank Public-Private Infrastructure Advisory Facility, SRC Global Inc., Haverford, PA.

SRC International. 1995. *Feasibility Study on the Introduction of Energy Service Companies in India*. Report prepared for USAID, SRC International, Birkerod, Denmark.

Sun Xiaoliang, Zhu Lin, and Bob Taylor. 2011. "China's ESCO Industry: Saving More Energy Everyday through the Market." Energy Management Company Association (China).

Taylor, Robert, C. Govindarajalu, J. Levin, A. Meyer, and W. Ward. 2008. *Financing Energy Efficiency: Lessons from Brazil, China, India and Beyond*. Washington, DC: World Bank.

Touhami, Myriem. 2006. "PROSOL Heats up Tunisian Solar Water Heating Market." UNEP, Paris.

USAID ECO-Asia Clean Development and Climate Program. 2009. "DSM Financing Annex: Financing DSM and Energy Efficiency Programs." USAID Regional Development Mission/Asia, Bangkok.

World Bank. 2002. *Project Appraisal Document on a Proposed GEF Grant of SDR 19.7 Million (US$26 Equivalent) to the People's Republic of China for the Second Energy Conservation Project*. Washington, DC: World Bank.

———. 2008. *Project Appraisal Document on a Proposed Loan in the Amount of US $200 Million and a Proposed Grant from the Global Environment Facility Trust Fund in the Amount of US$13.5 Million to the People's Republic of China in Support of the Energy Efficiency Financing Project*. Washington, DC: World Bank.

———. 2010a. *Implementation Completion and Results Report, Croatia Energy Efficiency Project*. Report No. ICR-1577, Washington, DC: World Bank.

———. 2010b. *Implementation, Completion and Results Report on a Grant from the Global Environment Facility Trust Fund in the Amount of US$10 million to the Republic of Bulgaria for an Energy Efficiency Project*. Report No. ICR00001575, Washington, DC: World Bank.

———. 2010c. *Project Appraisal Document on a Proposed Loan in the Amount of US $100 Million to the People's Republic of China in Support of the Energy Efficiency Financing Project*. Washington, DC: World Bank.

World Bank IEG (Independent Evaluation Group). 2010. "Assessing the Impact of IFC's China Utility-Based Energy Efficiency Finance Program." IEG Study Series, World Bank Independent Evaluation Group, Washington, DC.

PART 3

Financing Renewable Energy

CHAPTER 9

Barriers to Renewable Energy

The barriers to the penetration of renewable energy (RE) sources consist of cost disadvantages, uncertainties related to the properties of RE resources, power system interface issues, and newcomer disadvantages.

The *financial cost per megawatt-hour of output* of most RE technologies is higher than the cost of conventional sources of energy. The exceptions are mature technologies at resource-rich locations near centers of demand, for example, small hydropower with high-capacity factors at sites located near distribution grids, and RE technologies for specific, local applications such as bagasse-based power plants at sugar factories, and solar photovoltaic for telecommunications or for off-grid electricity supply to isolated households. The incremental financial costs of RE systems make their penetration dependent on support schemes and, thus, on unstable political preferences.

The preparation of utility-scale RE power involves *high transaction costs* and long lead times. Securing land rights, resource rights, construction permits, environmental permits, and the like can be a very time-consuming process, giving RE project preparation the reputation of being interminable A small hydropower project may need to secure 40–60 permits from different public authorities and agencies.

Price distortions on the bulk power market caused by *subsidized prices for fossil fuel* consumption by thermal power plants introduce artificial cost bias against RE. Fuel consumed at power plants is typically priced below its net-back value as an export product in fossil-fuel-exporting developing countries. Price distortions are also caused by *import duties and value added taxes on RE components* whereas components and fuels for thermal power production are exempted from import duties and value added taxes.

The *capital intensity* of RE systems makes the implementation of new projects dependent on efficient national financial markets and vulnerable to high costs of finance. Weak capital markets introduce a bias on the free market toward investments in fossil-fuel-based technologies. Because RE technologies are more capital intensive than conventional power technologies, high interest rates,[1] short maturities, and low gearing ratios[2] shift the financial price per kilowatt-hour of

RE upward relative to conventional power. The absolute absence of credit or equity capital may prevent potential RE projects from even trying to reach financial closure.

Resource dependency leads to substantial variations in annual output from wind farms and hydropower plants, and these variations need to be taken into account in financial planning and structuring. Security of fuel supply poses an absolute risk for dendro power plants during the operating phase. Developers of geothermal power projects must invest considerable financial resources up front in substantiating the existence of resources sufficient to make development of a plant feasible. However, even during operation, unexpected drops in the flow rate can take place.

RE power projects can face two different types of *off-take risks*. First, the creditworthiness of an RE plant with a long-term power purchase agreement is not higher than the creditworthiness of the off-taker, which can be undermined by a regulatory regime that fails to protect utilities' financial viability. Second, a generous feed-in tariff can be subject to downward retroactive changes.

The *intermittency of RE power supply*, in particular from wind energy, adds incremental costs to the power system in the form of backup power, spinning reserves, and control systems that lead system operators to resist the penetration of RE generation. In addition, intermittency makes system operators and regulators reluctant to recognize the capacity contribution of intermittent renewable technologies such as wind and solar in their planning processes, and thus to attribute any financial value to intermittent capacity.

The interface between *transmission and distribution grid planning* on the one side and *RE project preparation and implementation* on the other side creates difficulties in several countries. Wind farms stand idle because the connection line to be built by a utility has not been constructed yet, or incur low capacity factors attributable to grid downtimes because required investments in grid reinforcement were not carried out.[3] Disputes over the calculation of the total cost of connection (including "deep connection costs" for system reinforcement) and the allocation of payments for these costs between project developers and grid owners and operators need to be settled by the national regulator. Yet, regulatory economics does not provide clear-cut answers about the correct methodologies and payment principles to apply to this subject.

In some countries, *power market rules* are designed to secure new capacity on short to medium contracts and do not enable long-term supply contracts; no premium is given to contracts offering long-term price certainty. Thus, the portfolio value of including RE supply in the power mix is not taken into account.

In countries involved in the incipient stages of RE development, RE projects face multiple *newcomer handicaps:* new RE technologies lack an established track record; specialized skills are scarce because an efficient national supply chain for RE technology has not yet been built up; standard financial products specific for the RE and energy efficiency industry are not being offered by financial institutions; and the interpretation of new promotion laws and market regulations is uncertain. These factors increase investors' perceptions of the risk of RE projects and thus, their cost of capital. In a country with a small potential market for a specific technology, these handicaps impose a high cost penalty per future megawatt-hour of generated energy.

Still, RE has strong credentials. In the long run, RE-based supply is the most important carbon dioxide–mitigation tool. Simply from the point of view of national energy supply policy, the benefits of RE provide the portfolio advantage of a more diversified energy supply, reduced reliance on imported fuels, and productive employment creation.

Notes

1. High nominal interest rates in inflation-prone economies deter investment even if real interest rates at the time of project preparation are low.

2. In many developing countries, banks ask for 50 percent equity cofinance.

3. In July 2011, China set provincial quotas for wind energy generation in an effort to ease pressure on the power grids. As of the end of March 2011, the amount of inactive power from wind in the country totaled almost 25 percent of total installed capacity (*Bloomberg Energy Finance*, Week in Review, July 26, 2011).

CHAPTER 10

Government's Role in Promoting Renewable Energy

Generic Framework for Renewable Energy

A supporting framework for renewable energy (RE) comprises two interlinked pillars:

- RE-policy instruments composed of (a) subsidies to cover RE's incremental costs to bridge the gap between economic and financial viability of promoted RE technologies, thereby making otherwise financially unviable energy investments commercially attractive; and (b) a market-expanding regulatory framework that reduces risks, reduces RE projects' transaction costs, and gives supply from RE priority access to the power market
- Public finance instruments that enable RE projects to access commercial finance—equity and long-term debt—in sufficient quantities and at market-competitive terms and prices

Because of the interlocking obstacles to market development, effective frameworks to promote environmental finance are complex, consisting of packages of complementary and mutually reinforcing instruments. Although framework conditions vary from one country to another, the contours of a general policy framework for promoting RE finance can be established. Figure 10.1 groups government interventions by three major categories of instruments: demand pull, technology push, and finance push.[1] All three are needed for RE promotion to succeed.

The demand-pull instruments include incremental-cost finance instruments (support schemes that enable RE technologies to become financially viable on the national energy market), power market rules that facilitate the entry of RE, and environmental regulations and enforcement that increase the cost of fossil-fuel-based energy.

The objective of the technology-push instruments is to improve the economic and financial competitiveness of RE by reducing the cost and

Figure 10.1 Framework and Instruments for Promoting Renewable Energy Finance

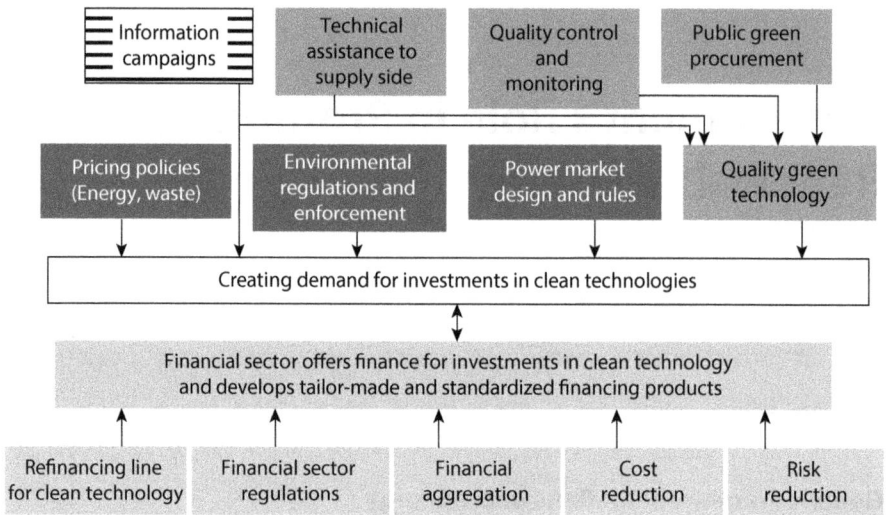

Note: blue = demand pull; orange = technology push; green = finance push.

improving the quality of the RE supply chain. Instruments include information campaigns to create consumer awareness[2]; technical assistance to actors
in the supply chain; monitoring and quality control of supply; public procurement policies for clean energy technologies; and in countries with "green
industrial growth" ambitions, RE supply chain development and cluster
policies.

Whether commercially viable RE investments succeed in attracting finance is
a separate issue, calling for public intervention using finance push instruments
during the initial market build-up phases. The aim of finance push is to increase
the supply of private finance by providing liquidity and reducing investor risks
and bank transaction costs. Instruments comprise refinancing lines, financial sector regulations that facilitate RE finance, assistance in establishing unconven-
tional financing channels, public cofinancing of project preparation and due
diligence costs, and sharing of lending risks.

Optimization Criteria for Incremental Cost Support

Incremental cost support boils down to subsidies. Subsidy schemes must fulfill
several policy objectives. The relevant design criteria for a subsidy scheme,
detailed in figure 10.2, are the following:

- *Impact effectiveness.* The scheme must lead to a significant expansion of the
  market, result in cost reductions in RE, provide portfolio benefits through risk
  reduction, and generate employment and foreign exchange earnings or
  savings.

Figure 10.2 Design of Subsidy Schemes for Clean Energy: Optimization Criteria

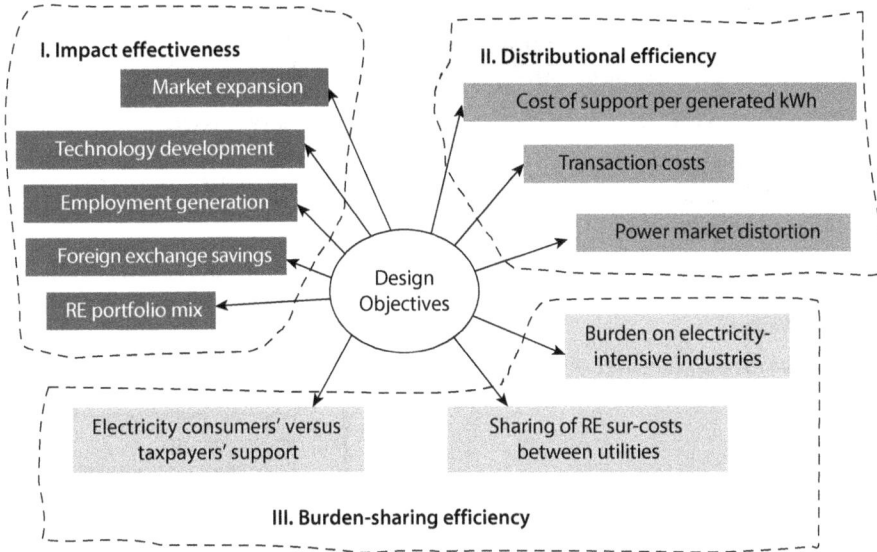

Note: blue = demand pull; Orange = technology push; Green = finance push.

- *Resource allocation efficiency.* Planners do not want to overcompensate investors, create big distortions on the market (e.g., by giving RE generators too many exemptions from the general rules of the power market), or set up a system that imposes high administrative costs on recipients and on the public administrator of the scheme.
- *Burden-sharing efficiency.* The schemes should not impose a heavy burden on low-income households or on energy-intensive industries that are subject to fierce foreign competition, nor lead to unwanted redistribution of income between firms and social groups; nor should the incremental cost be born mainly by utilities in RE-resource-rich regions.

Instruments for Leveraging Private Finance

Public finance instruments for green energy are instruments that seek to eliminate barriers in the finance sector that prevent commercially viable RE projects from accessing private equity and debt finance in sufficient quantities and on acceptable terms.

Basic Functions of the Finance Industry: Liquidity and Risk Cover

Public interventions to attract private investment finance to the RE sector aim to affect the direction of existing flows of private finance. Figure 10.3 helps to explain this process.

Figure 10.3 provides a basic model of the finance industry stripped of nonessentials. The financial sector has two core functions: to satisfy investor demand

Figure 10.3 Finance Sector: Core Functions and Operating Modality

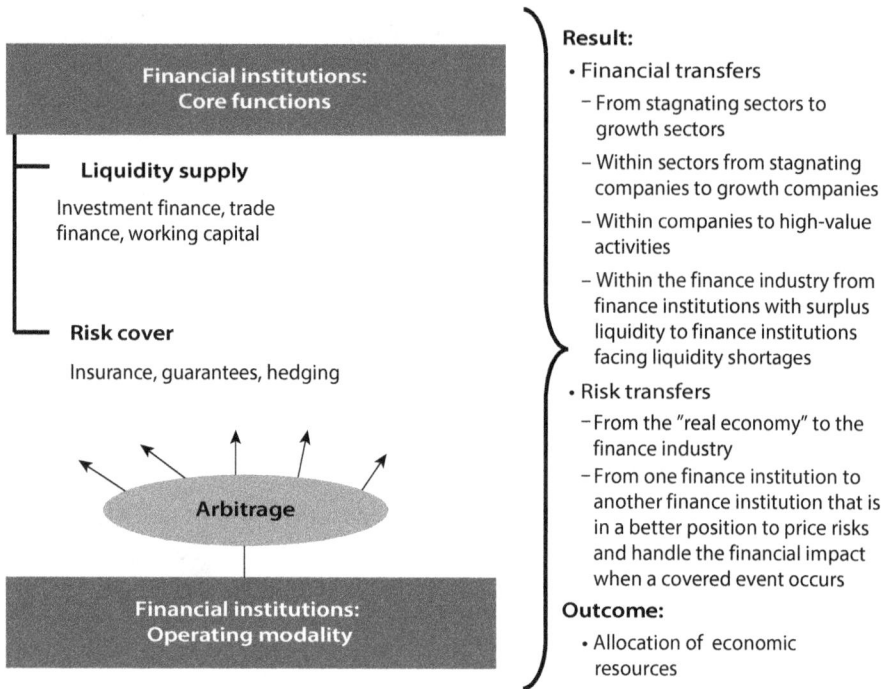

for liquidity and for risk cover. It does so by exploiting arbitrage opportunities—transferring finance from people with money to invest to people wanting to invest, conveying insurance cover from institutions having the financial strength to provide it to investors incapable of surviving financially if a catastrophe occurs, and so on. In an efficient financial and economic system, the transfer of financial resources through the finance industry leads to an optimal allocation of economic resources.

The objective of public finance interventions—to direct flows of private finance toward the RE sector—can thus be promoted in two ways. One is through instruments providing liquidity: debt and equity capital in forms and on terms not sufficiently available on the market. The second is through risk-sharing instruments that improve the risk-return profile of RE loans and equity investments as seen by the finance providers, thus improving the risk-weighted profitability of financing an RE project. Such instruments may be supported by grant-financed technical support to participating financial institutions and by grant funds for project preparation and due diligence reviews.

The use of a public finance instrument is subject to two caveats: (a) it must not replace private capital, out-competing private finance that otherwise would have been made available; and (b) the intervention must support the transformative goal of enabling the private investor and the finance community to undertake RE finance on their own, without continued support from public

Figure 10.4 Size of Renewable Energy Market and Scope for Private Financial Sector Engagement

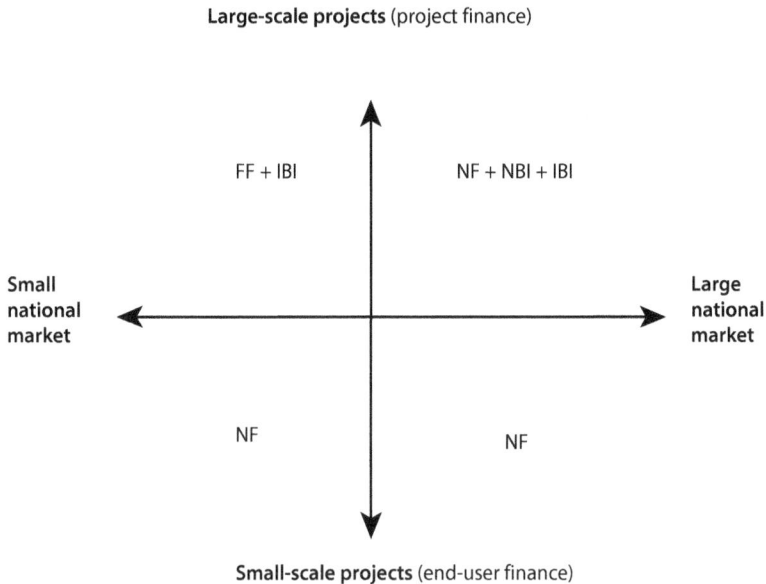

Large-scale projects (project finance)

FF + IBI   NF + NBI + IBI

Small
national   ◄─────────────────────►   Large
market   national
                                                    market

NF   NF

Small-scale projects (end-user finance)

Note: FF = foreign finance; IBI = international bond issue; NBI = national bond issue; NF = national finance.

finance instruments. The challenge is to use public finance instruments in a way that triggers the greatest amount of private funding for the smallest amount of public funds, while still attaining the politically defined RE penetration targets.

Size of RE Market and Scope for Financial Sector Engagement

The scope for financial sector transformation depends on the potential size of the RE market: the finance sector must be able to envision a large potential market to be motivated to commit resources specifically to RE investments in the development of finance products. A large potential market also entices more local entrepreneurs to engage in RE project development and to create a technical-commercial supply chain for RE. Figure 10.4 illustrates that the sources of private capital targeted by public finance programs depend on two parameters: the size of the national market and the size of the individual RE projects.

The implementation of a large project, for example, a 200 megawatt wind farm or geothermal plant, in a country with a small potential market for follow-up investment projects will be too large for the local finance sector and local entrepreneurs to handle. The aim of public finance instruments is, in this case, to attract foreign investment capital: foreign developer equity and commercial bank loans. The transformative impact is limited to building local know-how in the operation and maintenance of the supported technology.

Unlocking Commercial Financing for Clean Energy in East Asia • http://dx.doi.org/10.1596/978-1-4648-0020-7

The largest transformational impact can be achieved in countries with large potential markets for RE. China is the ultimate success story for obvious reasons—large RE market potential, strong national finance capacity, and an internationally competitive RE supply chain combined to turn China into the leading "green growth economy." The initial role of foreign public finance was to kick-start this domestication process: to overcome the newcomer disadvantage of initial low investment volumes and the business and developer communities' lack of familiarity with the technology and RE market conditions.

In countries with large established RE markets, public finance instruments are reduced to niche applications, for example, as tools to safeguard continuity of investment efforts or to increase the speed of financial closure in priority investments.

Notes

1. The framework is applicable for clean energy in general, that is, for the promotion of energy efficiency investment as well as RE.
2. The aim of some measures is to give consumers confidence in the products and advisory services, thereby overcoming the problem of asymmetric information between suppliers and consumers of clean technology. These measures are partly demand-pull, partly technology-push instruments.

CHAPTER 11

Policy Instruments for Covering the Incremental Cost Gap for Renewable Energy

Finance Sources and Targets

The Portfolio of Support Instruments

The portfolio of financial support instruments to increase the market share of renewable energy (RE)–generated electricity is summarized in the matrix in table 11.1. The rows identify *four potential financing sources* for subsidies to RE: (a) subsidies financed by the public budget, (b) subsidies raised through electricity invoices, (c) subsidized export credits for RE technologies and soft loans from development banks, and (d) payments for greenhouse gas reductions from the use of RE. The columns point out *three potential subsidy targets*: (a) subsidies to investments, (b) subsidies to output, and (c) subsidies to the cost of operation.

The difference between text in italic, in bold, and in regular font refers to two further categorizations:

- First is the distinction between direct and indirect support to investors. The instruments providing support to individual investments in an *indirect manner* are indicated in italics.
- Second is between price-based (market response determines the level of annual investment) and quantity-based (market response determines the output tariff or investment subsidy) support mechanisms; quantity-based mechanisms are indicated in bold.

The ideal subsidy package depends on its political acceptability and on the scope and scale of potential RE supply in the country. Different packages of subsidy instruments are needed for different stages of the technology introduction cycle:

Table 11.1 Sources and Targets of Renewable Energy Finance

Financing sources	Subsidy targets		
	Cost of investment	Price of output	Operating costs
Public budget finance instruments (taxpayer financed)	Grants to project preparation Investment grants per MW or in percent Investment tax credit Concessional or soft loans VAT exemption Import duty exemption Accelerated depreciation Tax holidays on income *Subsidies to exporters of RET equipment* *Subsidies to R&D&D*	Production tax credit per kWh Topping-up premium per kWh paid to generator Green kWh premium paid to consumers VAT or excise duty exemptions *Public green electricity purchases*	*Subsidies to the marketing of green electricity*
Electricity invoice financed instruments (ratepayer financed)	*Grid reinforcement (deep connection costs) paid by utilities* *Part of (shallow) connection costs paid by utilities* *R&D&D of power utilities on interfaces between wind farms and regional or national power system*	Feed-in tariffs (FITs) Green topping-up premiums Net or reverse metering Voluntary green consumer premium tariffs **Renewable portfolio standards** **Auctions or tenders for technology-specific PPAs (FITs)** *Eco-taxes on alternative fuels*	*Wheeling tariff below the true cost* *Balancing costs charged to consumers* *Use-of-system charges fixed below cost* *Subsidized administration of green invoicing*
Carbon market mechanisms		**CO$_2$ certificates (cap and trade)** CO$_2$ certificates (project-specific CERs or ERUs per MWh)	

Note: CER = certified emission reduction; CO$_2$ = carbon dioxide; ERU = emission reduction unit; kWh = kilowatt-hour; MW = megawatt; MWh = megawatt-hour; PPA = power purchase agreement; R&D&D = research and development and demonstration; RE = renewable energy; RET = renewable energy technology; VAT = value added tax. Quantity-based mechanisms are indicated in bold. Instruments providing support to individual investments in an *indirect manner* are indicated in italics.

- A "taxpayer pays" strategy is useful in the short term to get the development process started for a specific new RE technology. These strategies are used for end-user finance to promote stand-alone systems (e.g., solar home systems or solar water heaters) and to promote grid-connected RE in the research and development and demonstration (R&D&D) stages.
- The "electricity consumer pays" strategy is the solution for the large-scale commercialization phase of a grid-based RE technology.

Countries with ambitious RE programs employ both taxpayer-pays and energy-consumer-pays instruments because various RE technologies are at different levels of innovation and commercial market maturity. Combinations of taxpayer-pays and energy-consumer-pays instruments for RE investments can also be used to serve particular interests. The standard of living of low-income households is negatively affected by consumer-paid schemes; therefore, cofinancing of RE support from the public budget can be used to relieve problems of energy poverty, that is, households with limited ability to pay monthly utility bills. Some Spanish provinces added a premium to the feed-in tariff (FIT) if a certain percentage of total investment was locally sourced.

In Navarra, Spain, wind power investors could deduct up to 15 percent of their earnings from wind power from their tax returns if they located a wind farm in the province. In Denmark, wind turbine owners do not have to pay taxes on the level of production that equals their annual power consumption; this instrument was introduced to secure public backing for on-land wind turbine investments by widening their ownership base.

Shifting from Investment Subsidy to Tariff Support through Mandated Markets

The typical evolution for financial support of a grid-based RE technology is (a) a shift from taxpayer-paid to energy-consumer-paid support, (b) replacement of a capital investment subsidy by support to the output of power, and (c) strong focus on elimination of overcompensation, to support that is more compatible with general power market rules by, among other tactics, charging RE generators the full cost of auxiliary services that RE supply imposes on system operators.

A mandated market has three general features: (a) an obligation on transmission and distribution companies to connect RE generation; (b) an adequate power sales tariff level with a long-term power purchase agreement (PPA), and a right for commercial power suppliers to recover legally imposed surplus RE technology costs from consumers; and (c) a national (or state) policy target for the penetration of RE into the market. Mandated market schemes for RE systems fall into three main categories:

- FITs: Fixed tariff rates paid for several years to eligible generators.
- Tendering mechanism: By which RE project developers bid for long-term PPAs with the system operator or national transmission company, or for the level of required feed-in premium to be paid on top of the power market price.
- Renewable Portfolio Standard (RPS): Tradable green certificate (TGC) schemes, in which electricity suppliers are obliged to supply a certain quota of RE by investing in RE generation or by buying RE certificates from RE generators.

In the FIT schemes, policy makers fix the price, and the market determines the resulting quantity of new RE power supply. In tendering schemes and TGC schemes, policy makers fix the desired quantity of new RE power supply, and the market establishes the price for the desired quantity. The following sections review international experience with investment grants and then review experiences with the three types of mandated markets.

Investment Subsidy

Support for the R&D&D Stages of RE Technology

Expert and political opinion with regard to financial support to the R&D&D stages of an RE technology is divided between the relative merits of grants for specific technologies versus tax deductions for a more broadly defined range of technologies.

Proponents of the technology-specific grant approach underline two merits. First is the ability to focus on technologies that reflect national ambitions in RE policy. Second is that the approach can target the creation of regional and national know-how clusters.

Proponents of tax deductions for more broadly defined technologies argue that identifying the most promising technologies is left up to the creativity of private entrepreneurs, whereas grant-based programs for specified technologies entrust the capability to pick winners to public administrators.

Up-Front Investment Grants and Interest Rate Subsidies

Up-front investment subsidies are used mainly for three cases: (a) to support the initial development of a market for a new RE technology; (b) to support employment during the recession phases of a business cycle; and (c) to cover the incremental costs of RE to demonstrate the potential of RE technologies and to set cost benchmarks, in the absence of mandated market policies.

An example of the first is Australia's Photovoltaic Rebate Programme (PVRP).[1] The PVRP, initiated in 2000, makes cash rebates available to householders, owners of community-use buildings, display-home builders, and housing estate developers who install grid-connected or stand-alone PV (photovoltaic) systems. In 2007, PVRP provided a rebate of 8 Australian dollars ($A; US$6.60)[2] per watt for solar PV systems with a maximum of $A 8,000 (US$6,590). That year's federal budget allocated $A 300 million (US$247) for PVRP.[3] The support was allocated on a first come, first served basis. This type of scheme is of potential interest to emerging economies that want to begin development of distributed generation without high costs to the public budget. However, the same result can also be achieved by a very stingy FIT.

An example of the third case for the use of an up-front subsidy is the Chinese government's Golden Sun Demonstration Project, launched in July 2009 by the Ministry of Finance, the Ministry of Science, and the National Energy Board. In 2009, the global economic and financial crisis caused a significant decline in the export market for PV products; the scheme provided a lifeline market outlet for small PV manufacturers.[4] The scheme paid 50 percent of the investment costs for qualifying solar power plants and transmission and distribution projects; for projects in remote regions not connected to the grid, the subsidy was 70 percent. However, in the midst of the "first come, first served" boom, businesses engaged in false bidding and used low-quality products. To boost the government subsidies they received, a relatively large proportion of businesses declared their material costs to be higher than they actually were. That type of fraud risk is inherent in schemes that provide subsidies as a percentage of the cost of investment. Enterprises contracted under the Golden Sun project did their utmost to keep prices down, and suppliers did not hesitate to take a loss so as to obtain orders. However, some suppliers allowed second-class components and defective stock to be absorbed within Golden Sun projects. The use of low-quality products meant that the conditions for receiving the subsidy were not being met (Yuan 2011).

An investment subsidy can also be provided via a concessional loan. A concessional loan is a hybrid between an incremental cost cover instrument (the net present value of the interest rate subsidy could have been provided up front as an investment grant through a deduction in loan principle[5]) and a public finance instrument (enabling financial close). The instrument is used mainly in export credits and in loans to stimulate end-consumer purchases of RE technologies.

Investment Tax Credit versus Production Tax Credit

Investment tax incentives provide income tax deductions or credits for some portion of the capital investment made in an RE project. Income tax deductions reduce taxable income; tax credits directly offset taxes due. Two countries in particular have relied heavily on tax-code-based investment support for grid-connected RE—India and the United States.

Investment Tax Incentives
During the 1990s, almost all wind farm investments in India were undertaken by private corporations attracted by two complementary instruments. One was accelerated depreciation—the ability to write off 50–100 percent (depending on the date of putting in place the first foundations at the site) of the investment against taxable profits of the period during which the investment was made. The other was "wheeling," meaning transport of power at a fixed low rate through the transmission and distribution grid from the site of generation to the site of power consumption at company-owned plants.

Tax deductions and tax credits are economically attractive only to corporations with sufficiently large taxable income; however, they have proved to be powerful instruments for attracting and getting RE capacity installed. Their record with regard to the real policy objective—electricity generation from RE—is less convincing. Because investment tax incentives reward the installation of RE facilities, but not the production of electricity from those facilities, in California during the 1980s and in India during the 1990s, companies rushed to install wind turbines to capture the associated investment tax incentives, with little regard for choosing the best wind locations and the most efficient turbines. A significant fraction of installed wind farm capacity from those two periods represented misinvestment.

Several countries experimented with income tax incentives for customer-sited RE systems, giving investors the right to tax deductions or to tax credits for a percentage of the cost of the RE investment.

Property tax reductions can eliminate up to 100 percent of the property taxes on land and fixed assets used for RE production facilities.

Production Tax Credits

In the United States, the federal 10-year production tax credit of US$0.015/kWh given to wind farms (geothermal energy and solar PV get similar tax credits) is similar to an FIT premium in the sense that it is paid separately from the price for power received by an RE generator. But unlike RE generators receiving a feed-in premium, the RE generator receiving a production tax credit need not sell the power output at market prices. Normally, the generator will be paid a favorable RE tariff under a long-term PPA with a utility that needs to fulfill an RE quota. The production tax credit can be characterized as an investment grant that is paid up front over a 10-year period, but with the advantage that it encourages efficient production. It lowers the levelized life-cycle cost of wind power by about 25 percent. The production tax credit is a means of sharing the incremental cost of green power (a) between taxpayers and power consumers and (b) between the U.S. population as a whole and the state population where the off-taking utility is located. However, the volatility of U.S. production tax credit policy has negative impacts on the sustainability of the growth of RE industries (when Congress renews production tax credits, RE grows; when Congress does not renew production tax credits, RE growth stops). Continuity of the policy is essential for the sustainable and healthy growth of the RE industry.

Comparison of Investment and Production Tax Credits

Output-based incentives (production tax credits) are preferable to investment-based incentives (investment tax credits) because output incentives per kWh of power produced directly promote the desired outcome, which is to generate electricity from RE. The production tax credit focuses investors on maximizing output whereas the investment tax credit focuses them on getting the investment implemented. In India, the policy during the 1990s led to a series of investments in wind farms with very low capacity factors, either because wind resource quality had not been properly verified or because local grid quality had not been examined before investment in the wind farm.

Feed-In Tariffs

The term FIT is reserved for mandated market schemes in which the level of the tariff for new RE capacity is fixed by political decision. The tariff is assumed to reflect the full cost of the technology for private investors, including the market rate of return on investments with comparable risk profiles; thus, FITs are technology specific.

Design Challenges and Lessons Learned

The FIT as a policy instrument has two strong points. First is its market penetration impact: Because technology-specific FITs are fixed at a level that reflects the full cost of the technology for private investors, all potential project sites with generation costs equal to the FIT could, in theory, be initiated in the year in which the tariff comes into force. The market development potential fostered by FITs is, therefore, very strong. Second, if properly designed, FITs are very cost effective in the RE supply they trigger per dollar of incremental cost subsidy.

The weak point of the FIT is the risk of excessive subsidy costs because of stronger-than-expected market development caused by, among other things, economic rents generated by declining market prices for RE technologies that were not expected by policy makers when they fixed the FIT levels.

The design of a FIT poses a number of challenges:

- Which reference prices to use as benchmark for fixing the level of the FIT;
- How to keep demand expansion and associated support costs within manageable bounds;
- How to take "learning curve" cost reductions into account to avoid over-compensation;
- How to reduce resource rents from the best sites to a minimum, while allowing a broad range of sites to be developed;
- How to make the FIT scheme as compatible with general power market rules as possible; and
- How to handle the fuel element in FITs for biomass power.

Reference Prices for Setting the Level of a FIT

Three different reference prices are used as benchmarks for setting the level of a FIT: the estimated cost of generation per kWh of the supported RE technology at a site with a typical RE resource profile, the estimated avoided costs in conventional power supply per kWh of supplied RE power, and the cost per kWh of the average retail tariff.

As reflected in table 11.2, the benchmark price can be used either to fix the FIT that is received during a specific year of the FIT period or to fix the FIT for the whole FIT period of a project.[6] The fundamental lesson of the FIT is that the chosen method must reflect costs as closely as possible. The Ukrainian approach of fixing the RE FIT against retail tariffs in the base year, then multiplying it by some technology-specific factors (e.g., by 0.8 for one technology, and by 2.2 for another technology), is expensive for consumers. The U.S. Public Utility Regulatory Policies Act scheme of the late 1980s, which fixed RE tariffs according to an estimate of the avoided

Table 11.2 Reference Price and Cost Benchmarks for Setting the Level of a Feed-In Tariff

Period of FIT	Based on cost of RE technology	Based on avoided costs	Based on retail tariff
Annual tariff or revenue influenced by power market price during year	Feed-in premium	Variable, power system cost dependent	Tariff expressed in percentage of retail tariff Reverse metering
Fixed rate throughout FIT payment period	Fixed FIT (but may have inflation adjustment of individual components, e.g., biomass fuel cost)	Fixed FIT, derived from hypothetical long-run marginal cost of power supply	FIT fixed with reference to retail tariff in base year multiplied by RE–technology specific factor

Note: FIT = feed-in tariff; RE = renewable energy.

long-run marginal costs of conventional power based on an assumption of real annual fuel price increases, proved to be far off the price path for conventional fuels.

Risk of Excessive Market Expansion

The strength of the FIT—its ability to expand the market faster than any alternative—is also its highest risk. The market-expanding ability of the FIT risks pushing up the annual support bill quickly, to levels beyond what politicians expected and what the public budget or consumers can afford. Rapid expansion of RE power supply strains the adjustment capacity of the power system. Intermittent power increases the cost of system management, and distributed generation requires investment in the reinforcement of distribution grids. The mounting bill for incremental cost support is a particularly serious issue for solar PV because of its high cost of generation per kWh[7] and the absence of a natural limit on demand expansion: PV systems can be installed on rooftops and on open land and can be installed without resource investigation soon after making the decision to invest. The introduction of relatively generous (expected to give an 8 percent rate of return on investment) solar FITs in Germany led to such a massive increase in demand that some 60 percent of new solar PV capacity worldwide was installed in Germany during 2004–06. The upward shift in world demand reversed the steadily falling price trend: PV prices increased from 2004 to 2006 as a result of bottlenecks in supply. Then prices of installed PV systems dropped about 60 percent from 2007 to 2011 because of the considerable expansion in supply, in particular from China. Because the downward adjustments in solar FITs did not match the downward cost developments in the market, the windfall profits from investments caused an explosion in demand in Spain, Germany, and Italy. See box 11.1 for how France curtailed demand.

See box 11.2 for the potential unintended consequences of supporting a FIT with a specific tax.

Box 11.1 France's Approach to Limiting the Demand for Solar PV

Early in 2010, France cut its solar subsidies by 24 percent. In December 2010, France introduced a four-month suspension on FITs for new solar PV installations of more than 3 kW capacity. The 13,000 projects greater than 3 kW had accounted for 70 percent of capacity installed during 2010. In February 2011, a decree announced a strict limit on yearly installed PV capacity to 500 MW. The tariff for solar PV systems with capacity of more than 100 kW was reduced to €0.12/kWh (US$0.17/kWh), resulting in a reduction in the tariff for open-space systems of 57 percent and for rooftop systems of 70 percent. FITs for small PV systems were reduced by 20 percent. To limit the number of installations, a simplified Request for Proposal (RFP; a call for tender) is required for all rooftop projects between 100 kW and 250 kW. Winners are chosen on several nonprice factors and receive the fixed FIT. Solar PV projects greater than 250 kW were removed from the FIT program: rooftop projects greater than 250 kW and ground-mounted projects of any size have to respond to more conventional RFPs, where winners are picked based on price, environmental impact, innovation, and other factors.

Source: Bloomberg Newsletters.

Box 11.2 Tax-Financed Feed-In Tariffs

In Sri Lanka, an open-ended FIT regime with technology-specific tariffs was introduced in 2009. Two funds managed by the Sri Lanka Sustainable Energy Authority were to finance the support needed to attract private investments required for the national RE and energy efficiency policy to be realized: the Sri Lanka Sustainable Energy Fund (SLSEF) and the Sustainable Energy Guarantee Fund. A tax on oil imports was to be the main source of funding for the SLSEF. The SLSEF intended to use transfers to the national power utility (the Ceylon Electricity Board, or CEB) to finance the difference between the cost of the FITs received by RE plants and the value of the financial savings from avoided thermal power costs by CEB. However, this was not a feasible arrangement. First, the steady annual funding from an oil tax is incompatible with the large volatility in annual incremental costs from bursts in RE investment and fluctuating fossil fuel prices. Second, the compensation plan did not allow CEB to benefit from the portfolio value of RE power: the price stability of RE power provided under long-term PPAs with fixed tariffs. Instead, it reinforced the reduction in CEB's average cost of generated power when fossil fuel prices fell (the financial transfers from the SLSEF would increase because CEB imported more) and reinforced the increase in CEB's net financial costs of production when fossil fuel prices increased (higher avoided costs reduce the financial transfers from the SLSEF). Third, the Ministry of Finance would probably have opposed the introduction of a tax with a predefined use of revenue.

Keeping Demand Expansion within Manageable Bounds
The policy instruments introduced to control the explosion in demand and associated financial support caused by FITs differ by country.

- The huge costs of support in 2010 and 2011 led governments to reduce the FITs for PV systems, in some countries even several times per year. Yet, demand continued to increase: despite three tariff reductions during 2010, Germany installed a record 8 gigawatts (GW) of new capacity. Germany then attempted to set a soft target (without hard annual quantity limits) of 3.5 GW per year, but using a price mechanism to limit demand as it progressed beyond the targeted installment level. Germany reduces the solar FIT by a base rate of 9 percent each year plus a variable percentage that depends on how much new generation capacity is installed during the year: The FIT in 2011 and 2012 will be reduced by 3 percent if projected annual capacity additions, based on the previous three months' installation, pass the 3.5 GW target, plus a further 3 percent reduction for every 1 GW increment above the 3.5 target.
- The high demand led some governments to cap the amount of supported annual capacity. France introduced a strict annual limit of 500 MW for new PV installations; see box 11.1.[8]
- The Italian government targets about 2.5 GW in annual new PV capacity; however, 9 GW of capacity was installed in 2011. With the aim of stabilizing the annual subsidy bill at €6.5 billion (US$9.2 billion), Italy's 2012 RE law, the fifth Conto Energia, introduces three measures to contain subsidies; first,

cuts to the FIT: for a 3 kW rooftop PV installation from €0.274/kWh to €0.237/kWh (US$0.39/kWh to US$0.33/kWh) and for a 200 kW installation from €0.233/kWh to €0.199/kWh (US$0.33/kWh to US$0.28/kWh); second, an annual installation cap of between 2 and 3 GW on PV installations, systems of more than 12 kW must register with the government and are eligible for the FIT only when they fall within the limits of the cap; and third, installations of more than 5 MW are to be put through a competitive bidding process.

- Some governments scrapped the FITs for certain categories of supported investments (e.g., for open-land PV systems, while rooftop PV continued to be supported).
- Some countries dropped the open-ended FIT, replacing it with a tender regime for FITs.
- Spain, which financed a large part of the FIT through the public budget, scrapped all FIT support to RE generators in early 2012.

Adjusting FITs to the Downward Trend in RE Costs

During the 1990s, neither Germany nor Denmark changed FITs for new wind farms although the cost of production per kWh dropped steadily, by a total of 40 percent by the end of the decade. This led Germany to a pre-announced multiyear digression of tariffs in which the tariff for new plants is reduced by a certain percentage each year based on empirically derived progress ratios and forecasts for the different technologies. The digression system was expected to reduce the scope for investment bubbles caused by windfall profits. The failure of the approach to control solar PV led some experts to declare the death of the feed-in system. That is premature for three reasons:

- First, policy makers do not normally jump from one method to another when the alternative has its own weaknesses; instead, they adjust a given method in light of experience.
- Second, the multiyear price forecasts based on learning curve theory did not factor in either demand shocks (German PV demand leading to supply bottlenecks from 2004 to 2006; Chinese demand for commodities pushing up prices for metals used in wind turbines, while a jump in international demand led to bottlenecks in the manufacturing of wind turbines) or supply shocks (the entry of Chinese PV module manufacturers into the world market). Policy makers have learned the lesson: pricing formulas with fixed multiyear digression rates are out; tariff adjustments based on market monitoring are in.
- Third, the volatility of prices caught policy makers off guard. However, one must assume that the severity of the disequilibrium was abnormal.[9]

Minimizing Economic Rents Arising from Varied RE Resources

The differences in wind resources and of water resources at potential hydropower sites in a country result in great disparities in annual capacity factors of plants, which raises the issue of resource rents. Under a uniform FIT regime, projects at the best sites would reap substantial economic rents. In practice, these rents would be shared between the developers and the owners of the land at the sites, the latter receiving their share through increases in lease payments. To reduce the rents at the best sites, yet still enable projects at less attractive sites to be developed, several approaches are used. A simple approach is to award the FIT for a specific number of "full-capacity hours of production," for example, for the first 25,000 gigawatt-hour (GWh) per installed MW, after which the RE power plant has to sell its power into the power pool at market prices. In this approach, RE power plants with high capacity factors recoup their investment faster than plants with lower capacity factors, but the lifetime FIT payments are the same.

Another approach is to use tariff rates that decline stepwise with the expected GWh output per MW. In Germany, eligible projects are classified into three categories according to the quality of the wind resource at the project site. Wind farms located at "category 1" wind resource sites are paid the lowest tariff, which is valid only during the first five years. Projects at the other sites receive higher FIT tariffs until a defined GWh/MW production has been attained. Projects producing less than 60 percent of the "standard output" for a "category 3" wind resource site are not eligible for a subsidized FIT at all. In the French system of differentiated tariffs based on resource intensity, wind turbines are paid €0.082/kWh (US$0.12/kWh) for the first 10 years of a 15-year contract. During years 11 through 15, the tariff varies based on the productivity of the wind turbine. Wind turbines at windy sites are paid as little as €0.028/kWh (US$0.04/kWh), turbines at less windy sites are paid up to €0.082/kWh (US$0.12/kWh). In China, a regulation introduced by the National Development and Reform Commission in 2009 standardized FITs for new onshore wind projects. The regulation divided the country into four wind energy zones, with prices ranging from 0.51 yuan per kWh (US$0.07/kWh) to 0.61 yuan per kWh (US$0.09/kWh) according to available wind resources and construction conditions at the specific location.[10] The costs of the wind FIT program in excess of the cost of coal-fired generation are split between provincial grid operators and the central government.

The declining-rate FIT can also be tailored to the tenor of loans offered by banks on the national market, as done in Sri Lanka (see box 11.3).

Box 11.3 Adjust Feed-In Tariffs or Extend Loan Tenor?

Sri Lanka has a well-designed system of technology-specific FITs for RE up to 10 MW capacity. The system emphasizes reduction of economic rents by paying investors prices as close to their true cost of supply as possible. Developers have the choice between a fixed FIT for 20 years, or a three-tier tariff, with a high tariff during the first 8 years, a lower tariff for years 9–14, and a still lower tariff for years 15–20. The purpose of the three-step tariff is to facilitate local financing of projects: commercial banks in Sri Lanka only award loans with a tenor of up to six years.

Factoring in Fuel Price Volatility for Biomass FIT

The design of FITs for biomass-based power faces the challenge of adjusting for changes in the price of biomass fuel. This is a particular problem for dendro power plants because, unlike bagasse-based power, they contract for their biomass on a commercial basis from outside suppliers. The FIT for dendro power in Sri Lanka has a built-in adjustment for fuelwood equal to two-thirds of the rate of inflation—which is not realistic. This inflation-to-fuelwood price ratio is based on the behavior of fuelwood prices for industrial consumers in the past, when fuelwood was a marginal source of energy supply. If dendro power plants come onstream, fuelwood will become a commercial product subject to powerful demand pull on its prices from the high and increasing prices for oil; at a minimum, the fuelwood price component needs to track the national inflation rate on a one-for-one basis. In China, the government had to adjust the biomass FIT upward several times to reflect the rising cost of the fuel.

Applying FIT for Small-Scale RE Development

Several countries apply different FITS or a combination of methods to small and large RE generators. In 2010, the United Kingdom introduced a FIT for projects with a maximum size of 5 MW. Projects smaller than 50 kW receive the FIT; projects between 50 kW and 5 MW can choose support either under the Renewables Obligation or the FIT. Plants larger than 5 MW can only be supported through the Renewables Obligation. In 2009, Italy introduced a 15-year FIT for RE plants with capacity of less than 1 MW; for larger plants, the tradable green certificates system continues to apply.

Promoting a National RE Technology Industry

To justify the high cost of support to RE electricity, governments point to the employment advantages of a "green economy." To maximize the economic benefits from RE investments, governments seek to integrate RE policy with an RE industry promotion policy. Some countries add bonuses on top of the normal FIT to promote local green economic and new technology development. In Italy, projects receive a 10 percent bonus to the FIT if the value of European Union (EU)–based manufacturing amounts to at least 60 percent of the cost of modules and inverters. In addition, the Italian regime promotes technological innovation by offering extra-high FITs for PV systems using (a) innovative PV material, (b) glass PV surfaces, and (c) concentrated solar PV.

Countries such as China, India, and Spain have successfully developed national RE manufacturing capacity linking their RE support schemes with domestic content requirements. However, although the employment goal must be pursued, there are limits to this policy (see box 11.4 on Ontario). In July 2011, Japan and the EU filed complaints at the World Trade Organization (WTO) against Canada for inconsistency of the FIT with WTO obligations because it provides subsidies contingent on the use of domestic goods. The impact of FIT support on electricity bills became an issue in Ontario's elections and made regulators hesitant to approve FIT applications: less than one-fifth of submitted MW-capacity was approved by January 2011. This is a blow to the

---

Box 11.4 Ontario Feed-In Tariffs with Domestic Content Requirement

Ontario's Green Energy and Green Economy Act of May 2009 introduced a FIT for eligible projects. The Ontario Power Authority is responsible for implementing the program. The FIT pays up to Can$0.71/kWh (US$0.62/kWh) over 20 years for roof-mounted solar PV systems, with lower payments for ground-mounted solar and for other RE technologies. The dual objective is to phase out coal-fired electricity generation by 2014 and to boost economic activity by creating new green industries and jobs. The FIT has domestic content requirements to ensure that much of the RE technology comes from Ontario. For solar PV projects larger than 10 kW, developers must ensure that 50 percent of goods and labor are sourced in Ontario; the level increases to 60 percent in 2011.

The act has had the following impacts. A Green Energy Investment Agreement in 2010 between the Ontario government and Samsung called for the company to build four manufacturing plants in Ontario, invest Can$7 billion in the province, and develop 2.5 GW of wind and solar electricity generation, roughly 10 percent of Ontario's total electricity production. The Ontario Power Authority received 956 applications in October 2009 for the first round of FIT contracts; 510 were accepted, ranging from 10 kW to 500 kW in capacity, with total generating capacity of 112 MW (projects under a 500 kW threshold can be connected to the grid without detailed impact assessments). By January 2011, a total of 4,106 FIT applications had been filed for planned projects totaling 16,245 MW of renewable power. Of these, 1,263 resulted in executed contracts, for 2,630 MW.

---

market expectations of manufacturers that had set up operations in response to the domestic content regulations. Furthermore, in 2011, the agreement with Samsung (see box 11.4) was renegotiated. Samsung got a one-year extension of the commercial operation date of its generation facilities to 2014, the government reduced the incentives payable to Samsung by about 75 percent from a projected US$437 million to US$110 million and required that three of the four manufacturing plants be operational by the end of 2011.

Feed-In Premiums

Once RE power penetration reaches two-digit levels, policy makers and regulators try to better harmonize the terms offered to RE generators with general power market rules and conditions. Some countries then replace the FIT with a "feed-in-premium." In this scheme, RE generators sell their output into the power pool and are paid the daily market prices; in addition, they receive a separate feed-in premium per kWh sold. By selling to the pool, RE generators are subject to the same market requirements as fossil-fuel-based generation. Intermittent supply from wind farms, for example, must contractually acquire balancing energy to compensate for shortfalls in predicted supply.

Some countries, for example, Slovenia, apply a mixed scheme: generation plants with capacity up to 5 MW are supported through a FIT; larger plants are paid a feed-in premium on top of the market price.

The extent to which the system exposes RE generators to the full risk of the volatility of power prices on the bulk power market depends on the design of the scheme.

- In Denmark, onshore wind turbines connected to the grid after February 20, 2008, receive a fixed feed-in premium of 0.25 Danish kroner (DKr) per kWh (€33.6/MWh; US$0.05/kWh) for 22,000 full load hours. In addition, for 20 years wind turbine operators are paid DKr 2.3 per/kWh (€0.3/kWh; US$0.0046/kWh) to compensate for their expenses for balancing costs. Near-coast offshore wind turbines receive the same. Some states in India and Thailand also apply a fixed premium policy.
- In 2012, an amendment to the German Renewable Energy Sources Act (EEG) introduced a market premium as an option for RE generators. RE producers that market their electricity themselves under market supply and demand conditions—rather than receiving FITs—can claim the premium. The market premium is calculated as the difference between the EEG FIT and the monthly ex post average price at the energy exchange and includes a management fee.
- The Netherlands applies a sliding premium calculated as a function of the average electricity price. This system keeps the total support cost for consumers at a lower level than does a fixed premium.
- The United Kingdom intends to gradually replace its Renewables Obligation Certificate (ROC) scheme with a Contracts for Difference (CfD) scheme, under which RE generators receive a top-up on the wholesale price of electricity. The CfD guarantees generators a strike price for their electricity, the level of which depends on the RE technology. The top-up is added to the day-ahead wholesale electricity price for intermittent sources, such as wind, and on the year-ahead electricity price for dispatchable sources, such as biomass-fired power plants. If wholesale prices soar above the strike price, generators will have to give up some of their revenues.
- Spain applies a cap and floor system, in which the floor acts as a bottom limit to compensation as protection against steeply falling electricity prices.

The purpose of the feed-in premium is to turn producers of RE into market players that optimize production according to market prices. The exposure of RE generation to market prices acts as an incentive for RE generation to become more demand oriented: the premium adds value to production that meets the energy demands of the system, thus dissuading generators from just producing energy according to weather conditions. The ability of intermittent supply from wind farms and PV plants to react to changes in demand conditions is limited. However, RE generators can provide better supply estimates (with the help of weather forecasts), find least-cost arrangements for the contracting of balancing power, and find the appropriate economic balance between investing in energy storage and contracting for backup power. Efficiency improvements such as these gain importance when integrating large RE shares into an electricity system.

Tenders for PPA Contracts or for Feed-In Premiums

Tenders for Long-Term PPAs

Tenders for long-term PPA contracts for RE power are organized either by national or state regulators to fulfill national targets for new RE supply, or by utilities or power suppliers operating under an RE portfolio scheme not organized as a green certificate scheme. Tenders for power supply are also called reverse auctions.[11] The PPA rate fixed in an auction is equivalent to a FIT in the sense that a fixed favorable green tariff is paid and that the supply of RE enjoys preferential market access. But unlike a FIT, its level is not fixed by policy makers. See box 11.5.

The normal procedure is to organize technology-specific procurement auctions. Often a tender includes a call for supply from several RE technologies, each with a target quantity. In such cases, the amount of contracted biomass and small hydro typically falls below the expectations of the organizers, whereas more wind capacity is attracted than originally targeted. RE projects that are easier to prepare and implement within the supply deadlines specified in the tenders have a higher achievement rate than do more complex projects.

Technology-neutral auctions also occur, in which an RE volume is tendered and the projects offering the lowest rates are awarded the contracts irrespective of the RE technology used. See box 11.6.

Box 11.5 California's Renewable Auction Mechanism for Setting FITs

As a means to encourage development of midsize RE generation, the California Public Utilities Commission in August 2010 issued a proposal establishing a 1 GW pilot program for power from RE systems of 1–20 MW. The program requires Pacific Gas and Electric, Southern California Edison, and San Diego Gas and Electric to hold biannual competitive auctions for FITs into which RE developers can bid. The utility must award contracts starting with the lowest-cost viable project, moving up in price until the MW requirement is reached for that round. The state had had difficulty developing enough transmission to serve large-scale projects. This program encourages immediate activity for RE projects that can be incorporated into existing utility distribution infrastructure.

Source: Opalka 2010.

Box 11.6 Tenders and Size of Projects

A regulation from China's National Development Reform Committee (NDRC) that went into force in January 2006 provided that electricity prices for wind projects should be determined by tender. In practice, a two-tier pricing mechanism developed. Projects of more than 50 MW required approval by the NDRC, and pricing was set through tendering. For each project of less than 50 MW, the provincial counterpart of the NDRC determined pricing based on the project's production costs and then submitted the price to the NDRC for final endorsement.

The tender documents fix either the called-for quantity of power or the total available subsidy amount. In the first case, the winning bids will determine the financial cost of the tendered quantity. In the second case, the bids will establish how much power can be bought with the price support (Bauer and Barroso 2011).

Procurement auctions are open ended—bidders identify the sites for their projects. Concession tenders are for the development of the RE resource at a specific site; the bidders vie for the concession to develop the site and receive the long-term power supply contract for the output from the project.

In Brazil, the acquired power is fed into the power pool at the contracted price; thus, the green PPAs raise the average pool price. The increase in the pool price is subject to a politically fixed maximum: the average price of energy for end consumers can increase a maximum of 0.5 percent per year and 5 percent in total during the 20-year PPA period.

The tender procedure has three natural advantages:

- If completed successfully, a tender provides the amount of new RE generation targeted by policy makers; there is no risk of support costs getting out of control.
- The tariff is established by market forces; it involves no qualified guessing by the authorities about what levels of FITs are required to provide a targeted quantity.
- It controls economic rents. Tendering is effective at reducing costs. Competition ensures that only projects from the lowest-cost resource sites have a chance to win contracts in a given tender round. The average capacity factor of winning projects in initial rounds will be high and will decrease in later rounds because the best resource sites will have been progressively developed.[12]

The tender regime is subject to a number of risks and weaknesses not found in FIT regimes.

- The sector attracts inexperienced newcomers to the market. These new-comers submit low bids, which leads to the inability to implement the projects when the developers realize that their bid prices are below their costs of production.[13]
- The stop-and-go nature of tenders is not conducive to the stable conditions needed to develop a quality national supply chain.[14]
- Because the tender procedure enables only the least-cost projects to be implemented during early years, it leads to a high concentration of projects in the regions with the best RE resources. For wind farms this is a problem because local populations in wind-resource-rich areas begin to resist implementation of new projects.
- Because of the high transaction costs of tenders and the economies of scale of larger plant sizes, only major players are attracted. If policy makers want to encourage the development of small projects, too, the tender scheme is not the best choice.

In some countries, therefore, the tender mechanism has not been successful. The United Kingdom's Non-Fossil Fuel Obligation and China's RE tenders all failed to lead to substantial amounts of RE generation because many winning bids did not materialize.

Adjustments can be made in the tender structure to address such weaknesses.

- In Brazil's auctions, developers are required to put up 10 percent of the investment as assurance against the non-implementation of their projects, which serves as a penalty if they fail to supply the promised power.
- Green industry ambitions can be taken into account by organizing tenders for very large quantities that include minimum local content conditions; the scale of the investment provides the winning consortium with an initial guaranteed market for the output of the manufacturing plant it builds.
- To avoid overconcentration, region-specific tenders can be organized.
- To enable small-scale projects, some states carry out auctions specifically for small plants (see box 11.5). Others introduce open-ended FITs for small-scale plants while keeping larger plants within their quota or tender system.

Supporters of the tender regime insist that the competition for access to a limited number of PPAs drives the tariffs down to lower levels than under an open-ended FIT regime. However, the validity of that assertion depends on the existence of effective competition. Brazil's 2009 auction to contract for wind power for delivery in 2012 saw 13,000 MW of wind projects registering for the auction, but contracts were awarded for only some 1,800 MW of capacity. The average energy price of US$77/MWh was 21 percent below the initial auction price. A tender scheme operating under quasi-monopoly conditions will not generate such low prices. Second, the transaction costs associated with tenders are reflected in the bid prices. Therefore, the cost reductions per MWh of contracted RE power resulting from tenders will be modest. Reductions are highest when the information asymmetry between the developer's and the authorities' knowledge about the costs of production is high: the costs of a wind farm at an identified site can be estimated almost as well by outside experts as by the developer; for complex hydropower sites requiring in-depth studies, the information asymmetry is more acute.

Tenders for kWh Premium Payments

The Netherlands in 2010 announced its first tender for offshore wind energy of 700 MW of capacity. The award of the contract will go to the bidder asking for the lowest kWh premium (which will be financed from the annual state budget) to be paid on top of the conventional tariff paid through the electricity bills.

Renewable Portfolio Standards

Tradable Green Certificate Schemes to Fix RE Premiums

TGC schemes oblige either electricity generators or electricity suppliers to procure a certain percentage of their electricity supply from RE resources. The RE quantity expressed as a percentage of total supply increases year-on-year. Under the scheme, RE suppliers sell power on the bulk market and sell green certificates to suppliers in need of fulfilling RE quotas or to certificate traders.

The United Kingdom introduced its TGC scheme, called the Renewables Obligation, in 2002. The scheme imposes RE quotas on the suppliers of electricity to consumers: a 6.7 percent obligation in 2007, 7.9 percent in 2008, 9.1 percent in 2009, to reach the RE penetration target of 10 percent in 2010. ROCs are issued to generators per MWh generated from RE. At year's end, electricity suppliers must turn in certificates equal to the required RE percentage of their power sales to consumers. A fine is levied if the number of certificates is insufficient. The fine per missing certificate puts a cap on the price that certificates can fetch on the market. RE generators sign separate contracts for the sale of their power and the sale of their green certificates, either with the same off-taker or in separate sales.

The first quota schemes were hailed as the ultimate market-based instrument—the state creates the regulatory conditions for support, but not the terms of the support. In the United Kingdom, the state establishes the lifetime of the ROC system—until 2034—but not the length of the ROC sales contracts signed between RE generators and suppliers, nor their price, nor the price paid for electricity.[15] Therefore, as a result of the supposed superior ability of market forces to establish the right prices, tradable certificates were assumed to be capable of delivering RE at the lowest financial costs to electricity consumers.

That assumption overlooked the transaction costs imposed by the scheme on the cost of investment and the impact of price and revenue uncertainty on the cost of capital for RE projects. Countries switching from FIT regimes to green certificate schemes, for example, Sweden, saw that the price of the certificates was higher than the green premium implicitly provided under the previous FIT scheme.

The certificate scheme offers several advantages:

- The gradual, incremental penetration path prevents investment bubbles and their associated costs to consumers or to the public budget.
- The path provides a clear, quantified target for medium-term penetration of RE on the market.
- The scheme has, in theory, a lower risk of overcompensation than a FIT scheme: in well-functioning markets, falling prices for RE technologies lead to lower market prices for new certificates.
- It allows the cost burden of national RE penetration targets in federal states to be spread equally. Distribution companies in states with lower-than-average RE resource potential can purchase certificates issued to RE generators located in states with higher-than-average RE resource potential. This

burden sharing was the key motivation for the introduction of India's certificate scheme.

The certificate scheme has some weaknesses:

- It tends to favor least-cost RE technologies and established industry players unless separate technology targets or tenders are in place. It cannot easily handle the simultaneous promotion of multiple technologies, especially the introduction of new technologies still in the higher-cost end of development. The mechanism to promote a range of RE technologies with different production costs per kWh is rather awkward. In the United Kingdom, higher-cost RE technologies are awarded more certificates per generated MWh than lower-cost RE technologies: between 0.25 and 2 certificates more.
- As a result of the lack of price certainty in certificate schemes, countries with FIT policies tend to have lower RE tariffs than those with RPS policies.
- The complexity and high administrative costs of the scheme make it inadequate for small projects. The United Kingdom, therefore, introduced in 2010 a FIT for projects with a maximum size of 5 MW; other plants continue to be supported through the Renewables Obligation mechanism.
- Certificate schemes require an efficient and flexible supply chain and adequate high-quality RE resources to function properly. The mechanism is inefficient if only a limited number of RE projects are ready for development.
- The scheme must have a reasonably large RE market to provide the liquidity necessary for efficient price formation for the certificates. Denmark looked at the green certificate option in the early 2000s. Despite strong political interest, it was dropped. The Danish market was too small because the land-based wind farm potential was close to being fully exploited.

Renewable Portfolio Standard with Negotiated Supply

A directly negotiated PPA between a utility subject to an RPS and an individual RE project is feasible in some U.S. states, but the PPAs are subject to regulatory approval to ensure that the price is reasonable and does not impose an undue burden on consumers.

In March 2008, Chile adopted an RPS scheme, which went into force in 2010. The RPS is imposed on any generator company having an installed capacity of 200 MW or more. From 2010 through 2014, at least 5 percent of the energy traded by these generators must be produced by RE. Beginning in 2015 the quota increases 0.5 percent per year until reaching 10 percent in 2024. Only power from RE generation installed in 2007 or after qualifies.[16] To reach the target, generators can invest in their own RE capacity or purchase green electricity from independently owned RE generators or from utilities that have surpassed their obligations. Generator companies that fail to reach the RE share target are subject to a fine of US$28 for every MWh of RE power left undelivered. This amount rises to US$41/MWh if the target is missed a second time within three years.

Comparison of the Mandated Market Policies for Offshore Wind Farms

Denmark, Germany, and the United Kingdom apply different support mechanisms to make investments in offshore wind farms commercially viable. Germany applies its open-door FIT model, Denmark organizes single-site tenders for concessions that are awarded to the lowest tariff bid, and the United Kingdom organizes multisite tenders in which winners are identified through a "beauty contest"—a combination of quantitative and qualitative criteria used to identify the most suitable developer—and are remunerated through its ROC system.

In Denmark, the development of offshore wind farms follows a plan that has identified the most promising sites and the economic size of the wind farm at each site. To keep total support costs manageable, single-site tenders are arranged at intervals of several years. The Danish scheme relies on maximum transparency and simplicity to attract competitive bids. The 25-year concession for an offshore wind farm of a specific size in a specific area is offered to winning bidders through a tendering procedure, in which the only parameter is the price per kWh at which the bidder is willing to produce electricity. The area is not leased; the concession is only for the right to exploit the wind resources at the site. After the wind farm is connected to the grid, the wind farm will sell its power into the Nordic power pool; a premium will be paid on top of the market price so that the sum will be at the level of the bid price. For the 400 MW Anholt wind farm, which was awarded in 2010, the premium will be paid for the first 20 terawatt-hour (TWh (the output of the first 12–13 years), after which all revenue will come exclusively from the market price for the electricity sold.

The Danish Energy Agency is the single point of contact for interested bidders and for all administrative approval procedures. The agency ensures that the wind measurements at the site, preparatory geophysical investigations, and environmental impact assessments are completed before the tender and are part of the tender information, and that all required approvals have been secured. The Danish national transmission company is responsible for construction of the transmission line connecting the wind farm to the national and the European grid, which reduces construction risk and finance volume for the wind farm. The transmission company is required to pay compensation to the wind farm investor if the transmission infrastructure is not ready on time.

Denmark concluded its first two tenders at the low prices of DKr 0.0518/ kWh (about US$0.10/kWh) for a 200 MW farm in 2005 and of DKr 0.0629/ kWh (about US$0.12/kWh) at another 200 MW farm in 2007. These were the earliest larger-scale offshore wind farms and, therefore, attracted considerable interest among developers and wind turbine manufacturers wanting to gain experience and reference projects. By the time the 400 MW Anholt wind farm was tendered in April 2009, the situation had changed: it attracted only one bidder, the Danish energy company DONG, which in June 2010 was awarded the concession at its bid price of DKr 1.05/kWh (about US$0.20/kWh) for the first 20 TWh of production. Other potential bidders were discouraged mainly by the very short time given for the wind farm to become operational: the first wind turbine was to be operating by the end of 2012, the whole wind farm by the end of 2013.

The United Kingdom organizes multisite tenders of identified offshore wind farm sites for long-term leases with the British Crown Authority. The leasing fee is modest: £0.88/MWh (US$1.76/MWh)[17] for Round II projects. The United Kingdom has the largest and best wind resources in Europe and a much larger domestic power market than Denmark. These advantages make the multisite tenders feasible and economically rational. The size of the U.K. market and the long-term RE penetration targets allow large-scale investors to commit for the long term with a view to exploiting economies of scale and of scope in offshore wind farm development. General offshore environmental impact assessments and preliminary wind measurements are undertaken by the U.K. authorities before the tenders. The winners are selected on the basis of a beauty contest. Because the wind farms are compensated through the ROC system, which assigns two ROCs per MWh generated by offshore wind farms, the bidders are not asked to submit price bids for their output, but development plans for the site. The compensation level is based on the average price for ROCs during 2002–10 and average bulk power prices on the British market in 2010. The total revenue per kWh is about £0.134/kW (about US$0.22/kWh). The mechanism has proven its impact capability offshore: as of early 2011 about 1 GW of off-shore capacity was in operation, a further 4 GW was under construction, and concessions for projects with a total capacity of 32 GW were awarded in British Round III (Deloitte 2011).

Nevertheless, the British government is considering switching to FITs. Presumably, the complexity of the ROC system is one reason for the policy change. Price formation for the ROCs interacts with the EU's emissions trading system. When the prices for emission allowance units increase, the price for bulk power increases; therefore, the prices for ROCs should fall. But the impact is uncertain. Long-term price transparency is not a strength of the system and policy makers want to avoid the risk of heavy RE premiums.

The German open-door mechanism offers published FITs to the output of wind farms and leaves it to wind farm developers to identify relevant offshore sites, undertake all necessary investigations, and secure all approvals from involved authorities in both the state and national governments. Starting with a basic price of €0.13/kWh (about US$0.19/kWh), the FITs are graduated according to water depth and distance from the shore. At the end of 2010, Germany had 72 MW of offshore capacity in operation and 442 MW under construction. Applications have been submitted for projects totaling 26.5 GW; so far 7.5 GW have received approval.

See table 11.3 for a comparison of the policies.

Table 11.3 Renewable Energy Policy Review

	Quantity of RE development	Cost or price reduction	Resource diversity	Market sustainability	Local industry development	Investor certainty	Simplicity
FITs	Large amounts of RE in short time	Cost efficient if the FIT is periodically and wisely adjusted	Excellent	Technically and economically sustainable	Excellent	Can reduce investor risk with price guarantee and PPA	Simplest to design, administer, enforce, contract
RPS	If enforced, can meet realistic targets	RPS, if implemented through tenders, is better at reducing PPA tariffs for RE than if a "green certificate" scheme is used	Favors least-cost technologies	Technically and economically sustainable	Favors least-cost technologies and established industry players	Lack of price certainty difficult for investors; PPA can reduce risk	More complex to design and administer; complex for generators
Tendering	Related only to quantity of RE established by process	Good at reducing cost	Favors least-cost technologies	Tied to resource planning process; sustainable if planning supported and funding is stable	Favors least-cost technologies and established industry players	Can provide certainty if well designed (riskier than FIT)	More complex than FIT, simpler than RPS

Source: World Bank 2006.
Note: FIT = feed-in tariff; PPA = power purchase agreement; RE = renewable energy; RPS = Renewable Portfolio Standard.

Design and Implementation of Policies to Achieve Goals

Experiences with the different mechanisms indicate that no scheme is inherently superior to the others. None of the schemes enjoys a clear advantage. Each has its pros and cons. Sometimes countries switch from one mechanism to another, for example, from a FIT to a green certificate system or vice versa. However, it is more typical for a country to make adjustments to an applied mechanism to achieve, for example, a higher impact effectiveness, a more appropriate sharing of the subsidy burden, or a reduction in the cost of support per unit of power from new RE.

Impact Effectiveness
Market Expansion
The FIT is attractive to investors if (a) there is no market risk, (b) the project can be implemented any time during the year as soon as financial close has been secured, and (c) the formal procedure for signing the PPA with the system operator or local utility is simple. The FIT scheme, therefore, is capable of attracting a broader range of investors (small and large, professional project developers and ad hoc project developers, utilities, and independent power producers) than either RPS or tendering. The investor impact is one reason for the faster expansion of the market under a FIT—because of the larger number of investors, more projects and different categories of projects are implemented. The other reason is the absence of a limit on the amount of new capacity (except in schemes with caps on supported annual capacities). Because small players are included, the potential size of the market that can be developed is larger than in the other two mechanisms. The ability of the FIT to speed market development and maximize market size is unbeatable; it has a clear advantage in distributed generation. However, fast expansion is not attractive if it leads to a significant overshooting of the politically desired annual penetration target.

Green Industry Development
For early "green nations," the FIT proved to be the best instrument for promoting national green industries. Early entrants that succeeded in building sizable green industries—Denmark, Germany, and Spain—all used FITs. Those who used tenders or green certificates failed in their efforts to build green industries, for example, the United Kingdom and Ireland. Later entrants have found it more difficult to identify a clear winning mechanism, at least during the start-up phase. Emerging economies with potentially large national RE markets (and Ontario and Quebec among advanced economies) have used minimum domestic content requirements as a condition for accessing incremental cost support, using this as a means to promote transfer of technology and to build national green manufacturing know-how. Domestic content requirements can be and have been applied within both procurement tender regimes and FIT regimes.

Unlocking Commercial Financing for Clean Energy in East Asia • http://dx.doi.org/10.1596/978-1-4648-0020-7

Hedging against Volatility of Fossil Fuel Prices

The FIT and procurement tenders exploit one of the portfolio values of RE energy: to offer long-term fixed prices for power supply. Fixed FIT premiums provide zero-hedging benefits; flexible FIT premiums (full payment when the power market price hits a floor and zero payment when the market price hits a ceiling) provide some hedging benefits. The hedging benefit of RE power under a green certificate scheme is limited: in theory, green certificate prices should decline when power market prices go up; in practice, this feature is too uncertain.

Resource Allocation Efficiency

Transaction Costs

The FIT has the lowest transaction costs for investors and for public administrations; the green certificate scheme has the highest.

Cost of Support per Generated kWh

Supporters of procurement tenders and of green certificates emphasize the superiority of price discovery through the market. Supporters of the FIT, however, emphasize that the cost of capital (debt capital as well as equity capital) is lower for FIT schemes than for green certificate schemes and that this, together with low transaction costs, leads to lower overall compensation for RE power than under a green certificate scheme. This assertion was confirmed by an EU Commission study that compared experiences in Europe (Commission of the European Communities 2005). The average remuneration for RE power in a green certificate scheme promoting multiple RE technologies also suffers from the clumsy mechanism of allocating different quantities of RE certificates to RE technologies having different costs. The FIT, however, is vulnerable to political attempts at providing long-term price predictability for investors; but when tariffs are not changed in response to falling prices, or not changed sufficiently, high super-profits and runaway investment in new supply can result. This risk is particularly pronounced where the FIT has its strongest comparative advantage: grid-connected small-scale solar PV. Consumers can order and have systems installed on short notice. This is illustrated in figure 11.1.

Germany has implemented automatic price adjustments in response to demand development (an indirect method of price discovery). Italy, Spain, and the Czech Republic made ad hoc political decisions to reduce prices. Provided that there is sufficient competition—that is, that total supply exceeds the tendered quantity—the tender regime, as demonstrated by the reverse auctions in Latin America, is capable of providing RE supply at a lower cost than the FIT. In mid-2011, an auction in Peru resulted in prices ranging from US$69 per MWh for a wind farm to US$120 for a solar PV park; Uruguay's auction for wind power resulted in prices as low as US$63 per MWh, whereas wind developers in Brazil were awarded contracts averaging US$62 per MWh, making it the country's cheapest source of power. The same year, the FITs for onshore wind farms were €77/MWh (US$108/MWh) in Spain and €82/MWh (US$115/MWh) in France.

Figure 11.1 Net Present Value of European Feed-In Tariffs for Small Photovoltaic Systems and Average German Small System Cost

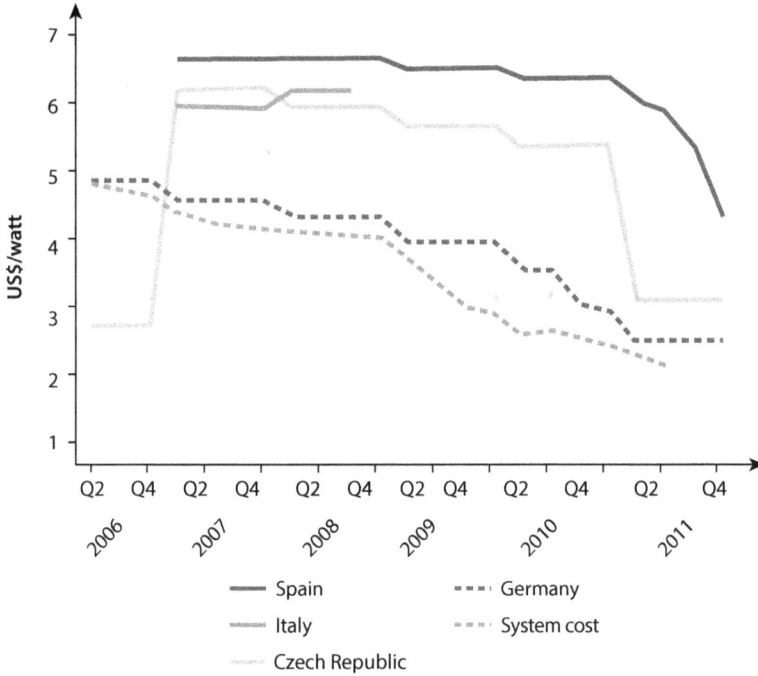

Source: BSW, Bloomberg New Energy Finance.
Note: Net present value calculated at 5 percent discount rate.

Table 11.4 Comparison of "Soft Costs" Affecting the Cost of Project Development

Scheme	Transaction costs	Investor risk
FIT	*Low:* No investment in tendering and in lengthy negotiations	*Low:* No market risk
Tradable green certificate (TGC)	*Medium:* Fees for TGC dealers and brokers; costs for negotiated long-term PPA prices or for day-to-day power pool sales	*Medium:* Risk of fluctuating market prices for electricity and for TGCs
Tender	*Medium/High:* Government for organization and implementation of tender; investor for preparation of bidding documents and time waiting for tender to take place	*Medium/High:* Risk of losing tender and that project implementation is delayed several years until tender prices have risen once the most resource-rich sites have been developed

The differences in risks and in transaction costs mean that projects have different financial cost curves under the three schemes (see table 11.4). The higher market risks and transaction costs of the mandated quantity schemes increase the cost of capital, and thereby, the RE plant's cost of production.

Market Distortion

Any mandated market scheme has a distortionary effect on the power market: RE output that is fed into the grid and supplied to the market irrespective of the prevailing demand-supply balance, and thus of the market price, distorts price formation in the market. Supporters of FIT premiums and of certificate schemes underscore that supply from RE generators is paid the prevailing market price. But this does not change the fact that RE supply, other than biomass-based power, is a function of resource conditions, not of market conditions.

Burden-Sharing Efficiency

Energy Poverty

Because of its dynamic deployment effect, in 2011 the FIT was costing German electricity consumers €13 billion (US$18.3 billion) in annual support; the cost for an average household amounted to €14 (US$19.70) per month. The income elasticity of demand for electricity is substantially lower than 1, meaning that increases in electricity prices impose a disproportionately large burden on low-income consumers. Taxpayer-pays mechanisms (investment grants, tax credits, and tax deductions) are, therefore, less onerous for low-income households than mandated market schemes. Among the taxpayer-pays instruments, the tender results in the lowest average tariff increase because of its ability to fix prices along the least-cost-first development path and because the amount of new supply each year is controlled. A FIT with prices fixed to achieve annual deployment close to the politically desired target will result in lower tariff increases than will a green certificate scheme. A FIT regime that is slow to react to changes in the market price for the supported technology results in runaway costs.

Regional Equity in Burden Sharing

In federal states, TGCs are seen as a way to encourage general RE portfolio standards to be applied in all states, with certificate trading allowing RE investments to take place in the states having the best RE resources. In countries applying national FITs financed via a public service fee on transmission, a regional burden issue occurs only in the sense that regions with the best resources receive the highest concentration of investments—and associated visual impacts on landscapes in the case of wind farms.

Hybrid Policy Approaches

FIT and RPS cannot be applied to the same RE technology, plant size, and market segment at the same time. However, Italy and the United Kingdom have implemented hybrid approaches in which a FIT is used for market segments, for example, small RE projects (less than 1–5 MW) that cannot be fully developed under an RPS system, whereas the RPS is used for larger, commercial-scale projects.

North-South Sharing of Incremental Cost Finance

The Global Energy Transfer Feed-in Tariffs for Developing Countries Program (GET-FIT) is a joint initiative of the German government and Deutsche Bank to assist the development of effective RE deployment strategies and schemes in developing countries. GET-FIT has developed an interesting concept for logically sharing the incremental costs of RE among the implementing countries. The basic premise is that clean energy provides global greenhouse gas mitigation benefits and conventional national energy policy benefits. Also, without a global warming issue, countries would invest in clean energy to pursue conventional policy goals such as security of supply, reduced dependence on imported fuels, local environmental improvement, price stability, employment creation, and development of new manufacturing and service industries. These ancillary effects of investments in clean energy provide benefits to the larger economy that partially or fully compensate for the incremental cost of clean energy compared with conventional power supply; they represent the "portfolio value" of RE power supply and of energy savings.

The *financial incremental cost* of RE power is equal to the difference between the revenue per kWh paid to RE power (RE cost of production) and the avoided financial cost of replaced conventional power supply. Because of the *external benefits (the portfolio value of RE power)*, the financial incremental cost exaggerates the economic cost of RE power to the national community. The *economic incremental cost* is equal to the financial incremental cost minus the portfolio value of RE power. GET-FIT suggests that the economic incremental cost be covered by donor grant financing, and that the national community cover the incremental cost equal to the portfolio value through various public finance instruments.

The mechanism can be implemented in various ways. Figure 11.2 shows one possibility. The chosen instrument is a FIT premium paid on top of the power market rate that the off-taking utility pays to the RE generator for power supply. Part of the premium is paid by the national state budget; the other part, the GET-FIT payment, by a donor-financed fund. A donor would guarantee the GET-FIT payment. Either the national government or a donor, depending on the national context, would guarantee the transfer of the premiums to the independent RE power producers.

Conclusions and Recommendations

Of three "mandated market" mechanisms, FITs have proven to be the most effective instrument for achieving high RE penetration in a short period. The green certificate scheme is clearly inferior—it imposes the highest transaction costs and the highest risk penalties on interest rates and on required returns on equity.

Investment grants and production tax credits can coexist with mandated market schemes to reduce the impact of an ambitious national RE deployment program on electricity tariffs.

Figure 11.2 Sharing of Incremental Cost Finance

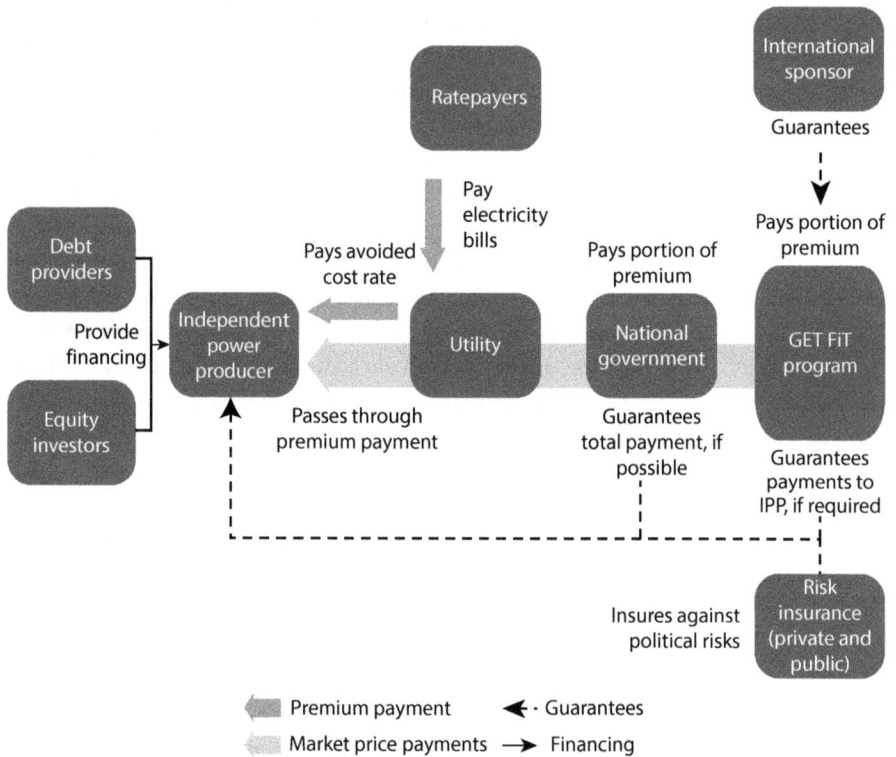

Source: DB Climate Change Advisors 2010.
Note: GET-FIT = Global Energy Transfer Feed-in Tariffs for Developing Countries Program; IPP = independent power producer.

The FIT's dynamic impact on market expansion has positive and negative aspects. The "explosion" of the German, Danish, and Spanish markets for wind energy in the 1990s, and later for solar PV in Germany and Spain, enabled the long-term cost-reduction potential of these new technologies to be realized. Cost reductions—at unchanged FITs—made less-attractive wind sites financially viable, expanding both the scope (geographic location) and the size of the potential market. A costly, but productive, interaction took place between the demand side, reacting to cost decreases with a high price elasticity of demand, and the supply side, reacting to the economies of scale generated by the increase in demand with further cost reductions, as predicted by learning-curve theory. However, the FIT requires deep pockets and high ambitions. When no limits are imposed on annual new capacity, FITs pose a risk of overshooting—the impact on annual market expansion might be higher than expected and higher than politically desired. The subsidy burden imposed on consumers (and in some countries, on taxpayers) by FITs that are higher than the cost of supply from conventional power plants can become politically intolerable.

The provision of support to grid-connected PV systems poses a problem for FIT schemes because solar PV is expensive and it is a mass-market technology; every house and landowner can become an investor. The market can expand very fast if generous tariffs are introduced. Between 2000 and 2009, global PV demand grew at an average annual rate of 51 percent, rising from 170 MW to 7,059 MW, reaching 19 GW in 2010 and 23 GW in 2011. Emerging economies wishing to apply FITs to solar PV systems must fix the rates at stingy levels to prevent subsidizing investments that would have taken place at a lower level of support, or even without support, and to control demand. Quarterly market monitoring is recommended so tariffs can be adjusted downward if demand exceeds the policy targets. The alternative of fixed annual caps with support being approved on either a first come, first served basis or through beauty contests dampens the positive impact of FIT and is less cost efficient.

Notes

1. Another example is the Chinese government's Solar Roofs Plan, under which the standard subsidy from the Ministry of Finance was 20 yuan per watt (US$2.93/watt).

2. US$ equivalents are provided for rough comparison throughout the chapter. Conversions are made using 2011 exchange rates unless the context clearly calls for a specific year.

3. The budget was also used for a targeted scheme to support the design and installation of solar systems on commercial, industrial, and iconic buildings, and to fund the training and accreditation of solar panel installers to meet the skills needs of the expanded program.

4. Larger manufacturers also participate, for demonstration effect reasons.

5. In fact, although not seen by the loan taker, this mechanism is used in the structuring of so-called mixed credits, wherein a third party pays a commercial bank the net present value of an interest rate reduction up front on a loan provided to an RE project.

6. There are also differences with respect to the FIT period: some countries pay the FIT for a specified number of years, others for a specified quantity of GWh per MW of installed capacity.

7. The Ontario FITS adopted in 2009 ranged from 104 Canadian dollars (Can$; US$91) per MWh for landfill gas plants larger than 10 MW to Can$802/MWh (US$702/MWh) for solar PV projects smaller than 10 kW.

8. France's solar PV program did not yield the expected green jobs impact because Chinese equipment modules captured the majority of the French market.

9. In Middle East and North African countries, the cost of investment per MW of new wind farms went up by two-thirds from €0.9 million (US$0.83) in 2003 to €1.5 million (US$1.39) in 2005–06; in the U.S. market the price of orders for new wind turbines fell 20 percent from 2008 to 2010. The spot price for PV system modules fell by 50 percent from third-quarter 2008 to first-quarter 2011. (As a rule of thumb, modules account for 50 percent of installed system cost.)

10. The prices set by the Wind Prices Notice do not differ substantially from the results of the fifth and last round of granted wind power concessions, and the pricing structure is similar to the on-grid prices that the National Development and Reform Commission had confirmed for provincially approved projects.

11. They are called reverse auctions because the buyer of the product organizes the auction, not the seller as in a conventional auction.

12. The average capacity factor of the winning bids for Brazil's auctions for power from wind farms in December 2009 and August 2010 is about 45 percent.

13. Of the 2.1 GW of wind power purchase agreements (PPAs) offered by Brazil in its 2009 and 2010 tender processes, about 670 MW are rated high risk from a deployment perspective because they offer expected returns on equity of less than 10 percent according to Bloomberg New Energy Finance.

14. The Irish and British RE tenders during the 1990s brought little in the way of manufacturing capacity.

15. An RE generator in the U.K. system is guaranteed ROC payments during a 20-year period. The annual price received for the ROCs is determined by market demand and supply. During 2002–10 ROC prices fluctuated between £39 and £54 (US$60 and US$83) per MWh; the average price was £45 (US$65). The average price for electricity on the British bulk power market in 2010 was £42 (US$67) per MWh (Deloitte 2011).

16. Reaching the 5 percent target is a challenge. As of mid-2009, Chile had commissioned 254 MW of hydro, 241 MW of biomass, and 20 MW of wind. But just 154 MW of this capacity was commissioned after January 1, 2007.

17. At 2007 exchange rates.

Bibliography

Bauer, Luiz, and Luiz Barroso. 2011. *Electricity Auctions and Overview of Efficient Practices*. Washington, DC: World Bank, ESMAP.

Commission of the European Communities. 2005. "Communication from the Commission: The Support of Electricity from Renewable Energy Sources." COM(2005) 627 final, European Commission, Brussels.

DB Climate Change Advisors. 2010. *GET-FiT Program: Global Energy Transfer Feed-in Tariffs for Developing Countries*. Frankfurt: Deutsche Bank Group.

Deloitte. 2011. "Analyse vedrørende fremme af konkurrence ved etablering af store havvindmølleparker i Danmark." Deloitte Business Consulting A/S. Medlem af Deloitte Touche Tohmatsu Limited, New York, NY. http://www.ens.dk/sites/ens .dk/files/politik/dansk-klima-energipolitik/politiske-aftaler-paa-energiomraadet/ energiaftalen-22-marts-2012/Deloitte%20-%20hovedrapport.pdf.

Opalka, Bill. 2010. "Feed-in Tariff Advances." *Renewable Biz Daily*, August 27.

World Bank. 2006. *Proceedings of the International Grid-Connected Renewable Energy Policy Forum*. Formal report 324/06. Washington, DC: World Bank.

Yuan Ying. 2011. "Burned by the Sun." *Chinadialogue* http://www.chinadialogue.net/ article/show/single/en/4232 April 14.

CHAPTER 12

Financing Mechanisms for Renewable Energy

Introduction

This chapter provides an overview of the financing mechanisms that can help overcome the barriers to renewable energy (RE) reviewed in chapter 9. The chapter discusses how the following instruments support the policy and regulatory framework for RE:

- Private sector innovations
- Liquidity support provided through public debt finance instruments
- Public support instruments for debt finance
- Mezzanine finance for both debt and equity support
- Financing of RE by consumers
- Public risk-sharing instruments
- Public RE funds and RE finance agencies

Private Sector Innovations in Renewable Energy Financing

This section provides examples of innovations in private finance for RE investments. The least expensive way to leverage private finance is to assist a country's finance industry in adapting successful models from elsewhere to local conditions.

Attracting Institutional Investors into RE Project Finance

Project finance hinges on finding investors looking for long-term assets to match the profile of their liabilities. The most important are institutional investors—insurance companies and pension funds.[1] Investments in RE are, in principle, an attractive asset class: they offer relatively good risk-adjusted returns and long duration, and are not highly correlated with capital markets. However, in many developing economies institutional investors either do not exist or limit their investment activities to the purchase of government debt. Getting their funds involved in RE finance requires some creative structuring of project finance by project sponsors.[2]

The financing of wind farms poses a particular challenge. Because they are large, more costly per MW of installed capacity, and riskier than onshore wind farms, putting together a financing package for an offshore wind farm is not easy. Project risks are highest in the planning and construction stages. Unlike onshore wind farms, offshore wind projects lack fixed-price turnkey contracts. Projects are developed under a multicontracting strategy in which the developer is liable for the interface risk between the contractual packages. For these reasons, investments in offshore wind farms have been funded primarily through utilities' balance sheets. Once the plant enters stable production, the risks are lower; at that point, institutional investor appetite arises for investments in operational assets. The new demand for investment in the operational assets is used by utilities to refinance their projects after commissioning.

DONG Energy used balance sheet financing to invest in its first wind farms, usually in partnership with other utilities. To finance the Anholt offshore wind farm, DONG, one of the world's most experienced offshore wind farm developers and operators, chose a different course (see box 12.1). The jointly owned special purpose vehicle elegantly manages the different rate-of-return expectations of the project developer (as high-risk investor) and of the pension funds

---

Box 12.1 Pension Fund Finance for Construction of the 400 MW Anholt Offshore Wind Farm

In 2010, the Danish company DONG Energy won the Danish Energy Agency's tender for the 25-year concession for the 400 MW Anholt offshore wind farm project. DONG's bid asked for a feed-in tariff of €0.135/kWh (US$0.18/kWh)[a] for the first 20 terawatt-hours (TWh) of production, after which the wind farm will sell its power in the commercial power market. The first turbine is to be operational by the end of 2012, the last by the end of 2013. The required investment was estimated to be DKr 10 billion (about US$1.9 billion). In March 2011, DONG sold ownership of the concession to a special purpose vehicle, a joint venture company (JVC) created by DONG (50 percent) and the two Danish pension funds PensionDanmark (30 percent) and PKA (20 percent) to finance and own the project. The pension funds acquired their stakes in return for a total joint investment of DKr 6 billion (US$1.1 billion). The JVC has signed a fixed-price construction contract and a 12-year operations and maintenance contract with DONG. DONG's rationale was to increase its investment capacity for the development of other wind farms, which is how DONG can create the most value. The pension funds improved the time and risk profiles of their financial investments because the construction and operation risks are taken by DONG; the average annual revenue can be predicted with high certainty. The return on investment compares favorably with alternatives. The average annual returns from Anholt over the wind farm's 20-year lifespan are expected to be at least double the current Danish bond yields of just above 3 percent.

a. US$ equivalents are provided for rough comparison throughout the chapter. Conversions are made using 2011 exchange rates unless the context clearly calls for a specific year.

(as low-risk investors). The special purpose vehicle has acquired the concession from DONG and finances the project investment. The pension funds purchased their 50 percent ownership stake in the joint venture company (JVC) for DKr 6 billion (US$1.07 billion) from DONG, which, therefore, needs to self-finance only 40 percent of the DKr 10 billion (US$1.78 billion) project finance. DONG collects its developer's premium up front (compared with selling shares in the project after commissioning) and limits its corporate debt exposure during construction to DKr 4 billion (US$0.17 billion) instead of DKr 10 billion (US$1.78 billion). The reduced debt exposure increases DONG's investment capacity for developing other wind farm projects—the activity for which DONG, the most experienced offshore wind farm developer and operator in the world, can achieve maximum value creation. Another important element of the offshore business is the construction contract between the JVC and DONG: it commits DONG to deliver the wind farm at a fixed price by a fixed date. This feature transfers the construction risk out of the pension funds' financial investment into the JVC. The JVC's operation and maintenance contract with DONG does the same for the operational risk. These two risk reductions enabled the pension funds to go into construction-stage financing. Structuring the finance for the Anholt project was not easy: the contracts comprise close to 10,000 pages.[3]

Institutional investors have an alternative entry point for construction-stage financing of RE projects: investment in an infrastructure investment fund. However, by directly investing in RE projects along with an industrial partner instead of via an infrastructure fund, institutional investors avoid paying high management fees and gain greater control. Therefore, it is not surprising that institutional investors expand their investments through individual RE projects. However, interesting new infrastructure fund mechanisms are evolving that improve their relative attractiveness. An example is New Earth, which invests in new waste treatment and recycling projects that are undertaken by a single industrial collaborating partner.[4] Financing projects that are developed, owned, and operated by a specific partner with a solid track record makes it easier for institutional investors to assess the associated risks.

Green Bonds for Attracting Retail and Institutional Investors

Climate bonds, also called green bonds, are issued to raise capital to fund specific projects aimed at reducing climate change risk. Some green bonds finance mitigation investments directly; some pay coupons tracking the performance of environmental indices such as the carbon price; some provide commercial and development banks with capital to finance green investment projects. Green bonds are increasingly being used to raise finance for RE and energy efficiency (EE) investments: as of early 2011, some US$12 billion of bonds backed by investments related to climate change solutions had been issued internationally.

When banks face constraints in providing long-term lending, green bonds, either company bonds or asset-backed securities backed by the cash flows generated by an RE project or by a portfolio of RE projects, are an interesting finance mechanism for RE project developers. Because they are considered safe assets, and some institutional and small-scale household investors want to have at least a certain percentage of their portfolios invested in sustainable and socially responsible assets, green bonds can attract premium prices from niche investors.[5] They are, therefore, a price-competitive means of raising long-term finance while offering socially conscious investors higher returns overall than government bonds. Asset-backed securities are generally used to refinance projects that are generating positive cash flows, but they can also be issued as project bonds ahead of construction.

Retail bonds are marketed to household investors and sold in small denominations to enable these investors to invest even with a small amount of start-up capital. The retail demand enables bonds to be issued in the €5 million (US$7.04) to €20 million (US$28.14) category, thereby allowing mid-size project developers to tap the bond market. Box 12.2 provides an example of a company retail bond. Box 12.3 gives an example of a project retail bond. Small bond issues are not tradable on capital markets, making them a very illiquid form of investment. However, in Japan, household demand for green bonds is large enough to provide a market for large bond issues[6] as well as for the creation of asset management funds that invest in green bonds collectively on behalf of household investors.[7]

Box 12.2 Green Company Retail Bond

Corporate bonds are essentially a loan to a company, under which the sum invested by the bondholders will be repaid at maturity. In May 2011, the RE company Wind Prospect Group, wholly owned by its 200 staff, launched a corporate retail bond onto the U.K. market with the aim of raising £10 million (US$14 million). The bonds are not tradable in capital markets. The bonds, launched under the name ReBonds, pay interest of 7.5 percent per year, with an additional 0.5 percent interest payable to bondholders that subscribe for £10,000 (US$16,200) or more; minimum investment is £500 (US$810). Interest is payable semi-annually until the original sum is repaid at maturity. The repayment date is four years after the issuance date, at the bondholders option, or each anniversary thereafter. Each bondholder wishing to be repaid must give at least six months written notice before the repayment date. Funds raised by the ReBonds are distributed to Wind Direct or to other U.K. subsidiaries within the Wind Prospect Group. Wind Direct specializes in providing green electricity directly to industrial and commercial clients, locating wind turbines on site, and supplying electricity directly to clients under long-term (up to 10 years), fixed-price, green electricity power purchase agreements. The first £6 million (US$9.7 million) of ReBond revenue are to fund Wind Direct's two–wind turbine, 2 MW wind farm project at South Staffordshire College. Output in excess of demand at the college is sold to the grid. In the end, Wind Direct managed to raise just £2.3 million (US$3.7 million) of the hoped for £10 million (US$16.2 million) bond.

Sources: ReBond Invitation Document (http://www.rebonds.co.uk/ReBonds_Invitation_Document_FINAL_230511.pdf); *Environmental Finance*, July 28, 2011.

Box 12.3 Unrated Retail Eco-Bonds to Finance Project Equity

As of mid-2011, the U.K. RE utility Ecotricity had 4,000 business and 41,000 residential customers and operational RE power capacity of 58.6 MW of wind turbines, with 152.3 MW in the planning stage. Ecotricity has a 15-year track record and a £44 million (US$71.2 million) balance sheet. Ecotricity's RE projects are typically financed with a mixture of 20 percent equity and 80 percent debt. Ecotricity raises the debt portion from banks, with an interest rate of about 6 percent. Ecotricity could access mezzanine debt carrying a 13–15 percent interest rate to finance the equity portion of its projects. However, since 2010, Ecotricity has turned to retail bond issues as a lower-cost way of raising finance for its equity needs. In December 2010, Ecotricity issued a £10 million (US$16 million) bond with the intention in 2011 to build 20 MW of wind and solar projects, investing a total of £35 million (US$56.7 million). Ecobond One closed in December 2010 almost two times oversubscribed: Ecotricity's retail customers as well as noncustomers bid to buy £9 million (US$14.6 million) of bonds. The company allocated 70 percent of the four-year bonds, paying 7.5 percent interest, to customers, and the rest to noncustomers at 7 percent interest. Although the bond was unrated, this handicap was overcome by the combination of a good track record, a good balance sheet, and interest rates far superior to those paid on bank deposits. Apart from raising capital, the bond issue served the strategic purposes of offering benefits to its customers and of advertising its existence to noncustomers. Ecobond Two closed in December 2011.

Source: Environmental-Finance.com (accessed July 2011).

Green bond issues of €100 million (US$140.7 million) and more target the international capital market, particularly institutional investors, offering the liquidity they require. Issuers of green bonds include RE project developers, development banks,[8] commercial banks,[9] state governments in the United States,[10] and municipalities.

Banks' willingness to engage in RE and EE lending would be increased if they had an exit route out of project finance, that is, if it were possible for primary loans issued by banks to RE and EE projects to be packaged and resold in secondary markets to pension funds, to institutional investors, and to individuals. However, since the subprime loan scandals in 2008–09, securitization has had a negative connotation. The intrinsic structural flaw in the loan-securitization market—the ability to earn substantial fees from originating and securitizing loans, coupled with the absence of any residual liability—skews the incentives of originators in favor of loan volume rather than loan quality. However, because the RE project market is much more transparent in its price setting and revenue generation than the housing market, the structural flaw poses a very low risk in RE securitization.

As a result of their flexibility on both the supply side and the demand side, green bonds can be introduced in quite a few countries as an effective instrument to attract national capital, from institutional investors as well as retail investors, into the financing of RE projects. The section on public risk-sharing instruments includes examples of finance-enhancing instruments enabling the introduction of green bonds for project finance.

Aggregation through Third-Party Finance

Providing limited-recourse finance for small RE projects is rarely possible. In general, small projects are too small for local banks to bother with on a project-finance basis. A portfolio of projects with a standard financing approach can create the necessary critical mass. Energy service companies are well-known aggregators for EE investments; third-party photovoltaic (PV) financing is a similar mechanism applied for RE.

In third-party PV financing, a solar power company or PV installer offers to install a PV system at no up-front cost to a customer on the customer's premises. In return, the customer signs a power purchase agreement (PPA) with the PV system installer for the purchase of the plant's output at rates guaranteed to be equal to or lower than the tariffs charged by the local utility. The solar power company retains ownership of the system and responsibility for maintenance; the PPA revenues serve as lease payment. At the end of the PPA, ownership of the PV system transfers to the customer. The length of the PPA is calculated to allow the installer to recoup the investment costs and earn a reasonable profit. Because the mechanism requires a minimum deal size to justify the transaction costs, third-party PV installers seek customers with unshaded roofs or site areas suitable for a 200 KW or larger PV system. Potential customers are commercial, residential, and public buildings with unshaded roof areas of at least 2,000 square meters.[11]

Private Insurance Products

The international insurance industry has reacted to the large volume of annual RE investment worldwide by introducing a range of insurance products tailor made for the needs of the RE industry.

Banks are concerned with the effect of the variability of annual output on the ability of generators to pay interest and installments on the loans. This concern has led to the introduction of weather derivatives and weather insurance. Insurance4renewables offers case-by-case coverage for RE projects, including carbon delivery guarantees, carbon counterparty credit risk insurance, and lack of sun or wind insurance.

Insuring green technology assets helps persuade banks to offer loans and technology firms to create investor confidence in their products. Munich Re, the world's biggest reinsurer, agreed in July 2011 to insure a Japanese solar module maker's liability for the performance of its products. Under the accord, Munich Re will insure the panel maker, Solar Frontier K.K., a unit of Showa Shell Sekiyu K.K., for as long as 20 years to cover any unexpected, substantial loss of quality. Solar Frontier started commercial operations in July 2011 at a 100 billion yen (US$1.26 billion) factory in southern Japan.

Public Debt Finance Instruments

Direct Project Finance from Development Banks
The Double Leverage Effect from Development Bank Loan Finance

Financial transfers from government budgets (raised from private citizens through taxation) provide development banks with the equity capital needed for reaching investment grade status, as long as the banks follow prudent loan practices. An investment grade rating enables a development bank to issue bonds on international capital markets, increasing finance options for its loans to investment projects and programs. The finance raised from international capital markets is the first-order leveraging effect of the government's original equity capital contribution. The second-order effect is achieved when loans from development banks to private RE projects attract cofinance—both private equity and commercial debt finance. (see figure 12.1).

Senior loans from development banks for RE investments are called for in any of five circumstances:

- To meet RE project demand for long-term finance in countries where national banks are prevented from doing so by finance sector regulations,
- To meet demand for RE finance in areas where commercial banks are not active yet,
- To act as bank syndicator for large-scale RE project finance,
- To serve as a safety net for a minimum of RE finance when overall lending is restricted in uncertain financial climates, and
- To provide long-term finance to RE projects at lower rates than the national capital market is capable of providing.

Figure 12.1 Development Bank as an Instrument for Leveraging Private Capital

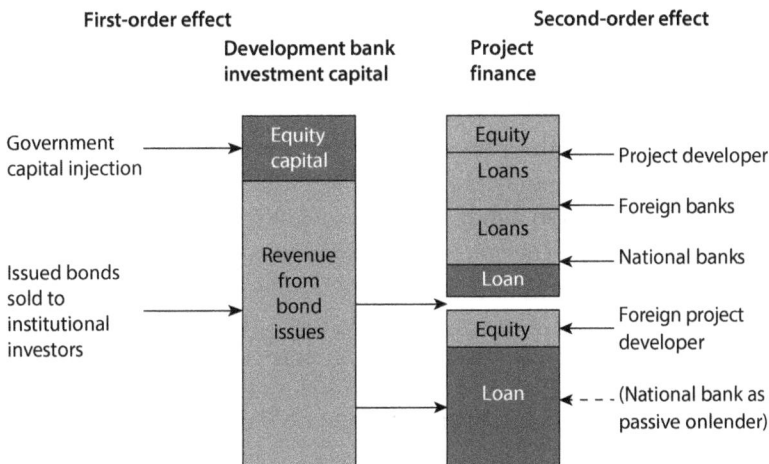

Project Finance from Multilateral Development Banks. Financial sector regulations in some countries restrict banks to maximum loan tenors of four to seven years. In the absence of local long-term finance, development banks may provide direct loans to RE projects without involving national banks.[12] The same approach can be used in the absence of limited-recourse finance, attributable to unfamiliarity either with the concept or with new RE technologies. Such a situation provides a clear goal and strategy for public finance interventions. The goal is to use the demonstration effect to attract commercial banks—investments in RE will become a recognized asset class based on the track record of sustained returns to RE projects. The loan investments will also be strategically used to introduce new RE technologies and, together with grant-financed technical assistance (TA), build technical and financing capacity, and develop commercial models and contracts for RE finance and project development. An example of the direct project finance mechanism is the European Bank for Reconstruction and Development's (EBRD's) Ukraine Sustainable Energy Lending Facility (USELF). USELF integrates its direct project financing with a comprehensive TA package (see box 12.4). Assembling a solid TA finance facility for building a project pipeline is key to the success of a direct lending facility. A second key factor is to have a competent manager who actively markets the finance facility in the country. In the USELF, the project development efforts of the facilitation team are closely monitored by a local ERBD officer as well by an officer in London who makes loan approval recommendations before formal decisions by the EBRD Board. The officer follows each project from the time it passes the facilitator's preliminary screening and has been issued a mandate letter.

Loan syndication is needed for financial close in large-scale projects. The participation of a development bank in loan syndication facilitates local bank participation because the local banks can piggyback on the development bank's experience in RE project finance; foreign banks find the participation of development banks in project finance politically reassuring. Examples of successful syndication in RE due to development bank participation are plentiful: the European Investment Bank (EIB) and the German development bank (KfW), participated in the financing of most offshore wind farms in Europe up to 2011. The Asian Development Bank (ADB) and the World Bank pioneered RE project finance in Asia, and the African Development Bank, among others, did the same in Kenya with the Lake Turkana project. The International Finance Corporation (IFC), the EBRD, the EIB, and KfW pioneered RE project finance in several Eastern European countries. A specific example is the syndication by the IFC and the EBRD of loans to wind farm projects in Romania developed by EDP Pestera Wind Farm, a wind energy company majority owned by a Romanian unit of EDP Renovaveis, a Portuguese clean energy developer. Commercial banks had been skeptical about Romania's regulatory framework and the country's willingness to honor the obligation to finance feed-in tariffs throughout the period stipulated in government regulations. However, because the IFC and the EBRD each lent some €91.1 million (US$128.2 million), commercial banks lent another €50 million (US$70.4 million).

Box 12.4 Technical Assistance to Accompany Direct Lending

Ukrainian energy policy includes targets for higher penetration of RE in the power supply. For a country of its size, Ukraine has relatively modest RE sources, and the regulatory framework for RE is still under development. The Ukraine Sustainable Energy Lending Facility (USELF) was established by the EBRD to foster RE power generation projects in Ukraine, including hydro, wind, biomass, biogas, and solar. Lending volume is a maximum of €50 million (US$70.4 million)[a] from EBRD and €20 million (US$28.1 million) from the Clean Technology Fund (CTF). USELF offers project developers loans ranging from €1 million (US$1.4 million) to about €15 million (US$21.11 million), with EBRD's loan share financing up to 50 percent of RE project investment; CTF's loan portion is additional (project developers see one combined loan). Interest rates are at market conditions and maturity is up to 12 years for the EBRD loan and possibly longer for the CTF loan, with the latter offering a grace period.

USELF is structured to provide financing directly from the EBRD for small and medium projects using a simplified and rapid approval process, thus reducing transaction costs. A facilitation team located in Kiev vets applications for finance from projects and assists project developers in making projects bankable for EBRD evaluation and approval. The no-cost TA from international and local experts provided through the team to project developers is comprehensive and includes improvement of feasibility studies and documents required for project appraisal, support in permitting and licensing processes, support in commercial negotiations related to agreements required by developers, legal support for preparation of loan documentation, and support for overall management of project development and preparation. In addition, training is provided to local consultancy firms and banks. A separate regulatory support project under USELF finances TA to Ukraine's National Energy Regulatory Commission. The TA is funded by a Global Environment Facility (GEF) grant of US$8.45 million.

Source: USELF website.
a. US$ equivalents are provided for rough comparison throughout the chapter. Conversions are made using 2011 exchange rates unless the context clearly calls for a specific year.

Project Finance from National Development Banks to Provide Low-Cost Finance. Specialized RE development banks such as the Indian Renewable Development Agency (IREDA) and New and Renewable Energy Authority in Egypt are used as on-lending conduits for foreign concessional loans. The intention is to kick-start a process that later brings in private capital. In the IREDA case, local commercial banks quickly became involved in financing wind farms (see box 12.5). During the 1990s and early 2000s, nominal interest rates in the finance markets in India were very high because of high inflation. IREDA's access to loans at concessional rates allowed it to offer loans at very competitive rates. But when falling inflation brought down the nominal interest rates offered by commercial banks, IREDA lost its competitive edge in its product pricing, and consequently market share. IREDA needs to charge interest rates and fees at close to market rates to survive as a viable lending institution. However, the demonstration effect of IREDA's initial investments had an impact on commercial banks. Even more important for commercial banks' involvement in RE lending was the RE support instrument

---

Box 12.5 The Indian Renewable Development Agency (IREDA)

IREDA was founded in 1987. Its business purpose is to promote environmentally friendly energy generation by granting loans. IREDA is a public limited company under the administrative control of the Ministry of New and Renewable Energy. IREDA functions as a specialized financial intermediary by operating a revolving fund for promoting and developing RE projects. IREDA receives its funds from loans from development agencies and international financial institutions, and from loan repayments from clients. IREDA offers innovative financing schemes, such as project financing of up to 80 percent of costs, equipment financing of up to 75 percent of costs, and other types of medium- to long-term debt (up to 10 years), with interest rates in 2010 in the range of 10.25–12 percent. During fiscal year 2008/09, IREDA disbursed 7.7 billion Indian rupees (US$160 million).

IREDA introduced initiatives to help overcome credit availability barriers in the rural market for solar photovoltaic (PV) systems, including arrangements for leasing systems and providing loans for PV through existing microfinance organizations. IREDA also assists the State Bank of India, Canara Bank, Union Bank of India, Bank of India, and Bank of Baroda to formulate schemes for EE lending to small and medium enterprises (SMEs) and is now extending special lines of credit to state electricity boards to implement projects to renovate and modernize thermal power stations.

As a result of IREDA's efforts, many commercial banks now play an active role in financing the established forms of RE (mainly wind energy) in India. Originally, IREDA was almost the only lending institution in this field, but its market share in RE financing decreased to 13 percent in fiscal year 2007/08 and to a mere 8.6 percent in wind energy. However, IREDA needs to maintain a presence in the established subsectors to generate income with which to promote less-established, higher-risk sectors such as concentrated solar power plants and other new RE technologies.

---

used by the Indian government during the 1990s and early 2000s—accelerated tax write-offs for wind farm investments and low wheeling charges to places of auto-consumption. Industrial corporations were thus able to invest in wind farms using balance sheet finance with loan finance provided by their normal commercial bank connections.

Project Finance from National Development Banks as a Tool to Promote National Manufacturing of RE. The Brazilian National Economic and Social Development Bank (BNDES) has a prominent position as a provider of finance to the RE sector. Its financing of RE power projects and bioethanol plants is part of the government's tender programs for RE projects, in particular the PROINFA program from 2002 to 2008 and ANEEL's tenders for RE power that started in 2009. BNDES gets its RE finance from a number of funds it manages, for example, the Constitutional Financing Fund of the Northeast (FNE) and the Northeast Development Fund (FDNE). Access to BNDES finance serves two policy objectives. One is to keep down the cost of RE power from winning bids. The other is to promote foreign investment in the RE value chain: to benefit from subsidies and BNDES finance, projects under PROINFA had to fulfill national content requirements. Law 10762 mandated a minimum national content of 60 percent in total construction costs. BNDES could finance up to 70 percent of capital costs (excluding site acquisition) at the basic national interest rate plus 2 percentage points and up to 1.5 percentage points. Interest is not charged during construction and tenor is 10 years. BNDES's RE lending amounted to US$2.4 billion in 2007, US$7 billion in 2008, and US$6.4 billion in 2009. Regionalization criteria limit each state's share to a maximum of 20 percent of total capacity for wind and biomass and 15 percent for small hydro.

Development Bank Finance to Accelerate Syndication and Safeguard Finance of a Steady Flow of Investments. The German government's decision in May 2011 to phase out nuclear power by 2022 adds to the urgency of realizing the country's potential for grid-connected RE power. The development of more than 20 GW of wind farms in the German North Sea and the Baltic Sea is a key element in the government's strategy. However, some experts doubt that the investments in the North Sea and in the required transmission systems to transport power from the north to southern Germany can be built in time. Thus, the primary objective of KfW's finance facility for offshore wind farms in Germany (see box 12.6) is not financial sector transformation: the German financial sector's expertise in RE project finance is strong.

Dedicated RE Credit Lines Provided by Development Banks

Dedicated RE credit lines finance smaller-scale RE projects such as grid-connected RE power plants up to 20 MW and end-user RE systems. They often finance end-user EE projects as well. In the RE credit line mechanism, a local commercial bank (or a number of banks) is used as an on-lending vehicle. The bank can be a "pure" on-lender of received funds or an active cofinancier: the award of the credit line to a participating bank is in most cases made conditional

---

Box 12.6 KfW's €5 Billion (US$7 Billion) Facility for Offshore Wind Farm Finance

KfW launched its program to support offshore wind development in June 2011. KfW can cofinance projects for up to 20 years in three ways: (a) direct lending as part of a bank syndicate, to a maximum of €400 million (US$563 million) per project or 50 percent of total capital requirements; (b) a financing package comprising a direct loan and an on-lent loan, via an intermediary, up to €700 million (US$984.9 million) per project and 70 percent of total financing; or (c) a direct loan for financing contingent additional costs arising during the installation phase, of up to €100 million (US$140.7 million). By August 2011, KfW had committed €264 million (US$371.5 million) to the Meerwind offshore wind farm project.

Source: KfW website.

---

on its topping up the received funds with 25–100 percent cofinancing from own funds.

Credit lines have three major uses in the removal of barriers to finance:

- To increase participating banks' commercial interest in RE finance through the liquidity impact of providing the banks with access to extra external sources of funds on attractive terms, enabling them to expand the volume of their lending business;
- To remove constraints on participating banks' ability to lend long term caused by mismatches between the average maturity of their in-loans and their out-loans; and
- To remove the obstacle of high costs of finance on the commercial market by combining the credit line with an investment grant facility.

The attraction of this mechanism is that participating banks will also continue their involvement in RE finance after termination of the credit line project. Transaction costs for project pipeline preparation may also be lower than in direct lending because the collaborating commercial banks' established networks can be used to identify and work with RE technology project developers.

The success formula for the RE credit line mechanism is well established: (a) carefully select participating financial institutions (PFIs) through a competitive process with well-defined criteria; (b) have at least three PFIs and preferably more, so developers can shop for the best deal; (c) have a grant facility for TA to support project pipeline building, capacity building of PFIs in due diligence appraisal of RE projects, and capacity building of local project developers and consultants; and (d) contract with a competent management team to operate the project management unit. If there are several PFIs, the project management unit is located independently; otherwise it is placed within the PFI.

The World Bank–financed Turkey Renewable Energy Project is an example of a well-designed project combining an on-lending facility with comprehensive TA support (see the case study in chapter 21). An example of a project offering a refinancing facility to participating banks is the World Bank–financed Vietnam Renewable Energy Development Project.

The World Bank and Global Environment Facility (GEF)–financed Renewable Energy for Rural Economic Development (RERED) project in Sri Lanka and its predecessor, the Energy Service Delivery project, are examples of a credit line to satisfy PFIs' need for long-term finance (see box 12.7). In Sri Lanka, interest rate subsidies or investment grants are not needed for grid-connected systems because the feed-in tariff regime was tailored to make investments commercially viable under market interest rates by providing a higher tariff during the initial years (see box 11.3 in chapter 11).

In the Dominican Republic, the longest repayment period banks are able to offer averages five to seven years, just as in Sri Lanka. A loan loss provision, determined by the Dominican Bureau of Internal Revenue, requires banks to set aside a high allowance in case of customer default (in the absence of a guarantee

---

Box 12.7 RERED Sri Lanka RE-Financing Credit

The RERED project was designed to on-lend funds through participating credit institutions (PCIs) to subborrowers undertaking RE subprojects (grid-connected RE power projects with capacity of about 10 MW or less, off-grid village-based RE power projects, solar home systems) and EE investments. The RERED project was supported by a US$115 million World Bank loan and a US$8 million grant from the GEF (for project support and investment grants for solar home systems) for the 2003–11 period. The government of Sri Lanka, in consultation with the World Bank, appointed DFCC Bank as the RERED Project Administrative Unit (AU) to implement the project. RERED had six PCIs, one of which was DFCC. To avoid conflicts of interest, the AU was independent of and separated from the PCI function of DFCC Bank. The AU, with a staff of six, was responsible for the administration of the International Development Agency (IDA) credit line and GEF grant funds, and provision of project support. Two Special Disbursement Accounts were maintained at the Central Bank of Sri Lanka to receive the proceeds of the IDA credit and GEF grant. The PCIs approved subloans to project beneficiaries using their own credit evaluation procedures. Once approved, PCIs forwarded loan refinance applications to the AU, requesting commitment for a maximum of 80 percent of the approved subloan amount. After the PCI disbursed funds against the approved subloan amount, the AU disbursed the approved 80 percent.

By mid-2011, the project had financed 130,721 solar home systems (SHS) with a cumulative capacity of 5.8 MW. Some 71 grid-connected projects with a capacity of 168 MW electrified 7,500 households through isolated grids served by micro-hydros with a total capacity of 2 MW.

---

facility) and makes banks hesitant to move into RE lending. Banco BHD is the only commercial bank that provides a credit line for RE, EE, and cleaner energy production. Its move into the sector was supported by loan finance from the IFC and a GEF grant for TA. BHD's credit line offers low-interest (about 5.5 percent) medium-term loans (repayment within five years with a one-year grace period) for small to medium project developers, with 80 percent of the project's investment cost available for financing. BHD markets the facility and is responsible for credit appraisal and approval. BHD has set up a TA facility for project development. The TA facility provides technical expertise (resource assessment, feasibility studies, and the like) and business assistance to developers through the project preparation process. As of mid-2011, BHD had started lending to fuel-switching projects but not yet to RE projects.

Contingent Project Development Grants

A contingent grant that transforms to a loan if the project is successful allows development activities to proceed without the developer risking defaulting on loans if the project cannot be implemented for reasons outside the developer's control. Contingent grants finance project development costs on a cost-shared basis, covering no more than 50 percent of estimated project development costs. To prevent overcharging, contingent grants are typically awarded as fixed amounts. The contingent grant addresses two barriers. First is the shortfall of finance for project preparation and development. The second is risk sharing: uncertain country environments make private developers reluctant to take on the full development risk; resource risks are particularly high in geothermal power projects; environmental risks can block hydropower; and wind farm projects suffer from the "not in my backyard" effect.

Some assistance programs apply a different philosophy by providing development support as a loan that converts to a grant if the project is successfully implemented. The stated philosophy for the approach is that it creates incentives for the developer to implement the project rapidly. The argument has a certain logic: some project developers are more interested in selling the rights for a project than in its construction and may delay project implementation waiting for better prices. However, this mechanism cannot be recommended because the risk sharing is too awkward—public finance participation has no upside if the project succeeds, and the investor faces a double financial hit if it fails.

Public Underwriting Support for High-Priority Infrastructure Projects

In July 2009, the government of the Australian state of Victoria selected a consortium for the construction and operation of a desalination plant at Wonthaggi, to be completed by the end of 2011. The project's construction costs were $A 3.5 billion (US$3.6 billion), making it the world's largest public-private partnership announced in 2009. A long-term off-take agreement with Melbourne Water, an entity wholly owned by the Victorian government, to purchase all water produced by the plant provides long-term revenue certainty for the project. Despite this arrangement, the project sponsor was unable to raise a significant part of the financing required by the time the winning consortium was announced. The shortfall was $A 1.7 billion (US$1.75 billion), equal to 46 percent of the project's capital costs. In response, the Victorian government provided a "Treasurers Guarantee of Syndication," by which the state government agreed to lend the funding shortfall at commercial rates if the project sponsor was unable to raise the amount by financial close. The debt shortfall was ultimately met by lending banks.

Public underwriting of project finance to ensure that high-priority infrastructure projects succeed is an exceptional instrument: participants in tenders are expected to be able to secure financial close. However, the outcome of the desalination project indicates it was a wise strategic decision that, in the end, cost taxpayers nothing, yet enabled the presumably best project for taxpayers and consumers to be implemented without delay.

Bank Deposit as Liquidity Guarantee

In 2002, a liquidity guarantee was structured for Uganda's West Nile rural electrification project as a means to overcome the hurdle of a regulation imposed by Uganda's central bank that limited the longest maturity of bank loans in Uganda to eight years. The government of Uganda had switched to a private sector–led approach to rural electrification, in which a multitude of agents were to develop and implement rural electrification projects. Engagement of commercial banks in the cofinance of rural electrification projects was a necessity for the sustainability of this decentralized electrification approach.

The West Nile Rural Electrification Company won a 20-year distribution concession for the isolated regional grid in the West Nile region, which included operating a 1.5 MW thermal generator and constructing a new 3.5 MW hydro generator. To enable the concession to be commercially viable under the feasible tariff revenue, roughly 80 percent of the total investment cost was covered by rural electrification grants financed by the government, assisted by a World Bank loan. The remainder of the finance was to be provided by investor equity and a bank loan from the investor's (the Aga Khan Foundation's) normal bank connection, Barclays Bank, through its Uganda branch. To match the conditions of the loan finance with the long-term nature of the investment, a two-step loan backed by a liquidity guarantee was chosen. The amortization profile of the 7-year loan was calculated as if it had a term of 14 years, but with a bullet payment of the outstanding principal to be paid at the end of the loan term. The bullet repayment was to be paid by a new 7-year loan provided by Barclays Bank to the concession holder at the end of the seventh year. The arrangement was to be backed by a liquidity guarantee as either a deposit placed by the project in a bank account, which, with interest payments, was to grow to the amount of the bullet payment within 7 years, or the purchase of a zero-coupon bond[13] by the World Bank with a redemption value, at the 7-year point, equal to the required bullet payment. If liquidity problems were to occur, Barclays could draw the amount, but otherwise it was expected that Barclays would provide the loan without calling on the liquidity facility, which then would be used to cofinance other rural electrification projects. In the end, Barclays Bank provided the loan without the liquidity facility being established.

The liquidity facility guarantee removes the risk for the project developer of the lending bank not having the liquidity to provide a new loan after eight years. However, establishing a liquidity facility guarantee for a single project is not an elegant solution: the transaction costs are too high and the leveraging effect too modest. Because a cash-type instrument was used, it required a large sum. After 7 years, the remaining principal on a 14-year loan will be in the range of 67 percent of the original loan principal. Depending on the effective yield on the zero-coupon bond, the purchase price of the bond will be in the range of 65 percent of the planned seventh year redemption value (based on a 6 percent yield). Therefore, the cash required to purchase the bond, or the original bank deposit, is on the order of 45 percent of the total loan amount.

In general, liquidity guarantees make sense only for a portfolio of projects, allowing the liquidity reserve to be lower than the total guaranteed liquidity reserve. The effort made in the West Nile case must be understood in view of the long-term strategic objective of giving commercial banks in Uganda experience in rural electrification finance.

Public Equity Finance

Medium and larger companies can fund RE project preparation and development through balance sheet finance. But balance sheet finance is not feasible for smaller-scale project developers and for start-up technology companies, meaning they have no access to bank loans to finance project preparation and development. Instead, they have to find sufficient equity, which can be difficult because few outside equity investors are willing to risk capital in early-stage projects or in small and medium enterprise (SME) business development activities. Public equity finance is thus used to cover two financing gaps: (a) capital for project preparation and development and (b) equity capital for start-up clean energy technology firms.

Direct Equity Investments in the Preparation of Larger-Scale Projects

Investors in large-scale RE projects can be reluctant to provide preconstruction support, needing to limit the amount of such investment on the balance sheet. For this reason, the Crown Estate in the United Kingdom participates with up to 50 percent in joint ventures for the development of offshore wind energy projects. The Crown Estate moves out of the project once it reaches financial close.

Equity Funds for Investing in RE Project Development

Equity funds for clean energy, ranging in size from US$50 million to US$250 million, typically invest a minimum of US$5 million and up to US$35 million in individual projects. Thus, they are relevant for medium to larger-scale RE projects only. Equity funds have high management costs. Fund managers typically charge a fixed annual management cost of 2–2.5 percent of committed capital and a performance fee of 20 percent of profits beyond a minimum. The equity fund instrument makes sense only in countries that have moved to a stage in their energy policies in which investors can see the emergence of a profitable and large clean energy market. Otherwise, there is no basis for the operation of private equity funds—the fixed annual management costs are too high to allow slow investment uptake.

Equity funds specializing in assistance to project developers and start-up RE technology firms offer the target group not only equity capital but often also management expertise.

Three approaches for public equity involvement can be seen. One is to invest in a fund of funds that, in turn, invests in private equity funds investing in clean energy projects. A second is direct investment in a private equity fund. The third is to set up a public-private equity fund to be managed either under a contract arrangement awarded through competitive bidding or by a private equity company co-investing from the beginning as lead investor.

The Global Energy Efficiency and Renewable Energy Fund (GEEREF), set up in 2008 by the European Union, Germany, and Norway, is a fund of funds that primarily invests in RE and EE infrastructure funds and similar investment structures in the African, Caribbean, and Pacific regions, non-EU Eastern Europe,

Latin America, and Asia. The committed €108 million (US$152 million)[14] is to be invested during 2009–12. GEEREF typically invests less than €10 million (US$14.1 million), a market niche usually ignored by private investors and international finance institutions. GEEREF is advised by the European Investment Bank Group, the EIB, and the European Investment Fund.

In 2010, Berkeley Energy's Renewable Energy Asia Fund (REAF)[15] received commitments from six emerging-market institutional investors—BIO, Commonwealth Development Corporation, Calvert, Deutsche Investitions und Entwicklungsgesellschaft, GEEREF, and FMO—enabling REAF's first closing of €50.7 million (US$67.3 million); the target fund size for REAF is €150 million (US$199.1 million).[16] With investments ranging from €5 million (US$6.6 million) to €25 million (US$33.2 million), REAF aims to take controlling stakes in project developers and in development-stage RE projects in wind, small hydro, biomass, and solar power, and in geothermal and landfill gas; transform these investments into operating portfolios; and generate superior returns through successful exits. The fund's geographical focus is primarily India with additional target markets including the Philippines, Sri Lanka, Thailand, and Vietnam.

InfraCo Asia Development Pte. Ltd. (InfraCo Asia) is managed by InfraCo Asia Management Pte. Ltd., a private sector infrastructure development company.[17] By acting as a principal project developer, InfraCo Asia aims to stimulate greater private investment in infrastructure development in low-income countries in South and Southeast Asia. InfraCo Asia focuses on smaller-scale projects (up to US$75 million). InfraCo Asia aims to reduce the entry costs of private sector infrastructure developers by acting as principal, taking an equity stake in the project to shoulder the risks of early-stage development costs, and providing development expertise through its team of experienced developers. InfraCo Asia also arranges project debt and equity capital from third parties, as well as from other InfraCo affiliate programs. InfraCo Asia retains an equity stake in the projects it develops to provide market confidence through the early operating period.

Equity Capital for Early-Phase RE Technology Firms and Clean Energy Businesses

The European Commission's 2007–13 Competitiveness and Innovation Framework Program has several schemes and a budget of more than €1 billion (US$1.4 billion) to facilitate access to loans and equity finance for SMEs where market gaps have been identified. The program's financial instruments are implemented for the commission by the European Investment Fund on a trust basis. The High Growth and Innovative SME Facility (GIF) provides risk capital for innovative SMEs, including clean energy firms, in their early stages. It has two windows.

- *GIF 1 covers early-stage (seed and start-up) investments in specialized venture capital funds* such as early-stage funds; funds operating regionally; funds focused on specific sectors, technologies, or research and technological development; and funds linked to incubators, which in turn provide capital to SMEs. Co-investment in funds and investment vehicles promoted by business angels is also permitted. The European Investment Fund can usually invest 10–25 percent of the total equity of the intermediary venture capital fund or up to 50 percent in specific cases.

- *GIF 2 covers expansion-stage investments by investing in specialized risk capital funds*, which in turn provide quasi-equity or equity to innovative SMEs with high growth potential in their expansion phase, avoiding buy-out or replacement capital for asset stripping. The European Investment Fund can invest 7.5–15 percent of the total equity of the intermediary venture capital fund or, exceptionally, up to 50 percent.

The ADB made an equity investment of US$20 million in the Clean Resources Asia Growth Fund, targeting private equity investments in promising clean energy technology companies. The private equity fund, sponsored by CLSA Capital Partners, a brokerage and investment group active in Asia since 1986, targets businesses engaged in clean energy–related operations in Asia, mainly focusing on China and India. It will make 12–14 investments, taking significant minority positions in the companies in which it invests. The targeted fund size is US$200 million.

The U.K. Innovation Investment Fund is a public-private fund of funds cofinanced by the U.K. government and private financiers. The managers are Hermes Private Equity and the European Investment Fund. It invests in funds covering low-carbon and clean technology, digital technology, information and communications technology, life sciences, and advanced manufacturing.

Attracting Private Equity Firms into Seed Finance

Seed finance is targeted to the early-stage investment phase of a clean energy business. The objective of the Seed Capital Assistance Facility (SCAF; see box 12.8) is to pull private equity capital funds and venture capital funds into the seed capital phase (which they normally would not consider), as a means to build portfolios of new projects for their own investment. The tool for this is cost-sharing grant instruments. SCAF has signed two SCAF Cooperating Fund Agreements in Asia, one with Berkeley Energy, a private equity fund focusing on wind and small hydro project development in the Philippines, Sri Lanka, and India, and the second with Aloe Group, a venture capital fund focused on new clean energy technologies and business ventures in India and China. SCAF provided support to five other fund managers to help develop new clean energy funds with an early-stage focus—Yes Bank, IndiaCo, E+Co, Low Carbon Investors Asia, and Conduit Capital. In 2011 in Africa, SCAF signed an initial Cooperating Fund Agreement with Evolution One, and results are just beginning to appear. In India, Aloe Group conducted an investment forum as part of the Renewable Energy Finance Forum–India conference, while IndiaCo has run

---

Box 12.8 Seed Capital Assistance Facility

Seed Capital Assistance Facility (SCAF) is a GEF-funded initiative of the United Nations Environment Programme (UNEP), the Asian Development Bank (ADB), and the African Development Bank, operating in cooperation with the European Investment Bank (EIB). SCAF helps venture capital and private equity fund managers to include portfolios of early-stage-focused seed transactions within their overall investment holdings. SCAF aims to mobilize private investment for early-stage project development and ventures. SCAF shares a portion of the project development and transaction costs for each seed investment that fund managers make in first-time clean energy projects. The SCAF Enterprise Development Support Line is used to share some of the elevated costs associated with deal sourcing, providing enterprise development services to and transacting seed-scale investments. Each cooperating fund manager decides which services to offer based on the local context; however, the common elements of these services generally involve (a) identification and training of new, precommercial, clean energy entrepreneurs and project developers; (b) targeted coaching or incubator services for specific promising investment opportunities; and (c) cofinancing of pre-investment feasibility studies.

Enterprise development support comes in the form of annual fees, limited to between two and three years, which is the normal time for seed-financed developments to become full-scale investments. This support is provided as a contingent grant, requiring that the cost-shared activities lead to corresponding investments by the fund's seed window. The SCAF Seed Capital Support Line is designed to help offset the higher perceived risks and lower expected returns when dealing with early-stage clean energy project and enterprise developments. The level of support is negotiated with each cooperating fund manager and then paid on a standard basis with each project. Typically, the support is in the range of 10–20 percent of each seed capital investment, paid at the time of investment disbursement. This support is used to cover some of the elevated project development costs that normally are charged to or financed by the developer, for example, technical assessments, contract negotiations for fuel-supply or off-take agreements, environmental impact analysis, and other aspects of the permitting process.

Cooperating fund managers to date are Evolution One (Southern Africa), the DI Frontier Market Energy and Carbon Fund (Southern and Eastern Africa), Berkeley Energy (South Asia), and Aloe Private Equity (India and China). In total, these four funds are capitalized at approximately US$550 million. Each public-private partnership arrangement involves about US$1 million of project development grants from SCAF disbursed against US$5 million of seed financing from the fund, helping leverage about US$200 million of construction-stage financing for RE or EE projects.

---

a business plan competition for new EE ventures, both providing enterprise development. In South Africa, the Evolution One fund has provided seed funding to a development company called RedCap to undertake permitting and other development for a 100 MW wind farm project in the Eastern Cape province.

Mezzanine Finance: Debt and Equity Support

Mezzanine finance is a term used for very flexible forms of debt finance that take higher risks than normal debt finance and are compensated by higher rates of return. Mezzanine finance is the most versatile of all public finance instruments. One major form is subordinated debt: a subordinated loan stands behind other investors upon insolvency or winding up. The second is quasi-equity in the form of convertible loans with patient and very flexible repayment terms. These instruments are used to cover two very different finance gaps.

- The first gap is the inability to secure debt because commercial finance institutions consider the risk of default too high. Subordinated debt provides 10–25 percent of a project's sources of funds. A subordinated loan reduces the amount of senior debt and improves the senior lender's loan-to-value and debt service coverage ratios.
- The second is an equity finance gap that occurs when the investor's equity is insufficient to comply with the minimum equity requirement for loan eligibility, or when a start-up technology company or a start-up project developer is unable to access commercial loan finance at all. A convertible loan is unsecured debt, requiring no collateral; instead, lenders have the right to convert their stakes to equity ownership in the event of default on the loan.

A mezzanine loan to a project can close both gaps, enabling an investor to get a project financed with a lower equity percentage (e.g., 20 percent instead of 30 percent) than is normal and with the senior loan financing a lower percentage (e.g., 55 percent instead of 70 percent) of total project cost than in an average RE project in the country.

Subordinated debt can also be used to extend the effective term of loans, thus improving both project cash flows and project viability.

Subordinate Loans to Leverage Senior Loan Finance

In normal circumstances, a bank's administrative costs for a loan transaction are the same regardless of whether another bank cofinances a project. Cofinance of project debt is of interest to commercial banks only when loan syndication is a necessity because the size of the required loan is larger than allowed by the bank's policy for exposure to individual loans. However, cofinancing by a development bank using a subordinated loan provides two benefits to the senior lender. One is the reduction in lending risk provided by the subordination, because the senior loan has priority access to a borrower's assets in case of loan default. The risk reduction can enable an RE project to come within the risk limit of a bank's lending policy, enabling the responsible loan officer to engage in a risk project the bank otherwise would have shied away from. The other is to allow the senior loan-giving bank to piggyback on the RE project experience of the development bank providing the subordinate loan. The fact that an experienced development bank has sufficient trust in a project to engage in subordination provides added comfort to the senior lender's decision to engage and reduces the bank's costs for due diligence.

The subordinated loan instrument can be useful in the early phases of RE promotion and in connection with the introduction of new technologies previously not tested in the project country. It is also useful in later phases if no partial risk guarantee (PRG) facility can be accessed.

Closing Equity Finance Gaps for Small-Scale RE Power Projects

A prime virtue of mezzanine finance provided as a convertible loan is its flexibility. Unlike conventional loans, its repayments need not be tied to a fixed amortization schedule. It can be structured with equity-like patient capital features. For example, the amortization on mezzanine finance for start-up SMEs developing RE technology or providing RE-related services can be structured as royalty payments: a fee per product sold until the mezzanine loan, including interest, is repaid.

In RE project finance, this flexibility is an advantage for RE power plants, such as wind farms or mini-hydropower plants, with variable resource flows from year to year. The Central American Renewable Energy and Cleaner Production (CAREC) mezzanine finance fund managed by E+Co assists in financing projects that are shut out of commercial financing by high collateral and project equity requirements. CAREC finances up to 25 percent of project capital costs for RE projects, offering either unsecured loans or additional project equity. The terms of CAREC finance are matched to a project's revenue stream, and loan payments come out of revenues net of operating costs and senior debt service.

The difficulty with equity finance is that small-scale power projects are not attractive to professional project development companies or to power utilities; both look for projects of 50 MW or greater. Entrepreneurial project developers who are interested in small-scale projects and often undertake the first steps toward their preparation frequently have insufficient equity capital to secure financial close. The French government's willingness to make mezzanine finance, rather than a partial credit guarantee, available, is probably linked to the long French tradition of public-private co-investments in industry; the U.S. government most likely would have chosen the partial credit guarantee instead. Management of Fonds d'Investissements de l'Environnement et de la Maîtrise de l'Energie (FIDEME) insists that the mezzanine finance investment provided a better— positive—return to public coffers. See box 12.9.

Consumer Finance of Renewable Energy

Finance Facilitated through Electricity Bill Invoicing

Several countries, as well as state and local governments in the United States, have given investment grants—or rebates, as they are called for consumer goods—to RE systems at homes and offices. Consumers apply for rebates at the time of purchase of equipment and systems. In some countries, the rebates are given under demand-side-management programs and paid for with public

Box 12.9 FIDEME

FIDEME (Fonds d'Investissements de l'Environnement et de la Maîtrise de l'Energie) is a public-private mezzanine fund open to French SMEs that face gaps in either debt or equity. FIDEME shows how "double-leveraged mezzanine finance" can address lack of investor equity in project finance. Although the French government had introduced feed-in tariffs for projects up to 15 MW for wind farms (among others), few projects were developed because interested project developers were unable to secure sufficient equity. In 2003, the French Environment and Energy Management Agency (ADEME) and the French commercial bank Natixis launched FIDEME, a €46 million (US$42.3 million)[a] public-private mezzanine fund. ADEME invested €15 million (US$13.8 million), one-third of FIDEME's capital, as a subordinated tranche within the private fund, providing a first loss guarantee to the private senior lenders in the fund. The fund then provided subordinated financing (convertible bonds or bonds with share warrants attached) to projects to help sponsors fill the gaps in debt or equity and attract senior lenders. A typical finance structure would be composed of 80 percent senior debt, a 10 percent FIDEME mezzanine loan, and 10 percent developer equity. The fund was open to French RE SMEs who faced gaps in debt or equity (or both) on their balance sheets, and was based on the concept of non-additionality, meaning that if FIDEME did not finance the project, it would not have been implemented.

The double-leverage structure allowed ADEME to mobilize €320 million (US$286.6 million) in investment, more than 20 times its public funding contribution. By the end of 2006, FIDEME had financed 27 RE projects with a total capacity of more than 300 MW in wind power, biomass, hydro, and geothermal energy. The estimated internal rate of return was 10 percent, whereas the initial target had only been 7 percent. This success led Natixis to establish a follow-up in 2008, EUROFIDEME2, this time on a purely commercial basis because the RE market in France had matured beyond the need for public finance support. Natixis put €25 million (US$36.6 million) into the fund, with a target of €250 million (US$366.2 million) including contributions by other financial institutions.

Source: Mostert 2010.
a. US$ equivalents are provided for rough comparison. Conversions are made using 2011 exchange rates unless the context clearly calls for a specific year.

benefit funds collected as fees on consumer purchases of electricity from utilities. In other countries, for example, for Tunisia's solar water heater support program, the rebates are financed by the state budget. See box 12.10.

Lowering Barriers to Bank Entry into RE Consumer Finance

The United Nations Environment Programme's (UNEP's) solar loan program in India (box 12.11) drew inspiration from innovations introduced by SELCO, a solar home system (SHS) developer active in several developing countries, including India. Equity investment for SELCO's subsidiary in India was provided by E+Co (along with others). E+Co also provided a bank guarantee allowing SELCO to access funds for direct consumer financing. SELCO pioneered several methods to engage local participating banks. First, using its own funds, and in some cases, grant funding, SELCO paid banks a small fee for each loan closed,

---

Box 12.10 Tunisia's PROSOL Program

In 1995, Tunisia's market for solar water heaters (SWH) was less than 1,000 square meters (m^2) per year. A GEF-supported project, which provided an up-front subsidy of 35 percent to the systems, succeeded in growing the market to 17,000 m^2/year by 2001. The disappearance of the GEF subsidy after 2001 led to a 50 percent drop in the annual market. A contributing factor was the perceived poor quality of the installed systems. This trend changed with the launch in 2005 of the PROSOL program, which applied a well-conceived and integrated approach combining demand-side and supply-side actions. PROSOL was implemented by Tunisia's Ministries of Industry, Energy, and Small and Medium Enterprises, and the National Agency for Energy Control in close collaboration with the National Power Company (NPC), the financial sector, and SWH installers.

PROSOL focused initially on the promotion of 200- and 300-liter SWH systems for residences, with the aim of installing 500,000 m^2 by 2009. The financial and technical assistance support provided by PROSOL was cofinanced by the state, the GEF, the UN Development Programme, and Italy's Mediterranean Renewable Energy Program. Financial support to SWHs comprised a direct investment subsidy as well as an interest rate subsidy. The subsidy for SWHs was TD 100 (€59) per m^2 up to a total of TD 400, which amounts to 19 percent of the installed price of a 200-liter, 2 m^2 SWH (priced at TD 1,100) and to 22–27 percent for a 300-liter, 4 m^2 system (priced at TD 1,500–1,800). The purchase of a 2 m^2 SWH costing TD 1,100 was financed by the subsidy of TD 200 and a consumer cash payment of TD 150; the remaining TD 750 was financed by a five-year bank loan with an interest rate of 7 percent instead of the usual 14 percent, which would be repaid through a surcharge on the consumer's monthly electricity bill. The interest rate reduction was achieved partly by a US$2 million GEF grant and partly by the power company administering amortization of the loan on behalf of the banks: it reduced the banks' transaction costs and eliminated the need for collateral. Supply-side actions were also undertaken to increase annual production capacity as well as the quality of SWH. In 2006, Tunisia had 11–13 SWH dealers (manufacturers and importers) and more than 380 "solar energy installers." In principle, the installers are authorized—the National Agency for Energy Control conducts short (1–3 day) training courses for installers—but in practice, the authorization criteria were applied softly to avoid slowing market development. The National Agency for Energy Control also provided training courses to SWH consultants to certify them for determining the appropriate systems for commercial buildings and for supervising the construction work. Consumers received one-year guarantees for installation, five years for the water tank, and ten years for the solar collector. The NPC, with offices in all districts in the country, provides information about the program to consumers. The residential program was later supplemented by a program targeting hotels.

---

helping to address high transaction costs and thus keeping loan pricing attractive for borrowers. Second, SELCO provided a small security deposit to the banks equal to two months of loan payments; these funds were deposited with the loan amount and applied to the borrower's last two monthly payments. The deposits, therefore, perform two functions, adding security for the lender and an incentive

---

Box 12.11 India–UNEP Solar Loan Program

The objective of the program was to motivate commercial financial institutions with large numbers of offices in rural areas to engage in financing SHSs. The program used two public finance instruments: an interest rate subsidy for borrowers, distributed through participating local banks, and transaction cost support in the form of a fee paid to participating local banks for each closed loan. Simplified application procedures were used to process the loans to make them more appealing to the targeted households. Grant funds were used for training and other capacity-building activities, including qualification of SHS vendors. The UNEP interest rate subsidy did not cover the interest rate per se, but was calculated as an amount to buy down the interest rate (for example, from a 12 percent commercial rate to 6 percent) over the term of the loan. The local banks still lent to borrowers on a commercial rate basis. The calculated subsidy amount, equal to two to six monthly loan payments on a five-year loan, was placed on deposit with the bank and applied to offset the borrower's last monthly payments. Hence, the customer would get the subsidy only after successfully repaying the loan. The banks received training and assistance in business planning and marketing of the SHS loans. The partnership between the vendors and the banks, and the subsidized loans, helped to increase the sales of SHSs to a level that made lending for SHSs commercially interesting for the banks even after termination of the program.

The program disbursed about 19,500 loans, with participation by 2,076 bank branches and five qualified vendors.

---

to the borrower to complete monthly payments so as to earn the discount represented by these funds. Third, SELCO also provided a buy-back guarantee to the local banks to repurchase the SHSs from borrowers that default. This is a contingent liability, not on SELCO's balance sheet.

Public Risk-Sharing Instruments

Finance institutions classify RE projects as higher risk for the following reasons:

- Lack of full competitiveness on the market, making the projects dependent on policy and regulatory support;
- Higher capital intensity than conventional energy technologies;
- Newer, less proven technologies; and
- In some cases, small project size by project finance standards.

These factors make risk-reduction instruments an effective tool for leveraging private finance.

Publicly Backed Guarantees to Attract Commercial Debt Finance

A publicly backed guarantee is a contractual obligation whereby a government, against payment of a fee, assures compensating payment to a lender or an investor in case of default on an obligation to which another party is committed. Whereas insurance involves two parties, guarantees involve interlocking contracts between three parties.

Partial credit guarantees are contracts between lender and borrower (loan agreement) and between guarantor and lender (guarantee agreement).

Partial risk guarantees (PRGs) are contracts between guarantor and investor or lender and between guarantor and the host country government (for example, a commitment to pass a law introducing feed-in tariffs).

Publicly backed guarantees can assist beneficiaries by providing them access to finance, reducing their cost of capital, and expanding loan tenor or grace periods to match project cash flows. In some cases, these qualities make publicly backed guarantees complementary to other public finance instruments; in others, publicly backed guarantees are the least-cost alternative as a stand-alone public finance instrument.

Guarantees to RE Project Loans

If a guarantee facility's ability to pay claims is to be credible, the facility must have a large portfolio and a solid capital base upon which to draw. Guarantors must keep enough money in an account to cover the contingent liability of the loan guarantee, that is, the present value of the expected payouts on the guarantee, inclusive of any recovery in liquidation (from selling the project's assets). An outside counter-guarantee facility could help establish the necessary credibility. The normal procedure, when a loan guarantee for a specific program with multiple loans is set up, is to establish a first loss guarantee facility.

The U.S. federal government's loan guarantee program has been a particularly important risk-reduction instrument for projects implemented in the wake of the 2008–09 global economic and financial crisis (see box 12.12). The eligibility criteria of the Section 1705 loan guarantee program were expanded to include RE projects using well-known technologies as a means to encourage RE investments when the willingness of banks to take on risk, and their lending ability, had become sharply reduced. A large number of wind farms, concentrated solar power plants, and solar PV power plants had signed committed PPAs with utilities, but without loan guarantees, private commercial banks could not have provided debt under the long terms and with the interest rates needed to match the PPA contracts. In addition, loan guarantees were a condition of drawing debt financing from the U.S. Federal Financing Bank.

Guarantees to Loans for High-Tech Start-Up Firms

To promote green job creation, the U.S. government's loan guarantee program also gave guarantees to the debt financing of investments in new clean technology firms. Three American solar power companies went bankrupt in August 2011: Solyndra, Evergreen Solar, and SpectraWatt. Solyndra and Evergreen suffered because they pursued innovative technologies whose competitiveness depended on their using less polysilicon, the main material for solar panels. That became less important because polysilicon prices tumbled more than 80 percent

---

Box 12.12 Guarantee to Multiyear PV Investment Program

NRG Energy Inc., an independent power producer, was awarded a conditional loan guarantee from the Financial Institutions Partnership Program of the U.S. Department of Energy for a US$2.6 billion distributed solar PV program, named Project Amp. The guarantee covers 80 percent of US$1.4 billion in debt facilities provided by the Bank of America, which will use a structured loan disbursement method that takes into account project size, risk, and capital intensity. The four-year program aims to install rooftop solar PV projects with a total capacity of 733 MW on 750 industrial buildings owned by Prologis Inc., the world's largest warehouse manager. The systems will feed electricity into the grid rather than supply power to the buildings upon which they are built. An initial 15.4 MW installation in southern California will sell power to Southern California Edison Co. NRG has agreed to provide equity financing for the program over 18 months and has a right of first offer to fund the remainder. Prologis also invests in each phase.

Source: Bloomberg New Energy Finance.

---

over three years as output caught up with demand. Because these companies had received loan guarantees for hundreds of millions of dollars—Solyndra received US$535 million in federal loan guarantees—the program was heavily criticized by Republican politicians as yet another example of wasteful use of taxpayers' money. Yet, one must expect that guarantees to high-risk but valuable projects will be called upon; in some cases high-tech gambles fail; for example, private investors risked US$1 billion on the Solyndra project, more than the government.

The Republic of Korea is setting up a US$97 million guarantee fund for investments in small RE companies. The fund can provide guarantees equivalent to 12 times its face value, meaning it could provide guarantees to as much as 1.24 trillion won (US$1.16 billion)[18] in debt finance. Finance for the fund is raised from power generators, energy distributors, and banks. The Korea New & Renewable Energy Association, acting on behalf of the contributors, receives applications, and an eight-member recommendation committee will create a short list and propose them to the two specialized guarantor organizations, the Korea Credit Guarantee Fund and the Korea Technology Finance Corporation, that manage the fund. Successful applicants will get five-year guarantees on as much as 10 billion won (US$9 million) in loans, and pay lower fees and interest rates.

Wrapping of Project Bonds to Attract Institutional Investors into RE Project Finance

Project bonds are issued after project commissioning to refinance the costs of project development and construction. Because of their risk characteristics, project companies are generally not able to issue investment grade bonds until completion of construction and confirmation of operating results. Compared with the United States, where projects in the energy and infrastructure sector have access to debt capital markets, the depth of the institutional market is low in other countries, making banks the major providers of RE project finance. However, the progress on the path toward low-carbon economies calls for more active involvement of institutional investors in project finance through the bond finance market, requiring that issued project bonds achieve investment grade status (at least a BBB rating from Standard & Poor's or a Baa rating from Moody's): financial sector regulations permit banks and institutional investors to invest only in investment grade bonds. Institutional investors have a preference for AAA and AA (high credit quality) bonds rather than for A and BBB (medium credit quality) bonds. Before the 2008–09 financial crisis, the investment grade status requirement was fulfilled by having capital market issuances in the RE sector be insured by monoline insurers with AAA credit ratings. The credit rating of the insurer was implicitly transferred to the insured bonds; insured or guaranteed bonds are called "wrapped bonds." The analytical work of the insurer permits institutional investors to invest in wrapped RE project bonds without having the specialist expertise to appraise complex RE project structures. However, most monolines lost their AAA credit ratings during the financial crisis, and this source of insurance cover dried up.

The Risk-Sharing Finance Facility (RSFF) was set up by the European Commission with a €1 billion (US$1.4 billion) contribution from the EIB and the same amount from the Commission's 7th Research Framework Programme (2007–13). The credit risk sharing between the European Community and the EIB extends the ability of the EIB to provide loans or guarantees to investments with higher risk profiles. Under the RSFF, the EIB can accept exposure to higher credit risks than under its normal lending activities, either in the form of counterparts with a higher risk profile or through transaction structures involving higher financial risks for the EIB. The RSFF enables the EIB to lend more than €10 billion (US$14.1 billion) for the targeted types of project investments. The share of EIB financing is limited to 50 percent of the total amount of eligible project costs.

The innovative project bond finance facilitated by the EIB for SunPower Corporation's Montalto di Castro solar park is one outcome of the RSFF (see box 12.13). The EIB and SunPower Corporation investigated the possibility of a loan syndication arrangement with private Italian banks, with the EIB providing its debt finance as a junior loan to the senior loans provided by private banks. That option was dropped for two pragmatic reasons. One was that the banks were unwilling to provide project loans with a tenor of 18 years on terms acceptable to the project owner. The banks insisted on either providing a senior loan of 18 years but retaining the right to revise its pricing after 8 years, or on the hard term of requiring a new loan to be negotiated after 8 years. The other reason was the banks' demand for higher equity cofinance than the project owner was interested in. Instead, it was decided to involve institutional investors in the finance by issuing a project bond, using RSFF resources to strengthen the project bonds to the rating required by institutional investors. Structuring the bond finance required

Box 12.13 Wrapped Tranche for Solar Power Project Bond for Montalto di Castro Solar Park

The U.S. firm SunPower Corporation manufactures solar energy systems and acts as a solar power project developer. In December 2010, SunPower sold €195.2 million (US$ 274.7 million) of bonds linked to a solar farm in Italy, which are understood to be the first such bonds of their kind. The proceeds were used to refinance the final two, completed, 44 MW phases of the company's Montalto di Castro solar park. The 18-year fixed rate bonds were issued in two €97.6 million (US$137.3 million) tranches. The first tranche was guaranteed by SACE, the state-owned Italian guarantee company, rated Aa2 by Moody's; it pays 5.715 percent and was sold to institutional investors. The second tranche was naked and rated Baa3; it pays 4.839 percent and was purchased by the EIB. The higher payment rate on the first tranche covers the costs incurred by institutional investors for the guarantee. The lead managers for the issue were BNP Paribas and Société Générale.

This was the world's first publicly rated bond issue for a solar project, as well as Italy's first rated project bond ever. Achieving investment grade ratings was a milestone for the solar sector, opening up a new global-scale pool of capital to fund solar projects beyond traditional project financing from banks.

Source: Environmental Finance, December 16, 2010.

hard work on the legal side. In Italy, the National Bank regulates bond issues, and regulation is heavily weighted toward investor protection, which required the project to create several vehicles to protect investors.

Liquidity Guarantee for Extension of Loan Tenor

The length of tenor can be a key limitation encountered by project developers seeking local financing. By covering certain risks, GuarantCo[19] can help extend tenors to more appropriately match the project developer's financing requirements. For example, assume the project developer is seeking 10-year money but a local bank is only able to provide 7-year money. The loan can be structured as a 10-year loan with GuarantCo providing a guarantee for the repayment of all outstanding debt in year 7. The fees and margin payable to the local bank and GuarantCo would be structured to provide an incentive for the local bank to continue with the financing for the full 10 years.

The World Bank issued a US$50 million partial credit guarantee in the China Ertan Power Project covering the later maturities of commercial loans to finance the expansion of a public sector hydroelectric power plant. The guarantee agreement expanded loan tenor from 7 to 15 years, although the guarantee covered payments only during years 13–15 (figure 12.2).

Put Option to Guarantee Payment of Principal in Bond Issue

The Leyte-Luzon geothermal power plant project was implemented by the National Power Company (NPC) and the Philippine National Oil Company

Figure 12.2 Partial Credit Guarantee for Increased Loan Tenor: China Ertan Power Project

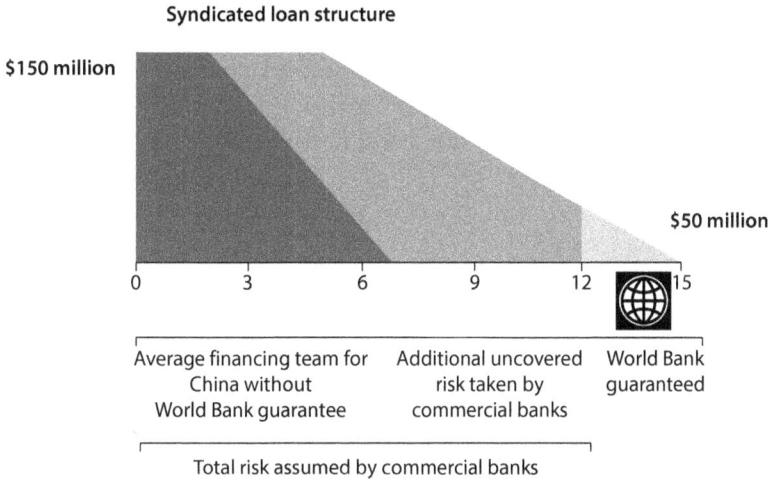

(PNOC), both state-owned companies. The NPC raised US$100 million in project finance through a 15-year bond issue on the international capital market. The World Bank provided a credit guarantee to the bond issue structured as a put option for principal repayment at maturity: it allowed bondholders to present or "put" their bonds to the World Bank at maturity for payment of principal. The purpose of the partial credit guarantee was to help the government entity access long-term financing on the international capital market and thereby to give the NPC access to debt with a longer tenor than the 10 years feasible on the national finance market.

Guarantees for Contingent Cost Overrun Facility

A partial guarantee has been provided to a US$75 million contingent cost overrun facility for an oil refinery in southern India. So far no RE project seems to have benefited from a similar guaranteed contingent cost overrun facility, but it is a feasible instrument.

Resource Risk Cover

Resource Insurance

For technologies inherently dependent on uncertain resources, wind and solar insurance can be used to provide coverage against unusually cloudy or still periods. Insurance is generally not available for hydrology risk or for biomass projects.

Commercial insurance can be taken out against lost revenue in event of lower-than-expected output due to lack of wind or sun.

Geological Risk Insurance

Although geothermal power projects in countries with high-quality resources can offer their output at rates that are reasonably cost competitive by RE technology standards, it has been difficult to get projects off the ground. High up-front investment requirements, geological risks associated with drilling, and a typical five-year development timeline from resource exploration to commercial operation present heavy obstacles.[20]

Geothermal energy poses two risks for investors. During the pre-investment phase, large investments are needed to establish the geological resource potential at the investigated site, and to determine whether it can be exploited commercially. During operation, the resource may turn out to be less attractive than estimated, with the result that peak production capacity declines after just a few years. See figure 12.3.

The case study in chapter 22 describes the experience of two World Bank–GEF GeoFund programs that provide guarantee facilities for geothermal resource exploration:

- The World Bank–GEF Europe and Central Asia Geothermal Energy Development Program, started in 2004, set up a Geothermal Energy Development Fund with three financing windows: a TA window, a PRG window, and an investment funding window. The PRG facility, endowed with US$12 million, partially insures project investors against the short-term, up-front geological risk of exploration or the long-term geological risk of lower-than-estimated temperature, higher-than-estimated mineralization, or difficult re-injectivity.

- The African Rift Geothermal Energy Development Facility Risk Guarantee Fund provides PRGs to early-stage exploration drilling, which has a considerable probability of being unsuccessful.[21] The recipient of a guarantee is charged a fee of 2–3 percent of the eligible drilling expense, payable up front upon signing. The guarantee premiums and fees to be charged to the applicants are not set at a level that would make the facilities financially self-sustaining. Depending on the frequency and severity of the payout events, the financial resources allocated to the guarantee cover will be depleted over time.

Figure 12.3 Geothermal Risk

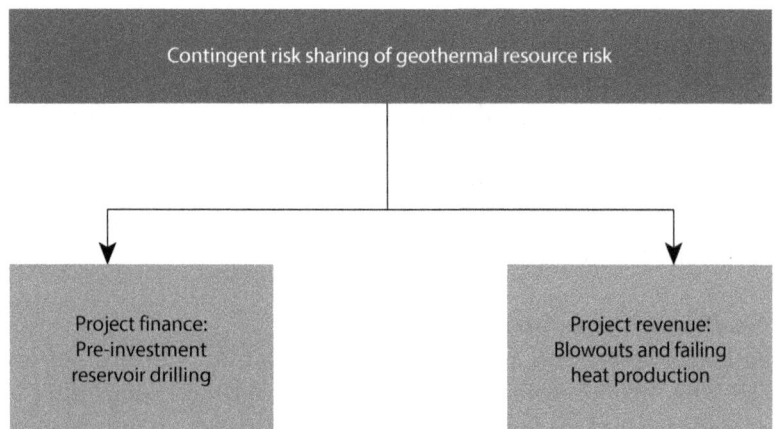

Because of the prolonged global financial crisis, the private sector risk insurance market for geothermal development has not expanded as expected when the GeoFund program was launched, limiting the opportunity for leveraging the private risk insurance market with GEF resources. Nor have the number of geothermal exploration projects been as high as expected when the fund was launched. However, this shortfall is more the result of the framework conditions for RE investment in the countries than the result of the instrument.

Chile has the potential to host about 3 GW in geothermal capacity, but geothermal exploration risk posed a barrier to its development. In 2009, the government of Chile announced a program to insure 30–70 percent of the costs of unsuccessful geothermal exploration wells. The dry-well insurance was to be made available to any company that managed to secure a geothermal exploration concession. The first unsuccessful well was to have 70 percent of its costs repaid by the government program, decreasing to 50 percent for the second and 30 percent for the third. Total liability is capped at US$8 million.

Credit Lines for High-Risk Investments in Geothermal Drilling

KfW is the implementing agency for the German Ministry of Environment's credit program Resource Risk in Deep-Geothermal Exploration Drilling. Projects comprising at least two deep-well drills in the business plan (production and injection drills) are eligible. KfW will lend to cover up to 80 percent of eligible costs, with a maximum loan amount of €16 million (US$22.5 million) per project, and no collateral is required. The maximum tenor is 10 years, and the grace period is 2 years.

An interesting aspect of the program is the collaboration with a commercial insurer, the Munich Counter-Guarantee Company (Münchener Rückversicherungs-Gesellschaft AG), which provides specialist advice and provides a partial counter guarantee for KfW loans to project developers. KfW must protect its AAA rating.

Tolling Arrangement for Removing Geothermal Risk

The tolling arrangement represents the extreme case of up-front risk sharing. In this arrangement, a government entity invests in the exploration and development of a geothermal resource. Once the commercial feasibility of the resource is established, the national energy regulator issues a tender for the electrification part of the project. The tender can be for

- A steam purchase contract, in which case the electricity generator sells the electricity on the power market, or
- A steam-to-electricity conversion contract, in which case the government entity—a state-owned power company—provides steam to the plant without cost and accepts power generated from the plant against a conversion fee.

The scheme has two drawbacks: no private capital is attracted to finance geothermal exploration and the geothermal plant, and the assumed efficiency advantage of private investors in the construction and operation of the plant is not exploited.

Other Insurance
Regulatory Risk Insurance

Project developers face the risk that a feed-in tariff awarded to a project could be taken away a few years after the project starts. An option is to buy an insurance policy for the project developer against the feed-in tariff disappearing. The policy can be structured similarly to a "put option."

Technology Risk Insurance

To promote entry of new technologies, insurance could be designed using private-public cooperation for RE technologies regarded as too risky for conventional insurances, providing protection against underperformance of a technology. Project developers would pay a premium for the insurance for the reparation or replacement of underperforming pieces of equipment and would receive liquidated damages up to the value covered by the policy. Insurers would provide the requested technical skills to assess specific technology risks and some of the finance for the insurance pool, and public funds would provide finance to the pool on a first loss basis.

Political Risk Insurance

The political or regulatory risks associated with many RE technology projects can be mitigated by political risk insurance or a PRG. Both of these instruments are offered by a number of multilateral institutions and bilateral credit agencies, including entities within the World Bank Group. Such a guarantee covers the risk of project defaults due to the actions of government or public sector agencies, including expropriation or breach of contract, such as failure to honor PPAs, that cannot be relieved by other means. PRGs offered by the World Bank Group's International Development Agency (IDA) and International Bank for Reconstruction and Development (IBRD) are secured against a matching counter guarantee from the host country government (so that if the PRG is called, the IDA or the IBRD then seeks recovery of the costs of the guarantee from the government), providing a very powerful incentive for the host country government to meet its obligations.

Public Renewable Energy Funds and Renewable Energy Finance Agencies

An emerging international trend is the creation of national RE funds with authority to decide how multiple public finance instruments can be used to achieve maximum impact from the fund's capital. The funds address two specific complexities of clean energy finance: first, different RE technologies pose very different finance challenges because of differences in technological maturity and financial competitiveness; and second, the technical supply chain for RE can have very specific financing gaps.

Funds and Specialized Agencies for RE Project Finance

The years since 2009 have witnessed a proliferation of RE funds. Some are national, for example, the U.K.'s Green Investment Bank (GIB), Kenya's Green Energy Fund, and Australia's Clean Energy Finance Corporation (endowed with $A 10 billion [US$10.3 billion][22] for the commercialization and employment of RE, EE, and low-carbon technologies).[23] Others are international, some created specifically to assist the pledged US$100 billion per year transfer of funds from Annex I countries[24] to developing countries.

Funds can be structured to invest directly in companies and projects, or as "funds of funds" (referred to as cornerstone funds) that invest in a number of commercially managed funds, each of which then invests in projects or companies. The cornerstone-funds approach can be more catalytic, leveraging private capital both into the fund itself and later into the investments that the fund makes.

On the *fund off-take side*, the creation of specialized public-private RE funds serves two purposes: (a) to promote initial RE market introduction and financial market development and (b) to serve as a safety valve against finance volatility, which is important in markets with high levels of uncertainty. On the *fund sourcing side*, the objective is to attract cofinance into the funds from private investors and to leverage further private resources when the funds invest in individual projects or in individual private finance institutions. Structured funds use risk reduction offered by public first loss equity to attract direct private equity investment into the fund. Nonstructured national funds attract finance from institutional investors through bond issues on international capital markets.

If they are to attract and not crowd out private capital, RE funds must operate in areas with identifiable and addressable market failures. For example, a fund could step in if the lack of an effective banking syndication market prevents projects from being financed.[25] Or, a fund could develop new, commercially priced insurance products for the construction phase that could attract equity in the short term and then be refinanced by traditional infrastructure investors once the projects are operating successfully. Not surprisingly, new funds typically employ a range of different public finance instruments, and fund managers are given discretion to decide which instruments to use to maximize achievement of the fund's objectives.

The U.K. Green Investment Bank

The discussions leading to the U.K. government's decision in 2011 to set up a GIB sheds light on present thinking in the RE community (developers, investors, finance sector, policy makers) about how public finance can drive low-carbon investment in Organisation for Economic Co-operation and Development countries with well-developed financial markets. The GIB will be endowed with an initial public capital commitment of £3 billion (US$4.9 billion) obtained from sales of public assets. From April 2015, the GIB will be able to borrow on its own against the credit of the government if the national debt is declining as a percentage of the economy. The GIB will be a statutory body and employ 50–100 people. The institutional rationale is distinct from the public finance instrument rationale for the creation of the GIB: the GIB is less a single financing mechanism than an umbrella government agency for increasing the availability of capital to low-carbon investment.[26]

A report by the National Audit Office in 2010 had criticized the uncoordinated proliferation of institutions providing public support to the RE and EE sector (National Audit Office 2010). Among other actions, the GIB will replace the Carbon Trust and the Marine Renewables Deployment Fund. Comments by industry participants were supportive of the centralization. Some argue that one of the biggest risks for all green projects is policy uncertainty and that the GIB could mitigate such uncertainty by improving the quality of advice being given to government about the impact its decisions and future actions will have on the investment community. Others believe that it will increase the quality of advice given to private industrial investors, including the right technologies in which to invest and which are likely to fail.

The report by the GIB Commission defines the public finance function of the bank as follows: "to work as part of overall Government policy to open up flows of investment by mitigating and better managing risk rather than simply increasing rewards to investors" (Green Investment Bank Commission 2010, viii). The report proposes that the GIB's primary focus should be on lowering risk for investors, rather than simply providing capital. It suggests the GIB could help catalyze low-carbon investment by unlocking project finance through equity co-investment, first loss debt, and insurance products for low-carbon technologies and infrastructure. Industry representatives also argue for guarantees for the early stages of projects, during which risks are highest, and that particular attention should be paid to the financing needs of small projects given that commercial banks steer clear of complex technologies at the small end of the market and, if they do engage, charge prohibitively high due diligence costs.

The GIB must have sufficient capitalization and funding to sustain its ongoing operations. The GIB would use the government's AAA rating to raise funds on international markets. Several finance experts underlined the importance of future asset-backed green bond issues from the GIB to make the large pools of capital held by institutional investors available for low-carbon investments. The argument is that green bonds would fit with the long-term investment horizons of pension funds and life insurance companies and would provide the scale of capital needed to fund the low-carbon transformation. The bonds would aggregate the debt from multiple RE projects to produce large bonds with significant liquidity. By forming liquid bonds, the GIB would enable fixed-income investors to purchase these bonds within the regulatory framework that poses limits on the risk investments of insurance and pension funds. It is claimed that institutional investors would prefer to finance RE projects through GIB liquid bonds rather than through private equity or project financing investments because of the risk diversification provided by the bonds.

InfraCo

InfraCo is a donor-funded infrastructure development company. It acts as an "honest broker" seeking to create viable infrastructure investment opportunities that balance the interests of host governments, the national and international private sector, and providers of finance. InfraCo acts as principal, shouldering much of the up-front costs and risks of early-stage development, thereby reducing the entry costs of later-stage private sector infrastructure developers. InfraCo operates in low-income developing countries, primarily located in Africa (InfraCo Africa) and parts of South and Southeast Asia (InfraCo Asia). It develops a pipeline of operations, giving priority to situations in which host country support for its involvement is strong and where it believes conditions exist to allow it to mobilize additional private investment. InfraCo is managed as a private sector infrastructure development company by InfraCo Management Services Ltd. InfraCo's capital is provided through share subscriptions by the Private Infrastructure Development Group (PIDG) donor group, made up of the development agencies of Austria, Ireland, the Netherlands, Sweden, Switzerland, and the United Kingdom, along with the World Bank. The above initiative is still relatively new; InfraCo Asia has only been operational since 2010. InfraCo Africa has successfully developed a wind turbine project in Cape Verde in which private developers had previously displayed no interest.

Funds Structured to Attract Multiple Sources of Finance

Structured funds can be established to attract private resources into publicprivate funds that invest in relatively high-risk regions or projects, yet need finance without risk premiums. Public finance within the fund is used to increase the risk-adjusted rate of return for private investors. Typical instruments are first loss equity and capped return. *First loss equity* means that the public sector takes the equity stake in a fund with a first loss position, thereby increasing the number of projects within a fund that can fail before the private sector investors lose money. In a *capped return* arrangement, the government's return on the capital investment is capped, allowing co-investors access to higher upsides on their investments.

The Global Climate Partnership Fund (GCPF) is a structured public-private partnership fund (see box 12.14). The European Fund for Southeast Europe (EFSE), based in Luxembourg, is also a public-private partnership fund with €756 million (US$1.1 billion) in commitments from donor agencies, international financial institutions, and private investors. The existing donor or public capital of €262 million (US$368.6) (35 percent) constitutes the first loss tranche—the first tranche to be used in the event of losses. Development finance institutions and international financial institutions invest in the mezzanine tranche, private investors in the senior tranche. Because of its investment structure, the EFSE is able to provide nearly unlimited access to long-term finance at

Box 12.14 The Global Climate Partnership Fund

The GCPF, founded in December 2009 as an initiative of the German Federal Ministry for the Environment, Nature Conservation and Nuclear Safety, and of KfW, provides refinancing resources to private local banks in developing and emerging countries for innovative lines of credit for climate projects by small and medium enterprises (SMEs) and households. The tenor of the loans is medium to long term. To a lesser extent, the fund invests directly in EE and RE projects as opportunities arise. GCPF's resources are deployed on a rotating basis: credit repayments are continually reinvested.

Because the GCPF invests in both high-risk regions (developing, transition, and emerging countries) and innovative sectors (financing of climate protection programs), the goal of attracting private cofinance into the fund required a creative solution. The GCPF is a structured fund, offering three tranches of shares and notes to its investors, each with a different risk and return profile. Bilateral donors invest in the equity capital tranche of the GCPF; the equity capital serves as the primary risk buffer against losses. Development banks invest in the mezzanine and senior tranches; among these is the World Bank Group's IFC with US$75 million. Private capital investors invest in the senior tranche. The fund is organized under private law and the fund manager is Deutsche Bank. A technical assistance facility is available to support the fund.

In 2011, GCPF resources totaled US$200 million and were projected to rise to US$500 million by 2015, mainly through the involvement of private investors.

market conditions for qualified financial institutions in Southeast Europe and in the Eastern subgroup of the European Union Neighbourhood. This leveraging potential is critical for the region, where capital markets are still developing. Although mezzanine and senior investors invest at a regional level, donor funds can be earmarked either to a specific country or to the region at large. Country-specific donor funds can facilitate a possible later transfer of ownership to local stakeholders. To undertake an investment, different sources of funds representing different risk tranches are pooled into a single source of financing for the EFSE. For the investment portfolio in each country, the proportion of the different risk tranches contributing to the total amount of pooled funds remains intact. Hence, donors and other investors hold a specific share of the pooled funds in the amount of their original nominal contribution to the EFSE.

Notes

1. The importance at a worldwide level can be illustrated by the following figures. In 2010, global bonds outstanding were valued at US$95 trillion; global equity market capitalization amounted to US$55 trillion. Some US$40 trillion of bond and equity assets were held by pension funds and insurance companies.

2. In some countries, changes in financial sector regulations may be required to allow pension funds to be formed.

3. Bank syndication is equally complex. In August 2011, the private equity group Blackstone reached financial closure for its 288 MW Meerwind offshore wind farm in the German North Sea. The project, to be completed by 2013, requires an investment of €1.2 billion (US$1.7 billion). Blackstone invests equity of €322 million (US$453 million). The debt financing of €822 million (US$1,157 million) is provided by a group of seven commercial lenders, alongside KfW and EKF, the Danish export credit agency.

4. The New Earth investment subfund designs, builds, finances, and operates waste treatment facilities, and generates renewable energy (RE) from waste-derived fuels. It was launched in 2008 by waste treatment facility operator New Earth Solutions Group and the Isle of Man–based fund manager Premier Group. The open-ended fund (investors include institutions such as pension funds as well as high-net-worth individuals) invests in U.K. recycling and waste treatment facilities operated by New Earth. Since its creation, the fund has raised £70.7 million (US$114 million) and invested in five waste management facilities across the United Kingdom. It aims to expand this portfolio to 40 waste treatment and energy-from-waste plants by 2016.

5. The green label, however, calls for certification. For this purpose, the Climate Bond Initiative is developing a Climate Bond Standard, designed to certify the environmental integrity of the underlying projects being financed.

6. Kommunalbanken Norway (KBN) is a bank collectively owned by the Norwegian municipalities to serve their needs for project finance. In 2011, KBN launched a US$180 million Clean Energy Bond on the Japanese uridashi market (non-Japanese-yen-denominated bonds sold directly to Japanese individual investors), the proceeds of which will be used to finance Norwegian municipal initiatives to reduce climate change.

7. Strong household demand in Japan has given rise to retail funds that collectively invest in green bonds of the capital market category; Nikko Asset Management has two funds that predominantly invest in World Bank Green Bonds.

8. The funds raised from green bonds issued by the World Bank are ring-fenced for World Bank–funded climate change projects such as EE, RE, and reforestation. The World Bank issued its first green bond in 2007. Since then, the European Investment Bank, the Asian Development Bank (ADB), the Nordic Investment Bank, and the African Development Bank have also issued green bonds.

9. An example is the Dutch/U.K. bank Triodos. It has branded itself as a green bank willing to invest directly in RE projects, and it raises capital explicitly for that purpose through retail climate bond issues.

10. Several US states also tap into this market to finance loan programs for RE and EE investments by residential and commercial property owners. The programs allow residential and commercial property owners to borrow the money for RE and EE investments from the state. The liability to repay the loan is attached to the property, rather than to the individual, as an assessment on real property. Loans are repaid through annual assessments on owners' property tax bills.

11. In the United States, third-party PV installers are also active in the single-family-home market. The installers have access to a number of tax benefits that are available to firms with cash flows from operations, but not to households.

12. Guarantee instruments to extend tenor are discussed in the section on public risk-sharing instruments.

13. A zero-coupon bond does not make periodic interest payments and its face value is paid at maturity. It is bought at a price lower than its par (or redemption) value: the difference between the discounted purchase price of the bond and its par value equals the compounded interest paid at maturity.

14. US$ equivalents are provided for rough comparison throughout the chapter. Conversions are made using 2011 exchange rates unless the context clearly calls for a specific year.

15. Berkeley Energy, based in the United Kingdom, is a private equity fund manager specializing in RE infrastructure investments in developing markets with an initial focus on Asia.

16. The ADB invested US$20 million in REAF in 2011.

17. InfraCo Asia is part of the InfraCo Group funded by the Private Infrastructure Development Group (PIDG), members of which include the development agencies of Austria, Ireland, the Netherlands, Sweden, Switzerland, and the United Kingdom, along with KfW and the World Bank Group. The ADB has invested US$20 million in InfraCo Asia.

18. US$ equivalents are provided for rough comparison throughout the chapter. Conversions are made using 2011 exchange rates unless the context clearly calls for a specific year.

19. GuarantCo was developed and is financed by the PIDG, a multidonor organization. Members include the U.K. Department for International Development, the Swiss State Secretariat for Economic Affairs, the Netherlands Ministry of Foreign Affairs, the Swedish International Development Cooperation Agency, the World Bank, and the Austrian Development Agency.

20. In some countries, good resources are located in national parks, imposing additional restrictions.

21. The failure rate for later-stage production drilling for advanced field assessment is much lower; therefore, insurance against this risk must be acquired on a commercial basis.

22. US$ equivalents are provided for rough comparison throughout the chapter. Conversions are made using 2011 exchange rates unless the context clearly calls for a specific year.

23. In addition, Australia's Renewable Energy Agency has $A 3.2 billion (US$3.3 billion) for research and development, demonstration, and commercialization of new technologies.

24. The industrial countries and economies in transition listed in Annex I of the UNFCCC. Their responsibilities under the Convention include a binding commitment to reducing their greenhouse gas emissions relative to 1990 levels by 2012.

25. The impact of the financial crisis in India provides an example. "Pre-crisis, an estimated $600 billion of RE investment in India had largely been through corporate balance sheets, backed up by guarantees. In 2007–08, the first 'non-recourse' RE project financing was successfully closed; however, by the peak of the crisis this had become 'last year's business.' Banks that were doing business under the constrained financial conditions were operating on the basis of short loan tenors, making raising longer-term debt to cover the duration of a project extremely difficult. Things were very difficult at the smaller scale end of the market" (Hamilton 2010, 11).

26. The government's medium-term requirement to meet the legally binding obligation established under the European Union Renewable Energy Directive 2009 is to increase the proportion of all the United Kingdom's energy needs—electricity, heat, and transport—that are supplied from renewable sources from 2.3 percent in 2008 to 15 percent by 2020. The government estimated in July 2009 that investment totaling some £100 billion (US$162 billion) would be required to achieve the 2020 target.

Bibliography

Aldersgate Group. 2010. *Financing the Future: A Green Investment Bank to Power the Economic Recovery*. London: Aldersgate Group.

Green Investment Bank Commission. 2010. *Unlocking Investment to Deliver Britain's Low Carbon Future*. London: GIB Commission.

Hamilton, K. 2010. "Scaling Up Renewable Energy in Developing Countries: Finance and Investment Perspectives." Chatham House, London.

Mostert, Wolfgang. 2010. *Publicly Backed Guarantees as Policy Instruments to Promote Clean Energy*. Sustainable Energy Finance Alliance of the UN Environment Programme, Nairobi.

National Audit Office. 2010. *Government Funding for Developing Renewable Energy Technologies*. London: National Audit Office.

CHAPTER 13

Selection of Financing Instruments for Renewable Energy

Introduction

Context matters: best practice is always circumstance based. The public finance instruments chosen must be tailored to the specific type of finance gap and to the characteristics of the technology, the finance sector, and the developer community. The required results will be obtained in the most cost-effective manner when instruments are selected based on a careful diagnosis of the finance and project situation in the country and when a range of public finance instruments are offered, each addressing a specific problem and targeting achievement of a specific objective.

Tailoring the Instrument to the Type of Barrier

A primary point of departure for the diagnostic is to determine whether lack of liquidity or lack of risk cover is the main problem blocking renewable energy (RE) project access to debt or equity capital, or whether a combination of risk cover and liquidity support instruments is needed. Used in their most straightforward manner as instruments to reduce the risk of conventional debt, subordinated debt, publicly backed guarantees (PBGs), and first loss reserves have very similar impacts on risk reduction. First loss reserves make sense for portfolio finance; subordinated debt and PBGs can also be used for individual project finance.

Investments by institutional investors are essential to providing stability in the supply of finance to RE projects. Therefore, attracting institutional investors into RE project finance will be a key objective of new public finance initiatives in countries with growing RE markets. Structuring the finance to achieve institutional investor entry is complex and requires substantial legal work; thus, contracting for good legal expertise is an important success factor. The main route to institutional investor finance is through the bond market, where wrapping is essential to strengthen project bond ratings to investment grade status. However, creative approaches are also being used in private finance to attract institutional investors to the construction finance phase.

Private insurance and guarantee companies and public-private funds offer risk cover on commercial terms to RE projects in emerging and developing economies. Thus, the availability on international markets of appropriate insurance and guarantee products should be determined before putting in place a specific risk product as part of a public finance program. Purchasing commercial risk products with program funds will be more cost effective.

Some public finance funds have suffered from the passivity of contracted fund managers who wait for project proposals to arrive instead of actively marketing the finance products. Although the risk of passive managers can be reduced by close monitoring, an incentive instrument will be more effective. Instead of basing the fund manager's typical 2 percent fee on capital paid into the fund, the fee should be based on committed investments out of the fund.[1] The formula will demonstrate the fund manager's confidence in the fund's business model, making it easier to convince potential investors to place money into the fund.

Publicly Backed Guarantees

A few conclusions can be drawn with regard to PBGs. First, guarantees can be essential for emerging and higher-risk technologies. Lenders often will not lend without PBGs (e.g., to next-generation ethanol projects), or only against payment of a high premium (e.g., interest rates on loans to offshore wind farms compared with loans to onshore wind farms). Second, in asset finance, PBGs can help lower banks' transaction costs for dealing with many requests for end-user finance. Third, PBGs are useful when policies require speedy implementation but the projects have above-average uncertainties. Fourth, guarantees are particularly valuable during times of tight credit and market uncertainty when banks are reluctant to lend, providing the grease that can ease provision of credit. Fifth, start-up small and medium enterprises (SMEs) have little access to bank credit, making them dependent on risk capital during their pre-seed, seed, and venture capital development phases. Several governments make PBGs available to three- to five-year-old SMEs, providing partial risk cover to share capital and mezzanine finance investments undertaken by business angels (BAs) and venture capitalists (VCs). The design of the PBG depends on the size and sophistication of the national BA and VC community. In countries with less-developed BA and VC communities, PBGs are designed to expand the pool of national investors and the pool of risk capital. Countries with well-developed BA and VC communities may opt to expand the pool of risk capital through direct public investments in BA and VC funds specializing in RE and energy efficiency investments. Sixth, some business finance PBGs solve special finance problems, for instance, PBGs for mortgages on laboratory buildings that would be difficult to sell if a company were to enter bankruptcy.

However, PBGs are not a panacea, even though they tend to have the largest theoretically feasible leveraging ratios, for example, a portfolio guarantee with a

5 percent default rate can leverage debt finance 20 times larger than the loss-cover amount that must be deposited. In some applications, PBGs are effective, for instance, as a bond-wrapping tool to attract institutional investors or to allow the launch of an issue onto the international bond market. However, in conventional debt guarantee applications, the effect of PBGs depends on the sophistication and the psychology of the local finance market. The United States uses PBGs as instruments in energy policy more frequently than any other country.[2] European Union countries implement broad energy efficiency and RE initiatives without including PBGs in the package of measures. The higher use of PBGs in U.S. energy policy is due to three factors. First, the more sophisticated the financial market is, the more potential applications that can be identified for PBGs, and the easier it is to influence the flow of funds through subtle changes in arbitrage opportunities. Second, promarket ideology gives PBGs more "market flavor" than does direct grant finance. Third is habit formation—once a subsidy product like a PBG has entered the market, soon neither the providers nor the off-takers can imagine conducting business without it.

Importance of Framework Conditions

No matter how well designed a scheme is, its impact on RE investments will always depend on the quality of the overall framework conditions in the target country. The World Bank's insurance scheme for geothermal resource exploration risk, promoted by the GeoFund projects for Eastern Europe and Central Asia and for East Africa, illustrate this point. In Hungary, the rate of return on geothermal projects was not sufficient to attract more than the one project insured by the program (and it failed to find adequate resources); in East Africa the resources are good, but the general framework conditions are too uncertain.

Increasing Venture Capital

Venture capital for RE can be increased in a number of ways: (a) by partial guarantees to equity provided by private investors in VC funds, (b) by direct public equity capital investments in existing VC funds, (c) by newly developed public-private equity and mezzanine finance funds (with or without caps on returns on private capital), and (d) by incentives to equity funds to engage in early-stage finance. The choice depends on three main factors.

- Belief in what works fastest. Public investments in VC funds directly provide new risk funds, including from the private sector, because public resources are provided on a 50/50 matching fund basis.
- Whether the development of a broad-based BA and VC community is a major ancillary objective. PBGs to equity investments are an instrument to attract more individuals and firms to become interested in becoming BAs.
- Whether public investors strongly desire to share in the upside potential of supported investments. Upside potential is "automatic" for public co-investments

in VC funds. In PBG schemes, upside potential can be built in through success-dependent fee rates; however, this avenue does not allow for the windfall profits that accrue to VC capital investments when a highly profitable technology is developed.

See table 13.1 for a summary.

Table 13.1 Objectives for Public Finance Instruments by Stage of RE Market Development in a Country

Public finance instrument	Initial market	Developing market	Mature market
Debt finance			
National development bank project finance	Provide low-cost finance to RE projects to serve as showcase for commercial banks (IREDA, India)	Provide low-cost finance and incentives to investments in national manufacturing of RE (BNDES, Brazil)	Accelerate loan syndication and provide finance safety net to safeguard a steady flow of investment (KfW, Germany) Allow commercial financial institutions to piggyback on RE project experience in new and higher-risk RE projects with good prospects for further similar projects
Multinational development bank project finance	Build capacity in RE finance at collaborating commercial financial institutions	Loan syndication of large-scale RE projects	n.a.
Dedicated RE credit lines	Build capacity in RE finance at collaborating commercial financial institutions End-user RE finance Finance small-scale RE projects of less than 10–20 MW (USELF, Ukraine)	Finance small-scale RE projects of less than 10–20 MW (RERED/ ESD in Sri Lanka) End-user RE finance Provide loans with long-term tenor	End-user RE finance (KfW)
Public underwriting support	n.a.	Avoid delay in securing finance for high-priority infrastructure projects	Avoid delay in securing finance for high-priority infrastructure projects
Mezzanine finance as subordinated debt	Encourage commercial financial institutions to test loan finance to RE projects	Introduction of new RE technologies previously not tested in the project country, encouraging commercial financial institutions to provide loan finance	Securing financial close for high-priority infrastructure projects
Transaction cost support	Attract commercial financial institutions into RE consumer loan finance (UNEP Solar Loan Program, India)	Attract commercial financial institutions into RE consumer loan finance (UNEP Solar Loan Program, India)	n.a.

table continues next page

Table 13.1 Objectives for Public Finance Instruments by Stage of RE Market Development in a Country *(continued)*

Public finance instrument	Initial market	Developing market	Mature market
Contingent project development grants, transforming to loan at success	Facilitate loan finance to preparation of high-risk investments and reduce risk of these investments (e.g., investment in exploration and drilling of geothermal projects)	Facilitate loan finance to preparation of high-risk investments and reduce risk of these investments (e.g., investment in exploration and drilling of geothermal projects)	Facilitate loan finance to preparation of high-risk investments and reduce risk of these investments (e.g., investment in exploration and drilling of geothermal projects)
"Green Investment Banks" with freedom to employ different finance instruments	n.a.	n.a.	Flexibly meet ad hoc finance challenges in an environment characterized by rapid technological change and shortage of bank finance
Equity finance			
Public equity investment	Preconstruction support	Preconstruction support	Preconstruction support to development of offshore wind farms and geothermal projects
Investment in equity funds and funds of funds	Expand number of smaller-scale private project developers (GEEREF and InfraCo Asia)	Expand number of smaller-scale private project developers (GEEREF and InfraCo Asia)	n.a.
Mezzanine finance as quasi-equity	n.a.	Close equity gaps for smaller-scale project developers and for SME RE technology companies (CAREC, Central America)	Closing equity gaps for smaller-scale project developers (FIDEME, France)
Venture capital			
Investment in venture capital funds	Stimulate creation of innovative clean energy service firms (African Rural Energy Enterprise Development)	Stimulate creation of innovative clean energy technology firms (CRAGF of ADB)	(High Growth and Innovative SME Facility, EU)
Grant cofinancing of transaction costs of seed-finance investments	n.a.	Provide incentives to private equity capital funds and venture capital funds to invest in the seed capital phase to stimulate creation of innovative clean energy technology firms (SCAF)	n.a.
Risk cover or reduction			
Partial credit guarantees to RE projects	n.a.	Promote investment in leading-edge RE demonstration plants, transmission for RE-connected power, and smart grids	Promote investment in leading-edge RE demonstration plants, transmission for RE-connected power, and smart grids (US DOE loan program 2009)

table continues next page

Unlocking Commercial Financing for Clean Energy in East Asia • http://dx.doi.org/10.1596/978-1-4648-0020-7

Table 13.1 Objectives for Public Finance Instruments by Stage of RE Market Development in a Country *(continued)*

Public finance instrument	Initial market	Developing market	Mature market
Partial credit guarantees to RE investment programs	n.a.	n.a.	Allow economies of scale in finance, in RE technology procurement, and in installation (Project Amp, United States)
Publicly backed guarantees (PBGs) to RE technology start-up firms	Partial credit guarantees to attract bank loans to innovative SMEs in renewable energy	PBGs to equity investments by business angels and venture capital	PBGs to encourage equity investments by business angels and venture capital
PBGs for technology transfer	Insure against political risks: war and civil disturbance, expropriation, currency transfer risks, and breach of contract (Multilateral Investment Guarantee Agency)	Insure against political risks: war and civil disturbance, expropriation, currency transfer risks, and breach of contract (Multilateral Investment Guarantee Agency)	n.a.
Wrapping of project bonds	n.a.	n.a.	Pull institutional investors into RE finance (Montalto di Castro solar park, Italy)
Credit guarantee to bond issue structured as a put option for principal repayment at maturity	n.a.	Enable RE investor to launch bond issue on international capital market	n.a.
Liquidity guarantee	Extend tenor to match the financing requirements of the project developer (GuarantCo)	Extend tenor to match the financing requirements of the project developer (GuarantCo)	n.a.
Partial risk guarantee	n.a.	Facilitate loan finance to preparation of high-risk investments and reduce risk of these investments (e.g., investment in exploration and drilling of geothermal projects) (African Rift Geothermal Energy Development Facility)	Facilitate loan finance to preparation of high-risk investments and reduce risk of these investments (e.g., investment in exploration and drilling of geothermal projects)
Resource insurance	Mitigate annual variations in revenue	Mitigate annual variations in revenue	Mitigate annual variations in revenue
Geological risk insurance	Sharing the risk of high project development costs, provide protection against losses of revenue during operation	Sharing the risk of high project development costs, provide protection against losses of revenue during operation	Sharing the risk of high project development costs, provide protection against losses of revenue during operation

Note: ADB = Asian Development Bank; BNDES = Brazilian National Economic and Social Development Bank; CAREC = Central American Renewable Energy and Cleaner Production; CRAGF = Clean Resources Asia Growth Fund; FIDEME = Fonds d'Investissements de l'Environnement et de la Maîtrise de l'Energie; GEEREF = Global Energy Efficiency and Renewable Energy Fun; IREDA = Indian Renewable Energy Development Agency; KfW = Kreditanstalt für Wiederaufbau (German development bank); n.a. = not applicable; RERED/ESD = Renewable Energy for Rural Economic Development/Energy for Sustainable Development; SCAF = Seed Capital Assistance Facility; SME = small and medium enterprise; UNEP = United Nations Environment Programme; US DOE = United States Department of Energy; USELF = Ukraine Sustainable Energy Lending Facility.

Notes

1. The performance payment of a 20 percent share of profits above a benchmark would be paid on top of the management fee.

2. Some East Asian countries, for example, the Republic of Korea, use publicly backed guarantees (PBGs) much more than does the United States, but as subsidy instruments in industrial policy.

PART 4

Clean Energy Financing Case Studies

Financing instruments	Energy efficiency case studies	Renewable energy case studies
Dedicated credit line	• China Energy Efficiency Financing Project (CHEEF); Chapter 14 • Thailand Government Energy Conservation Fund (ENCON); Chapter 15	• Turkey Renewable Energy Project; Chapter 21
Partial risk guarantee	• China Second Energy Conservation Project; Chapter 16 • China Utility-Based Energy Efficiency Finance Program (CHUEE); Chapter 17 • Commercializing Energy Efficiency Financing (CEEF); Chapter 18	• Geothermal Funds in Eastern Europe and Africa; Chapter 22
Dedicated funds	• Bulgarian Energy Efficiency Fund (BEEF); Chapter 19 • South Africa Eskom Standard Offer Program for Energy Efficiency and Demand-Side Management; Chapter 20	

CHAPTER 14

Case Study: China Energy Efficiency Financing Project (CHEEF)

Introduction

The China Energy Efficiency Financing (CHEEF) Project consists of three phases. The first phase is the CHEEF I project, approved by the World Bank Board in May 2008 to improve energy efficiency (EE) of medium and large industrial enterprises in China, and thereby reduce their adverse environmental impacts on climate. The project is designed to achieve the objective through (a) two International Bank for Reconstruction and Development (IBRD) loans of US$100 million each to the Export-Import Bank of China (China EXIM Bank) and to Huaxia Bank; and (b) a Global Environment Facility (GEF) grant of US$13.5 million for technical assistance to the government and two participating banks. The second phase, the CHEEF II project, an IBRD loan of US$100 million to Minsheng Bank, was approved in June 2010. The third phase, the Additional Financing for CHEEF (CHEEF III) with an IBRD loan of US$100 million to China EXIM Bank, was approved in October 2011 to expand the target market segments of CHEEF by piloting energy service company (ESCO) lending and expanding EE investments in the building sector.

Country Context

The government of China has made energy conservation one of the highest national priorities and is committed to a target of reducing energy intensity of gross domestic product (GDP) by 20 percent during the 11th Five-Year Plan (2006–10) and 16 percent during the 12th Five-Year Plan (2011–15). To achieve these targets, the central government reached an agreement with the 30 provincial governments on their provincial energy saving targets for 2006–10, and held provincial leaders accountable for reaching these targets. Second, the central government signed responsibility contracts on specific enterprise energy savings targets with the nation's top 1,000 energy-consuming enterprises, which account for one-third of China's total energy use. These "sticks" are also combined with "carrots." The central government provided 105 billion Chinese yuan (Y; US$15 billion) during 2007–09, with additional funds from provincial governments, as incentives for EE investments and technology research and development.

The estimated energy conservation investments needed to achieve the 20 percent EE target surpass US$50 billion, most of it in the industrial sector. A large financing gap remains for medium and large energy conservation investments in the industrial sector, which range from US$5 million to US$25 million per project.

In 2010, the State Council issued new policies to provide strong support to the growth of the ESCO industry, offering subsidies, awards, and generous tax incentives for ESCOs, and encouraging lending to ESCOs by allowing banks to use and recognize ESCO project assets, contracts, and revenues as loan security. In addition, the government plans to expand the focus of its energy conservation efforts in the industrial sector to the building and transport sectors because energy demand for buildings and transport will increase rapidly—tripling for the building sector and more than quadrupling for the transport sector—during the next two decades as a result of China's rapid urbanization.

Barriers

Four key barriers have impeded development of the lending market for medium and large industrial energy conservation investments, despite its large potential:

- Most local banks usually rely on balance sheet financing that requires borrowers to have good credit ratings or high levels of collateral, thus favoring large-scale borrowers. The concept of project-based financing focused on energy savings has not yet been widely accepted by financial institutions. Many attractive EE investments, particularly those to be undertaken by small and medium enterprises (SMEs) that are not creditworthy, often have difficulty in accessing finance, despite the high savings rates in the East Asia and Pacific region.
- EE investments also involve perceived performance risk because investors are not sure whether the expected future savings will be realized or captured by financiers.
- EE investments tend to be small, with high transaction costs.
- Financial institutions lack the required expertise and interest in developing the EE business line.

CHEEF focused on addressing these barriers through (a) establishing a dedicated credit line to build capacity and confidence of domestic banks for EE lending and (b) supporting the government in the design and implementation of energy conservation programs under the 11th and 12th Five-Year Plans.

Objectives

The project development objective of CHEEF I was to improve the EE of medium and large industrial enterprises in China, and thereby reduce their adverse climate impacts. The objective of CHEEF II is to improve the EE of selected enterprises, and thereby reduce their adverse global environmental impacts, by scaling up commercial lending for EE investment. The objective of CHEEF III is to improve the EE of selected energy end users in key energy-consuming sectors, thereby reducing their adverse climate impacts.

Design

The program consists of two major parts. The first part is a dedicated EE credit line totaling US$400 million that IBRD funds through three Chinese banks—China EXIM Bank, Huaxia Bank, and Minsheng Bank. The second part is technical assistance with support from the GEF to (a) support national EE policy with a focus on market-based mechanisms such as energy savings certificate trading schemes and (b) build capacity in the three participating banks.

Key Features of Energy Conservation Investment Lending
Subborrower Eligibility
Beneficiary enterprises borrowing from the participating financial institutions (PFIs) should be large and medium industrial enterprises whose total annual revenues are at least Y 30 million (US$4.7 million). The annual revenues of the beneficiary enterprises are based on the income statements from the latest audited financial statements, which have to be for a fiscal year no more than two years before the current fiscal year.

In CHEEF III, subborrower eligibility was expanded to include (a) industrial enterprises of all sizes; (b) ESCOs (including leasing companies), which are companies that provide a wide range of services to implement EE projects with performance-based agreements under which the end users pay for the services from the demonstrated energy savings; and (c) owners of buildings (including office buildings, shopping centers, multifamily residential complexes, and other commercial and public buildings), government agencies, government end users, and district heating or cooling system operators.

Project Eligibility
Subproject investment is limited to renovation and rehabilitation (adjustment, replacement, or extension) of existing physical components and systems with the objective of achieving higher EE. Such renovation and rehabilitation is confined to the end user's existing premises; any new construction has to be within the boundaries of existing premises so that no new land is acquired for the subproject.

The cash flow benefit arising only from energy savings associated with the subproject, as estimated using the subproject financial projections prepared by the subborrower and reviewed by PFIs, has to be adequate to repay the total investment cost of the subproject in 10 years.

Unlocking Commercial Financing for Clean Energy in East Asia • http://dx.doi.org/10.1596/978-1-4648-0020-7

PFI Underwriting Criteria
PFI underwriting criteria still rely heavily on the subborrowers' credit rating and follow the eligibility criteria in the CHEEF Operational Manual. PFIs assume all risks.

Average Size, Payback Period, and Type of EE Investment
The average project size is about US$20 million, consisting of equity from end beneficiaries, the IBRD loan, and debt contributions from PFIs. Enterprises are expected to contribute equity financing up to about 30 percent of project costs. The required leverage ratio of the IBRD loan to PFI contribution is 1:1 under CHEEF I, and increased to 1:2 under CHEEF III. The average investment cost through the end of 2011 is about US$300/ton of coal equivalent of energy savings, with a payback period of two to three years. However, the low-hanging fruit (subprojects such as waste heat recovery investments in the cement, iron and steel, and chemical sectors) have been harvested, so the cost is increasing.

Terms and Conditions
The IBRD loan is on-lent by the government to the three PFIs: US$200 million to China EXIM Bank, US$100 million to Huaxia Bank, and US$100 million to Minsheng Bank, using IBRD terms and conditions. The PFIs, in turn, on-lend the funds to industrial enterprises and ESCOs for energy conservation investment subprojects at market rates.

Key Features of Technical Assistance
Technical Assistance to PFIs
The GEF grant is used for (a) training and capacity building for PFIs; (b) developing new financial products for ESCO lending, and adaptation of loan appraisal and underwriting criteria tailored to EE investments; (c) conducting specific market segment studies to broaden the end-user sectors and EE technologies in the portfolio; (d) building partnerships and engaging selected bank branches for marketing development and generating deal flows; and (e) developing market-aggregation tools for SMEs and projects.

Technical Assistance for National Policy Support and Capacity Building
Technical assistance at this level focuses on (a) supporting the National Development and Reform Commission to develop market-based mechanisms such as energy savings certificate trading schemes and (b) identifying and implementing priority energy conservation programs during the 12th Five-Year Plan, along with strengthening the institutional capacity of the National Energy Conservation Center.

Implementation Results

At the end of 2012, after three years of project implementation under the CHEEF I project, two PFIs had invested US$825 million in industrial EE, of which US$175 million was from IBRD, which leveraged US$650 million from two PFIs and industrial enterprises, achieving a 1:4 leverage ratio. These investments are expected to result in energy savings of 2 million tons of coal equivalent and to reduce carbon dioxide emissions by 4.8 million tons.

The project is playing a significant role in increasing the PFIs' capacity, interest, and confidence in mainstreaming the EE financing business line and played a catalytic role in leveraging additional financing for EE to the two participating banks from the German and French development agencies and from the European Investment Bank.

Lessons Learned

Experience demonstrates that a dedicated EE credit line, together with technical assistance, can contribute significantly to increasing the capacity, interest, and confidence of PFIs and their EE investments through a learning-by-doing process. This approach yields high leverage, achieving a 1:4 leverage ratio. The PFIs will also revolve repaid loans back into EE investments, a double leverage effect. Early evidence indicates that the PFIs have progressed from little understanding of the EE lending business to mainstreaming EE and green financing business lines, and becoming leaders in EE financing in China.

The technical assistance program has been critical. Providing technical assistance to and capacity building of staff for evaluation of EE investments, and having a dedicated team within the PFIs, are crucial to successful project implementation. Strong management commitment within the PFIs is also critical. It is important to mobilize and engage the branches by assigning dedicated staff, conducting training, and providing bonus incentives. Specifically targeted market studies in subsectors or subborrower groups are important for finding business deals. Building partnerships with industrial and ESCO associations is also helpful in identifying business deals. Following the PFIs' internal processes is important for mainstreaming EE investments in PFIs' main business. Hiring specialists for due diligence is necessary until in-house capacity is built.

The government's EE commitments and policies are vital. The government's EE commitments and policies have been a major contributing factor in the success of this program. The aggressive energy intensity reduction targets, incentives for EE investments and technology research and development, and contracts with the country's top 1,000 industrial enterprises to reduce energy intensity have created an environment that is favorable for EE actions by industrial firms. These government initiatives have also led to increased interest in EE lending on the part of financial institutions.

The PFIs still rely heavily on subborrowers' credit rankings as primary financing criteria. Changing PFIs' underwriting criteria from balance sheet financing to project-based financing that focuses on energy savings (thus increasing access to financing for ESCOs and SMEs) has been a major challenge. PFIs have focused narrowly on a few main heavy industries (iron and steel, cement, and chemicals) and a few EE technologies (predominantly waste heat recovery). As a result, they are facing increasing difficulties in finding projects. However, market needs and opportunities exist to expand lending to a wider range of energy user sectors and EE technologies. Therefore, CHEEF III strongly emphasizes innovative ESCO financing and expanding the project scope to include EE in buildings.

Bibliography

World Bank. 2008. "Project Appraisal Document on a Proposed Loan in the Amount of US$200 Million and a Proposed Grant from the Global Environment Facility Trust Fund in the Amount of US$13.5 Million to the People's Republic of China in Support of the Energy Efficiency Financing Project." World Bank, Washington, DC, April 21.

————. 2010. "Project Appraisal Document on a Proposed Loan in the Amount of US$100 Million to the People's Republic of China in Support of the Energy Efficiency Financing Project." World Bank, Washington, DC, April 6.

————. 2011. "Project Paper on a Proposed Additional Loan in the Amount of US$100 Million to the People's Republic of China for an Additional Financing for the Energy Efficiency Financing Project." World Bank, Washington, DC, January 12.

CHAPTER 15

Case Study: Thailand Energy Conservation (ENCON) Fund

Introduction

The Energy Conservation Fund (ENCON Fund) established under Thailand's Energy Conservation and Promotion Act 1992 has been the Thai government's key financial mechanism for supporting energy efficiency (EE) and renewable energy (RE) development. The source of funds for the ENCON Fund is a sales tax of 0.04 Thai baht (B; US$0.001) per liter on petroleum products (gasoline, diesel, fuel oil, and kerosene) sold in Thailand. This tax provides annual inflows of approximately US$200 million (Sinsukprasert 2010).

Financial support provided by the ENCON Fund is monitored under the framework of the government's Energy Conservation Plan. Two phases of the Energy Conservation Plan have been completed (the first phase covered 1995–99 and the second phase covered 2000–04). These two phases were designed primarily to support the mandatory energy managers program[1] and voluntary measures. They achieved limited success—US$630 million in investment from the ENCON Fund resulted in estimated energy savings of US$696 million. Much of the planned investment in designated factories and buildings did not materialize. The third phase, covering 2005–11, had a budget of US$2,930 million, representing a major scale-up from the first two phases.

The Energy Efficiency Revolving Fund (EERF) and the Energy Service Company (ESCO) Fund are two featured funds under the ENCON Fund that aim to address the issue of access to finance, which has been the key barrier to scaling up EE and RE projects in Thailand.

The EERF was established in 2003. Although it was initially structured for a three-year period, because of its success, the program was extended and was in its fifth phase in 2011. The ESCO Fund was established by the Ministry of Energy in 2008 with initial capitalization of US$30 million from the ENCON Fund and was extended for a second phase.

Country Context

Despite the policy frameworks and financing mechanisms the government has put in place to promote EE in Thailand, energy intensity has not changed much since 2000, largely because of the increasing share of energy-intensive industry in the economic structure and little improvement in EE at the sector level. The transport and industry sectors embody the largest energy-savings potential in Thailand. The rising energy intensity of industry is primarily driven by the increasing share of manufacturing in the economy and continuing use of inefficient industrial plants. The transport sector is among the most energy intensive, mainly due to the country's high level of motorization, heavy dependence on road transport, and lack of fuel economy standards.

The government's 20-Year National Energy Efficiency Development Plan commits to reducing energy intensity by 25 percent compared with 2005 levels by 2030, or to 12.1 thousand tons of oil equivalent (ktoe) per billion Thai baht of GDP in 2030 from its 2005 level of 16.2 ktoe per billion Thai baht of GDP. Nearly half of the energy-savings potential is in the transport sector, followed by the industry and building sectors.

The Thai government has also been making efforts to promote RE in Thailand in the heating, power, and transport sectors to diversify its fuel sources and enhance energy security. The 15-year Renewable Energy Development Plan set a target to increase the share of alternative energy from 6.4 percent in 2008 to 20 percent in 2022. RE for heating is on track to meet the target. Although RE currently accounts for less than 2 percent of total power generation, because of the attractive tariffs under the RE adder scheme,[2] the total proposed investments under the small power producer (SPP) and very small power producer (VSPP) scheme have already far exceeded the RE target, particularly for solar photovoltaic and wind power. Alternative fuel for transport—both biofuel and natural gas—is the only subsector that lags behind the RE target. In addition, the SPPs and VSPPs need technical assistance and access to finance to make the proposed RE investments a reality.

Barriers

Many EE measures are financially viable for investors at current prices but do not come to fruition because of a number of market failures and barriers:

- *The current energy managers program and voluntary measures to improve EE have not achieved their intended results.* The energy managers program requires energy-intensive factories or buildings to appoint energy managers, but the managers have no incentive to turn the planned EE investments to achieve energy savings into reality.

- *Despite their lifetime "negative" costs (fuel savings are greater than additional investments), obtaining finance for the up-front investments in EE is a major challenge.* EE investments tend to be small, but with high transaction costs.

They are also perceived to be risky because investors are not sure whether the expected future savings will be realized. Financial institutions lack the required expertise and interest in developing the EE business line. As a result, domestic banks in Thailand provide inadequate EE lending, particularly to small and medium enterprises and to energy service companies (ESCOs). Although lack of domestic capital is rarely a problem, inadequate policy frameworks and institutional capacity are significant constraints to financing EE in Thailand.

- *RE development in Thailand also continues to face significant implementation barriers.* Despite the high level of private sector interest in RE power investment, the Ministry of Energy has expressed concern about whether the submitted proposals will actually materialize, given that some SPPs and VSPPs do not have much experience with RE and have difficulty accessing finance. The ministry has been revising application criteria to screen out investors with no real expertise or experience. A complicated approval process for several types of RE resources also delayed implementation of a number of projects.

Objectives

The objective of the EERF is to stimulate and leverage commercial financing for EE projects and to help commercial banks develop streamlined procedures for project appraisal and loan disbursement. The fund provides capital to Thai banks to fund EE projects, and the banks provide low-interest loans to EE projects.

The objective of the ESCO Fund is to supply start-up capital to ESCOs and clean energy project developers by providing for the government to co-invest with private investors. It aims to address the problem of access to equity for smaller-scale RE and EE projects. The fund seeks to promote more than US$40 million of RE and EE investments resulting in at least 10 ktoe in energy savings or US$8 million.

Design of the Energy Efficiency Revolving Fund

The EERF was established to promote EE lending by Thai banks. The EERF extends credit lines to participating banks at a low interest rate to stimulate bank lending for EE projects.

Financing Instruments

The EERF provides credit lines to 11 participating Thai banks (expanded from the six participating banks in 2005) at a zero interest rate with the requirement that the funds be on-lent to project borrowers at an interest rate of not more than 4 percent to cover their management and administration costs and risk. The repayment period is not more than seven years. The maximum loan size from the EERF per project is B 50 million (US$1.25 million). The EERF has no fixed conditions regarding the leverage ratio in each project. In practice, projects requiring funding of less than B 50 million normally borrow 100 percent from the EERF. For projects requiring funding greater than B 50 million, the commercial banks provide the rest.

The initial size of the fund was B 2 billion (about US$55 million at the then current exchange rate). Six participating banks were initially selected as partners in the EERF. Each bank was provided a credit line in the range of B 100 million to B 400 million (about US$2.5 million to US$10 million). The Department of Alternative Energy Development and Efficiency (DEDE) reserved the right to adjust the credit lines according to the actual requirements for the EE investments made by each bank. It was planned that funds would only be released from the EERF to each bank as required to meet loan drawdowns.

Loan repayments flow back to the ENCON Fund and not to the EERF itself. When each phase is committed, a proposal for replenishment of the EERF is submitted to the ENCON Fund. According to DEDE, the repayment rate has been highly satisfactory.

A summary of the characteristics of the EERF is provided in table 15.1.

The participating banks use their standard credit evaluation and project appraisal criteria for evaluating the loans. Loan applications are assessed mainly on the basis of the project proponent's balance sheet and assets rather than on the cash flows and savings from the EE project itself. Therefore, the finance is asset-based rather than project-based lending.

Project Beneficiaries and Selection of Participating Institutions
The eligible projects (EE measures) are as defined in the ENCON Act and focus on industries and buildings. Any commercial bank interested in participating in the program is eligible.

Implementing Agency
The banks are responsible for the overall lending process, including marketing, appraisal, and credit approval, and for loan collection and enforcement of all

Table 15.1 Summary of Thailand Energy Efficiency Revolving Fund

Fund size	Phase I, US$100 million
	Phase II, US$66 million
	Phase III, US$65 million (including renewable energy)
	Phase IV, US$13 million
	Phase V, US$17 million
Eligible borrowers	Industrial and commercial facility owners, ESCOs, and project developers
Eligible projects	EE and RE
Loan size	Up to 100% of project costs
	Less than US$1.4 million per project
Loan term	7 years
Interest rate	Up to 4% (negotiable)
Number of participating banks	11

Sources: Sajjakulnukit 2008; Sinsukprasert 2010.
Note: Exchange rate is B 30/US$.

remedies in default events. DEDE executes a standard contract with each partici-pating bank for the implementation of the EERF. The contract defines the terms and conditions for the fund's operations.

Technical Assistance Program

DEDE provides technical assistance in project appraisal and supports energy audits and feasibility studies. DEDE has retained a group of technical consultants from the Energy Research Institute at Chulalongkorn University to carry out technical assessments. Regardless of who conducts the technical assessment and appraisal, the participating bank assumes all project risk.

Design of the ESCO Fund

Financing instruments. The ESCO Fund can provide equity investment, venture capital, and credit guarantees; can facilitate equipment leasing; and can support project development. As of the end of 2011, most of the funds have been pro-vided as equity investments. Although a credit guarantee is listed as one of the instruments, none have been provided.

Project beneficiaries. Project beneficiaries are factory owners and ESCOs that would like to develop EE projects or would like to replace conventional energy with RE.

Implementing agency. Two fund managers have been selected—the Energy Conservation Foundation of Thailand and the Energy for Environment Foundation.

Technical assistance program. The program will provide technical assistance on EE and RE projects to developers from the start to the completion of project implementation.

Implementation Results

The EERF supported more than 335 EE and 112 RE projects during 2003–10 and resulted in a total investment of about US$453 million, includ-ing US$210 million in financing from the EERF. (See figure 15.1 for a break-down by project type.) This represents an average leverage ratio of about 1:1 for the total portfolio. The leverage ratio of the total portfolio has been increasing to about 2:1 as banks become more familiar and confident with participating projects, and thus are willing to take on more risk on these projects. Total energy savings through 2009 are estimated to be more than US$154 million per year. The average payback period is approximately three years.

So far, the EERF has completed four phases in which 100 percent of the fund has been committed. By the end of 2011, the fund was in its fifth phase, at which time 90 percent of the funds had been committed, and the remainder was expected to be committed in 2012, with several projects in the pipeline for

Figure 15.1 Projects Supported by the Energy Efficiency Revolving Fund during 2003–09 by Type of Technology
Percent

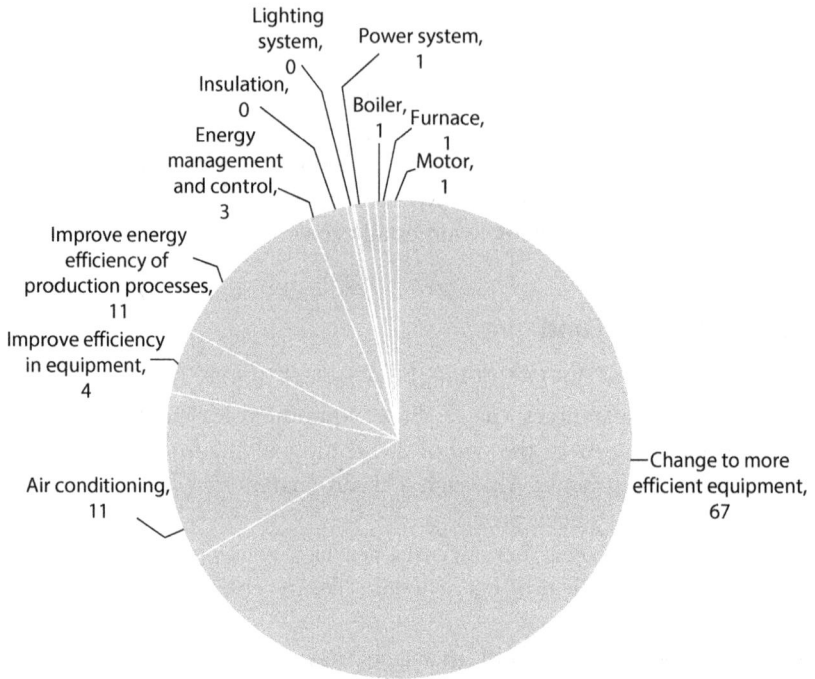

Source: Sinsukprasert 2010.

approval. The proposal for a sixth phase for an amount of B 1,000 million was submitted in 2011 to the ENCON Fund Committee for consideration and approval.

As of April 2010, the ESCO Fund had supported 26 projects, mostly RE investments, with a total investment of US$145 million. (See figure 15.2 for a breakdown by project type.) The US$12 million from the ESCO Fund resulted in 32 ktoe of energy saved, or US$18 million per year.

Lessons Learned

The ENCON Fund has made substantial contributions to mainstreaming energy conservation and RE development in the energy sector, as well as to prioritizing RE and EE issues in the national agenda. The later period of the ENCON Fund included increasing efforts to tackle barriers in RE and EE development, particularly access to finance through the EERF and the ESCO Fund.

The EERF has been successful in increasing participation from commercial banks and the private sector in EE and has supported many clean energy projects. Key success factors are provision of low-cost capital (zero-interest funds)

Figure 15.2 Projects Supported by the ESCO Fund
Percent

Biomass thermal, 1.47
Biogas, 1.80
Solar power, 13.21
Solar hot water, 0.29
Energy efficient equipment, 1.88
Biomass power, 81.34

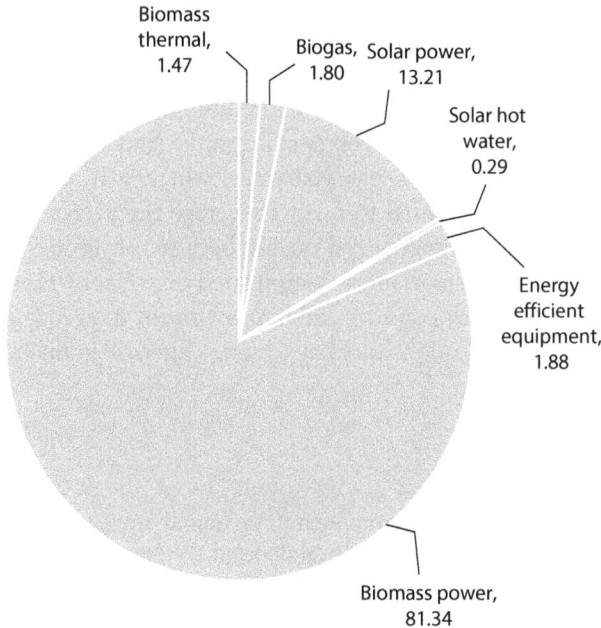

Source: Sinsukprasert 2010.

to the commercial banks, and simplified procedures for project application, appraisal, and loan processing. The banks found the program attractive because they were able to obtain "deal flow" by offering loans at below-market interest rates and therefore saw an opportunity to leverage new business. Project proponents, particularly large industrial and commercial energy users, were able to obtain external finance from banks when they could not access internal funds.

However, the EERF required the banks to assume all of the credit risk. Consequently, banks generally used asset-based financing and provided loans only to customers with strong balance sheets or other assets. These customers are generally larger-scale companies. The EERF did not facilitate credit enhancement and simply provided low-cost funds to the creditworthy borrowers. The result was that very few ESCO projects were financed (only three in Phases I and II combined) because most of the ESCOs in Thailand have limited financial capacity and weak balance sheets. Smaller-scale businesses and newcomers in the sector also faced limited access to finance because of banks' asset-based evaluation criteria.

Moving forward, there is room to enhance the operations of the EERF to further leverage untapped potential, particularly small and medium industrial EE and building EE projects. The terms and conditions (interest rate and repayment period), financial instruments (guarantee and credit enhancement), and design (loan size, technical assistance, and capacity-building program) of the EERF are likely be reviewed to meet changing local market conditions and to provide finance to untapped potential.

The ESCO Fund has also been well received by the private sector because it is suitably designed to tackle the lack of equity financing for smaller-scale RE projects. The fund's size, however, is still limited and could be expanded. Innovative instruments such as a risk guarantee, which is in the scope of the ESCO Fund and has the potential to further leverage the private sector investment, has not yet been operationalized mainly because of limited funding and the capacity of fund managers in more complicated financial markets and transactions. The government may consider combining current fund managers' strong sectoral expertise with institutions that have strong expertise in financial transactions and markets.

Notes

1. Thailand's Energy Conservation Promotion Act required "designated" industrial consumers (defined as facilities with electrical demand greater than 1.0 MW or annual energy use of more than 20 terajoules per year of electrical energy equivalent) to appoint an energy manager, submit data on energy use to the Department of Alternative Energy Development and Efficiency (DEDE) every six months, submit preliminary and detailed energy audits to DEDE, and submit targets and plans for increasing energy efficiency to DEDE.
2. The "adder" is a scheme analogous to the feed-in tariff.

Bibliography

Sajjakulnukit, Boonrod. 2008. "Thailand's Experience with Its Energy Conservation Fund and Revolving Fund." Paper presented at the Asia Clean Energy Forum, June 3.

Sinsukprasert, Prasert. 2010. "Financing Energy Efficiency and Renewable Energy: Thailand's ENCON Fund." Paper presented at the International Energy Efficiency Forum, Astana, Kazakhstan, September 27–30.

CHAPTER 16

Case Study: China Second Energy Conservation Project

Introduction

The China Second Energy Conservation Project (EC II) was approved by the World Bank Board in October 2002. The project's objective was to expand domestic investment in energy efficiency (EE) projects through the aggressive development of China's nascent energy management company (EMC) industry, thereby achieving large-scale EE improvements and associated reductions in the growth of carbon dioxide (CO_2) emissions and other pollutants. The project was designed to achieve the objective by establishing an EMC loan guarantee program to enhance new and emerging EMCs' credit so they could access commercial financing and by forming an EMC association to provide technical assistance and capacity building to EMCs. The project was successfully completed in June 2010.

Country Context

Improving EE has been a cornerstone of China's energy policy since the early 1980s, and China increasingly uses market-based mechanisms to promote EE. In particular, the joint European Commission, Global Environment Facility, and International Bank for Reconstruction and Development China Energy Conservation Project (1998–2006) introduced a market-based approach to financing energy conservation investments through energy saving performance contracting (ESPC)—a practice typical for an energy service company (ESCO) or an EMC.[1] The program involved three newly established pilot EMCs in Beijing, Liaoning, and Shandong. As a follow-on project, the US$26 million Global Environment Facility's EC II was implemented during 2003–10 as a major dissemination and expansion effort to help overcome the barriers to rapid and efficient development of China's EMC industry.

Barriers

The first China Energy Conservation Project successfully demonstrated that the ESPC concept is viable under Chinese conditions. However, four main barriers still constrained new EMC development:

- *Lack of awareness of the basic concept.* Despite steady efforts to publicize the concept of ESPC, the idea remains unknown except to some businesses specializing in energy conservation work.

- *Lack of knowledge and skills to operate EMC businesses.* ESPC, as operated by the EMCs, is a novel and sophisticated business concept. Key capacities required include (a) excellent and up-to-date knowledge of energy conservation technologies and their practical application, to provide value added to customers and minimize technical risks; (b) the ability to assess and minimize host-enterprise credit risks, employing various credit appraisal techniques and a variety of options to secure repayment prospects; (c) sophisticated corporate financial management, including project portfolio risk management; and (d) contract, procurement, and project implementation management. In principle, these comprehensive abilities could be obtained through business practice, good staffing, incentive mechanisms, training, and a variety of other avenues. However, new EMCs still find it difficult to obtain these abilities.

- *Lack of credit financing for EMC business development.* Chinese commercial banks focus primarily on loan security issues and are particularly risk averse. They do not fully understand the ESPC mechanism, and are not familiar with EE technologies and projects. Also, EMCs do not have track records to be considered creditworthy by the banks, and it is usually difficult for EMCs to provide the mortgages or guarantees required by commercial banks. Thus, loans either to EMCs or to the host enterprises that implement ESPC projects are perceived to be highly risky and unacceptable to financial institutions.

- *Difficulties securing sufficient equity financing.* Equity finance is especially important if EMCs are to provide at least some finance for their projects. Securing equity investment is often subject to the problems noted above, and obtaining credit finance becomes a chicken-and-egg problem—if credit financing can be secured, equity investments are easier to obtain, and vice versa.

Objectives

The objective of the EC II project was to expand domestic investment in EE projects through the aggressive development of China's nascent EMC industry, thereby achieving large-scale EE improvements and associated reductions in the growth of CO_2 emissions and other pollutants.

Design

The project had three components: (a) an EMC service component, designed primarily to provide in-depth, practical technical assistance to new and emerging EMCs on setting up and developing their businesses; (b) an EMC loan guarantee program, designed to provide new and emerging EMCs with enhanced opportunities to receive loans from domestic banks, and to engage the banks in the development of a sustainable EMC industry; and (c) a project monitoring, reporting, and evaluation component designed to support the coordination and evaluation work. The EMC service component was implemented by the ESCO Committee of the China Energy Conservation Association, also commonly known as China's Energy Management Company Association (EMCA); the EMC loan guarantee program was implemented by the China National Investment and Guarantee Co. Ltd. (I&G) as the sole implementing agency.

Key Features of the EMC Loan Guarantee Program
Guarantee Beneficiaries
EMCs are the key guarantee beneficiaries and must be the borrowers. Guarantees cannot be provided if the borrower is an end user.

Project Eligibility
Projects were eligible if savings on the customer's energy bill would account for more than 50 percent of total project benefits and the project was implemented using the ESPC mechanism.

One of objectives of EC II was to popularize the ESPC mechanism under market conditions and improve EE; therefore, the projects supported by the guarantee program had to be implemented using the ESPC mechanism. In an ESPC project, the investment, any net increase in operating costs, and reasonable profits are covered by the energy savings, and the customer's cash flow remains positive throughout the project's lifetime.

Participating Banks
The guarantee program was open to all banks. A total of 12 Chinese banks with 37 branches participated. The Bank of Beijing was among the most active commercial banks in the EMC loan guarantee program, with 20 of its branches issuing loans to 68 percent of the ESPC projects.

Characteristics of Guarantee Mechanism
- Guarantee coverage and risks: The program provided a loan guarantee of up to 90 percent of the principal of a single project loan. The participating banks covered the remaining risks. The risk coverage level was determined during project design. If the borrower defaulted, I&G had the recourse right. The program's projected loss rate was 2.54 percent, and the actual loss rate was 1.08 percent. Five projects defaulted with subrogation of 23.5 million Chinese yuan (Y; US$3.7 million), of which Y 10.4 million (US$1.6 million) was recovered.

- Counter guarantee: Counter guarantees were required, but the stipulations were often less stringent than banks usually demanded and involved EMC assets, collateral, and diversified portfolio security; third-party partial counter guarantees; and various methods for using specific EMC contracts with host enterprises as security.
- Guarantee fee: The guarantee fee was about 1.0–1.5 percent of the loan amount, based on project-specific risks and costs.
- Deal flow: Deal flow was mainly generated from I&G branches, EMCA members, and partner banks.
- Average size, payback period, and type of EE investments: The average loan size was US$3.9 million. The average payback period was between two and four years. Most were industrial projects.

Key Features of Technical Assistance

The EMC service component consisted of a large capacity-building and technical assistance program to raise broad awareness of the EMC mechanism, assist new EMCs to grow into established businesses, and help develop policy support. The core of the technical assistance was the establishment and development of EMCA into a permanent, self-sustaining institution, so it could fulfill its function over the short and long terms. EMCA's main activities include the following:

- Training and cross-exchange events for its members and prospective new EMCs,
- Information compilation and dissemination through a variety of channels,
- Support for expansion of the ESPC market and sensitizing market players to the potential role of EMCs,
- Advocacy with the government and promotion for policy support, and
- International exchange and cooperation.

Implementation Results

EC II fully achieved its objectives and played a key role in the successful development of the nascent EMC industry in China. ESPC investment in 2009 totaled about US$2.7 billion. China's ESPC business has grown much more strongly than originally expected. Direct energy-savings benefits from ESPC investments in 2009 totaled about 116.1 million tons of coal equivalent, which equates to 82.7 million tons of CO_2, and exceeded its target by 16 times. The project fostered the broad development of the EMCs operating in China.

The EMC loan guarantee program implemented by I&G helped to address inadequate access to commercial financing, which is a leading problem in EMC development in virtually all countries. I&G issued loan guarantees for 148 EMC projects during 2004–09 totaling Y 517 million (US$80 million), supporting Y 910 million (US$142 million) in ESPC project investments. The lending support to China's new EMCs was important; however, the special value of I&G's program was to operationally introduce new EMCs to the financing world, and the new ESPC business to the banking industry. The guarantee company guaranteed loans to 42 different EMCs, most of which were privately owned. Almost all of these EMCs received their first-ever bank loan under the program.

EMCA has been a focal point for (a) fostering the legitimization of the EMC industry in China, (b) providing general and practical technical assistance for newly emerging and potential EMCs, (c) helping EMCs overcome obstacles in technology or business at start-up, (d) building a platform for communications between EMCs and the government, and (e) assisting the government in development of supportive policies for the EMC industry (e.g., EMCA played a key role in the development of the new national special support policies for the EMC industry approved by China's State Council in 2010). EMCA membership rose from 89 entities in 2004 to 450 in 2009. EMCA has established itself as the principal institution representing China's EMC industry both in China and internationally.

Lessons Learned

The government's EE commitments and policies are essential. Broad government support for the promotion of EE in general and specific support for the development of the EMC industry were the determining factors in the success of this program. The attention given to EE by government authorities and enterprise managers at all levels in response to the government's insistence on achieving its national target of reducing energy use per unit of gross domestic product (GDP) by 20 percent during the 11th Five-Year Plan (2006–10) increased demand for EE services and project investment. In addition, specific government support for the ESPC mechanism was also important, including its clear and steady backing for all of the project's promotional activities, and research and support for policy issues.

Phased international support is an effective approach. The design and implementation of a long-term project approach involving two strategically phased projects to introduce, and then expand, the adoption of the mechanism in China, implemented over a 12-year period, was a key factor in the successful development outcome of the project. The results of the demonstration EMCs supported under Phase I were reviewed and incorporated into this second project. To encourage the market underpinnings for expansion of the industry under EC II, that project subsequently aimed to avoid direct grants to new or emerging EMCs, and substituted the Chinese commercial banking industry, supported with suitable risk-mitigation and technical assistance measures.

The technical assistance program (EMCA component) was critical. The creation of a new, permanent EMC industry association to deliver technical assistance to newly developing EMCs, foster mutual assistance between EMCs, and represent the industry to government and others proved to be a good decision.

Key factors underlying EMCA's success included (a) clear association with, but independence from, the government; (b) success in managing relations between companies within the association; and (c) substantial, stable—but declining and finite—source of finance for operations provided under the project. A critical factor was the quality of EMCA's leadership, who proved capable of balancing a series of conflicting interests and demands, and steering the new entity onto a stable and sustainable path.

Collaboration with financial sector institutions helped finance ESPC projects. The EMC loan guarantee program was a first trial of the use of Global Environment Facility funds by the World Bank to support an in-country guarantee reserve fund. The mechanism proved successful in generating deal flow, involving 12 Chinese banks in ESPC projects for the first time. Specific strong points include preservation of reserve fund capital and successful outreach to 42 different EMCs, the majority of which received their first-ever bank loan under the program. Deal volume could have been increased greatly if the program had been opened up to cover a wider variety of EE lending opportunities, and not just those involving the relatively narrow field of ESPC. However, limiting the program to ESPC proved to be the right decision because the specialization resulted in both remarkable coverage of the program within the EMC industry and innovation in developing finance products especially for EMCs.

Careful selection of implementing agency is essential. I&G is the largest state-owned insurance company in China. It is quite risk averse, with little appetite for credit risk. During the initial project implementation stage, deal flows were limited. I&G required 90 percent counter guarantees, which drove away many ESCOs that were interested in the product. However, technical assistance helped I&G develop new product lines and lower its counter guarantee requirements. The success of the initial ESCO projects also increased its confidence. Subsequent to project completion, the I&G ESCO guarantee team stayed in place at its own expense, an early sign of program sustainability.

Note

1. An ESPC involves a turnkey service for purchasing a complete package of EE improvements, usually with minimal or no up-front cost to the client. A typical ESPC project is delivered by an ESCO that guarantees that the savings produced by the improvements will be sufficient to finance the full cost of the project. Although ESCOs have been active on a large scale since the late 1980s—originating in Europe and North America—many countries, such as China, adopted the concept in the late 1990s and began to achieve successful market development. The terms ESCO and EMC are interchangeable in this case study.

Bibliography

Project Management Office of the China WB/GEF Energy Conservation Project. 2003. "Operations Manual to the Second WB/GEF Energy Conservation Project." Washington, DC: World Bank.

World Bank. 2002. "Project Appraisal Document on a Proposed GEF Grant of SDR 19.7 Million (US$26 Equivalent) to the People's Republic of China for the Second Energy Conservation Project." World Bank, Washington, DC, September 25.

————. 2010. *Implementation Complementation Report for China Second Energy Conservation Project.* Report No. ICR00001480, World Bank, Washington, DC.

CHAPTER 17

Case Study: China Utility-Based Energy Efficiency Finance Program

Introduction

The China Utility-Based Energy Efficiency Finance Program (CHUEE) was initiated in 2006 by the International Finance Corporation (IFC), in collaboration with the Global Environment Facility (GEF), to stimulate energy efficiency (EE) investments in China. The program relied on two main financial instruments: bank guarantees for EE loans and technical assistance to market players including utilities, equipment vendors, and energy service companies to help implement EE projects. Both types of interventions depended on subsidies funded by donor agencies. The IFC drew upon the success of its similar programs worldwide, which had been designed to target barriers similar to those encountered in China. The lessons learned from these programs helped in designing and conducting a detailed assessment of the EE market situation in China.

The IFC decided to implement a risk-sharing facility in partnership with several local banks. The initiative was supported by the Chinese government's increased energy conservation efforts defined in its 11th Five-Year Plan. The program initially identified three existing IFC clients to be partner companies: Xinao Gas Holdings Ltd., a private natural gas distribution company; China Minsheng Banking Corp. Ltd., based in Beijing; and Industrial Bank (IB), based in Fuzhou in the Fujian Province. The IFC was supposed to provide guarantees and technical assistance to the banks, market partners, and end users (customers). However, Minsheng decided not to participate in the program and there was a mismatch between IB and Xinao. Consequently, the initial utility-based business model was abandoned, and the program was implemented featuring financial institution partners that provided loans to end users. The participating financial institutions comprised IB, Bank of Beijing (BOB), and Shanghai Pudong Development Bank.

Country Context

China is now the world's largest energy-consuming nation and largest source of global greenhouse gas (GHG) emissions. China's total demand for energy—and resulting GHG emissions—is rapidly increasing to support the country's continuing economic growth. The primary energy demand in China increased by more than 100 percent in less than 10 years, exceeding 2,920 million tons of coal equivalent in 2009. Meanwhile, China's gross domestic product (GDP) more than tripled, from 9,920 billion Chinese yuan (Y; US$1.5 trillion) in 2000 to Y 34,050 billion (US$5.5 trillion) in 2009. About 75 percent of China's primary energy supply is sourced from coal, and more than 50 percent of its energy consumption occurs in the industrial sector. If economic growth continues at the projected rate of 7.2 percent per year, total consumption would grow to exceed 12 billion tons of coal equivalent by 2030, leading to massive increases in coal consumption and substantial increases in related GHG emissions. The government of China has recognized the challenges posed by continuing increases in energy consumption and GHG emissions, and has made a national commitment to a less energy-intensive development path. China has made unprecedented efforts to improve the energy efficiency (EE) of its economy by setting and achieving energy-intensity-reduction targets in its 11th Five-Year Plan and has now established ambitious targets for the 12th Five-Year Plan.

The investments in EE improvement required to meet the 12th Five-Year Plan targets are estimated to be in excess of US$50 billion, and there is a large financing gap for medium and large energy conservation investments in the industrial sector. Given the economic and financial appeal of such projects, since the late 1990s the government has gradually eliminated public funds earmarked for industrial energy conservation project financing, expecting Chinese enterprises to invest their own resources and banks to build energy conservation lending business lines. Recognizing the major barriers to scaling up private investments in EE, the government has been seeking innovative financing approaches to leverage commercial financing of EE.

Barriers

In January 2004, the government requested the IFC to provide assistance for developing new private sector initiatives in financing renewable energy and EE projects. After two years of research, the IFC launched the program, which was approved by the IFC Board in May 2006. In designing the program, the IFC identified the following market failures and barriers to EE investment in China:

- Lack of information, which limits end users' ability to gain adequate knowledge on EE technologies and equipment and to assess the risks of financing such projects;
- Lack of awareness and experience among Chinese commercial banks about the financing of EE projects;

- Lack of financial and technical skills on the part of industries to prepare investment grade or bankable EE project proposals; and
- Risk aversion in the Chinese banking sector, which customarily makes credit decisions based on fixed asset collateral. Consequently, EE players such as equipment suppliers and energy service companies (ESCOs) faced difficulties accessing finance for their EE projects because they did not have strong balance sheets.

Program Objectives

The principal objective of CHUEE was to catalyze EE investments in China, thus supplementing China's efforts to conserve energy and to reduce GHG emissions. The program had two components: (a) a guarantee for EE loans and (b) provision of technical assistance to financial institutions, to market partners including ESCOs and equipment suppliers and vendors, and to end users of energy.

Specific project objectives included the following:

- Provide a risk-sharing facility through a partial credit guarantee to banks, supplemented by technical assistance to banks for capacity building, business development, and relationship brokerage to build the banks' knowledge and capacity, overcome their risk perceptions, and help develop customized appraisal procedures for EE projects;
- Provide technical assistance to the market partners in the development of bankable project proposals and help foster relationships with banks to facilitate access to financing; and
- Provide technical assistance to energy end users to increase their knowledge and awareness of the EE opportunities, the requirements of the banks, and the ESCO models to help them understand the various financing options and increase their interest and capacity to identify EE projects and access financing for the projects.

CHUEE Program Design

To achieve the objectives and overcome the barriers outlined above, CHUEE was designed to have three major components:

- Partial credit guarantee, to address financial risk issues and reduce risk averseness of the participating banks;
- Technical assistance to EE stakeholders, to assist them in properly assessing the EE potential of their facilities and structuring their EE projects; and
- Market outreach and information dissemination, to create market momentum and increase general awareness of the market.

The program was designed as a US$215.5 million facility, which included a US$16.5 million grant component from the GEF and another US$3 million from other donors.

Partial Credit Guarantee

CHUEE was designed to apportion the EE project risk between the IFC and the partner banks by providing credit risk guarantees, which were expected to provide incentives to the banks to lend to EE projects. The objective of this risk-sharing structure was to give some confidence to the local banks to develop and try different flexible EE financing products, while taking less risk. The risk-sharing structure is illustrated in the table.

Risk	Risk sharing
First 10 percent of the loss	75 percent covered by the IFC
	25 percent borne by the participating bank
Remaining 90 percent of the loss	40 percent covered by the IFC
	60 percent borne by the participating bank

Technical Assistance to Market Partners

The program conducted various studies and provided training and marketing support to various EE participants. The marketing studies commissioned by the program helped to fine-tune the target areas for the intervention; this was important because the program's target sectors shifted when the utility-based approach was abandoned. The technical assistance covered various aspects of the EE business and provided assistance to the key market stakeholders. Significant portions of the technical assistance were designed to assist Chinese banks to develop their knowledge of the EE market and familiarize them with the different structures applied to EE deals. This effort included introducing project finance lending products, lending to ESCOs, and savings-based lending. Consultants hired by the program also provided project-by-project reviews of the EE projects for the banks that used the risk-sharing facility.

Technical assistance was also provided to build the capacity of project proponents and ESCOs by providing training and advice to project developers so they could be credible partners for financial institutions. The program conducted

- Seminars on obtaining bank loans and preparing loan applications;
- Training on business and management, including direct help to access finance by introducing ESCOs to banks or other financing windows (the Clean Development Mechanism, carbon trade, and others);
- Annual meetings and various fairs, which provided briefings on new and innovative domestic and foreign EE technologies; and
- Training sessions to equipment suppliers to market the program, build staff capacity, and assist customers in preparing EE projects for financing and in marketing their equipment in partnership with banks.

Market Outreach and Information Dissemination

A significant component of the program, contributing to achieving market momentum and sustainability, was increasing general market awareness of EE technology, services, and successful projects. CHUEE attempted to demonstrate the benefits of EE finance and the approach to accessing EE finance. The program also helped to overcome the asymmetry of information about EE, whereby only ESCOs, equipment vendors, and engineering companies had sufficient knowledge of EE, and their clients and financiers had little or none.

Structure and Governance

The program was operated by the designated project team within the IFC Beijing Office and was comanaged by the IFC regional, financial markets, and environment departments. The IFC's investment officers from the financial market department exerted limited managerial control and oversight, and the risk-sharing facility was mainly handled by the program team.

The evaluation of the project concluded that oversight and an accountability framework were lacking, which contributed to irregular processing in project approval and service provisioning (World Bank Independent Evaluation Group 2010). For example, the IFC was supposed to conduct technical reviews of only the first five projects, and then hand over the responsibility for technical review to the client banks. This handover did not take place, and when IB requested more reviews by the program team, the legal agreement was not clear about the arrangement.

The contractual arrangements between the IFC and the partner banks left room for different interpretations of maximum exposure limits per project and client, which led to a portfolio biased toward one of the borrowers, rather than being well diversified.

Implementation Results

At the start of the program, it became clear that the interests of the initial partners targeted by the IFC were not in alignment, and the program design was changed from a utility-based model to guarantee-backed bank lending.

IB, the first banking partner, rapidly built up its portfolio of EE project lending and, within less than a year, had fully used the guarantee facility of Y 460 million (US$60 million), financing 50 loans to 35 companies. Consequently, the IFC modified the program in December 2007 to enhance the guarantee portion by reallocating GEF resources from technical assistance to additional guarantees and adding supplemental IFC resources (referred to as the second guarantee facility or "CHUEE II").

EE financing activity by commercial banks has been increasing in China in recent years, and even without the program, the participant banks likely would have grown their EE business. However, the program evaluation indicated that with the program, IB's EE lending grew at twice the rate of comparator banks, and the quality of its EE lending portfolio was very good (zero defaults). Its faster growth relative to comparator banks was helped by the support provided by CHUEE for establishing a dedicated EE lending department—a unique feature among Chinese banks—and for preparing guidelines and procedures for EE loans, and by capacity building for applying project-finance tools to EE finance.

Upon completion of the program evaluation in June 2009, the following results had been obtained (sum of IB and BOB):

- Number of projects: 98
- Number of participating companies: 78
- Total loan amounts: US$512 million
- Total project investments: US$936 million
- Guarantees provided: US$197 million

Although the program design had assumed a default rate of 2.5 percent, no defaults occurred under the guarantee program. In comparison, China's commercial banks' default rate was 1.14 percent in 2010.

CHUEE's technical assistance and outreach activities were provided to 47 banks and financial institutions, 14 utilities, 67 equipment suppliers, 72 end users, and 135 ESCOs.

The projects financed were primarily in the heavy industries, with steel representing the largest portion (37 percent), followed by chemicals (20 percent) and cement (17 percent). Other industries included coking, food, and glass. Non-industrial applications (such as municipal buildings, hospitals, and the like) accounted for very few projects. Almost all the projects were very large—the average loan size was US$5.7 million—and paybacks ranged from two to four years.

The estimated GHG reductions (based on engineering calculations) were 14 million tons of CO_2 equivalent.

Lessons Learned

The major lessons learned as documented by the program evaluation are summarized below:

- Careful selection of private sector partners is needed to meet strategic program objectives. CHUEE demonstrated that when the interests of the partners are not aligned with each other and with the overall program objectives, the results are likely to be affected and project objectives not met.
- A guarantee by itself is not an adequate incentive to increase EE lending. Collateral requirements are only one reason for the lack of dedicated EE financing products in China. Building the capacity of the commercial banks is equally important so they can properly assess project risks.
- Flexibility is needed in program design to respond to unexpected challenges and opportunities. The program design cannot always perfectly match market conditions after the program is launched. More often than not, from the time a program is designed to the moment it is implemented, the market experiences changes that might require adjustments to the program structure.
- Government policies and market readiness are important factors in determining program design. The timing of CHUEE coincided with the Chinese government's focus on EE, which was outlined in the 11th Five-Year Plan.

- In emerging markets, caution is needed in applying a utility-based EE finance model. As became clear in the beginning of the program, the gas utility eventually backed out of the program.
- An exit plan is critical. Although generating EE financing opportunities was the immediate objective of the program, sustainability was equally important. Therefore, an exit strategy must be developed at the beginning of the program. Developing a network of resources for technical evaluation of projects is often the most important component of the exit strategy.

Bibliography

World Bank Independent Evaluation Group. 2010. *Energy Efficiency Finance: Assessing the Impact of IFC's China Utility Energy Efficiency Finance Program.* Washington, DC: World Bank.

CHAPTER 18

Case Study: Commercializing Energy Efficiency Finance (CEEF)

Introduction

The Commercializing Energy Efficiency Finance (CEEF) Program was launched in April 2003 as a joint program of the International Finance Corporation (IFC) and the Global Environment Facility (GEF), with the IFC acting as the executing agent for the GEF. The CEEF program was based on experience gained from the Hungarian Energy Efficiency Co-financing Program (HEECP), which had been initiated in Hungary in 1997. The countries included in the CEEF program were the Czech Republic, the Slovak Republic, Estonia, Latvia, and Lithuania. In 2005, Hungary was added and HEECP was merged into the CEEF program. The CEEF program was successfully completed in December 2008.

Country Context

Although substantial potential for improvement of energy efficiency (EE) had been identified in the targeted countries, very few EE projects were being implemented in the 1990s, primarily because of a lack of availability of finance for such projects. Conditions during this period indicated that a number of market factors would be favorable to the implementation of EE projects:

- Prevailing energy prices were high and increasing,
- Energy utilization was substantially and inherently inefficient,
- A number of energy service providers were entering the market, and
- Financial markets were evolving.

However, finance for EE projects was limited, and few projects were being financed and implemented.

Barriers

The IFC identified the following important barriers to implementation of EE projects in the target countries:

- Weak credit and unfamiliar risk profiles of energy users and energy service companies (ESCOs),
- Extremely cautious financial institution (FI) lending practices,
- Lack of collateral value of EE project equipment,
- Lack of relevant expertise and capacity in local FIs,
- Poor capability on the part of project hosts and ESCOs to prepare bankable EE projects,
- Relatively high transaction costs associated with EE project development and finance,
- Lack of medium- to long-term finance needed to allow EE projects to be self-financing through savings, and
- High interest rates.

The CEEF program focused on addressing these barriers through a combination of risk sharing and technical assistance.

Program Objectives

The CEEF program was designed to meet the GEF's objectives of promoting and enhancing commercial finance of EE projects, thereby leading to a reduction of greenhouse gas emissions and creation of a sustainable market in the CEEF countries for EE project development and financing.[1] The two key tools introduced by the CEEF to achieve these objectives were (a) risk sharing and risk management through partial credit guarantees provided to local FIs for loans to EE projects and (b) technical assistance for capacity building within FIs, ESCOs, project developers, and project hosts.

The primary short-term measures used to achieve the CEEF objectives were reduction of credit risk, lowering of transaction costs, and development of institutional capacity of the EE and financial services industries in the CEEF countries to develop and finance EE investment projects.

The program's specific objectives were to

- Reduce the credit risk of EE finance for eligible local FIs (making transactions possible and gaining credit approval for use of the FI's own funds);
- Provide targeted technical assistance to stimulate deal flow and uptake of financial products offered under the guarantee facility (in support of partner FI marketing and delivery of EE financing services and of ESCOs in the preparation of projects and programs for investment);
- Reduce transaction costs borne by project participants;
- Enable longer-term financing (to lower annual finance payments, finance longer payback "deep retrofit" projects, and make EE projects more

attractive to the end user by allowing them to be self-financing from energy cost savings); and

- Help create a sustainable market for finance of EE projects.

Market Structure and Regulatory Environment

The IFC determined that the existing market structure and energy-related policies and regulations were conducive to the implementation of the program. Generally, the CEEF countries were characterized by

- Liquidity in local currency capital markets, including for medium- to long-term financing;
- Existence of credit risk barriers as a limiting factor in mobilizing these local financial resources;
- Macroeconomic conditions that were otherwise reasonably attractive for adequate borrowing and investment, that is, interest rates to end-borrowers in the mid to high teens, and reasonably positive outlooks for inflation and economic growth;
- A capable FI sector (including commercial banks and nonbank FIs) interested in the EE market;
- Strong economics and high technical potential for EE;
- An existing base of EE service providers (including ESCOs) that could deliver EE projects and respond effectively to technical assistance to structure and prepare projects for investment; and
- Policy and institutional support for EE (including previous market preparation activities) and for business investment generally.

Program Design

The CEEF program was designed to work in partnership with local FIs by providing partial guarantees to share in the credit risk of EE loans that the partner FIs would fund with their own resources. The transactions eligible for the program included capital investments aimed at improving the efficiency of energy use in buildings, industrial processes, and other energy end-use applications. Even though many EE investments were economically attractive and could be developed and structured so that the energy cost savings enjoyed by the end users exceeded their loan repayments, most financial intermediaries, especially in emerging markets, were reluctant to finance these transactions because of their unfamiliarity with such projects and the perceived weak client and project credit profiles.

The program, therefore, assisted the banks and FIs in financing EE projects in many areas where they had previously been unwilling to do so. Such projects not only lead to obvious environmental and economic benefits, but often confer considerable social benefits. Some of the projects targeted by the program included EE investment projects by small enterprises, street lighting projects by small towns and villages, and replacement of outdated heating technologies in hospitals.

Risk Sharing

Risk sharing was achieved through an innovative partial guarantee structure under which the IFC guaranteed 50 percent of the project risk equally with the participating FIs. The GEF committed US$17.25 million to the program, of which US$15 million was for the guarantee facility. (The remaining US$2.25 million was used for program operating costs and for technical assistance.) A portion of the GEF contribution was set aside as a first loss reserve.

The IFC committed an additional US$75 million for guarantees, so up to US$180 million in loans from private FIs could be guaranteed. Equity contributions from project sponsors (30 percent) would add another US$57 million, thereby enabling total project investments of US$237 million. This investment was expected to contribute to the competitiveness of these economies as well as to improved local and global environmental conditions. The program was an important tool for supporting each of the countries' national strategies for meeting European Union accession goals and targets.

Technical Assistance

The second major program component was technical assistance to FIs, ESCOs and other project developers, and project hosts. GEF funds for technical assistance leveraged funds from bilateral funding agencies. The technical assistance program had two main purposes: (a) to help prepare projects for investment and (b) to build EE and FI industry capacity in each country. Technical assistance was designed at several levels:

- For FIs participating in the guarantee program, to help market their EE finance services, prepare projects for investment, develop new EE finance products, and build their capacity to originate EE project finance;
- For EE and ESCO businesses, to build their corporate capacity for developing EE projects; and
- For targeted EE market-promotion activities, generally undertaken in cooperation with other organizations.

In addition, the technical assistance program funded the necessary monitoring and evaluation activities to define baselines and confirm post-installation energy and emissions savings achieved by supported projects.

Key Design Elements

The program design differed from other approaches taken in the region to promote EE and was devised to ensure a sustained development impact. The CEEF program was highly market oriented with market-based pricing and availability to multiple financial intermediaries. The program also sought to catalyze investment across a broad range of end-user groups and market segments. In addition, the program's technical assistance components were targeted at building EE finance expertise in the financial sector and hence the ability of ESCOs to market and obtain finance for EE projects. By creating incentives for local FIs to enter the EE finance market, the program helped to increase the local financial sectors' experience and capacity to provide EE project finance on an ongoing and, eventually, on an independent basis.

Specific project design elements included the following:

- Increasing the awareness and interest of Estonian, Latvian, Lithuanian, the Czech Republic, and the Slovak Republic[2] FIs in financing EE projects;
- Establishing guarantee facility agreements with participating FIs and documenting the procedures for approving and providing individual project guarantees (transaction guarantees);
- Reducing the credit risk of individual EE project finance;
- Lowering transaction costs related to project development and financial structuring;
- Assisting FIs in developing specialized financial products targeted at certain end-use market segments;
- Assisting end users and EE companies to prepare bankable EE projects;
- Fostering institutional capacity in the EE and financial services industries to develop and finance EE investment projects; and
- Encouraging the establishment of cooperative relationships between FI and EE companies to increase the deal flow of EE projects.

Implementation Results

Under the CEEF program, the IFC signed guarantee facility agreements with 14 participating FIs. A total of 829 projects were financed using the guarantees. Of these, 72 were individual projects and 757 were portfolio projects (mostly apartment buildings in Hungary). A total of 41 project developers and ESCOs were involved in implementing the guaranteed projects. The total amount of the guarantees provided to the projects was US$49.5 million. These projects represent a total investment of approximately US$208 million. The projects were implemented in five of the six target countries—the Czech Republic, Hungary, Latvia, Lithuania, and the Slovak Republic.[3] The projects have generated carbon dioxide (CO_2) reductions of 145,700 tons per year and energy savings of 846 terajoules per year.

None of the project guarantees provided under the CEEF were called,[4] and the GEF cost per ton of CO_2 reduction for the guaranteed projects was US$2.50 based on losses through the end of 2008. If the leveraged or indirect projects are included, the GEF cost is reduced to US$1.2 per ton of CO_2 reduction.

The program achieved significant progress toward the objective of expanding the availability of commercial financing for EE projects in the target markets. The guaranteed projects are estimated to have led to additional implementation (leveraged projects or indirect effects) of projects by FIs and ESCOs (without the IFC guarantees) of project investments of US$80 million and CO_2 reductions of 164,800 tons per year. Thus, the total guaranteed and leveraged projects resulting from the CEEF program account for US$330 million of investment, annual reductions of 310,500 tons of CO_2, and annual energy savings of 1,956 terajoules. In addition, the program directly led to a separate IFC guarantee for a US$250 million contract between the Hungarian Ministry of Education and a consortium of project developers (which included a bank and an ESCO) to provide EE services to schools throughout Hungary.

The program evaluation concluded that the technical assistance provided by the CEEF program led to substantial capacity building in the FIs as well as in the ESCOs and project development companies (Danish Management Group 2010). The country-specific results were very good relative to the goals in Hungary, the Czech Republic, and the Slovak Republic. Progress in Latvia and Lithuania was more limited.

The program evaluation also concluded that the commercial EE financing activities of the participating FIs increased substantially as a result of the program, and the FIs have developed new financing products tailored to the EE market. Furthermore, the EE financing activities of these FIs continued after the end of the CEEF program, thereby demonstrating the sustainability of the program.

Lessons Learned

The major lesson learned from the CEEF program (and its predecessor HEECP) is that a risk guarantee program can be successful in leveraging finance from commercial FIs. The risk guarantee mitigates the FIs' risk perceptions, allowing them to undertake EE project finance. Many of the participating FIs (particularly in Hungary and the Czech Republic) that gained experience with project financing for EE have provided additional financing without the IFC guarantee and have continued and expanded their financing of EE projects subsequent to conclusion of the CEEF program.

The key factors that appear to have influenced the success of the program in the different countries are (a) EE market maturity and acceptance of the guarantee product; (b) attitudes and interests of FIs; (c) FI staff knowledge, experience, and contacts; and (d) FI staff capability and enthusiasm. The program was more successful in Hungary, the Czech Republic, and the Slovak Republic than in the Baltic countries, where the EE market is in the development stage, FIs have little interest in EE project financing, and fewer ESCOs are in the market.

Some of the other important lessons learned are summarized below:

- The IFC's local presence in each market was important to program success because continual follow-up was required to ensure program take-off. It took at least a year to convince each bank to join the program and to conclude the guarantee facility agreement, and then another year to launch the program in the bank.

- The skills, capabilities, experience, and enthusiasm of the IFC field staff contributed significantly to the success of the program in Hungary and the Czech Republic. Also, the field staff's knowledge and understanding of local market conditions and FI and ESCO characteristics was very useful in program operations.

- The technical assistance component, although performed on an ad hoc basis, was an important element in program success. The seminars and training conducted as a part of the technical assistance activities in response to market needs were reported by the program staff to have been successful and effective and appreciated by the participants. The ad hoc element, while seeming unstructured, permitted for flexibility and adaptation to market needs in the very different participating countries.

- The IFC made changes to improve the flexibility and responsiveness of program operations to be able to react more effectively and promptly to market changes, to create new products and delivery mechanisms, and to develop better relationships with the FIs and other program stakeholders. These changes were appreciated by the field staff and the stakeholders and led to large project volumes.

Notes

1. The first initiative, the HEECP program, started as a pilot phase with HEECP1, in place from 1997 to 2001 in Hungary. An evaluation of HEECP1 conducted in 2000 concluded that the program had developed and used innovative financial products to address credit risk barriers and had contributed to the improvement of the knowledge and capability of financial institutions and project developers, thereby leading to successful mobilization of increased amounts of finance for EE projects. Based on these results, the IFC, in cooperation with the GEF, launched HEECP2 in 2001, providing additional funding for credit guarantees and technical assistance. The CEEF program presented in this case study was initiated in 2003 based on the same setup. In 2005 HEECP2 was merged with the CEEF program.

2. Hungary was added to this list when HEECP was merged with CEEF in 2005.

3. There were no guarantee agreements and projects in Estonia.

4. In HEECP, US$153,000 was paid out for guarantees that were called.

Bibliography

Danish Management Group. 2010. *Final Process and Impact Evaluation, Commercializing Energy Efficiency Finance (CEEF) and Hungarian Energy Efficiency Co-Financing Program (HEECP)*. Report submitted to IFC, February 2010.

CHAPTER 19

Case Study: Bulgarian Energy Efficiency Fund (BEEF)

Introduction

The Bulgarian Energy Efficiency Fund (BEEF) was established with support from the Global Environment Facility (GEF) in accordance with the provisions of the Bulgarian Energy Efficiency Law of 2004, which sought to create broadly based, sustainable commercial financing for energy efficiency (EE) projects. The fund was designed as a dedicated, revolving EE facility with in-house technical and financial evaluation capabilities. The BEEF was to be operated as a not-for-profit organization, managed by a professional fund manager (FM), and income from fees charged to clients of the fund needed only to cover the operating costs and losses from defaults. The BEEF aimed to complement local commercial banks' existing lending facilities and then to achieve higher leverage on its investments.

The BEEF was capitalized with US$10 million of GEF funding, which was designed to support the establishment and operation of the BEEF as a commercially oriented public-private finance facility. GEF funds were used to provide seed capital for the BEEF and to cover setup and operating costs until the BEEF reached financial self-sufficiency, and also to cover partially the initial costs of EE capacity building. Additional financing was secured from the Bulgarian government (US$1.8 million), and the Austrian government provided US$2.0 million.

Country Context

At the initiation of the BEEF in 2005, Bulgaria's energy intensity was more than twice the average value for the European Union and was also considerably higher than that of many transitional economies in Europe. Bulgaria's National Energy Saving Action Plan (2001–2003) (Government of Bulgaria 2001a) identified the significant energy-savings potential—as much as 50 percent of annual energy demand for existing building stock, 40 percent for district heating, and 30 percent for industry. Even though many of the most promising energy saving projects had attractive payback periods of less than three years, very few of them had been carried out. During the period of the Action Plan, commercial finance of EE projects amounted to only US$13 million, or a mere 5 percent of the annual requirements for EE investments included in the National Energy Saving Program to 2010 (Government of Bulgaria 2001b).

Therefore, the government of Bulgaria initiated serious efforts to progress (a) from policy formulation to implementation; (b) from a focus on the supply side to the demand side; (c) from isolated EE projects to coherent programs; (d) from an ineffective EE Agency to a national center of excellence in policy and implementation; and (e) from almost exclusive funding by the government and bilateral donors to the creation of an EE finance market.

The new government policies assigned a high priority to improved EE, creating a supportive policy framework for EE, especially through addressing price distortions in the economy, and promoting the emergence of an EE finance market by establishing a commercially oriented revolving EE fund.

The World Bank's Country Assistance Strategy for Bulgaria was designed to support reforms that assisted the country in meeting its European Union accession requirements concerning EE and environmental protection, and the energy sector was considered important in meeting these requirements. The potential for greenhouse gas (GHG) emission reduction offered by EE investments in Bulgaria was estimated to be high. The country's energy inefficiency and financing barriers to EE, along with the government's credible commitment to addressing them, provided a compelling case for the GEF to support a contingent financing operation in Bulgaria. The financing operation would help to build sustainable market-based capacity to develop and finance EE projects on commercial terms.

Barriers

The major barriers to the uptake of commercial EE finance in Bulgaria were the following:

- Commercial bank intermediation relative to the size of the economy was low by international standards. Insufficient competition allowed banks to manage risks by limiting lending volume, demanding high collateralization (in some cases 200 percent or higher), charging high interest rates to local businesses (between 10 percent and 18 percent, despite inflation of about 4 percent), and focusing on short-term lending (with loan maturities of one to two years).
- Commercial banks were generally not familiar with the technical and economic aspects of EE projects. Also, the financial and technical skills needed for the preparation of sound, bankable EE project proposals were largely missing.
- The relatively small size of EE projects compared with energy supply projects or other conventional bank loans made them unattractive for commercial financing.
- Commercial banks perceived the risks and transaction costs of EE projects to be too high. The perception of high risk constrained finance to the potential

EE projects of small and medium enterprises, housing cooperatives, municipalities, hospitals, and similar energy consumers.

- Information about EE technologies, the effectiveness of EE measures, and project development and financing techniques was unavailable, partly because of the lack of a strong institutional focal point within the government for effective information dissemination, including "good practices" for EE.
- Innovative financing approaches, such as energy performance contracting, were not being used because of the lack of a mature and competitive energy services industry.

The BEEF was designed to address these barriers through a combination of increased capital availability, risk sharing, and technical assistance.

Program Objectives

The principal objective of the BEEF was to support a large increase in EE investments in Bulgaria through development of a self-sustaining, market-based financing mechanism, ultimately to provide sustainable and increasing reductions in GHG emissions without reliance on continuing public funding.

Because Bulgarian banks lacked both liquidity and credit risk assessment tools to extend dedicated EE finance to borrowers, the BEEF was designed to provide both loans and partial credit guarantees (PCGs) for EE projects. At least half of the benefits of BEEF-supported projects were to result from measurable energy savings.

Specific objectives included the following:

- Mitigation of the perceived high risk and transaction costs of EE investments by directly supporting the implementation of a number of EE projects on fully commercial terms, demonstrating the ability to overcome the barriers and make profits on such projects;
- Facilitating, through demonstration and explicit partnerships, expanded investment by other market participants, such as commercial banks, energy service companies (ESCOs), and leasing companies;
- Providing targeted technical assistance to stimulate deal flow and uptake of financing offered (in support of partner financial institution marketing and delivery of EE financing services and of ESCOs in preparing projects and programs for investment); and
- Increasing the number of active financial institutions and ESCOs engaged in development, implementation, and financing of EE projects.

BEEF Program Design

The BEEF had three main components:

- *PCGs* to share in the credit risk of EE finance transactions and to improve loan terms for project sponsors. A guarantee account was established in a competitively selected commercial bank. The PCG covered potential loan loss claims up to 70 percent of the outstanding loan principal (of the portfolio) of the financial institution. The individual guarantee commitments could not exceed US$500,000.

- *Investment (subloan) financing facility* to cofinance bankable EE projects on a commercial lending basis using a loan account.
- *Technical assistance* to provide initial funding on a grant basis to a portion of EE project development, capacity building, information barrier removal, and administrative costs of the BEEF.

Building on Best Practices

The project design used "best practices" for EE programs in Central and Eastern Europe, drawing inspiration from the GEF's Romania EE Project and the IFC and GEF–supported Hungary Energy Efficiency Co-financing Program (HEECP). The design attempted to incorporate lessons from the U.S. Agency for International Development (USAID)–financed Municipal Energy Efficiency Program in Bulgaria. The latter project provided PCGs to the United Bulgarian Bank for small-scale municipal EE projects. The designers of the BEEF concluded that the USAID-financed project had suffered from two shortcomings: the non-revolving nature of the PCG facility and the financing monopoly position of United Bulgarian Bank, which kept the interest rate and collateral requirements at relatively high levels. The BEEF attempted to correct these deficiencies in its guarantee structure.

Project Funding

The GEF supplied grant financing of US$10 million for (a) providing seed capital for the BEEF, (b) defraying the initial setup and operating costs until the BEEF reached financial self-sufficiency, and (c) partially defraying the initial costs of EE capacity building (project development, financial packaging, and the like).

The GEF amount for the guarantee account was US$4.5 million, which was expected to trigger a total of US$31.1 million in project financing. Individual guarantee commitments were not to exceed the equivalent of US$500,000 (the guarantee liability limit).

The GEF amount for the loan account was US$4 million, which was expected to trigger investments of US$16.34 million. The GEF allocation for technical assistance was US$1.5 million. Additional funding of US$1.8 million was provided by the government of Bulgaria. The Austrian government contributed an additional US$2.0 million to the fund.

Structure and Governance

The BEEF was established as an independent legal entity specialized in financing EE investments on a commercial basis. The recipient of the GEF's grant on behalf of the government of Bulgaria was the Ministry of Energy and Energy Resources (MEER). The World Bank, as the implementing agent for the GEF, signed a grant agreement with the MEER. The final grant beneficiary was the BEEF under a subsidiary grant agreement with the MEER and a project agreement with the World Bank.

The management of the BEEF was entrusted to an FM, selected on a competitive basis. The FM comprised a consortium of three companies—Elana Holding, a leading Bulgarian nonbanking financial institution; EnEffect, a leading Bulgarian nongovernmental organization; and the Canadian EE consulting firm Econoler.

Market Changes

Soon after the initial implementation of the BEEF, a number of significant changes occurred in the market environment that affected the program's design and performance.

A Bulgarian Energy Efficiency Agency initiative to accredit energy auditing companies resulted in an increase in the number of ESCOs. The accreditation of energy auditors strengthened the credibility of EE investment projects and reduced the risk that projects would be nonperforming. This development lessened the need for banks to collaborate with the BEEF to cofinance EE investments to benefit from the BEEF's technical expertise in renewable energy and EE.

The purchase by foreign banks of majority shares in several major Bulgarian commercial banks resulted in greater access to credit from these foreign partners. Liquidity shortages that existed during BEEF project design and appraisal were substantially reduced, obviating the need for BEEF loan financing. Also, strong competition among banks for market share drove down interest rates and margins to such low levels that banks saw no room for accommodating a guarantee fee within the margins. The BEEF had to reduce its guarantee fees to a very low 0.1 percent to find clients for its products.

The European Bank for Reconstruction and Development (EBRD) launched the Bulgaria Energy Efficiency and Renewable Energy Credit Line (BEERECL) for on-lending to private sector companies for industrial EE and small-scale renewable energy projects. The BEERECL started in 2004 with a credit line to one major bank and was soon extended to two others. The EBRD provided credit finance of €55 million (US$71 million). A €35 million (US$45 million) grant from the Kozloduy International Decommissioning Support Fund (KIDSF) provided free consulting services to borrowers and gave them a completion fee of up to 15 percent of the BEERECL loan amount for EE or 20 percent for renewable energy. The free consultancy services undermined the comparative advantage of the BEEF in technical expertise.

The EBRD also launched the Bulgaria Residential Energy Efficiency Credit Line for banks to finance small-scale residential EE projects. This credit line also had a supporting grant facility from KIDSF. In addition, the EBRD provided a senior loan of €7 million (US$9.1 million) to the Energy and Energy Savings Fund, a special purpose investment company set up in 2006 to finance the ESCO business of the construction and engineering group Enemona.

These developments promoted the ultimate goal of establishing a sustainable EE financing market in Bulgaria, but they directly competed with the BEEF in the EE marketplace.

The BEEF FM took a number of actions to adjust the financial products in response to these market developments.

- The FM offered credit products with attractive financing conditions for the initial BEEF projects to develop a sustainable project pipeline in the early years of the fund. As an initial approach, this was the most efficient way to provide an attractive set of services.

- The FM concluded, based on early fund experience, that demand for the US$4.5 million fund allocation for guarantees was insufficient, and that US$2.5 million would be enough to maintain the guarantee business. Therefore, US$2 million was transferred to the loan component. The BEEF managed in the following years to sell a limited number of project guarantees and a greater number of portfolio guarantees. It had to lower its guarantee fees to 0.1 percent to find takers, and even that took some arduous selling efforts. In some of the cases, project developers whose guarantee requests had been processed backed off from the deals and received loans from banks that would accept their projects without a guarantee. Overall, the market indicated that Bulgarian banks rarely required PCGs for small projects.

- The FM also identified the obstacles to concluding deals with commercial banks for cofinancing. Banks were not interested in BEEF cofinancing for small projects because the transaction costs became too high relative to the loan amounts. However, the cofinance of large projects was beyond the scope of the BEEF. A further issue was that the client base—municipalities, hospitals, and universities—were all considered by banks to be reliable and creditworthy borrowers.

The BEEF then focused on identifying certain niche markets.

- One of the important niche markets was the provision of finance to EE projects for public buildings owned by local authorities (administration buildings, schools, and the like), hospitals, or universities, and street lighting. To reduce the administrative burden on municipalities for financing EE projects, the FM initiated, together with the Ministry of Energy and Economy, changes in the EE Act. Adopted in June 2007, the revised EE Act stipulates that local authorities are not obliged to adhere to procurement procedures when seeking finance for EE projects; they can negotiate directly with the BEEF.

- Despite the EBRD's ESCO loan to Enemona, the BEEF kept Enemona as a customer by providing loans for the implementation of ESCO projects and portfolio guarantees to a pool of 29 ESCO contracts that were loan-financed by a commercial bank with which the BEEF had a collaboration agreement.

The BEEF FM also developed and introduced some innovative financial products:

- Through its information campaign and media initiatives, the BEEF advised that ESCO contracting was an effective means of implementing and managing EE investments. Three ESCOs entered the market with the BEEF's technical assistance and financing. The BEEF's ESCO portfolio guarantee scheme provided an ESCO with a guarantee against defaults and a liquidity guarantee to cover disruptions in the flow of receivables.
- In 2010, the BEEF reached an agreement with the EBRD to receive a €40 million EBRD credit line to be used by the BEEF to purchase receivables from ESCO contracts.
- The BEEF introduced two other innovative guarantee schemes: (a) a Residential Portfolio Guarantee scheme that covers the first 5 percent of defaults on individual end-user loans used to finance a joint EE project for an apartment building (or portfolio of such buildings) and (b) a standardized EE financing product with the International Asset Bank, called "Energy Asset," which provides a PCG of up to 80 percent of the amount of the principal.

Implementation Results

By the conclusion of the project in March 2010, the BEEF had accomplished the following:

- Awarded 81 loans (with another four or five being processed for final approval). The total loan volume was US$16 million, and the total investment financed by these loans was US$24 million.
- The lifetime energy savings from these loans was 0.09 million tons of oil equivalent, and the GHG savings were 0.9 million tons of carbon dioxide equivalent.
- Entered 31 guarantee deals covering about US$2 million, triggering an investment volume of US$15 million. With no more guarantee agreements to be signed as of the end of July 2010, the entire guarantee category net allocation of US$2.5 million will have been used. The resulting lifetime energy savings are 0.02 million tons of oil equivalent, and the GHG savings are 0.1 million tons of carbon dioxide equivalent.
- The average simple payback period was 4.7 years. The typical loan size was US$250,000–500,000.
- The BEEF's financial self-sufficiency ratio (defined as the annual income from project operations divided by project annual operating costs) was 133 percent in 2009, demonstrating that the BEEF achieved its self-financing target and would be able to sustain its operations.

- Contributed to EE financing for public sector projects in local municipal governments and other public institutions that commercial banks were unwilling or too slow to finance.
- Contributed, along with a number of initiatives by EBRD and others, to increasing the number of ESCOs from 14 to 38 and the number of banks extending loans to EE projects from 2 to 13.

Lessons Learned

The major lessons learned are summarized below:

- The BEEF survived as a viable financial mechanism, despite major changes in the market environment, as a result of the built-in flexibility of the initial project design and the quality of the BEEF's professional FM, who adjusted the BEEF's interventions to the market conditions. Close supervision by the World Bank played an important role in helping to identify and tackle key strategic issues and ensured ownership and coordination with government counterparts.
- Before introducing new financial instruments in a market, it is important to assess carefully why and under what circumstances the instrument is expected to work and to test the underlying assumptions through a market survey. An innovative approach implemented successfully in one country may not be effective in another if market conditions are significantly different.
- Innovative projects are likely to be vulnerable to developments in the external environment that differ from what was expected at appraisal. Provision should therefore be made in the program design to review the changing market conditions and make adjustments as appropriate. The BEEF was originally conceived as a private finance engagement instrument, but it had limited success in this objective. However, it found a niche in providing loans to public sector EE projects and in actively encouraging preparation of EE projects.
- The BEEF's loan activities were expected to consist primarily of cofinancing with commercial banks. However, commercial banks only find cofinancing attractive as a means to reduce their exposure to a single client when financing very large projects. Because EE projects are relatively small (the BEEF loans were typically in the range of US$250,000–500,000), commercial banks have limited interest in cofinancing.
- Risk-sharing programs such as PCG funds have been a popular choice for several financing programs in developing countries. The BEEF was designed with the expectation that commercial banks would take advantage of a PCG to engage in EE financing. However, the Bulgarian finance community did not see much need for a PCG. In Bulgaria, public sector borrowers have good repayment records, and corporate borrowing is based on balance sheets and the banks' previous experience with clients. As a result, Bulgarian banks were unwilling to incur the costs of the guarantees.

- The development of the market for EE in the multi–apartment building sector depends on the creation of well-functioning condominium associations and on the introduction of "energy poverty" schemes to solve the issue that arises when poor households living in those apartment buildings are unable to access loans to pay for their shares of the total cost of the EE investment. General portfolio PCGs for ESCO projects cannot solve such issues.

Bibliography

Government of Bulgaria. 2001a. "National Energy Saving Action Plan (2001–2003)." Sofia.

———. 2001b. "National Energy Saving Programme to 2010." Sofia.

Klev, Kolio. 2007. "Policy or Energy Efficiency Implementation and Integration of EU Directives in Bulgaria." Paper presentation delivered in Beijing, China, January 10–15.

World Bank. 2005. "Project Appraisal Document on a Proposed Grant from the Global Environment Facility Trust Fund in the Amount of US$10.0 Million to the Republic of Bulgaria for an Energy Efficiency Project." World Bank, Washington, DC.

———. 2010. "Implementation, Completion and Results Report on a Grant from the Global Environment Facility Trust Fund in the Amount of US$10 mil to the Rep of Bulgaria for an Energy Efficiency Project." World Bank, Washington, DC.

CHAPTER 20

Case Study: South Africa Eskom Standard Offer Program for Energy Efficiency and Demand-Side Management

Introduction

The Standard Offer is a mechanism for acquiring demand-side resources (energy efficiency [EE] and load management) under which a utility (or a government agency) purchases energy savings or demand reductions (or both) using predetermined and prepublished rates. Any energy user (utility customer) or energy service company (ESCO) that can deliver energy or demand savings is paid the fixed amounts per kilowatt-hour (kWh) or kilowatt (kW) (the Standard Offer amounts) upon completion of the EE or demand-side management (DSM) project and verification and certification of the achieved savings by an authorized measurement and verification (M&V) organization. A Standard Offer Program (SOP) treats energy-savings projects analogously to customer generation of electricity, and considers the energy or demand reductions to be resources for which the utility will pay. The mechanism is comparable to the feed-in tariffs (FITs) used to promote increased implementation of renewable energy resources. The amounts to be paid for the energy savings or demand reductions under a SOP are generally based on the value of these reductions to the utility system.

The South African government's EE policies and regulations (Department of Energy 2009, 2010) have led to designation of the Standard Offer as the optimum mechanism for implementation of EE measures. The SOP is now the preferred process for implementation of the incentives from the EE/DSM Fund, which was established by Eskom through an electricity tariff surcharge approved by the National Energy Regulator of South Africa (NERSA). Eskom implemented a pilot SOP in 2010 and launched a three-year program under the mandate of NERSA in 2011.

Country Context

South Africa's economy is driven by large, highly energy-intensive mining and related industries that rely on coal as the predominant fuel source. South Africa has also placed an emphasis on rural electrification, which has led to increased demand for primarily coal-based electricity. South Africa's historically low-cost energy supplies together with the predominance of extractive industries have created an energy-intensive economy. South Africa is the largest contributor to greenhouse gas emissions in Africa. On a per capita basis, its greenhouse gas emissions are higher than those of most other major emerging economies, including Brazil, China, and India.

A combination of factors, including supply-side problems (coal availability), delays in construction of new generation capacity, maintenance needs, and unplanned outages, resulted in an acute power crisis in South Africa beginning in January 2008 that caused power system reserve margins to fall, virtually overnight, from 10 percent to almost zero. The size of the power shortage was staggering—about 3,500 megawatt (MW) or about 10 percent of peak demand, every weekday from 6 a.m. to 10 p.m. This shortage was expected to last until new capacity could be built.

The South African government has recognized the importance of EE and DSM as key elements in a strategy to minimize environmental impacts and contribute to a sustainable development strategy. The 1998 *White Paper on the Energy Policy of the Republic of South Africa* emphasized the goal of providing the nation with wider access to energy services while ensuring that the environmental impacts of energy conversion and use are minimized as much as possible (Department of Minerals and Energy 1998). The need for EE and DSM led to the formulation of specific policies and regulations, such as the EE Strategy and a new Regulatory Policy on Energy Efficiency and DSM, which established the EE/DSM Fund, to be administered by Eskom, and defined the rules and procedures for its implementation.

The initial EE/DSM programs faced a number of issues, including limited staff capacity; a complex, nontransparent, and time-consuming project evaluation process; and an adversarial negotiation process with ESCOs. Thus, the implementation of EE/DSM projects fell far short of what was expected and possible, and substantial modifications and enhancements were needed to make the EE/DSM process more efficient and effective. A World Bank team, working in cooperation with Eskom, the Department of Minerals and Energy, NERSA, and other stakeholders including the South African Association of ESCOs, developed and proposed the concept of the Standard Offer to overcome some of the issues and challenges (World Bank 2011).

Barriers

Although the importance of EE had been recognized in the South African energy market, energy users and ESCOs were facing many barriers to implementation of EE projects, including low electricity prices, lack of commercial financing for

EE projects, and limited capacity for implementation. The National Electricity Regulator (NER)[1] made EE/DSM planning and implementation one of the license conditions of all major electricity distributors and defined their responsibilities and obligations (NER 2004). It also defined the potential roles of ESCOs and created an independent M&V body, accountable to NER, to conduct all of the M&V functions related to EE/DSM implementation. NER established the EE/DSM Fund to be administered by Eskom (the Eskom EE/DSM Fund) and defined the rules and procedures for its implementation. The fund provided incentives (50 percent of the capital cost as a grant) to EE project developers.

However, the implementation of EE projects under the EE/DSM Fund encountered many challenges and barriers (World Bank 2011):

- Eskom's DSM group was understaffed and overburdened.
- Eskom used a cumbersome, slow, and nontransparent process to evaluate and process EE/DSM proposals. The proposal process—a sequence of technical, financial, and procurement reviews conducted by separate Eskom committees—led to substantial delays and costs to the project developers, and often erected a major disincentive to applying for EE/DSM funds.
- Eskom's project approval criteria appeared to be unclear and inconsistently applied, and the proposal evaluation process had suffered from misunderstanding, poor communication, and insufficient feedback, particularly regarding why proposals were rejected.
- Eskom's evaluation teams had been overly concerned about and spent inordinate amounts of time on the details of the energy-savings calculations and costs of the EE/DSM measures.
- Eskom's contract negotiation process was complex, time consuming, and adversarial.

The uncertainty and delays in the Eskom evaluation process created large risks and made many projects difficult to finance and implement. Eskom maintained that it had to devote sufficient time and resources to proper due diligence of every project given that they were responsible for ensuring that "ratepayer" proceeds in the Eskom EE/DSM Fund were spent fairly and judiciously. Both Eskom and the ESCOs agreed that the goals of the EE/DSM Fund were not being met.

Program Objectives

To overcome the issues related to the implementation of the Eskom EE/DSM program, the SOP approach was recommended by the World Bank following consultation with stakeholders in South Africa. The objectives of the SOP were to

- Provide customers and ESCOs a predetermined payment for delivered energy or demand savings, allowing them to structure and propose EE/DSM projects efficiently and rapidly;

- Streamline the project approval process and scale up project development and implementation;
- Simplify the contracts between the utility and the ESCOs or customers;
- Reduce the burden on the utility staff for project evaluation and processing;
- Provide transparency to project proponents on payments for delivered savings;
- Leverage commercial financing for EE projects; and
- Reduce the utility's risk by making the payments performance based to ensure it paid only for measured and verified savings.

Program Design

The SOP replaced the procedures being used by Eskom's DSM group to identify and approve EE/DSM projects and allowed Eskom to purchase energy savings from energy users and ESCOs using a predetermined and prepublished price. This approach streamlined evaluation of project proposals and disbursement of the incentives or subsidies, thus reducing the burden on Eskom staff and facilitating a larger pipeline of projects. The greater transparency, shorter processing times, and reduced transaction risk of the SOP also facilitated mobilization of commercial financing, essential to achieving a substantial scaling up of EE/DSM investment.

Eskom's Integrated Demand Management Program

Under the regulatory initiatives of the 2009 second Multi-Year Price Determination period, NERSA approved 5.4 billion South African rand (about US$700 million) over a three-year period for EE and DSM (NERSA 2010). The target is to deliver 1,037 MW of demand savings and 4,055 gigawatt-hours (GWh) of energy savings. The regulatory order stated "These funds will be applied for project implementation and administrative costs for DSM, EE and demand-reduction programmes, including a portion of the solar water heating (SWH) initiated by the Department of Energy (DoE)" (Etzinger 2011, 4). Eskom established the Integrated Demand Management Program to implement this order. Under the program, Eskom offers the following SOPs (Skinner 2012):

- Standard Offer Program
- Standard Product Program
- Performance Contracting Program
- Solar Water Heating Program

Brief descriptions are provided below.

Standard Offer Program

This program offers payments for delivered savings form EE projects at a fixed rate for the Eskom peak period (16 hours per day from 6 a.m. to 10 p.m.

on weekdays) for three years. The typical technologies implemented under this program include efficient lighting and fixtures, light-emitting diodes, hot water systems, solar systems, and industrial process optimization. A standard amount is paid per kWh saved, based on the technology, and is up to 85 percent of the NERSA benchmark for avoided costs. The level of payment is between US$0.05 and US$0.08 per kWh, depending on the technology.

The eligible projects are between 50 kW and 5 MW. Payments are made to the project developers in installments, with 70 percent of the payment upon project completion and 10 percent at the end of each of the three years. M&V is required each year, and payments are adjusted based on the M&V results.

Standard Product Program

The Standard Product Program covers small projects (under 100 kW) and provides pre-approved rebates for energy savings achieved through specified technologies, such as efficient lighting, shower heads, air conditioners, solar water heaters, and heat pumps.

Payments for these projects are made per product installed and are based on a standard value per item. The values are up to 100 percent of the NERSA benchmark, and the level of payment is between US$0.05 and US$0.09 per kWh, depending on the technology. Full payment is made upon installation and based on M&V.

Performance Contracting Program

The Performance Contracting Program applies to larger projects in commercial and industrial facilities (producing savings of more than 5 MW). Project developers are invited to bid through a tender process and payments are made at a prepublished rate, which was, in January 2012, about US$0.07 per kWh saved during Eskom's peak period and about US$0.012 per kWh during off-peak hours. The contract period is three years.

Solar Water Heating Program

The Solar Water Heating Program provides a standard, prespecified rebate per unit for replacement of residential electric water heaters with pre-approved SWHs. The rebate values are capped within size bands for the SWHs. The program is designed to help achieve the South African government's goal of installing 1 million solar water heaters by 2014.

Applicant Eligibility

The following types of organizations (called project developers) are eligible to provide proposals to Eskom under these programs:

- Any customer of Eskom or of municipal electricity providers in the commercial and industrial sectors;
- Any ESCO, defined as a business entity that provides any or all of the following services: energy engineering, EE measure design, equipment installation,

equipment maintenance, and financing services on a performance-contracting basis.

If the project developer is not the energy consumer or facility owner, an agreement between the energy consumer or facility owner and project developer is required, which should transfer ownership of verified energy savings from the energy consumer or facility owner to the project developer. It is a requirement of the program that the project developer be registered with Eskom as a vendor.

Pre-approved Technologies

Eskom has prepared and published a list of pre-approved EE/DSM technologies or measures eligible for payment under the Standard Offer and Standard Product Programs. Eligible EE and load-management measures must reduce electric energy consumption at the project site during some or all of Eskom's peak period (6 a.m. to 10 p.m. on weekdays), and this reduction must be measurable and verifiable. In addition, Eskom invites technology and equipment or appliance manufacturers and suppliers to propose new or innovative technologies under the Performance Contracting Program.

Pricing the Standard Offer Programs

Payment procedures under the SOP are intended to be simple, standard, and transparent. Payment amounts are prespecified for the eligible technologies and products so that project developers know exactly how much they will receive upon successful delivery of monitored and verified savings. The payment schedule has been determined for specific technologies and measures based on the following factors:

- Benefits to the electricity system of reduced energy and demand during various time periods (time of day, month, and so on),
- Energy and demand savings provided by the project during various periods,
- Tariff category of the Eskom customer,
- Annual hours of use by time period,
- Lifetime of the technology or measure, and
- Expected persistence of the energy and demand savings over the lifetime.

Implementation Results

The results of Eskom's programs through the end of 2011 are summarized here:

Program	Number of projects	Demand savings (MW)	Energy savings (GWh)
Standard offer	61	31.4	148.1
Standard product	572	19.7	86.9
Performance contracting	16	131	2,076
Solar water heating	172,784	—	—

Source: Skinner 2012.
Note: — = not available.

Lessons Learned

The major lessons learned from Eskom's implementation of the SOP follow:

- The Eskom programs have been well received by energy users and ESCOs, and the number of projects implemented increased substantially.
- The program was structured to last three years, and Eskom's role beyond the second Multi-Year Price Determination period is unclear.
- Eskom faced many challenges in developing the right incentive structure for the various programs and the technologies and products covered by these programs.
- Successful implementation of the SOP requires a sound, multifunctional management and implementation approach.
- Business processes, systems, and controls for the programs addressing the commercial and residential markets need to be streamlined and automated.
- Staff and advisers need to be trained on the complexities of the SOP incentives.
- Although many ESCOs have participated, most of the projects have been developed by a small number of large ESCOs; the capacity of the smaller ESCOs for project preparation needs to be developed.
- The fixed incentives offered under the SOP appear to be more attractive to project developers than the tendering process.

Note

1. This agency was later renamed the National Energy Regulator of South Africa (NERSA).

Bibliography

Department of Energy. 2009. "Electricity Regulation Act, 2006: Determination Regarding the Integrated Resource Plan and New Generation Capacity." Department of Energy, Pretoria.

———. 2010. "Policy to Support the Energy Efficiency and Demand Side Management Program for the Electricity Sector through the Standard Offer Incentive Scheme." Department of Energy, Pretoria.

Department of Minerals and Energy. 1998. *White Paper on the Energy Policy of the Republic of South Africa*. Pretoria: Department of Minerals and Energy.

Etzinger, Andrew. 2011. "Energy Efficiency Financing Policy: South Africa's Standard Offer Program." Presentation, Johannesburg, South Africa, December.

NER (National Electricity Regulator). 2004. "Regulatory Policy on Energy Efficiency and Demand-Side Management for South African Electricity Industry." NER, Pretoria.

NERSA (National Energy Regulator of South Africa). 2010. "Revision of Regulatory Rules for Energy Efficiency and Demand Side Management (EE/DSM) including Standard Offer Programme (SOP)." NERSA, Pretoria.

Skinner, Tom. 2012. "An Overview of Energy Efficiency and Demand-Side Management in South Africa." Presentation to the World Bank/IFC Workshop on Appropriate Incentives to Deploy Renewable Energy and Energy Efficiency, Washington, DC, January 30–February 1.

World Bank. 2011. "Implementing Energy Efficiency and Demand Side Management: South Africa's Standard Offer Model." ESMAP Briefing Note 007/11, World Bank, Washington, DC.

CHAPTER 21

Case Study: Turkey Renewable Energy Project

Introduction

The Turkey Renewable Energy Project was approved by the World Bank Board in March 2004 to expand privately owned and operated distributed power generation from renewable sources within the market-based legal framework. The project was designed to achieve its objective by establishing a commercial financing mechanism for renewable energy (RE) projects and demonstrating the feasibility of private development of economic and financially viable RE projects within a competitive market framework. The Turkey RE project was successfully completed in June 2010.

Country Context

Until the 2008–09 global economic and financial crisis, Turkey had recorded impressive economic accomplishments. During the period 2002–07, annual economic growth was nearly 7 percent on average, inflation was brought down to single-digit levels, and public debt fell to less than 40 percent of gross domestic product (GDP).

The Turkish government embarked on a comprehensive electricity reform program beginning in 1996 to establish a competitive electricity market with the goals of increasing private investment, improving supply- and demand-side efficiency, and ensuring energy supply security in an environmentally sustainable manner. The originally vertically integrated state-owned electricity monopoly had been split into two state-owned companies: a generation and transmission company (TEAS) and a distribution company. In 2001, the government passed the Electricity Market Law (Law 4628), which, among other actions, further split TEAS into three companies: the Turkish Electricity Transmission Company, the Turkish Electricity Trading and Contracting Company, and the Electricity Generating Company. It also established the Electricity Market Regulatory Agency (EMRA) as an independent regulatory commission that provides generating licenses and sets tariffs. The law also laid the basis for the establishment of a wholesale electricity market and gradual opening of the retail electricity market.

Barriers

The following barriers prevented implementation of RE projects:

- *Lack of a sustainable framework to attract private investment into RE generation.* Several approaches had been employed in the past to attract private investment into generation, including the build-operate-transfer (BOT) model, the build-own-operate (BOO) model, the auto-producer model, and the transfer of operating rights (TOOR) model. The first three models (BOT, BOO, and auto-producer) had been used to encourage private investment in new power plants. The TOOR model was used to transfer existing generating assets and distribution companies to private investors. The BOT and BOO approaches attracted substantial new investment in power plants. However, the energy prices from BOT plants were high. The auto-producer model, which is a form of self-generation employed by industries that also sell surplus energy to the national grid, was, in many respects, the most successful because it had created a substantial amount of capacity without any associated liabilities. However, its use was limited because it was primarily aimed at self-generation and not for supplying the outside market.

- *Critical reform steps yet to be implemented to achieve a smooth reform transition,* including the following:
  - resolving the problems of inadequate tariffs and revenue deficits in the power sector;
  - dealing with the potential stranded costs that arose from the above-market price contracts signed with BOT and BOO project sponsors;
  - achieving regulatory certainty and clarity; and
  - coordinating reform implementation across multiple agencies, including the Ministry of Energy and Natural Resources, the EMRA, Treasury, the Privatization Agency, the Turkish Electricity Transmission Company, the Turkish Electricity Trading and Contracting Company, the Electricity Generating Company, and the distribution company.

- *Lack of long-term financing to exploit the economic RE resources.* The capital-intensive nature of most renewable technologies results in a high demand for capital and a long payback period, and therefore a greater exposure to market and regulatory risks. Commercial banks were unwilling to take on the risks of providing long-term loans, especially to small and medium enterprises, for renewable projects.

By pioneering a new financing mechanism and supporting institutional development activities for the introduction of laws, mechanisms, and procedures for private investment in RE, the project would help Turkey mobilize additional sources of finance from commercial banks and international financial institutions to provide long-term finance for RE development.

Objectives

The project objective was to increase privately owned and operated distributed power generation from renewable sources, without the need for government guarantees, and within the market-based framework of the new Turkish Electricity Market Law.

Design

The project's main component was the Special Purpose Debt Facility (SPDF) for renewable generation financing in the amount of US$202.03 million (including a US$2.03 million front-end fee). The SPDF was a term lending facility established and operated by two financial institutions (FIs). The two FIs selected were the privately owned Turkish Industrial Development Bank (TSKB) and the government-owned Turkish Development Bank (TKB). The World Bank loan for the SPDF was on-lent from the Turkish Treasury (the borrower) to the FIs (US$50 million to TKB and US$150 million to TSKB). The FIs used the SPDF to provide long-term debt financing to private sponsors of RE projects. The SPDF was intended to leverage equity investment from local private developers, export credit financing, and other financing for the construction and operation of qualified renewable generation projects.

Key Features of the SPDF
Selection of Participating Banks
The two FIs were selected based on their financial strength and their capacity to appraise and supervise project implementation. In addition, their status as development banks allowed the Turkish Treasury to on-lend public funds to these organizations.

Sponsor Eligibility
Beneficiary enterprises borrowing from the FIs had more than 50 percent private ownership and undertook investments to generate electricity from renewable resources as defined in EMRA's Licensing Regulation. Per the Environmental Impact Assessment Regulation, this included hydro electric projects under all of the following thresholds: (a) 50 megawatt (MW) installed capacity (increased to 100 MW in 2006), (b) reservoir area less than 15 square kilometers, and (c) reservoir storage volume of less than 100 million cubic meters.

Project Eligibility
- Minimum 25 percent sponsor equity financing.
- Minimum debt coverage ratio of 1.2 calculated on a three-year moving average after completion of the investment and throughout the life of the loan.

- Financial rate of return of at least 10 percent.
- Certification from the relevant local or national authorities that the proposed project met all environmental laws and regulations in force in Turkey, as well as the World Bank policy on environmental assessment (defined in the operational manual).
- Eligible projects were to be built on river basins agreed on in the project agreements between TKB, TSKB, and the World Bank.
- Projects involving involuntary resettlement would not be eligible for financing from the SPDF.
- Compliance with World Bank procurement procedures for the procurement of goods and civil works to be financed under the SPDF subloans.

Subloan and Financial Lease Terms and Conditions
- Subloans were made to finance plant and equipment, goods, and civil works for investment purposes (where applicable, subloans could be extended as a leasing facility). Financial leases were for equipment only.
- Subloans extended to beneficiary enterprises were to have a minimum total maturity of six years with a minimum grace period of two years. Financial leases were to be for a minimum duration of six years.
- The SPDF could finance up to 50 percent of the investment cost. The aggregate amount of subloan or financial leases to a single subproject could not exceed US$20 million (increased to US$40 million in 2006).
- Total aggregate value of multiple subloans or financial leases (from TSKB and TKB) made to any beneficiary enterprise and its affiliates could not exceed US$40 million.
- Subloans were to be evaluated in accordance with the FIs' regular project and credit evaluation guidelines and were to include (where applicable) criteria in the "Guidelines for Sub-loan/Eligible Project Evaluation" specified in Section V of the operational manual.
- Subloans were denominated in U.S. dollars; the foreign exchange risk was borne by the beneficiary enterprise.
- The FIs determined subloan pricing based on the risks of the particular beneficiary enterprise and eligible project being financed. The spread was expected to be no greater than 300–350 basis points for the riskier projects or sponsors with tight debt service ratios.

Technical Assistance
To support implementation of the project, the government agreed to a number of institutional development activities, including (a) improving the collection, evaluation, and dissemination of technical data and information about potential renewable project sites to prospective private sector developers; (b) developing RE legislation; and (c) improving public-private cooperation in developing hydropower. The World Bank provided support and assistance to the government to pursue these institutional development activities both before and during project implementation.

Institutional and Policy Reforms Supported before Implementation
- Licensing definition of renewable generation: The term "generation facilities based on renewable resources" was clearly defined and incorporated into EMRA's Licensing Regulation. This definition clarifies the types of resources, as well as size limits (for hydro), on renewable generation plants that would qualify for preferential and fast-track treatment within the market-based principles of the Electricity Market Law.

- Project processing procedures: Streamlined procedures were established for publishing project potential, receiving applications from private sponsors, reviewing the applications and feasibility studies, and granting conditional and then final resource-use rights after EMRA licensing. These procedures were implemented for hydroelectric projects through regulations of the State Hydraulic Agency under the Ministry of Energy and Natural Resources. The regulation is consistent with the Electricity Market Law and clearly defines the rights, responsibilities, and accountability of all the involved agencies—specifically the State Hydraulic Agency, the Electrical Power Resources Survey and Development Administration, and the private sponsors.

- Market-based renewables obligation: A market-based RE obligation was implemented that required retailers to purchase energy from renewable generators if the price of this energy was less than the allowable wholesale energy price pass-through to consumers.

- Implementation of environmental impact assessment and mitigation procedures for all renewable generation projects of less than 10 MW equivalent to the more stringent procedures for projects greater than 10 MW.

Institutional and Policy Reforms to Be Supported during Implementation
- Building an institutional mechanism and capacity to support investment lending for renewables and to attract further sources of bilateral or multilateral debt.
- Preparing the Renewable Energy Law.
- Regulating dam safety and private hydraulic infrastructure.
- Enhancing the institutional capacity of both the State Hydraulic Agency and Electrical Power Resources Survey and Development Administration to ensure that a continuous pipeline of economically feasible and environmentally beneficial RE projects was identified.

Implementation Results

The project surpassed its original targets for increasing private investment in renewable generation and reducing carbon dioxide emissions as a result of clean energy development 10 months before the expected closing date. By project completion, the loan had supported 19 private sponsors in developing 23 RE plants, including one wind plant, one landfill gas plant, three geothermal power plants, and 18 hydropower plants. The total generating capacity developed amounted to 618.5 MW as compared with the original target of 500 MW. The annual electricity generation from these new renewable power plants under normal hydraulic and wind conditions was estimated to be 2,320 gigawatt-hours (GWh) as compared with the original target of 2,200 GWh. The resulting reduction in carbon dioxide emissions was estimated to be 1.7 million tons per year, significantly exceeding the original target of 932,000 tons. The US$200 million World Bank loan leveraged an additional US$555.4 million in private investment, indicating a leverage ratio of 2.65, which is higher than the target of 1.48 envisaged at project appraisal.

As the first major international assistance project to Turkey aimed at accelerating the development of renewable power generation, the project successfully demonstrated a financial intermediation mechanism and generated significant interest among other domestic and international financial institutions in providing long-term finance to various RE projects. This financial intermediation mechanism was replicated by other international financial institutions, such as the European Investment Bank, the Council of Europe Development Bank, Agence Francaise de Development, and others, to channel their funds through TKB, TSKB, and other Turkish banks to finance RE in Turkey. Long-term financing dedicated to RE and energy efficiency projects that TSKB and TKB received from other international financial institutions amounted to about US$404 million (TSKB) and US$200 million (TKB) since the project began.

Given the continued strong demand for RE finance, as requested by TKB and TSKB and supported by the Turkish government, a new project—the Private Sector Renewable Energy and Energy Efficiency Project—was approved by the World Bank Board in May 2009. The financing included US$500 million from the International Bank for Reconstruction and Development and US$100 million from the Clean Technology Fund. It was the first project to use resources from the newly established Clean Technology Fund. The new project closely followed the previous project design and experience, and consists of a term lending facility with the TSKB and TKB for financing RE (including hydro, wind, biomass, and solar), as well as energy efficiency investment.

Lessons Learned

The long-term, programmatic approach that Turkey adopted and the World Bank supported contributed to the success of the project by creating the enabling environment, building capacity, and catalyzing investment. The Turkish experience suggests that the development of RE often faces an array of barriers, including institutional, capacity, and financing challenges. Promoting the use of renewable resources requires a thorough understanding of the sector background, long-term efforts, and a strategic mix of policy and investment interventions to overcome these barriers.

A predictable policy and regulatory environment is a critical precondition for private sector investment in RE development. Having a supportive policy environment, including predictable feed-in tariffs and transparent rules for electricity trading, is critical for attracting private sector investment. Other favorable policies include facilitation of developer access to land and adoption of transparent and streamlined procurements for obtaining licenses and water-use rights for hydropower development. For RE projects, developing a coherent strategy that integrates the establishment of an enabling policy and regulatory environment within the overall framework of the project design is important.

Technical assistance is critical for project success. Under the RE project, the World Bank provided to EMRA and DSI a range of technical assistance to help clarify and enact a number of RE policies and regulations. These measures included the development of regulatory procedures for the allocation of water-use rights, procedures for licensing renewable power plants, power purchase obligations of the distribution companies, tariffs for RE, and so on. The World Bank loan also assisted TSKB and TKB in developing their capacity for financing RE projects. Through the implementation of the project, both of the banks gathered substantial knowledge and experience in managing complex RE investments and developed suitable levels of staff with requisite qualifications and experience to market the new facility, appraise and evaluate project proposals, and monitor implementation. In addition, the World Bank provided extensive professional training and awareness building on environmental and social issues, which enabled TKB to improve its capacity in safeguards compliance. The technical assistance activities were financed through internal resources at the assisted institutions as well as grants such as the Policy and Human Resources Development project preparation grant.

RE development could have been leveraged to achieve greater impact. First, the project's demonstration effect sparked interest among other financial institutions in investing in the sector. Second, the World Bank supported the strengthening of project management and safeguard capacity of the participating FIs. The FIs have rapidly increased their RE portfolios by working with other commercial banks and international financial institutions. Third, the World Bank assisted the development of government administrative capacity in regulating the renewables industry. The government can leverage its strengthened institutional capacity to further promote the development of RE.

It is important to develop friendlier policies for small, first-time renewable developers to overcome the financing challenge. The subproject sizes ranged from US$4 million to US$117 million, with an average of US$66.5 million. Most of the project beneficiaries were small and medium enterprises (fewer than 99 employees) that faced more challenges in gaining access to bank finance. The high levels of required sponsor collateral initially prevented small renewable developers with low collateral value from accessing finance. With technical assistance from the project team, TSKB was able to accept the concept of project financing and relaxed the collateral requirements whereas TKB required guarantees from other commercial banks to overcome the challenge.

Careful selection and high performance of FIs also contributed to project success. In addition to their status as development banks, the two FIs were selected based on their financial strength and their capacity to appraise and supervise project implementation. Both FIs were able to commit and fully disburse all of the funds to viable projects about a year ahead of schedule and meet the environmental and social safeguards requirements. In particular, TSKB developed its unique mix of technical, risk assessment and management, and business marketing skills and established itself as a leading Turkish institution providing finance to RE projects.

Bibliography

World Bank. 2009. *Turkey Renewable Energy Project Appraisal Document (PAD)*. Report 46808-TR, World Bank, Washington, DC.

———. 2011. *Turkey Renewable Energy Project Implementation Completion Report (ICR)*. Report ICR1789, World Bank, Washington, DC.

CHAPTER 22

Case Study: Geothermal Funds in Eastern Europe and Africa

Introduction

To promote the use of geothermal energy, the World Bank has supported two geothermal guarantee funds to address technology risks.

The first is the US$25 million Geothermal Energy Development Program (GeoFund) in the Europe and Central Asia (ECA) region, which was approved by the World Bank Board in October 2006. The GeoFund is being implemented in a series of individual subprojects over a period of eight years. The first phase (Adaptable Program Loan 1, or APL1) of the GeoFund was completed in December 2009 and included two subprojects: (a) a grant of US$810,000 to the International Geothermal Association (IGA) for regional technical assistance (TA) activities and (b) a geological risk insurance (GRI) grant of US$3.72 million to MOL (the Hungarian Oil and Gas Company). The second phase (Adaptable Program Loan 2, or APL2) of the GeoFund, which is still ongoing, has provided US$1.5 million for the Armenia Geothermal Project, which focuses on TA; it was endorsed by the Global Environment Facility (GEF) on February 4, 2009. Out of the US$25 million GeoFund program, US$10 million was allocated to the International Finance Corporation for geothermal development projects involving the private sector in Turkey. The remaining US$9.5 million was returned to the GEF because the GEF administrative budget had been exhausted and no additional GEF subprojects are envisaged under the GeoFund program implemented by the Bank.

The second geothermal guarantee fund is the US$11 million Risk Mitigation Fund established under the US$18 million African Rift Geothermal Development Program (ARGeo). The project became effective in June 2010 and will run for five years. A pipeline of eligible projects was developed for each country and a US$5 million guarantee grant for the Assal Geothermal Power Project in Djibouti was approved. Because of long delays in the approval of the project as a whole, new developments have taken place, and as of mid-2012, the original proposed projects need to be revised and new ones submitted for consideration.

Context

GeoFund in ECA

Many countries of the ECA region lag behind the original 15 European Union (EU) countries in the use and development of renewable energy (RE) resources. Significant barriers impede the increased use of RE in these countries, and more specifically geothermal energy (GeoE), including expertise, know-how, energy market issues, and high transaction costs attributable to the typically small size of RE projects. Although technological barriers are common to all ECA countries, financial barriers related to the availability of public and private equity finance, the performance of the banking system, general investment climate, and economic development tend to be less significant in the western parts of the ECA region than in former Soviet Union countries. Legislative support to the development of RE in the ECA region has been growing and has reached different levels in different countries. The strongest support is found in Turkey. Some of the countries that recently joined the EU exhibit various degrees of support for RE. Non-EU countries, for the most part, do not have any favorable rules and regulations toward RE in place.

The first GeoFund operation was the Hungary MOL Geothermal Power Pilot Project. Hungary is known to have favorable geothermal resources—most measured geothermal gradients are higher than the worldwide average. Although the use of GeoE in Hungary is significant, compared with the worldwide average it remains relatively low given the resource base. This imbalance is largely due to the typical barriers of high up-front investment requirements and the geological risks associated with drilling. The value added of the Bank's assistance for the Hungary MOL Geothermal Power Pilot Project is the covering of the geological risk. Without this guarantee, which is unique on the market, the project's profitability was not attractive enough for the project developer. Neither conventional lending nor straight grants suit the needs of this kind of operation. Although loans were available from various commercial sources and were part of the financing package, they did not improve the risk-adjusted internal rate of return. Straight grants on a scale that would push the project above the hurdle rate were not justifiable for private investors.

African Rift Geothermal Fund[1]

GeoE is a key energy resource for East Africa, estimated at more than 6,000 megawatts (MW) of electricity generation potential in the region. This indigenous, environmentally friendly resource has a proven track record with more than 25 years of continuous operation in Kenya at affordable cost and with greater than 85 percent availability. However, only Kenya and Ethiopia have installed a variety of large and small power generating units with a total capacity of 210 MW. Many of the countries in the region are suffering from acute energy crises driven by a combination of large oil price fluctuations, increasingly persistent droughts linked to climate change, and booming demand stemming from rapid population increase and healthy economic growth rates. In this context,

GeoE stands out as one of the most promising and sustainable long-term alternatives for low-cost bulk electricity baseload production to complement the regional energy mainstays of hydro power and petroleum-based thermal generation. The ARGeo project covers six countries: Djibouti, Eritrea, Ethiopia, Kenya, Tanzania, and Uganda. Although there are many differences between these countries, all of them have, as part of the African Rift Valley system, considerable potential for GeoE, and they all need significant additional power generation capacity to meet growing demand and to expand access to electricity services.

The first proposed operation under ARGeo was the Assal Geothermal Power Project in Djibouti. The power sector in Djibouti is relatively small and highly dependent on thermal generation based on hydrocarbons. Tariffs are among the highest on the continent at US$0.28/kWh. Generation costs are higher than utility revenues. To avoid price escalation, the government of Djibouti is forced to support operations with recurrent budget subsidies. The high cost structure and limited supply make it difficult to extend services to the remaining 50 percent of the population who have yet to gain access to electricity. Private sector growth and competitiveness are also constrained by the lack of electricity, severely affecting Djibouti's attractiveness to foreign direct investment. The energy supply situation, however, was improved in 2009 when the transmission line from Ethiopia was completed. The interconnection enables Djibouti to import up to 300 GWh of hydro-based electricity from its neighbor. To reduce the growth in imports, the government of Djibouti aims to develop domestic energy resources rapidly. GeoE is the only domestically viable resource for large-scale energy development in Djibouti because no hydro, biomass, or hydrocarbon resources are available. However, the Assal project, which was to be developed by Reykjavik Energy Invest (REI) of Iceland did not proceed as planned, and an alternative project may be selected to be covered by the risk mitigation fund.

Barriers

In addition to common barriers impeding the development of RE projects, two technology barriers in particular are specific to the development of geothermal deposits:

- High up-front costs associated with identifying the geothermal deposits and drilling the high-cost wells, and
- Associated geological risks of not finding sufficient resources during exploration or premature resource depletion during operation.

Geological risks appear to be among the most difficult to tackle. Special knowledge pertaining to the assessment and handling of geological risks is often beyond the experience and capacity of both potential energy investors and lenders, which reduces their willingness to undertake or participate in geothermal projects.

Objectives

The objective of both funds was to promote and accelerate the use of GeoE in each of the regions.

Design of the GeoFund

The GeoFund originally included three components: (a) TA (US$7 million) to address information and capacity barriers; (b) direct investment funding (US$8 million) to support project developers by providing low-cost loans, straight grants, or contingent grants; and (c) geological risk insurance (US$10 million) to mitigate the geological risks associated with GeoE exploration and operation. The first phase of the GeoFund program included two GEF subprojects: (a) a grant of US$810,000 to IGA for regional TA activities and (b) a GRI grant of US$3.72 million to MOL, Hungary.

Key Features of the GRI
APL Triggers
Two sets of triggers applied under the horizontal APL: project triggers that determined when an individual investment was eligible to receive Bank funds, and policy triggers that determined the eligibility of an individual country to receive Bank assistance under the APL program.

- Policy triggers
  - Proven country commitment by GEF focal point endorsement of the GeoFund program
  - Established country program on RE development (or program in the process of being established)
- Project triggers
  - Project sponsor cofinancing in a ratio of approximately 1:5 to prove commitment to the project
  - Use of a sound screening package to prove project readiness

Guarantee Structure
GRI parameters. For each type of GRI, insurance coverage was defined against the key parameters of GeoE production, such as reservoir temperature, wellhead pressure, wellhead flow rate, geothermal fluid chemistry, and the like. The GRI parameters are specified in the grant agreement. For example, in the Hungary MOL Geothermal Power Plant Pilot Subproject, "success" was defined as 2,100 cubic meters per day or more and "failure" was defined as 1,200 cubic meters per day or less.

Coverage. GRI would cover up to 85 percent of the eligible cost. Eligible costs are defined as the actual loss incurred by the project developer due to drilling results other than expected. The project developer covers the remaining drilling expenses as well as all of the predrilling expenses.

Tenor. The tenor of each GRI would be up to nine months from the start of drilling of the well.

Premium and fee. The premium was between 3 and 5 percent of the eligible cost of drilling and payable up front upon signing. The applicable fee was determined based on the risk assessment of individual projects. For the Hungary MOL Geothermal Power Plant Pilot Subproject, MOL paid to the GeoFund an up-front processing fee of US$10,000 and a 3 percent premium on the insured amount (US$131,254).

Risk-management measures. The GRI is managed by the Bank's GeoFund Coordination Team. The risks of excessive defaults were managed through conservative forecasts and technical due diligence.

Technical Assistance

The TA component was implemented by IGA based on a work program prepared jointly by IGA and the Bank's GeoFund Coordination Team. The TA included a capacity-building subcomponent and a policy-development subcomponent. The capacity-building subcomponent comprised the following elements:

- Review and assessment of geothermal resources, modes of occurrence, and methods of use;
- Training of local experts in the preparation and implementation of GeoE projects;
- Transfer of know-how through the establishment of a roster of international geothermal experts and implementation of targeted international studies;
- Support to the organization and execution of conferences and workshops; and
- Dissemination of information through support for the creation of knowledge resource centers and support to publications.

The policy-development subcomponent consisted of three elements:

- ECA country policy support activities to identify key barriers to the use of RE resources:
  - Support of governments' policy and framework reforms, including taxation in favor of GeoE development;
  - Development of national geothermal programs and action plans;
  - Creation of domestic financial mechanisms for support of GeoE projects;
  - Creation of and secretariat support to the GeoFund Advisory Forum, consisting of experts from the ECA countries; and
  - Creation of and secretariat support to the GeoFund Group Scientific and Technical Experts.
- Demonstration projects.
- Management and administration to support the contracting of an implementation specialist to manage the TA funds.

Design of the ARGeo Fund

ARGeo has three components: (a) TA for exploration and regional network, (b) a financial risk-mitigation instrument, the RMF, and (c) a TA facility for post-drilling activities, which include, among others, feasibility studies, policy, regulation, and transaction advice and support. The first two aim to support exploration activities, the latter to support production drilling and operation.

The TA program for upstream scientific assessment, surface exploration, and regional cooperation is managed by the United Nations Environment Programme the other two components are managed by the World Bank. Allocation of the GEF grant between the Bank's two facilities can be adjusted during implementation, if necessary, depending on changes in client demand and market conditions. Because the objectives of the facilities are independent of one another, a project developer, private or public, can enjoy a combination of support from any of the three facilities as appropriate.

Key Features of the RMF

Guarantees are awarded on the basis of appropriate criteria complying with the state of the art. Project applications are required to provide sufficient surface-based exploration data to justify investment in exploratory drilling in the concerned geothermal field. The eligibility of the drilling site is judged by an independent Geothermal Advisory Panel, which also monitors drilling execution and assesses possible events of default.

The design of the RMF is based on the GeoFund and follows a similar structure. The main differences follow.

- *Coverage.* Up to 85 percent of the eligible drilling expenses will be covered. The actual payout ratio will be determined based on achievement of defined geological parameters. No payment will be made in a success case. Maximum payment will be made in a total failure case. Partial payment may be made for partial failure, as specifically defined for each project.
- *Premium and fee.* The recipient will be charged an RMF fee of 2–3 percent on the eligible drilling expense, payable up front upon signing. The fees to be charged to the applicants are not set to make the RMF financially self-sustainable. Depending on the frequency and severity of the payout events, the resources allocated to the RMF will eventually be depleted.

Technical Assistance

The World Bank TA facility will be executed by IGA. It will primarily offer support to address and mitigate the capacity constraints of participating client countries and local utility project sponsors to proceed in geothermal power plant development and the postdrilling stage. Specifically, it will

- Provide funding to seek equity participation and financing of plant feasibility studies, project implementation planning, financial analysis and transaction advisory services, bidding and contract preparation, negotiation advice for power purchase agreements, and others;

- Provide support to local government ministries and agencies to strengthen their technical, financial, legal, and institutional capacity;
- Provide a small portion of the grant to client countries in the predrilling phase, to complete specific information to qualify for RMF coverage; and
- Support the creation of an East African Regional Branch of the IGA to coordinate activities on GeoE development in the African Rift countries and beyond, together with United Nations Environment Programme implemented TA.

Implementation Results

GeoFund

Under the GRI subproject, the results of the exploration and testing activities indicated that the two wells would not produce adequate flow rates for any geothermal-based operation. This outcome was verified in the technical report produced by MOL, and further verified by a team of independent experts hired by the Bank. The expenses for the payment claim were verified by an international auditing firm. After verification in accordance with the grant agreement, a payment of US$3,305,577.63 was made to MOL on December 17, 2007. The remaining US$414,422.37 was cancelled, and the MOL grant account was closed in 2007.

Although the project did not directly contribute to a reduction of greenhouse gas emissions, the GRI component worked as envisaged for unsuccessful drilling. MOL has assured the Bank of its continued commitment to geothermal development and is exploring two additional geothermal projects, which, if successful, may result in future reductions of greenhouse gas emissions. The Geothermal Workshop in Istanbul resulted in 19 prospective subprojects for geothermal development. However, the depletion of the GEF administrative budget forced the GeoFund Coordination Team to decline to finance any of the 19 subproject proposals, except for the seven candidate subprojects in Turkey, which have been transferred to International Finance Corporation execution.

As a result of the prolonged global financial crisis, the private sector risk insurance market for geothermal development has not expanded as expected when the GeoFund program was launched, which limited the opportunity for leveraging GEF resources with the private risk insurance market.

Experiences and lessons learned from GeoFund were used in preparation of the ARGeo Fund. Close work between the ECA GeoFund Coordination Team and the ARGeo team resulted in beneficial synergies between the two regional geothermal development programs, and saved time and resources.

ARGeo Fund

The first project, the Assal Geothermal Power Project in Djibouti under the Rift Valley Program did not move forward because the investment from Iceland was called back when that country's economy sank.

Lessons Learned

- GeoFund was the first GEF region-wide program for geothermal development, and as such carried high transaction costs. It took 58 months from concept to Board approval, and the GEF administrative budget was depleted earlier than expected.
- Given that pipeline development is critical to the success of a regional program, it should be pursued as early as possible during project preparation.
- It is important to find a suitable operational modality (or an executing agency with region-wide operating capacity as a project vehicle if available) for successful multicountry program implementation.
- Close cooperation between regions on similar innovative geothermal development programs resulted in synergy and efficiencies in knowledge and product innovation.
- Sector-specific region-wide programs like the GeoFund program, solely supported by GEF resources, tend to lack country unit ownership and linkages to country-based programs. Such a structure incurs high transaction costs under the Bank's operation procedures, which are designed for countries and not for regions.
- Country RE policy is a prerequisite for geothermal development and should be part of the policy triggers for the risk guarantee fund.
- TA is critical and should be part of program design.
- A systematic approach in support of GeoE development is essential. A mechanism is needed to support the entire project cycle from identification to preparation to implementation of GeoE projects.
- Technical lessons learned include the following: (a) a technical definition of the triggering geological parameters (temperature, flow rate, and so forth) and testing and measuring methodology are critical for designing a workable instrument; (b) before commitment of the funds, the project proposal and the pre-exploratory geological studies and assessment techniques to be deployed should be subject to technical due diligence, the outcome of which will strongly affect the success of the exploration activities; and (c) systematic monitoring and supervision of the drilling activities are important to avoid potential disputes over the cause of a geological risk event at the time of payment claim.

Note

1. See Mwangi (2010) for a short review.

Bibliography

IFC (International Finance Corporation). 2010. "Turkey GeoFund GEF Project Appraisal Document." Washington, DC.

Mwangi, Martin Njoroge. 2010. "The African Rift Geothermal Facility (Argeo) – Status." Paper presented at "Short Course V on Exploration for Geothermal Resources," Lake Bogoria and Lake Naivasha, Kenya, October 29–November 19.

World Bank. 2010. *ECA GeoFund Project Implementation Completion Report*. Report ICR00001516, Washington, DC.

Environmental Benefits Statement

The World Bank is committed to reducing its environmental footprint. In support of this commitment, the Office of the Publisher leverages electronic publishing options and print-on-demand technology, which is located in regional hubs worldwide. Together, these initiatives enable print runs to be lowered and shipping distances decreased, resulting in reduced paper consumption, chemical use, greenhouse gas emissions, and waste.

The Office of the Publisher follows the recommended standards for paper use set by the Green Press Initiative. Whenever possible, books are printed on 50% to 100% postconsumer recycled paper, and at least 50% of the fiber in our book paper is either unbleached or bleached using Totally Chlorine Free (TCF), Processed Chlorine Free (PCF), or Enhanced Elemental Chlorine Free (EECF) processes.

More information about the Bank's environmental philosophy can be found at http://crinfo.worldbank.org/crinfo/environmental_responsibility/index.html.

green
press
INITIATIVE

www.ingramcontent.com/pod-product-compliance
Lightning Source LLC
Chambersburg PA
CBHW080230270326
41926CB00020B/4196